Lecture Notes in Artificial Intelligence   3955

Edited by J. G. Carbonell and J. Siekmann

Subseries of Lecture Notes in Computer Science

Vito Di Gesù Francesco Masulli
Alfredo Petrosino (Eds.)

Fuzzy Logic
and Applications

5th International Workshop, WILF 2003
Naples, Italy, October 9-11, 2003
Revised Selected Papers

 Springer

Series Editors

Jaime G. Carbonell, Carnegie Mellon University, Pittsburgh, PA, USA
Jörg Siekmann, University of Saarland, Saarbrücken, Germany

Volume Editors

Vito Di Gesù
Università degli Studi di Palermo
Dipartimento di Matematica ed Applicazioni
Via Archirafi, 34, 90123 Palermo, Italy
E-mail: digesu@math.unipa.it

Francesco Masulli
Polo Universitario di La Spezia, DISI
Via Dodecaneso 35, 16146 Genoa, Italy
E-mail: masulli@disi.unige.it

Alfredo Petrosino
University of Naples "Parthenope"
Department of Applied Science
Via A. De Gasperi 5, 80131 Naples, Italy
E-mail: alfredo.petrosino@uniparthenope.it

Library of Congress Control Number: 2005938510

CR Subject Classification (1998): I.2.3, I.5, F.4.1, F.1, F.2, G.2, I.2, I.4

LNCS Sublibrary: SL 7 – Artificial Intelligence

ISSN   0302-9743
ISBN-10   3-540-31019-3 Springer Berlin Heidelberg New York
ISBN-13   978-3-540-31019-8 Springer Berlin Heidelberg New York

Springer is a part of Springer Science+Business Media

springer.com

© Springer-Verlag Berlin Heidelberg 2006

Typesetting: Camera-ready by author, data conversion by Scientific Publishing Services, Chennai, India
Printed on acid-free paper   SPIN: 10983652   06/3142   5 4 3 2 1 0

Preface

The present volume contains the contributions delivered at the 5th International Workshop on Fuzzy Logic and Applications (WILF 2003), hosted by the Istituto Italiano Studi Filosofici, Palazzo Serra di Cassano, Naples (Italy) and held on October 9-11, 2003.

The volume includes the more recent achievements in the domain of theoretical, experimental and applied fuzzy logic and related techniques. To emphasize the particular connotation of the modern applications of fuzzy logic, special attention has been devoted to the recent trend of integrating and complementing fuzzy logic with rough set theory, neural networks, genetic algorithms and other formal theories and methodologies in order to define flexible and "intelligent" systems, based on the so-called paradigm of soft computing. The capabiblity of these techniques to incorporate imprecision and incomplete information, and to model complex systems, makes them useful tools in many scientific areas.

Among these areas, WILF 2003 dedicated a Special Session on "Soft Computing in Image Processing." Image processing has been a major topic in many areas of research and development, particularly in computer vision and pattern recognition. The majority of the methods were based on probabilistic paradigms, such as the well-known Bayesian paradigm and evidence-based decision-making systems, and just recently soft-computing techniques have gained a relevant role in the leading techniques to tackle image-processing problems. The special session was organized in cooperation with the SCIP group (http://fuzzy.rug.ac.be/SCIP).

The volume consists of peer-reviewed papers, selected out of more than 50 papers submitted to the workshop and given as oral contributions at the workshop. The conference also included three presentations from keynote speakers, Isabelle Bloch from ENST, France, Antonio Di Nola from the University of Salerno, Italy, and Sankar Pal from the Indian Statistical Institute, India.

Thanks are due to Programm Commitee Members and Referees, who took care of the unexpected load of reviewing work. Thanks are also due to the sponsors, with special mention of Antonio Gargano and Gerardo Marotta, director and president of IISF respectively, for supporting the workshop with their financial and organizational help.

Vito Di Gesú, Francesco Masulli and Alfredo Petrosino
Program Chairs
WILF 2003

Organization

WILF 2003 was jointly organized by the Istituto Italiano Studi Filosofici, IISF, the IEEE Neural Networks Society - Italian RIG, the INNS International Neural Network Society, SIG Italy, and SIREN, and by the National Group of Scientific Computing (GNCS), Italy

Executive Committee

Conference Chairs:
Vito Di Gesú (University of Palermo, Italy)
Francesco Masulli (University of Pisa, Italy)
Alfredo Petrosino (University of Naples "Parthenope", Italy)

Program Committee

Jim Bezdek (University of West Florida, USA)
Palma Blonda (CNR-Bari, Italy)
Andrea Bonarini (Politecnico di Milano, Italy)
Piero Bonissone (General Electric, USA)
Ernesto Damiani (University of Milano, Italy)
Antonio Di Nola (University of Salerno, Italy)
Silvio Giove (University of Venezia, Italy)
Marco Gori (University of Siena, Italy)
Ugur Halici (METU, Ankara, Turkey)
Jim Keller (University of Missouri-Columbia, USA)
Etienne Kerre (Ghent University, Belgium)
Ludmilla Kuncheva (University of Wales, UK)
Carlo Morabito (University of Reggio Calabria, Italy)
Gabriella Pasi (CNR-Milano, Italy)
Witold Pedrycz (University of Alberta, Canada)
Roberto Tagliaferri (University of Salerno, Italy)
Settimo Termini (University of Palermo and CNR-Naples, Italy)
Ronald Yager (Iona College, New York, USA)
Hans-Jurgen Zimmermann (RWTH-Aachen, Germany)

Sponsoring Institutions

Istituto Italiano Studi Filosofici (IISF), Naples, Italy
National Group of Scientific Computing (GNCS), Italy
ICAR, National Research Council, Section of Naples, Italy

Table of Contents

Neuro-fuzzy Systems

Fuzzy Decision Theory and Application

Soft Computing in Image Processing

Rough-Fuzzy Granular Computing, Case Based Reasoning and Data Mining

Sankar K. Pal

Machine Intelligence Unit,
Indian Statistical Institute, Kolkata, India
sankar@isical.ac.in

Abstract. Data mining and knowledge discovery is described from pattern recognition point of view along with the relevance of soft computing. Key features of the computational theory of perceptions (CTP) and its significance in pattern recognition and knowledge discovery problems are explained. Role of fuzzy-granulation (f-granulation) in machine and human intelligence, and its modeling through rough-fuzzy integration are discussed. Merits of fuzzy granular computation, in terms of performance and computation time, for the task of case generation in large scale case based reasoning systems are illustrated through examples.

Keywords: soft computing, fuzzy granulation, granular computation, rough sets, case based reasoning.

1 Introduction

In recent years, the rapid advances being made in computer technology have ensured that large sections of the world population have been able to gain easy access to computers on account of falling costs worldwide, and their use is now commonplace in all walks of life. Government agencies, scientific, business and commercial organizations are routinely using computers not just for computational purposes but also for storage, in massive databases, of the immense volumes of data that they routinely generate, or require from other sources. Large-scale computer networking has ensured that such data has become accessible to more and more people. In other words, we are in the midst of an information explosion, and there is urgent need for methodologies that will help us bring some semblance of order into the phenomenal volumes of data that can readily be accessed by us with a few clicks of the keys of our computer keyboard. Traditional statistical data summarization and database management techniques are just not adequate for handling data on this scale, and for extracting intelligently, information or, rather, knowledge that may be useful for exploring the domain in question or the phenomena responsible for the data, and providing support to decision-making processes. This quest had thrown up some new phrases, for example, *data mining* [1, 2] and *knowledge discovery in databases (KDD)* which are perhaps self-explanatory, but will be briefly discussed in the following few paragraphs. Their relationship with the discipline of pattern recognition (PR), certain challenging issues, and the role of soft computing will also be mentioned.

V. Di Gesú, F. Masulli, and A. Petrosino (Eds.): WILF 2003, LNAI 2955, pp. 1–10, 2006.

The massive databases that we are talking about are generally characterized by the presence of not just numeric, but also textual, symbolic, pictorial and aural data. They may contain redundancy, errors, imprecision, and so on. KDD is aimed at discovering natural structures within such massive and often heterogeneous data. Therefore PR plays a significant role in KDD process. However, KDD is being visualized as not just being capable of knowledge discovery using generalizations and magnifications of existing and new pattern recognition algorithms, but also the adaptation of these algorithms to enable them to process such data, the storage and accessing of the data, its preprocessing and cleaning, interpretation, visualization and application of the results, and the modeling and support of the overall human-machine interaction. What really makes KDD feasible today and in the future is the rapidly falling cost of computation, and the simultaneous increase in computational power, which together make possible the routine implementation of sophisticated, robust and efficient methodologies hitherto thought to be too computation-intensive to be useful. A block diagram of KDD is given in Figure 1 [3].

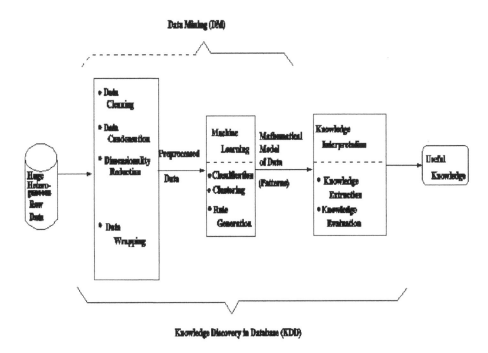

Fig. 1. Block diagram for knowledge discovery in databases [3]

Data mining is that part of knowledge discovery which deals with the process of identifying valid, novel, potentially useful, and ultimately understandable patterns in data, and excludes the knowledge interpretation part of KDD. Therefore, as it stands now, data mining can be viewed as applying PR and machine learning principles in the context of voluminous, possibly heterogeneous data sets. Furthermore, soft computing-based (involving fuzzy sets, neural networks, genetic algorithms and rough sets) PR methodologies and machine learning techniques hold great promise for data mining. The motivation for this is provided by their ability to handle imprecision, vagueness, uncertainty, approximate reasoning and partial truth and lead to tractability, robustness and low-cost solutions [4]. An excellent survey demonstrating the significance of soft computing tools in data mining problem is recently provided by Mitra et al. [5]. Some of the challenges arising out of those posed by massive data and high dimensionality, nonstandard and incomplete data, and over-fitting problems deal mostly with issues like user interaction, use of prior knowledge, assessment of statistical significance, learning from mixed media data, management of changing (dynamic) data and knowledge, integration of different classical and modern soft computing tools, and making knowledge discovery more understandable to humans by using linguistic rules, visualization, etc.

Web mining can be broadly defined as the discovery and analysis of useful information from the web or WWW which is a vast collection of completely uncontrolled heterogeneous documents. Since the web is huge, diverse and dynamic, it raises the issues of scalability, heterogeneity and dynamism, among others. Recently, a detailed review explaining the state of the art and the future directions for web mining research in soft computing framework is provided by Pal et al. [6]. One may note that web mining, although considered to be an application area of data mining on the WWW, demands a separate discipline of research. The reason is that web mining has its own characteristic problems (e.g., page ranking, personalization), because of the typical nature of the data, components involved and tasks to be performed, which can not be usually handled within the conventional framework of data mining and analysis. Moreover, being an interactive medium, human interface is a key component of most web applications. Some of the issues which have come to light, as a result, concern with - (a) need for handling context sensitive and imprecise queries, (b) need for summarization and deduction, and (c) need for personalization and learning. Accordingly, web intelligence became an important and urgent research field that deals with a new direction for scientific research and development by exploring the fundamental roles and practical impacts of machine intelligence and information technology (IT) on the next generation of web-empowered products, systems, services and activities. It plays a key role in today's IT in the era of WWW and agent intelligence.

Bioinformatics which can be viewed as a discipline of using *computational methods to make biological discoveries* [7] has recently been considered as another important candidate for data mining applications. It is an interdisciplinary field mainly involving biology, computer science, mathematics and statistics to analyze biological sequence data, genome content and arrangement, and to predict the function and structure of macromolecules. The ultimate goal is to enable the discovery of new biological insights as well as to create a global perspective from which unifying principles in biology can be derived. There are three major sub-disciplines dealing with the following three tasks in bioinformatics:

a) Development of new algorithms and models to assess different relationships among the members of a large biological data set;
b) Analysis and interpretation of various types of data including nucleotide and amino acid sequences, protein domains, and protein structures; and
c) Development and implementation of tools that enable efficient access and management of different types of information.

First one concerns with the mathematical and computational aspects, while the other two are related to the biological and data base aspects respectively. Data analysis tools used earlier in bioinformatics were mainly based on statistical techniques like regression and estimation. With the need of handling large heterogeneous data sets in biology in a robust and computationally efficient manner, soft computing, which provides machinery for handling uncertainty, learning and adaptation with massive parallelism, and powerful search and imprecise reasoning, has recently gained the attention of researchers for their efficient mining.

While talking about pattern recognition and data mining in the 21st century, it will remain incomplete without the mention of the *Computational Theory of Perceptions (CTP)*, recently explained by Zadeh [8, 9], which has a significant role in the said tasks. In the following section we discuss its basic concepts and features, and relation with soft computing.

2   Computational Theory of Perceptions and F-Granulation

Computational theory of perceptions (CTP) [8, 9] is inspired by the remarkable human capability to perform a wide variety of physical and mental tasks, including recognition tasks, without any measurements and any computations. Typical everyday examples of such tasks are parking a car, driving in city traffic, cooking meal, understanding speech, and recognizing similarities. This capability is due to the crucial ability of human brain to manipulate perceptions of time, distance, force, direction, shape, color, taste, number, intent, likelihood, and truth, among others.

Recognition and perception are closely related. In a fundamental way, a recognition process may be viewed as a sequence of decisions. Decisions are based on information. In most realistic settings, decision-relevant information is a mixture of measurements and perceptions; e.g., the car is six year old but looks almost new. An essential difference between measurement and perception is that in general, measurements are crisp, while perceptions are fuzzy. In existing theories, perceptions are converted into measurements, but such conversions in many cases, are infeasible, unrealistic or counterproductive. An alternative, suggested by the CTP, is to convert perceptions into propositions expressed in a natural language, e.g., it is a warm day, he is very honest, it is very unlikely that there will be a significant increase in the price of oil in the near future.

Perceptions are intrinsically imprecise. More specifically, perceptions are f-granular, that is, both fuzzy and granular, with a granule being a clump of elements of a class that are drawn together by indistinguishability, similarity, proximity or functionality. For example, a perception of height can be described as very tall, tall, middle, short, with very tall, tall, and so on constituting the granules of the variable 'height'. F-granularity of perceptions reflects the finite ability of sensory organs and, ultimately, the brain, to resolve detail and store information. In effect, f-granulation is a human way of achieving data compression. It may be mentioned here that although information granulation in which the granules are crisp, i.e., c-granular, plays key roles in both human and machine intelligence, it fails to reflect the fact that, in much, perhaps most, of human reasoning and concept formation the granules are fuzzy (f-granular) rather than crisp. In this respect, generality increases as the information ranges from singular (age: 22 yrs), c-granular (age: 20-30 yrs) to f-granular (age: "young"). It means CTP has, in principle, higher degree of generality than qualitative reasoning and qualitative process theory in AI [10, 11]. The types of problems that fall under the scope of CTP typically include: perception based function modeling, perception based system modeling, perception based time series analysis, solution of perception based equations, and computation with perception based probabilities where perceptions are described as a collection of different linguistic *if-then* rules.

F-granularity of perceptions puts them well beyond the meaning representation capabilities of predicate logic and other available meaning representation methods. In CTP, meaning representation is based on the use of so called constraint-centered semantics, and reasoning with perceptions is carried out by goal-directed propagation of generalized constraints. In this way, the CTP adds to existing theories the capability to operate on and reason with perception-based information.

This capability is already provided, to an extent, by fuzzy logic and, in particular, by the concept of a linguistic variable and the calculus of fuzzy if-then rules. The CTP extends this capability much further and in new directions. In application to pattern recognition and data mining, the CTP opens the door to a much wider and more systematic use of natural languages in the description of patterns, classes, perceptions and methods of recognition, organization, and knowledge discovery. Upgrading a search engine to a question- answering system is another prospective candidate in web mining for CTP application. However, one may note that dealing with perception-based information is more complex and more effort-intensive than dealing with measurement-based information, and this complexity is the price that has to be paid to achieve superiority.

3   Granular Computation and Rough-Fuzzy Approach

Rough set theory [12] provides an effective means for analysis of data by synthesizing or constructing approximations (upper and lower) of set concepts from the acquired data. The key notions here are those of "information granule" and "reducts". Information granule formalizes the concept of finite precision representation of objects in real life situation, and reducts represent the core of an information system (both in terms of objects and features) in a granular universe. *Granular computing* refers to that where computation and operations are performed on information granules (clump of similar objects or points). Therefore, it leads to have both data compression and gain in computation time, and finds wide applications. An important use of rough set theory and granular computing in data mining has been in generating logical rules for classification and association. These logical rules correspond to different important regions of the feature space, which represent data clusters.

For the past few years, rough set theory and granular computation has proven to be another soft computing tool which, in various synergistic combinations with fuzzy logic, artificial neural networks and genetic algorithms, provides a stronger framework to achieve tractability, robustness, low cost solution and close resembles with human like decision making. For example, rough-fuzzy integration can be considered as a way of emulating the basis of f-granulation in CTP, where perceptions have fuzzy boundaries and granular attribute values. Similarly, rough neural synergistic integration helps in extracting crude domain knowledge in the form of rules for describing different concepts/classes, and then encoding them as network parameters; thereby constituting the initial knowledge base network for efficient learning. Since in granular computing computations/operations are performed on granules (clump of similar objects or points), rather than on the individual data points, the computation time is greatly reduced. The results on these investigations, both theory and real life applications, are being available in different journals and conference proceedings. Some special issues and edited volumes have also come out [13-15].

4   Rough-Fuzzy Granulation and Case Based Reasoning

Case based reasoning (CBR) [16], which is a novel Artificial Intelligence (AI) problem-solving paradigm, involves adaptation of old solutions to meet new demands, explanation of new situations using old instances (called cases), and performance of reasoning from precedence to interpret new problems. It has a significant role to play in today's pattern recognition and data mining applications involving CTP, particularly when the evidence is sparse. The significance of soft computing to CBR problems has been adequately explained in a recent book by Pal, Dillon and Yeung [17] and Pal and Shiu [18]. The CBR cycle consisting of four REs (namely, Retrieve, Reuse, Revise, Retain) [16] is shown in Figure 2. The different tasks involved are case selection/generation, case representation and indexing, case matching, case adaptation, and case base maintenance.

In this section we demonstrate an example [19] of using the concept of f-granulation, through rough-fuzzy computing, for performing the task of case generation in large scale CBR systems. A case may be defined as a contextualized piece of knowledge representing an evidence that teaches a lesson fundamental to achieving goals of the system. While case selection deals with selecting informative prototypes from the data, case generation concerns with construction of 'cases' that need not necessarily include any of the given data points. For generating cases, linguistic representation of patterns is used to obtain a fuzzy granulation of the feature space. Rough set theory is used to generate dependency rules corresponding to informative regions in the granulated feature space.

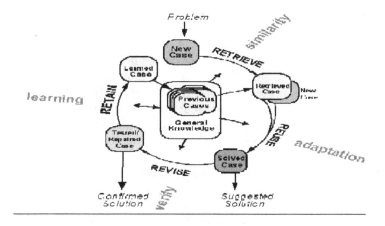

Fig. 2. The CBR Cycle

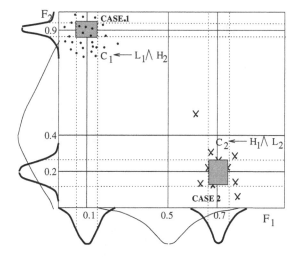

Fig. 3. Rough-fuzzy case generation for a two dimensional data [15]

The fuzzy membership functions corresponding to the informative regions are stored as cases. Figure 3 shows an example of such case generation for a two dimensional data having two classes. The granulated feature space has $3^2 = 9$ granules. These granules of different sizes are characterized by three membership functions along each axis, and have ill-defined (overlapping) boundaries. Two dependency rules: class1 L1 H2 and class2 H1 L2 are obtained using rough set theory. The fuzzy membership functions, marked bold, corresponding to the attributes appearing in the rules for a class are stored as its case.

Unlike the conventional case selection methods, the cases here are cluster granules and not sample points. Also, since all the original features may not be required to express the dependency rules, each case involves a reduced number of relevant features. The methodology is therefore suitable for mining data sets, large both in dimension and size, due to its low time requirement in case generation as well as retrieval.

The aforesaid characteristics are demonstrated in Figures 4 and 5 [19] for two real life data sets with features 10 and 649 and number of samples 586012 and 2000 respectively. Their superiority over IB3, IB4 [16] and random case selection algorithms, in terms of classification accuracy (with one nearest neighbor rule), case generation (tgen) and retrieval (tret) times, and average storage requirement (average feature) per case, are evident. The number of cases considered for comparison are 545 and 50 respectively.

Figures 6-7 show another application of the aforesaid concept of fuzzy granular computing to multispectral image segmentation problem [20]. Here, the incorporation of rough set theoretic knowledge encoding is seen to improve the performance in terms of b segmentation quality index [20] and computation time when applied on other methods like k-means algorithm, expectation maximization algorithm, and minimal spanning tree.

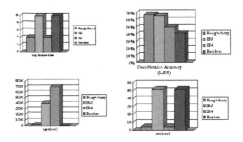

Fig. 4. Performance of different case generation schemes for the forest cover-type GIS data set with 7 classes, 10 features and 586012 samples

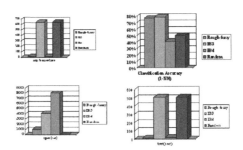

EM/KM: Random initialization + EM/K-means,
REM/RKM: Rough set theoretic initialization + EM/K-means,
KMEM: K-means initialization + EM, EMMST: Random init. + EM + MST
FKM: Fuzzy K-means, REMMST: Rough set init. + EM + MST

Fig. 5. Performance of different case generation schemes for the handwritten numeral recognition data set with 10 classes, 649 features and 2000 samples

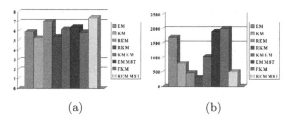

(a)   (b)

Fig. 6. (a) Segmentation Quality (in terms of β index) and (b) Computational Time (in CPU secs on a Sun Workstation)

Fig. 7. Segmented image of a part of the city of Calcutta with β index value of 7.37

5 Conclusions

Data mining and knowledge discovery in databases, which has recently drawn the attention of researchers significantly, have been explained from the view-point of pattern recognition. As it appears, soft computing methodologies, coupled with computational theory of perception (CTP), have great promise for efficient mining of large, heterogeneous data and solution of real-life recognition problems. Fuzzy granulation, through rough-fuzzy computing, and performing operations on fuzzy granules provide both information compression and gain in computation time; thereby making it suitable for data mining applications. We believe the next decade will bear testimony to this in several fields including web intelligence/mining which is considered to be a forefront research area in today's era of IT.

References

1. J.G. Shanahan, *Soft Computing for Knowledge Discovery: Introducing Cartesian Granule Feature*, Kluwer Academic, Boston, 2000.
2. S.K. Pal and A. Pal, Eds., *Pattern Recognition: From Classical to Modern Approaches*, World Scientific, Singapore, 2002.
3. A. Pal and S.K. Pal, Pattern recognition: Evolution of methodologies and data mining, In *Pattern Recognition: From Classical to Modern Approaches*, Eds., S.K. Pal and A. Pal, World Scientific, Singapore, 2002, pp. 1-23.

4. L.A. Zadeh, Fuzzy logic, neural networks and soft *computing, Communications of the ACM*, vol. 37, pp. 77-84, 1994.

5. S. Mitra, S.K. Pal and P. Mitra, Data Mining in Soft Computing Framework: A Survey, *IEEE Trans. Neural Networks*, vol. 13, no. 1, pp.3-14, 2002.

6. S.K. Pal, V. Talwar and P. Mitra, Web Mining in Soft Computing Framework: Relevance, State of the Art and Future Directions, *IEEE Trans. Neural Networks*, vol.13, no.5, pp.1163-1177, 2002.

7. P. Baldi and S. Brunak, *Bioinformatics: The Machine Learning Approach*, MIT Press, Cambridge, MA, 1998.

8. L.A. Zadeh, A new direction in AI: Toward a computational theory of perceptions, *AI Magazine*, vol. 22, pp. 73-84, 2001.

9. L.A. Zadeh, Foreword, *Neuro-Fuzzy Pattern Recognition: Methods in Soft Computing*, (Authors: S.K. Pal and S. Mitra), Wiley, New York, 1999.

10. B.J. Kuipers, *Qualitative Reasoning*, MIT Press, Cambridge, 1984.

11. R. Sun, *Integrating Rules and Connectionism for Robust Commonsense Reasoning*, Wiley, N.Y., 1994.

12. Z. Pawlak, *Rough Sets: Theoretical Aspects of Reasoning about Data*, Kluwer Academic, Dordrecht, 1991.

13. S.K. Pal and A. Skowron, Eds., *Rough-Fuzzy Hybridization: A New Trend in Decision Making*, Springer-Verlag, Singapore, 1999.

14. S.K. Pal, L. Polkowski and A. Skowron, Eds., *Rough-neuro Computing: A Way to Computing with Words*, Springer, Berlin, 2003.

15. S.K. Pal and A. Skowron, Eds., *Special issue on Rough Sets, Pattern Recognition and Data Mining, Pattern Recognition Letters*, vol. 24, no. 6, 2003.

16. J.L. Kolodner, *Case-Based Reasoning*, Morgan Kaufmann, San Mateo, CA, 1993.

17. S.K. Pal, T.S. Dillon, and D.S. Yeung, Eds., *Soft Computing in Case Based Reasoning*, Springer, London, 2001.

18. S.K. Pal and S.C.K. Shiu, *Foundations of Soft Case Based Reasoning*, John Wiley, NY, 2003.

19. S.K. Pal and P. Mitra, Case generation using rough sets with fuzzy discretization, *IEEE Trans. Knowledge and Data Engineering*, 2003 (to appear).

20. S.K. Pal and P. Mitra, Multispectral image segmentation using the rough set initialized EM algorithm, *IEEE Trans. Geoscience and Remote Sensing*, vol. 40, no. 11, pp. 2495-2501, 2002.

VHDL High Level Modelling and Implementation of Fuzzy Systems

A. Barriga[1], S. Sanchez-Solano[1], P. Brox[1], A. Cabrera[2], and I. Baturone[1]

[1] Instituto de Microelectronica de Sevilla, Spain
barriga@imse.cnm.es
[2] Instituto Superior Politecnico José Antonio Echeverría (ISPJAE),
Ciudad de La Habana, Cuba

Abstract. In this paper we illustrate a fuzzy logic system design strategy based on a high level description. Employing this high level description, the knowledge base is described in a language in appearance close to the natural language with the particularity that it uses a hardware description language (VHDL) directly synthesizable on an FPGA circuit. In addition, we analyze FPGA implementations of different fuzzy inference hardware architectures in order to characterize them in terms of area and speed.[1]

1 Introduction

Natural language uncertainty and the approximate reasoning mechanism of the human brain can be modelled through the use of fuzzy logic. The knowledge base of a fuzzy system is described by a set of rules as in an expert system. However, the rule computation is performed numerically as in a neural network. This double view (symbolic description and analytic processing) means that fuzzy logic is useful for modelling those systems in which it is difficult to achieve a mathematical behaviour.

Electronic implementation of fuzzy systems is necessary to create specific hardware at a low cost but with a high performance, in terms of speed and power. Thus, our design methodology has to cover the different design stages, from system specification up to the implementation and testing of the circuit. Our design methodology is based on the fuzzy system development environment called Xfuzzy [1], [2]. The tools included in this environment share a fuzzy system description language (XFL [3]) for the rule base and structure specification. Xfuzzy includes tools that make the description of fuzzy system easier. There are also simulation tools and learning tools for adjusting the system parameters. The realization of the system can be achieved by using the synthesis tools, both software (C, C++ and Java) or hardware synthesis. Hardware synthesis is performed on a specific architecture of the fuzzy system [4], [5], [6]. This architecture exploits the active rule concept, programmability, and uses simplified

---

[1] Partial founded by projects 58/02 de DGAECE (Junta de Andalucía) and TIC2001-1726 (CICYT).

V. Di Gesú, F. Masulli, and A. Petrosino (Eds.): WILF 2003, LNAI 2955, pp. 11–18, 2006.

defuzzification methods to optimize the implementation. In other to avoid the restrictions imposed by the architecture, it is useful for some applications to model the fuzzy system with VHDL [7] while the synthesis tools perform the implementation of the circuit. The aim of our paper is to depict a fuzzy logic modelling. We will show a fuzzy logic modelling style based on VHDL starting from a high level description and the implementation on FPGAs devices.

2   Introduction VHDL System Modelling

In this paper we achieve two aims. First we propose a fuzzy system description style based on the description of the structure of the fuzzy system in an easy way (linguistic variables, rule base, fuzzy operators). Secondly, we analyze a set of hardware architectures in order to characterize them in terms of speed and area. Our starting premise implies that the fuzzy system description must be synthesizable because we are interested in hardware realizations. Thus we will use VHDL as the working platform for our systems. But VHDL language imposes some limitations, compared with the flexibility and expressiveness of other fuzzy logic oriented languages (such as XFL [3]). On the other hand, it is necessary to adapt the characteristics of the system (types of membership functions, inference algorithms, defuzzification mechanisms) to its hardware implementation.

To achieve the first objective we use the XFL description format. In this language the system structure description (fuzzy sets, rule base) and the operator description (connectives, fuzzy operations) are defined separately. This allows us to describe independently both the fuzzy system structure and the processing algorithm.

2.1   Rulebase

Figure 1 shows an example of the VHDL architecture body of a fuzzy system. It contains the rule base structure. In this example there are 9 rules. Each rule structure can be divided into two components: the antecedent of the rule and the consequent. The antecedent of the rule is an expression of the input variables related to their linguistic values. The consequent sets the linguistic value of the rule output.

The rule in Figure 1 must be read as follows:

$$if\ x\ is\ low\ and\ y\ is\ low\ then\ z\ is\ half \tag{1}$$

where x, y, z are the input and output variables, *low* and *half* are linguistic labels.

The processing mechanism of the fuzzy operation is (=), connective and, inference then (rule(,)) is not defined in the VHDL description. Only the structure of the rulebase is defined. Such a description is a high level description because it does not assume any specific implementation criteria. It only describes the knowledge base in terms of a behaviour rule base.

Figure 2 shows an example of a rulebase in which rules are grouped using the connective or and the linguistic hedges greater than ($>$) and less than ($<$). Using these kinds of operators we can reduce the rulebase. The equivalent rulebase of Figure 1 will thus contain only five rules instead of nine.

```
architecture specification of example1 is
. . .
begin
    R(1) <= rule( (x = low)    and (y = low),    half);
    R(2) <= rule( (x = low)    and (y = middle), strong);
    R(3) <= rule( (x = low)    and (y = high),   very_strong);
    R(4) <= rule( (x = middle) and (y = low),    weak);
    R(5) <= rule( (x = middle) and (y = middle), half);
    R(6) <= rule( (x = middle) and (y = high),   strong);
    R(7) <= rule( (x = high)   and (y = low),    very_weak);
    R(8) <= rule( (x = high)   and (y = middle), weak);
    R(9) <= rule( (x = high)   and (y = high),   half);
    Z  <= defuzz(R);
end specification;
```

Fig. 1. VHDL description of the rulebase

```
architecture specification of example2 is
. . .
begin
R(1) <= rule(((x = middle_low)  and (y = very_low)) or
             ((x = middle)      and (y < middle_low))  or
             ((x = middle_high) and (y < middle)) or
             ((x = high)        and (y < middle_high)) or
             ((x = very_high)   and (y < high)), very_weak);
R(2) <= rule(((x = very_low)    and (y > low)) or
             ((x = low)         and (y > middle_low))  or
             ((x = middle_low)  and (y > middle))or
             ((x = middle)      and (y > middle_high)) or
             ((x = middle_high) and (y = very_high)), very_strong);
. . .
end specification;
```

Fig. 2. Rulebase using linguistic hedges

2.2   Membership Function

Linguistic labels represent a range of values within the universe of discourse of input and output variables. These labels can be described by functions in order to compute the membership degree of a certain input value. Membership functions associated to a linguistic label can be triangular or trapezoidal. Figure 3 shows the definition of such membership functions.

A triangular or trapezoidal membership function is characterized by a name (linguistic label) and three points defining the triangle (or four points defining the trapezoid). In the example of Figure 3 there are three constants related to the membership functions of the input variables x and y (*low, middle* and *high*) and five singleton membership functions of output variable z (*very_weak, weak, half, strong* and *very_strong*). Figure 4 shows these function sets.

```
architecture specification of example1 is
-- MF for x and y
constant low    : trapezoid := (0, 0, 15, 31);
constant middle: triangle   := (15, 31, 47);
constant high   : trapezoid := (31, 47, 63, 63);
-- MF for z
constant very_weak  : integer := 0;
constant weak       : integer := 15;
constant half       : integer := 31;
constant strong     : integer := 47;
constant very_strong: integer := 63;
 . . .
begin
 . . .
end specification;
```

Fig. 3. VHDL membership function definitions

Fig. 4. Membership function representation

2.3   Data Types and Fuzzy Operators

Data types and fuzzy operators are defined independently of the system description. They are inserted in a VHDL package as a type and function library. Fuzzy operators are defined using overloaded functions.

Figure 5 shows the VHDL package containing the definition of some data types and functions. Most of the functions overload VHDL operators. We can get compact specification of the rulebase using overloaded operators, as shown in Figure 1.

Another characteristic of the function library is the definition of linguistic hedges (greater, greater or equal, less, less or equal). We can get more linguistic expressiveness and compact rulebases using these operators, and as result we get a better optimization of the resulting circuit (this will be discussed in Section 4).

```
package xfvhdfunc is
type triangle is array (1 to 3) of integer range 0 to TOP;
type trapezoid is array (1 to 4) of integer range 0 to TOP;
function "=" (x: integer; y: triangle) return integer;
function ">" (x: integer; y: triangle) return integer;
function ">=" (x: integer; y: triangle) return integer;
function "<" (x: integer; y: triangle) return integer;
function "<=" (x: integer; y: triangle) return integer;
function "and" (x,y: integer) return integer;
function "or" (x,y: integer) return integer;
function "not" (x: integer) return integer;
function rule (x: integer; y: integer) return two_integer_vector;
function defuzz(x: consec) return two_integer_vector;
end xfvhdfunc;
```

Fig. 5. VHDL package containing data type definitions and functions

3   Fuzzy System Architectures

The set of fuzzy system architectures we have considered is shown in Table 1. The two first architectures share the same entity (input and output ports). Both are combinational circuits implementing the rulebase in parallel. An example of the first architecture is the rulebase of Figure 1. In this example there are 9 rules executing concurrently. As a result of the synthesis process, the final circuit computes all the rules simultaneously.

The second architecture of Table 1 is also implemented as a combinational circuit. The main difference between the previous architecture and this one is

Table 1. Architectures being considered

Architecture	Entity
1 Combinational system with parallel rule processing	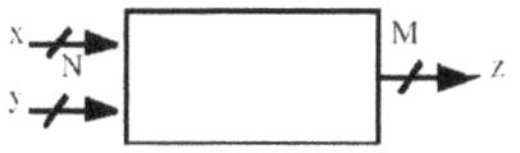
2 Combinational system with parallel rule processing, rule aggregation and linguistic hedges	
3 Sequential rule processing	

the use of the connective or and the linguistic hedges, as shown in Figure 2. As mentioned in a previous section, these operators were implemented using overheaded VHDL operators.

The resulting synthesis of both architectures produces very similar circuits. The main difference is related to the number of rules (Architecture 2 has only 5 rules, one for each consequent). Thus, the antecedent part of the rules can be optimized better in Architecture 2, and as a result, the final circuit requires less hardware resources.

Architecture 3 is based on sequential execution of the rulebase. The description uses a finite state machine with a machine state for each rule. The entity includes a start signal (input capture, machine initialization) and a finish signal.

4   Implementation Result

As an implementation example we will consider the following function:

$$z = \frac{1}{1 + e^{10(x-y)}} \tag{2}$$

It consists of a two-input function (x, y). The surface representing the function is shown in Figure 6. We have analyzed two set of realizations. A first set is composed of systems containing 3 membership functions (3 MF) for the input variables and 5 membership functions for the output. We have shown along this paper some examples of these kinds of systems. Membership functions were described in Figures 3 and 4. The rulebase is described in Figure 1 and we have considered different realizations according to Table 1. All cases use 6 bits for input variables, membership degree and slopes.

The right surface of Figure 6 shows an approximation using 7 membership functions (7 MF) for antecedents and 5 for consequents. Both kind of approximations allow us to compare realizations of less complex systems (case using 3 MF) and more complex systems for more precision (case 7 MF). The rulebase for Architecture 1 using 3 MF requires 9 rules while using 7 MF requires 49 rules. We

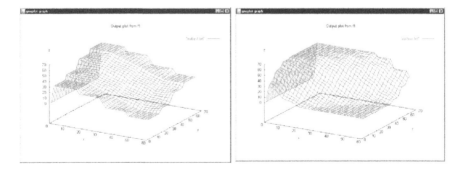

Fig. 6. Function surface (Equation 2) using 3 and 7 membership functions for antecedents

Table 2. Some FPGA implementation results on Spartan IIE xc2s200e-pq208 device

MF	Description	Rules	Area (slices)	Max delay (ns)
	Without connective/linguistic hedges	9	217	35
3	With connective/linguistic hedges	5	176	42
	With connective/linguistic hedges and sequential rules execution	5	1323	34
	Without connective/linguistic hedges	49	975	108
7	With connective/linguistic hedges	5	358	61
	With connective/linguistic hedges and sequential rules execution	5	1084	60

have implemented all the systems on Xilinx FPGAs (4000 and Spartan family devices).

Table 2 shows some implementation results on Spartan IIE devices. Comparing Architectures 1 and 2 of Table 1 we have observed a reduction in terms of hardware resources and maximum delay when we reduce the rule number using the connective or and linguistic hedges. The reason is that in Architecture 2 the aggregation rule stage is simpler because the aggregation is implemented summing the outputs in parallel by means of a combinational circuit.

Architecture 3 means a sequential execution of rules. The realization based on this architecture increases hardware costs. The reason is related to the overhead of the finite state machine.

As a final conclusion, Architecture 2 (description shown in Figure 2) provides better implementation results in terms of area and speed. Such systems have a more compact rulebase which allows for the optimization of the output stage of the circuit (rule aggregation and defuzzifier). We can thus conclude that one of the main design criteria for fuzzy system implementation is the reduction of the rulebase.

We are currently developing a CAD tool under the *Xfuzzy* [2] fuzzy system development environment which produces the VHDL description of the XFL specification.

5   Conclusions

High level description of fuzzy systems allows the designer to focus on the structure of the system and the behaviour specification and not on the implementation features of the processing functions. The use of a hardware description language with a predefined function library has the advantage of a direct approach to the circuit through a synthesis tool. FPGA implementations allow us to run the design cycle automatically in order to obtain the circuit in a short time.

In this paper we have shown the modelling of fuzzy systems using VHDL and we have analyzed various architectures. This study is the base for developing tools in order to automate the design and select the best choice for a specific problem.

References

1. F.J. Moreno Velo, I. Baturone, S. Sánchez Solano, A. Barriga: FUZZY 3.0: A developement environment for fuzzy systems. International Conference in Fuzzy Logic and Technology (EUSFLAT'2001), pp. 93-96, Leicester, Sept. 2001
2. Xfuzzy home page: http://www.imse.cnm.es/Xfuzzy
3. F.J. Moreno Velo, S. Sánchez Solano, A. Barriga, I. Baturone, D.R. López: XFL3: A new fuzzy system specification language. WSES/IEEE Multiconference on Circuits, Systems, Communications and Computers (CSCC'2001), pp. 361-366, Creta July 2001.
4. Hollstein, T., Halgamuge, S.K., Glesner, M.: Computer-Aided Design of Fuzzy Systems Based on Generic VHDL Specifications. IEEE Trans. on Fuzzy Systems, vol. 4, no. 4, Nov. 1996.
5. Sánchez-Solano, S., Barriga-Barros, A., Jiménez, C.J., Huertas, J.L.: Design and Application of Digital Fuzzy Controllers. 6th IEEE International Conference on Fuzzy Systems (FUZZ-IEEE'97), pp.869-874, Barcelona, 1-5 July. 1997.
6. S. Sánchez-Solano, R. Senhadji, A. Cabrera, I. Baturone, C.J. Jiménez, A. Barriga: Prototyping of fuzzy logic-based controllers using standard FPGA development boards. Proc. 13th IEEE Int. Workshop on Rapid System Prototyping (RSP'2002), Darmstadt, Jul. 2002.
7. Zamfirescu, A., Ussery, C.: VHDL and Fuzzy Logic If-Then Rules. Proc. of Euro-VHDL, pp. 636-641, Hamburg 1992.

Some Complexity Results
on Fuzzy Description Logics

Piero A. Bonatti[1] and Andrea G.B. Tettamanzi[2]

[1] Università di Napoli "Federico II",
Dipartimento di Scienze Fisiche — Sezione di Informatica,
Complesso Universitario di Monte Sant'Angelo,
Via Cinthia, Napoli, Italy
bonatti@na.infn.it
[2] Università degli Studi di Milano,
Dipartimento di Tecnologie dell'Informazione,
Via Bramante 65, I-26013 Crema (CR), Italy
andrea.tettamanzi@unimi.it

Abstract. We present and discuss some novel and somewhat surprising complexity results for a basic but significant fuzzy description logic (DL) which extends the classical $\mathcal{ALC}$ language. In particular we show that checking the consistency of a concept or a KB in fuzzy DLs has a complexity which jumps from linear-time to EXPTIME-complete, while the subsumption problem is always (at least) as hard as in crisp DLs.

1   Introduction

Description logics (DL) [1] are a family of logic-based knowledge-representation formalisms emerging from the classical AI tradition of semantic networks and frame-based systems. DLs are well-suited for the representation of and reasoning about terminological knowledge, configurations, ontologies, database schemata, etc.

The need of expressing and reasoning with imprecise knowledge and the difficulties arising in classifying individuals with respect to an existing terminology is motivating research on nonclassical DL semantics, suited to these purposes. Recently, a quite general fuzzy extension of description logics has been proposed, with complete algorithms for solving the entailment problem, the subsumption problem, as well as the best truth-value bound problem [4]. All these algorithms have been shown to be PSPACE-complete, i.e., fuzzification of description logics has no impact from a computational complexity point of view.

The properties of the fuzzy extensions of DLs proposed so far are not yet completely understood. In this paper we note that there is no unique way of generalizing concept consistency in a fuzzy setting, and prove complexity results for this and other reasoning tasks of interest in the fuzzy extension of the DL $\mathcal{ALC}$. We obtain rather surprising results: the complexity of concept and knowledge base consistency checking in fuzzy DLs may range from linear-time to EXPTIME-complete, while the subsumption problem is always (at least) as hard as in crisp DLs.

V. Di Gesú, F. Masulli, and A. Petrosino (Eds.): WILF 2003, LNAI 2955, pp. 19–24, 2006.

2 Fuzzy $\mathcal{ALC}$

$\mathcal{ALC}$ is a basic yet significant representative of DLs. The syntax of the $\mathcal{ALC}$ language is very simple: a *concept* (denoted by C or D) is built out of primitive (or *atomic*) concepts according to the grammar

$$
\begin{aligned}
C, D \rightarrow\ & C \sqcap D\ | \\
& C \sqcup D\ | \\
& \neg C\ | \\
& \forall R.C\ | \\
& \exists R.C\ | \\
& \top\ |\ \bot\ |\ A
\end{aligned}
$$

where A denotes an atomic concept, and R denotes an atomic role. From a logical point of view, concepts can be seen as unary predicates, whereas roles can be interpreted as binary predicates linking individuals to their attributes.

Fuzzy $\mathcal{ALC}$ retains the same syntax, only semantics changes. A fuzzy interpretation $\mathcal{I}$ consists of a non-empty domain $\Delta^{\mathcal{I}}$ (the universe of discourse), and an assignment $\cdot^{\mathcal{I}}$, which maps every atomic concept A onto a fuzzy subset $A^{\mathcal{I}}$ of $\Delta^{\mathcal{I}}$, every atomic role R onto a fuzzy binary relation $R^{\mathcal{I}} \subseteq \Delta^{\mathcal{I}} \times \Delta^{\mathcal{I}}$, and every individual name a onto an element $a^{\mathcal{I}} \in \Delta^{\mathcal{I}}$. The special atomic concepts $\top$ and $\bot$ are mapped respectively onto $\Delta^{\mathcal{I}}$ (the function that maps every individual onto 1) and the empty set (the function that maps every individual onto 0).

The semantics of compound concepts is defined as follows: for all $x \in \Delta^{\mathcal{I}}$,

$$(C \sqcap D)^{\mathcal{I}}(x) = \min\{C^{\mathcal{I}}(x), D^{\mathcal{I}}(x)\}; \tag{1}$$

$$(C \sqcup D)^{\mathcal{I}}(x) = \max\{C^{\mathcal{I}}(x), D^{\mathcal{I}}(x)\}; \tag{2}$$

$$(\neg C)^{\mathcal{I}}(x) = 1 - C^{\mathcal{I}}(x); \tag{3}$$

$$(\exists R.C)^{\mathcal{I}}(x) = \sup_{y \in \Delta^{\mathcal{I}}} \min\{R^{\mathcal{I}}(x, y), C^{\mathcal{I}}(y)\}; \tag{4}$$

$$(\forall R.C)^{\mathcal{I}}(x) = \inf_{y \in \Delta^{\mathcal{I}}} \max\{1 - R^{\mathcal{I}}(x, y), C^{\mathcal{I}}(y)\}. \tag{5}$$

Axioms and queries can be of two kinds: inclusions and assertions. An inclusion is a statement of the form $C \sqsubseteq D$, which is true (i.e., 1) in $\mathcal{I}$ if for all $x \in \Delta^{\mathcal{I}}$,

$$C^{\mathcal{I}}(x) \leq D^{\mathcal{I}}(x), \tag{6}$$

and false (i.e., 0) otherwise. By $C \equiv D$ we abbreviate the pair of assertions $\{C \sqsubseteq D, D \sqsubseteq C\}$. If $C \sqsubseteq D$ is valid (true in every interpretation), then we say that D *subsumes* C. An assertion can be either of the form $C(x) \leq \alpha$, or $C(x) \geq \alpha$, where C is a concept, x is an individual constant and α is a rational number. The two kinds of assertions are true in $\mathcal{I}$ if $C^{\mathcal{I}}(x^{\mathcal{I}}) \leq \alpha$ (resp. $C^{\mathcal{I}}(x^{\mathcal{I}}) \leq \alpha$), and false otherwise.

3 Concept Satisfiability

It is proven in [4] that given acyclic inclusion axioms plus assertions like $C(x) \leq \alpha$ and $C(x) \geq \alpha$, fuzzy inference is PSPACE-complete; however, the discussion of concept consistency provided there is incomplete, because in fuzzy $\mathcal{ALC}$, concept consistency can be formulated in two ways, namely

- checking whether $C \not\sqsubseteq \bot$, and
- checking whether C is satisfiable to a given degree α.

As a matter of fact, the complexity of checking whether $C \not\sqsubseteq \bot$ or, equivalently, $C \not\equiv \bot$, which is PSPACE-complete in the classical case, turns out to be linear-time in fuzzy $\mathcal{ALC}$. However, unlike in the classical case, this version of consistency checking cannot be taken as the basis for other reasoning problems, i.e., it is less complex but also less expressive.

The proof goes as follows: given the definition of compound concept C, rewrite it by using the following equivalence-preserving rewriting system:

1. $\neg\top \to \bot$;
2. $\neg\bot \to \top$;
3. $\top \sqcup C \to \top$;
4. $C \sqcup \top \to \top$;
5. $\bot \sqcup C \to C$;
6. $C \sqcup \bot \to C$;
7. $\exists R.\bot \to \bot$.[1]

Repeatedly applying the above rewrite rules yields a concept in what we might call *Top-Bottom Normal Form* (TBNF), i.e., $\top$, $\bot$, or a $\bot$-free concept where $\top$ occurs only in subconcepts of the form $\exists R.\top$ (*nontrivial* TBNF).

By a simple structural induction on the concept C we obtain:

Lemma 1. *Let $\mathcal{I}_{0.5}$ be any interpretation that maps every atomic concept (resp. role) onto the constant function $\lambda x.0.5$ (resp. $\lambda x \lambda y.0.5$). For all nontrivial TBNF concepts C, $C^{\mathcal{I}_{0.5}} = \lambda x.0.5$.*

In other words, the interpretation in which all membership degrees are one half, renders all nontrivial TBNF concepts "half-satisfiable". A direct corollary of this property is that

Lemma 2. $C \equiv \bot$ *iff* $C \to^* \bot$.

Furthermore, the rewriting process is confluent and eliminates one connective at each step; therefore, we derive the following result.

Theorem 1. *In fuzzy $\mathcal{ALC}$, the inclusion $C \sqsubseteq \bot$ can be checked in linear time.*

The second version of consistency, called α-consistency (cf. [2, 3]), is defined as follows: a compound concept C is α-consistent, iff there exist an interpretation $\mathcal{I}$ and an individual $x \in \Delta^{\mathcal{I}}$ such that $C^{\mathcal{I}}(x) \geq \alpha$.

---

[1] Note that there is no corresponding rewrite rule for $\exists R.\top$.

Theorem 2. *If $\alpha \leq 0.5$ then α-consistency can be checked in linear time.*

Proof. If $\alpha = 0$ then every concept is α-satisfiable. If $0 < \alpha \leq 0.5$ then note that C is 0.5-satisfiable (hence α-satisfiable) iff its TBNF is not $\perp$ (by the above lemmata). The latter test takes linear time, hence the theorem holds. $\square$

If, however, $0.5 < \alpha \leq 1$, then α-consistency turns out to be PSPACE-complete, like in the case of crisp $\mathcal{ALC}$. This is an unusually abrupt complexity jump.

The PSPACE-completeness proof requires some preliminaries:

Definition 1. *For all interpretations $\mathcal{I}$, let $\sharp\mathcal{I}$ be the crisp interpretation such that $\Delta^{\sharp\mathcal{I}} = \Delta^{\mathcal{I}}$ and for all atomic concepts A and all $x \in \Delta^{\mathcal{I}}$*

$$A^{\sharp\mathcal{I}}(x) = \begin{cases} 1 \text{ if } A^{\mathcal{I}}(x) > 0.5 \\ 0 \text{ otherwise} \end{cases}$$

and similarly for (atomic) roles.

Lemma 3. *For all C, $\mathcal{I}$, and $x \in \Delta^{\mathcal{I}}$,*

$$C^{\mathcal{I}}(x) > 0.5 \text{ iff } C^{\sharp\mathcal{I}}(x) = 1,$$
$$C^{\mathcal{I}}(x) < 0.5 \text{ iff } C^{\sharp\mathcal{I}}(x) = 0.$$

We are thus able to reduce α-satisfiability, for $\alpha > 0.5$, to classical satisfiability: for all $\alpha > 0.5$, C is α-consistent iff C is classically consistent. As a consequence (by standard complexity results) we have:

Theorem 3. *If $0.5 < \alpha \leq 1$ then checking α-consistency is PSPACE-complete.*

4   KB Satisfiability

We now address the problem of checking whether a general, terminological knowledge base (KB) is satisfiable, i.e., whether there exists an interpretation satisfying simultaneously a given set of inclusions.

First of all, we can use the special interpretation $\mathcal{I}_{0.5}$ and Lemma 1 to prove that:

Corollary 1. *If all compound concepts C_{ij} are nontrivial TBNF concepts then the KB $\{C_{i1} \sqsubseteq C_{i2} \mid 1 \leq i \leq n\}$ is satisfiable.*

Furthermore, it is possible to prove that the general problem is much harder.

Theorem 4. *Checking whether an arbitrary set of inclusions is α-satisfiable is EXPTIME-complete.*

The proof sketch is as follows: after normalization, all cases are trivial but $\top \sqsubseteq C$ and $C \sqsubseteq \perp$. Such inclusions are satisfiable iff they are classically satisfiable (use the crisp interpretation $\sharp\mathcal{I}$ and the results from the previous section). The latter problem is known to be EXPTIME-complete (for arbitrary inclusions).

5   Subsumption

In crisp $\mathcal{ALC}$, checking whether $C \sqsubseteq D$ is valid (i.e., D subsumes C) can be reduced to a concept consistency check. However, adding fuzziness to $\mathcal{ALC}$ destroys this equivalence, and it can be shown that checking whether $C \sqsubseteq D$ is valid is at least as hard as in the classical case, even under the assumption which makes satisfiability checking of $C \sqsubseteq D$ a linear-time problem.

Theorem 5. *In fuzzy $\mathcal{ALC}$ the subsumption problem is PSPACE-hard even if the concepts involved are nontrivial TBNF concepts.*

The proof of this theorem consists in reducing crisp unsatisfiability of a concept C (PSPACE-complete) to the fuzzy subsumption problem $C \sqsubseteq \neg C$ using the crisp interpretation $\sharp\mathcal{I}$ and the results of the previous section. If C is not in nontrivial TBNF, it can be first reduced to this form by replacing $\top$ and $\bot$ with $A \sqcup \neg A$ and $A \sqcap \neg A$, respectively, where A is any atomic concept.

6   Conclusions and Future Work

Careful investigation of the computational complexity of inference in fuzzy DLs unveils unusual complexity results, some of which are reminiscent of properties of disjunctive logic programs, namely:

- concept satisfiability of the first kind is easy (linear-time);
- the complexity of concept satisfiability of the second kind, i.e., α-satisfiability, depends on α, and jumps from linear-time to PSPACE-complete as $\alpha > 0.5$;
- KB satisfiability is linear-time if all concepts are in nontrivial TBNF, and EXPTIME-complete otherwise;
- subsumption is (at least) as difficult as subsumption in crisp DLs, even in those cases where satisfiability is easy.

The proofs of these result made clear that there exist simple and strong relationships between the semantics of fuzzy DLs (the fuzzy interpretations $\mathcal{I}$) and the semantics of crisp DLs (the corresponding "defuzzified" interpretations $\sharp\mathcal{I}$).

Several important issues remain still open. Having proved that subsumption in fuzzy DLs is at least as hard as in crisp DLs, a precise complexity characterization for it will have to be the subject of further investigation. Another interesting problem is evaluating lower and upper bounds for the membership value of a given individual to a given concept.

Fuzzy $\mathcal{ALC}$ could be extended in a variety of ways to make it a usable tool for a vast range of real-world application domains: cardinality-based quantifiers and compound roles could be added, alternative t-norms and co-norms could be used to define the basic connectives, and other types of assertions about individuals could be allowed.

References

1. Franz Baader, Diego Calvanese, Deborah McGuinness, Daniele Nardi, and Peter Patel-Schneider, editors. *The Description Logic Handbook: Theory, implementation and applications.* Cambridge, 2003.
2. D. Butnariu, E. P. Klement, and S. Zafrany. On triangular norm-based propositional fuzzy logics. *Fuzzy Sets and Systems*, 69:241–255, 1995.
3. Mirko Navara. Satisfiability in fuzzy logics. *Neural Networks World*, 10(5):845–858, 2000.
4. U. Straccia. Reasoning within fuzzy description logics. *Journal of Artificial Intelligence Research*, 14:137–166, 2001.

An Evolutionary Approach
to Ontology-Based User Model Acquisition

Célia da Costa Pereira[1] and Andrea G.B. Tettamanzi[2]

[1] Genetica S.r.l.,
Via S. Dionigi 15, I-20139 Milano, Italy
dacosta@genetica-soft.com
[2] Università degli Studi di Milano,
Dipartimento di Tecnologie dell'Informazione,
Via Bramante 65, I-26013 (CR), Italy
andrea.tettamanzi@unimi.it

Abstract. In this paper we propose a new approach to User Model Acquisition (UMA) which has two important features. It doesn't assume that users always have a well-defined idea of what they are looking for, and it is ontology-based, i.e., we deal with *concepts* instead of *keywords* to formulate queries.

1 Introduction

Research in User Model Acquisition (UMA) has received considerable attention in the last years. The problem of information overload leads to a demand for automated methods to locate and retrieve information with respect to users' individual interests. Unfortunately, methods developed within information retrieval [7, 8] leave two main problems still open.

The first problem is that most approaches assume users to have a well-defined idea of what they are looking for, which is not always the case. We solve this problem by letting fuzzy user models evolve on the basis of a rating induced by user behavior. The second problem concerns the use of *keywords*, not *concepts*, to formulate queries. Considering words and not the concepts behind them often leads to a loss in terms of the quantity and quality of information retrieved. We solve this problem by adopting an ontology-based approach.

The approach described in this paper has been implemented and successfully tested in the framework of the Information and Knowledge Fusion (IKF) Eureka Project E!2235.

2 Data Representation

We deal with the problem of learning user interests from user behavior in a document retrieval system. Therefore, a suitable representation has to be found for documents, concepts and their relations, and user interests.

V. Di Gesú, F. Masulli, and A. Petrosino (Eds.): WILF 2003, LNAI 2955, pp. 25–32, 2006.

We assume concepts and their relations to be organized in a formal ontology [6, 9]. A lexical database like WordNet[1] or one of its derivates, will provide the link between words appearing in a document and the concepts they may refer to (i.e., their senses/meanings).

2.1   Document Representation

We have been inspired by the method proposed in [3], and we extended it to work with ontological concepts. In this framework, a document can be represented as a vector, whose components express the "importance" of every concept.

However, passing from an unstructured space of words seen as independent entities to an ontology of concepts, structured by the hierarchical *is-a* relation into a lattice, is not trivial. Suppose, for example, that we find in a document the three related concepts of *cat*, *dog*, and *animal*: now, *animal* is a super-class of both *cat* and *dog*. Therefore, mentioning the *animal* concept can implicitly refer both to *cat* and *dog*, although not so specifically as mentioning *cat* or *dog* directly would. Therefore, we need to devise a system to take this kind of interdependence among concepts into account when calculating levels of importance.

The main idea is to consider but the leaf concepts in the ontology, i.e., the most specific concepts only, as elements of the importance vector for a document. This choice can be justified by thinking that more general concepts (i.e., internal concepts) are implicitly taken account of through the leaf concepts they subsume, by "distributing" their importance to all of their sub-classes down to the leaf concepts in equal proportion [2] (this ensures that the components of a document vector are independent, or orthogonal, with respect to each other):

$$N(c) = \text{occ}(c) + \sum_{c \in \text{Path}(c,...,\top)} \sum_{i=2}^{\text{length}(\mathbf{c})} \frac{\text{occ}(c_i)}{\prod_{j=2}^{i} \|\text{children}(c_j)\|},$$

where $N(c)$ is the count of explicit and implicit occurrences of concept c, and $\text{occ}(c)$ is the number of occurrences of lexicalizations of c.

Since an ontology can contain a huge number of concepts (e.g., in the order of the hundreds of thousands), it is convenient to limit ourselves, for the purpose of calculating document importance vectors, only to the top-level ontology, whose size may be in the thousands of concepts [3]. Anyway, it is important to remark that the approach described below is absolutely independent of which subset of the ontology one decides to restrict to, and that what we call "leaf concepts"

---

[1] URL: http://www.cogsci.princeton.edu/~wn/.

[2] The assumption that the importance of an internal node is distributed to all subclasses in equal proportion is convenient in case of lack of further information on which subclass is more "typical" or "usual". However, taking that kind of information into account would significantly complicate the model and it is not clear what the gain in accuracy would be.

[3] Of corse if the ontology doesn't contain a huge number of concepts this limitation is not necessary.

can be defined in any way that is consistent with our premise, that is, that they form a set of mutually independent concepts (i.e., none of them subsumes, or is subsumed by, any other). The ontology lattice, cut this way, can be treated as a direct acyclic graph (*dag*), having $\top$ as its root.

The quantity of information info(c) given by the presence of some concept c in a document is given by

$$\text{info}(c) = \frac{N_{doc}(c)}{N_{rep}(c)},$$

where $N_{doc}(c)$ is the number of times a lexicalization of c appears in the document, and $N_{rep}(c)$ is the total number of its occurrences in the whole document repository.

Each document is then represented by a document vector I, whose jth component is

$$I(c_j) = \frac{info(c_j)}{\sum_{i \in \mathcal{L}} \text{info}(i)},$$

where c_j is a leaf concept, and $\mathcal{L}$ is the set of all leaf concepts.

We define similarity between documents on the basis of their vector representation, and we group them into clusters according with their similarity, in order to express user interests with respect to clusters instead of all individual documents. Any fuzzy clustering algorithm, like fuzzy c means [2], can serve this purpose. Furthermore, we characterize each cluster by a set of *key concepts*, i.e., the most important concepts in the vector representation of its member documents.

2.2 Representing User Interests

What we expect from a model of user interest is the ability to tell to which degree a given document or concept interests a user. Therefore, a natural abstract representation for a user interests is a fuzzy set of document clusters. We should observe that by knowing to which degree each given cluster belongs to the user interests, it is possible to derive the degree to which every document interests a user. We propose tree propositions for defining the interest of a document $I(d)$:

- the *optimistic* one which has been inspired by the optimistic utility proposed by Yager in [10].

$$I(d) = \max_C \min(\mu_C(d), I(C)).$$

  Where $I(C)$ represents the interest of the user for the cluster C and $\mu_C(d)$ is the degree of membership of the document d in the cluster C. This definition says that only a small membership degree of a document to all very interesting clusters can decrease its interest degree. If the document doesn't belong to any cluster in the user profile then its interest is equal to 0.
- the *pessimistic* one which has been inspired by the pessimistic utility function defined by Dubois and Prade in [5] which at its turn has been inspired by the Yager's optimistic utility.

$$I(d) = \min_C \max(1 - \mu_C(d), I(C)).$$

– the *mean value based* one

$$I(d) = \frac{\sum_C \mu_C(d) \cdot I(C)}{\sum_C \mu_C(d)}$$

In practice, a model of user interests is represented by a vector of membership values, one for each document cluster, i.e., of cluster interests.

3   Evolving User Models

The principle of our approach to UMA is the following. When a user logs in the system, there are two possibilities: it is either a new user or a known user. In the former case, the user will be asked to enter their personal data and a description of their interests (optional). In both cases, an evolutionary algorithm [1] is automatically set to run in the background, its objective being to optimize a model for the current user, with minimal user input.

Information gathered directly from the users at the time of their registration is used to generate an initial population of user models. From then on, it is the evolutionary algorithm which is responsible for tracking their interests as they interact with the system. Every action taken by a user in response to any proposition made by the system on the basis of a user model is interpreted as a rating of that user model.

3.1   Initialization

The first step concerns the case when a user is not yet known by the system. Our approach consists then in using the set of interest clusters which groups similar documents to initialize the list of interest clusters in the user profile. Summarizing, a user whose profile does not contain any group of interests (a new user), is asked (optionally) to describe, with key concepts, document titles, short phrases or others, their center of interest. The profile of the user is then set up by adding in the list of its interest groups, instances of clusters with characteristics similar "enough" to those requested by the user. To each of these groups of interests there is associated a degree corresponding to the importance the user attributes to that cluster. This importance depends on the interest degree of the documents in the cluster and their respective membership degree.

Let $\mathcal{U}$ be the set of the key concepts concerning the request introduced by the user, and $\mathcal{C}$ the set of key concepts associated to a document d. The importance $I(d)$ that this document has for the user is estimated by:

$$I(d) = \frac{|\mathcal{U} \cap \mathcal{C}|}{|\mathcal{U} \cap \mathcal{C}| + |\mathcal{U} \setminus \mathcal{C}| + |\mathcal{C} \setminus \mathcal{U}|} \qquad (1)$$

As we said previously, the interest for a cluster C depends on the interest of documents in the cluster and their membership degree. Here, we define tree possibilities for computing this interest:

– the *optimistic possibility*

$$I(C) = \max_d \min(\mu_C(d), I(d)).$$

If all documents of C belong completely to C ($\mu_C(d) = 1 \; \forall \; d \in C$) then $I(C)$ corresponds to the degree of the most interesting document in C.
– the *pessimistic possibility*

$$I(C) = \min \max_d (1 - \mu_C(d), I(d)).$$

With this definition we can see that the less a document belongs to a cluster the less its interest degree influences the general interest of the cluster. If all documents of C belong completely to C ($\mu_C(d) = 1 \; \forall \; d \in C$) then $I(C)$ corresponds to the degree of the least interesting document in C.
– the *mean based possibility* which is simply computed using the mean weighted value of the document's interests.

$$I(C) = \frac{\sum_d \mu_C(d) \cdot I(d)}{\sum_d \mu_C(d)}.$$

Let $\mathcal{C}_i$ be the set of key concepts associated with documents d_i in the cluster C. The list of concepts associated to this cluster in the user profile contains only the concepts in $|\mathcal{U} \cap_i \mathcal{C}_i|$. We can see that if the user doesn't insert its preferences, the interests of all clusters are initially set to zero. Their set up are made with the evolution of the acquisition process.

The second step deals with the case in which the user is not new. In this case, the user interests are obtained automatically using an evolutionary algorithm to optimize a set of models (propositions) to the user. Summarizing, a user profile contains:

– the personal data of the user,
– a list of fuzzy clusters which interest the user and their respective documents,
– the degree to which each cluster interests the user (its importance for the user).

3.2   Representation

A user model is represented as a vector of membership degrees in $[0, 1]$, which describe the model's guess at the extent to which the user is interested in each document cluster. This is the most natural representation, given the abstract model of a user interests as a fuzzy set of document clusters.

3.3   Fitness Calculation

The evolutionary algorithm is on-line: each time the user interacts with the system, one of the models in the current population is randomly chosen to make its proposition to the user. If the user is satisfied (resp. unsatisfied), the fitness of the chosen model increases (resp. decreases), as well as the fitness of all other models with the same proposition. The fitness of the other models is not changed. The on-line property of our algorithm poses some interesting problems, in that a precise calculation of fitness is not available for every individual at any moment. We invite the reader to see [4] for more details.

3.4 Genetic Operators

The algorithm is elitist, i.e., it always preserves a copy of the best individual unchanged. The *mutation* operator affects each individual with a probability inversely proportional to its fitness.

The *recombination* operator is uniform crossover: each child has a 0.5 probability of inheriting each gene from either parent. We tried several probability crossover rates and 0.5 is the probability which assures a non homogeneous population after few generations.

Deterministic tournament *selection* with a tournament size of 3 is responsible for selecting the pool of parents for the next generation. This tournament size value has been choose after many experiments. It avoids to have, at any generation step, an homogeneous population essentially constituted by the current best individual.

4   Validation of the Approach

The approach described above has been implemented and experimentally validated as follows. A simulation was set up whereby user interests are randomly created and used to simulate user interaction with the system. Precisely, initially a reference model is created. While evolving, the algorithm makes propositions, which are rated according to the reference model. This allowed us to effectively verify that the evolutionary algorithm was capable of learning user interests from user feedback. Figure 1 shows a graph of the distance between the reference model and those used by the system to make its propositions during one of the tests.

In a subsequent phase, a drift effect was applied to the simulated user interests, and the ability of the algorithm to effectively track changing user interests was experimentally proved.

5   Discussion

The evolutionary algorithm described above will not be always running. It will run only when a request is made by the user. In this case, once a feedback from the user is received, evolution will advance by one generation and then pause, waiting for the next user interaction.

This work is a significant step ahead toward the definition of a UMA approach suited for an ontology-based knowledge management framework, like the one

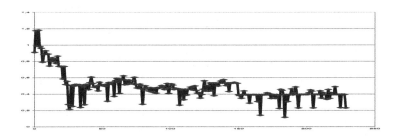

Fig. 1. Distance between the model to learn and the models obtained during the evolutionary process

developed in the IKF Project. This approach is novel, although inspired by several works in the literature.

We have first established the representation for the data of the problem. We have redefined the notion of document vector to consider concept, rather than keyword, occurrences in a document. Thus, a document is represented by a vector containing the importance of all the leaf concept obtained when considering the ontology only to a given depth. We have also defined a similarity function for two documents to use a fuzzy clustering algorithm.

A user model is essentially made up of personal data, a set of document clusters grouped according to their similarity and, for each of these document clusters, an associated degree corresponding to the interest of the user in that document cluster. The user models evolve in time tracking changes of user preferences. An evolutionary algorithm has been devised to obtain this behavior. The goal of that algorithm is to find, at each stage in evolution, the best models, i.e., the ones capable of making the best propositions to the user.

References

1. T. Bäck, D. B. Fogel, and T. Michalewicz, editors. *Evolutionary Computation (in two volumes)*. Institute of Physics, Bristol, Philadelphia, 2000.
2. J. Bezdek. *Pattern Recognition with Fuzzy Objective Function Algorithms*. Plenum, New York, 1981.
3. B. Crabtree and S. Soltysiak. Identifying and tracking changing interests. *International Journal on Digital Libraries*, 2(1):38–53, 1998.
4. E. Damiani, A. Tettamanzi, and V. Liberali. On-line evolution of fpga-based circuits: A case study on hash functions. In A. Stoica, D. Keymeulen, and J. Lohn, editors, *Proceedings of the First NASA/DoD Workshop on Evolvable Hardware*, pages 26–33, Pasadena, CA, July 19–21 1999. IEEE Computer Society.
5. Didier Dubois and Henri Prade. Possibility theory as a basis for qualitative decision theory. In *IJCAI*, pages 19–25, Montreal, 1995.
6. Nicola Guarino. Formal ontology and information systems. In Nicola Guarino, editor, *Formal Ontology and Information Systems: Proceedings of the first international conference (FOIS'98)*, Amsterdam, 1998. IOS Press.

7. Bernardo Magnini and Carlo Strapparava. Improving user modelling with content-based techniques. In *Proc. 8th International Conference on User Modelling*, pages 74–83. Springer-Verlag, 2001.

8. Andrea Rodriguez and Egenhofer. Determining semantic similarity among entity classes from different ontologies.

9. John F. Sowa. *Knowledge Representation: Logical, Philosophical, and Computational Foundations*. Brooks/Cole, Pacific Grove, CA, 2000.

10. R. Yager. An approach to ordinal decision making. *International Journal of Approximate Reasoning*, 12:237–261, 1995.

Mathematical Modeling of Passage Dynamic Function

Anna Esposito[1,2], Eugène C. Ezin[3,4], and Maria Marinaro[2,3]

[1] Department of Psychology, Second University of Naples,
Via Vivaldi 13, I-81100 Caserta, Italy
[2] Department of Physics, Salerno University and INFM,
Via S. Allende, I-84081 Baronissi (Salerno), Italy
[3] International Institute for Advanced Scientific Studies,
Via Pellegrino 19, I-84019 Vietri sul Mare(Salerno), Italy
[4] Institut de Mathématiques et de Sciences Physiques,
BP 613 Porto-Novo, Benin
eugene.ezin@imsp-uac.org

Abstract. In this paper, we report on a mathematical modeling of the passage dynamics we defined as the description of the environment through which the noise waves go before corrupting the speech signal in our implementation of a neuro-fuzzy system for noise cancellation [2, 3, 4]. We restricted our analysis in establishing rigourously that passage dynamics can be considered as linear dynamical systems under some limitations in introducing the concept of forced linear passage. Finally, we did some experiments to validate the theoretical results obtained from our analysis.

1 Introduction

In our previous works, in designing an adaptive neuro-fuzzy system for canceling noise from speech signal, we defined the passage dynamics as the modeling of the environment through which the noise waves go before corrupting the speech signal [2, 3]. We have experimentally shown how important is such a modeling problem through the system performance in proposing some nonlinear passage dynamic functions based on the statistical properties of the noise sources and the inference noise signal that corrupted the speech signal [2, 3]. Moreover we defined a passage dynamic function with free parameters[1] for the system we implemented for noise source identification [4]. At a first glance, the process of modeling the passage dynamic is nonlinear with many not well-known parameters. The analysis we will develop is done under certain assumptions. We assumed that the process is linear and tried to set up the mathematical background for defining linear passage dynamic functions.

---

[1] Free parameters are managed by the user such that the noise sources and the inference have more or less the same mean and standard deviation.

V. Di Gesú, F. Masulli, and A. Petrosino (Eds.): WILF 2003, LNAI 2955, pp. 33–38, 2006.

2   Linear Passage Dynamic Functions

Given a noise source $n(t)$ and its delayed version $n(t-1)$, we are seeking for a set of functions ϕ such that

$$\phi : \mathbb{R}^d \times \mathbb{R}^d \quad \rightarrow \quad \mathbb{R}^d$$
$$(n(t), n(t-1)) \longmapsto z(t) \tag{1}$$

where $z(t) = \alpha\, n(t) + \beta\, n(t-1) + \vec{\gamma}$ represents the inference noise wave that corrupts the speech signal, α and β are constants, and $\vec{\gamma}$ is a constant vector belonging to $\mathbb{R}^d$ (in practice, d is about 50.000). The noise source $n(t)$ and its delayed version $n(t-1)$ are zero mean and are strongly correlated with $z(t)$ [1, 2]. Let be Z, N_1 and N_2 the random variables that describe the inference $z(t)$, $n(t)$ and $n(t-1)$ respectively. N_1 and N_2 are not correlated. Without loss of generality, we can consider N_1 and N_2 centered. Denoting $\mathbb{E}$ the expectation function and cov the covariance function, the previous requirements lead to the following system

$$\begin{cases} cov(N_1, \alpha N_1 + \beta N_2 + \Gamma) \neq 0 \\ cov(N_2, \alpha N_1 + \beta N_2 + \Gamma) \neq 0 \\ cov(N_1, N_2) \qquad\qquad\;\; = 0 \\ \mathbb{E}(N_1) \qquad\qquad\qquad\;\; = 0 \\ \mathbb{E}(N_2) \qquad\qquad\qquad\;\; = 0 \end{cases} \tag{2}$$

where α and β are unknown parameters, and Γ the random variable that describes $\vec{\gamma}$.

Theorem 1. *The constant vector $\vec{\gamma}$ in $\mathbb{R}^d$ associated to the random variable Γ is null and therefore the function ϕ is homogenous.*

Proof : Let's consider $\vec{\gamma} = {}^{\perp}(\gamma_1\ \gamma_2\ \dots\ \gamma_d)$ where $\perp$ denotes the transposition operator. One has $Z = \alpha N_1 + \beta N_2 + \vec{\gamma}$. That leads to $\mathbb{E}(Z) = \alpha\mathbb{E}(N_1) + \beta\mathbb{E}(N_2) + \Gamma$. As a requirement of the neuro-fuzzy system, $z(t)$ must have the same statistical properties with $n(t)$ and $n(t-1)$ [2, 3, 4]. which are zero mean vectors. Therefore $\mathbb{E}(Z) = 0$. Hence $\vec{\gamma} = \vec{0}$ since $\Gamma = 0$. In conclusion, the fonction ϕ is homogenous and we have : $\exists\ \alpha,\ \beta \in \mathbb{R}$ such that $Z = \alpha N_1 + \beta N_2$.

The problem under examination can then be formulated in the following terms: *Under which conditions on parameters α and β, the system (2) can be solved on such parameters in the way that the inference noise signal $z(t) = \alpha n(t) + \beta n(t-1)$ becomes a good linear passage dynamic function modeling ?*

3   Case-Study of Normal Distribution

Let us consider the probability space $(\mathbb{R}, \mathcal{P}(\mathbb{R}), p)$. We assume here that N_1 and N_2 are Gaussian variables with parameters $(0, \sigma_1)$ and $(0, \sigma_2)$ respectively. The variable Z is centered[2] and the following theorem holds:

---

[2] Since it is a linear combination of centered random variables N_1 and N_2.

Theorem 2. *The standard deviation σ_Z of the random variable Z is*

$$\sigma_Z = \sqrt{\alpha^2 \sigma_{N_1}^2 + \beta^2 \sigma_{N_2}^2} \tag{3}$$

where σ_{N_1} and σ_{N_2} are standard deviations of N_1 and N_2 respectively.

The probability that $N_i(\omega) \in \,]j\sigma_i, (j+1)\sigma_i[\; \forall \, i = 1, 2, \; \forall j \in \mathbb{N}$, is given by

$$p\left(j\,\sigma_i < N_i < (j+1)\,\sigma_i\right) = \phi^\star(j+1) - \phi^\star(j), \, \forall \, i = 1, 2 \tag{4}$$

where $\phi^\star$ is the normal distribution with parameter $(0,1)$ defined as

$$\phi^\star(x) = \frac{1}{\sqrt{2\pi}} \int_{-\infty}^{x} e^{\frac{-t^2}{2}}\, dt. \tag{5}$$

Considering $j, l \in \mathbb{N}$ one can prove the following inequalities

$$\alpha j\, \sigma_1 + \beta l\, \sigma_2 < \alpha\, N_1 + \beta\, N_2 < \alpha\,(j+1)\,\sigma_1 + \beta\,(l+1)\,\sigma_2. \tag{6}$$

In particular, for $j = l = 1$, one has

$$\alpha\, \sigma_1 + \beta\, \sigma_2 < \alpha\, N_1 + \beta\, N_2 < 2\,\alpha\,\sigma_1 + 2\,\beta\,\sigma_2. \tag{7}$$

Under the assumptions that $\alpha \geq 0$ and $\beta \geq 0$, we have $\sigma_Z^2 \leq \alpha\,\sigma_1 + \beta\,\sigma_2$. The probability that $Z(\omega) \in \,]\alpha\sigma_1 + \beta\sigma_2, 2(\alpha\sigma_1 + \beta\sigma_2)[$ cannot be easily calculated since we do not know its probability density function. However, under the assumptions made above, this can be calculated.

3.1 Probability Density Function (pdf) of Z

Let f_1 and f_2 be the pdfs of N_1 and N_2 respectively. One has

$$f_1(x) = \frac{1}{\sigma_1\sqrt{2\pi}}e^{\frac{-x^2}{2\sigma_1{}^2}} \quad \text{and} \quad f_2(y) = \frac{1}{\sigma_2\sqrt{2\pi}}e^{\frac{-y^2}{2\sigma_2{}^2}}. \tag{8}$$

Changing N_1 and N_2 into M_1 and M_2 respectively by $M_1 = \alpha N_1$ and $M_2 = \beta N_2$, one has $Z = M_1 + M_2$. In order to determine the pdf of Z, let recall two theorems[3] we applied from probability theory [5, 6].

Theorem 3. *Given the random variable X with $f(x)$ as its pdf, and $Y = \Phi(X)$ a random variable depending upon X where Φ is a monotonous function, with ψ as its inverse, the probability density function of Y is given by the formula*

$$g(y) = f\left[\psi(y)\right] \times |\psi'(y)|. \tag{9}$$

Theorem 4. *Given the random variable X that follows the normal distribution law with parameters (m_x, σ), where m_x denotes the expectation value and σ the standard deviation, the random variable $Y = a\,X$ where a is a fixed numerical constant, follows the normal distribution law with parameters $(a\,m_x, |a|\sigma)$.*

---

[3] We kindly refer the reader to [5, 6] for their proofs.

Denoting $g_1(x)$ and $g_2(y)$ the probability density functions of M_1 and M_2 respectively, and applying theorems (3) and (4), one obtains

$$g_1(y) = \frac{1}{|\alpha|\sigma_1\sqrt{2\pi}}e^{\frac{-y^2}{2\alpha^2\sigma_1^2}} \quad \text{and} \quad g_2(y) = \frac{1}{|\beta|\sigma_2\sqrt{2\pi}}e^{\frac{-y^2}{2\beta^2\sigma_2^2}}, \tag{10}$$

with $y = \Phi_i(x) = k_i\,x$ and $x = \psi_i(y) = \frac{y}{k_i} \,\forall i = 1, 2$ $(k_1 = \alpha, k_2 = \beta)$. Therefore, M_1 and M_2 follow the Gaussian distribution law with parameters $(0, |\alpha|\sigma_1)$ and $(0, |\beta|\sigma_2)$ respectively. Let us consider now $Z = M_1 + M_2$, and $f(x, y)$ its probability density function. Its distribution function $G(z)$ is defined by

$$G(z) = p(X + Y < z) \tag{11}$$

$$= \iint_{\mathcal{D}} f(x, y)\,dx\,dy \tag{12}$$

$$= \int_{-\infty}^{+\infty}\int_{-\infty}^{z-x} f(x, y)\,dx\,dy \tag{13}$$

$$= \int_{-\infty}^{+\infty}\left(\int_{-\infty}^{z-x} f(x, y)\,dy\right)dx \tag{14}$$

where the domain $\mathcal{D} = \{(x, y) \in xOy$ such that $x + y < z$, z is fixed$\}$. The derivative of $G(z)$ respect to z is the pdf of Z. Therefore, one has

$$g(z) = \int_{-\infty}^{+\infty} f(x, z - x)\,dx = \int_{-\infty}^{+\infty} f(z - y, y)\,dy. \tag{15}$$

The variables M_1 and M_2 are independent as N_1 and N_2. That leads to $f(x, y) = g_1(x)g_2(y)$. Then, the pdf $g(z)$ in (15), becomes

$$g(z) = \int_{-\infty}^{+\infty} g_1(x)\,g_2(z - x)\,dx = \int_{-\infty}^{+\infty} g_1(z - y)\,g_2(y)\,dy. \tag{16}$$

That is the convolution of g_1 with g_2 we can write on the form $g = g_1 \star g_2$. In simplifying $g(z)$, the following equalities hold :

$$g(z) = \int_{-\infty}^{+\infty} g_1(x)\,g_2(z - x)\,dx \tag{17}$$

$$= \int_{-\infty}^{+\infty} \frac{1}{\alpha\,\sigma_1\sqrt{2\,\pi}}e^{\frac{-x^2}{2\,\alpha^2\,\sigma_1^2}}\frac{1}{\beta\,\sigma_2\sqrt{2\,\pi}}e^{\frac{-(z-x)^2}{2\,\beta^2\,\sigma_2^2}}\,dx \tag{18}$$

$$= \frac{1}{2\,\alpha\beta\,\sigma_1\sigma_2\,\pi}\int_{-\infty}^{+\infty}e^{-A\,x^2 + 2\,B\,x - C}\,dx \tag{19}$$

where $A = \dfrac{\alpha^2\,\sigma_1^2 + \beta^2\,\sigma_2^2}{2\,\alpha^2\,\beta^2\,\sigma_1^2\,\sigma_2^2}$ $\quad B = \dfrac{z}{2\,\beta^2\sigma_2^2}$ $\quad C = \dfrac{z^2}{2\beta^2\,\sigma_2^2}.$

Using Euler–Poisson's formula [7], one has

$$\int_{-\infty}^{+\infty}e^{-A\,x^2 + 2\,B\,x - C}\,dx = \sqrt{\frac{\pi}{A}}e^{-\frac{A\,C - B^2}{A}}. \tag{20}$$

Therefore, the function $g(z)$ in (19) becomes

$$g(z) = \frac{1}{2\alpha\beta\,\sigma_1\sigma_2\,\pi}\frac{\sqrt{2\pi}\,\sigma_1\,\sigma_2}{\sqrt{\alpha^2\,\sigma_1^2 + \beta^2\,\sigma_2^2}}e^{-\left(\frac{z^2}{2\,\beta^2\,\sigma_2^2} - \frac{z^2}{4\,\beta^4\,\sigma_2^4} \times \frac{2\,\alpha^2\beta^2\,\sigma_1^2\,\sigma_2^2}{\alpha^2\sigma_1^2 + \beta^2\sigma_2^2}\right)} \tag{21}$$

$$= \frac{1}{\sqrt{2\,\pi}\sigma_Z}e^{-\frac{z^2}{2\,\sigma_Z^2}}. \tag{22}$$

We can conclude that the random variable Z has a normal distribution with parameters $(0, \sigma_Z)$ in which $\sigma_Z = \left(\alpha^2\sigma_{N_1}^2 + \beta^2\sigma_{N_2}^2\right)^{\frac{1}{2}}$.

3.2   Forced Linear Passage

Since $\alpha > 0$ and $\beta > 0$, one has $\sigma_Z^2 \leq \alpha\,\sigma_1 + \beta\,\sigma_2$. Therefore the following property holds : $\exists\,\rho \geq 0$ such that $\alpha\,\sigma_1 + \beta\,\sigma_2 = \rho + \sigma_Z^2$. To force the linear function to be a simple passage dynamic for the problem under examination, the parameter ρ should be equal to 0. That leads to

$$\alpha\,\sigma_1 + \beta\,\sigma_2 = \alpha^2\,{\sigma_1}^2 + \beta^2\,{\sigma_2}^2. \tag{23}$$

where α and β are unknown. The equation (23) becomes

$$\beta^2\,{\sigma_2}^2 - \beta\,\sigma_2 + \alpha^2\,{\sigma_1}^2 - \alpha\,\sigma_1 = 0 \tag{24}$$

$$\left(\sigma_2\,\beta - \frac{1}{2}\right)^2 + \left(\sigma_1\,\alpha - \frac{1}{2}\right)^2 = \frac{1}{2} \tag{25}$$

$$\left(\frac{\beta - \frac{1}{2\sigma_2}}{\frac{1}{\sigma_2\sqrt{2}}}\right)^2 + \left(\frac{\alpha - \frac{1}{2\sigma_1}}{\frac{1}{\sigma_1\sqrt{2}}}\right)^2 = 1 \tag{26}$$

The set of points (α, β) is the first quadrant of an ellipse since $\sigma_1 \neq \sigma_2$, $\alpha > 0$ and $\beta > 0$. In polar coordinates system, the equation (26) becomes

$$\begin{cases} \alpha = \frac{1}{2\sigma_1} + \frac{1}{\sigma_2\sqrt{2}}\,\sin(\theta) \\ \beta = \frac{1}{2\sigma_2} + \frac{1}{\sigma_1\sqrt{2}}\,\cos(\theta), & \theta \in \mathbb{R}. \end{cases} \tag{27}$$

In this form, it is sufficient to know $\theta \in [0, \frac{\pi}{2}]$ to determine the parameters α and β that depend upon σ_1 and σ_2 and the angle θ. Applying the previous results to the babble, car, traffic, and white noise sources, we plot in Figure 1 the corresponding passage dynamic function (PDF) for each noise source sample.

4   Concluding Remarks

Our mathematical analysis provides a set of numerical values for α and β, that defined a linear passage dynamic function. One can observe that the system of constraints defined in (2) is not completely solved since the hypotheses of strongly correlation between noise sources and the inference $z(t)$ is not completely solved. For modeling such a function, it appears from our result that a linear passage dynamic function is strongly dependent on the noisy source distribution (see 1).

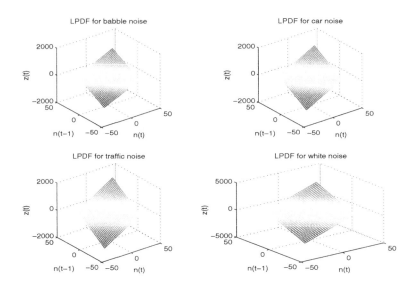

Fig. 1. Plot of linear passage dynamic function (LPDF) for different noise sources. We chose $\theta = 25°$.

References

1. J.-S. R. Jang, C.-T. Sun, E. Mizutani, *Neuro Fuzzy and Soft Computing, A Computational Approach to Learinig and Machine Intelligence* Prentice Hall Upper Saddle River, NJ 07458.
2. E. C. Ezin, *Neural Networks and Neural Fuzzy Systems for Speech Applications,* PhD. Dissertation, Institut de Mathématiques et de Sciences Physiques, Université d'Abomey-Calavi, Bénin, March 2001.
3. A. Esposito, E. C. Ezin, C. Reyes-Garcia, *Speech Noise Cancellation, Based on a Neuro-Fuzzy System: Experimental Results*, in Proceedings of the IEEE on International Workshop on Intelligent Signal Processing, pp. 342-347, Budapest, September 1999, ISBN 963 420 607 7.
4. A. Esposito, E. C. Ezin, C. Reyes-Garcia, *A Neuro-Fuzzy Inference System for Noise Source Identification*, in Proceedings of International Workshop, Speech and Computer, SPECOM, St.-Petersburg, Russia, pp.53–56, September, 2000.
5. E. S. Ventsel, *La théorie des Probabilités*, Traduction Française, Edition Mir, 1982.
6. W. Feller, *An Introduction to Probability Theory and Its Applications*, vol. I and vol. II, second and thrid edition, John Wiley & Sons, 1968 and 1971.
7. Press H. William et al., *The Art of Scientific Computing*, Second Edition, Cambridge University Press, 1999.

Bi-monotonic Fuzzy Sets Lead to Optimal Fuzzy Interfaces

Giovanna Castellano, Anna M. Fanelli, and Corrado Mencar

CILAB – Computational Intelligence LABoratory,
Department of Informatics, University of Bari,
v. E. Orabona, 4 – 70126 Bari, Italy

Abstract. In this paper, we address the issue of designing optimal fuzzy interfaces, which are fundamental components of fuzzy models. In particular, we prove that for a class of so-called bi-monotonic fuzzy sets, optimal interfaces can be guaranteed if mild conditions hold. The class of bi-monotonic fuzzy sets covers a broad range of fuzzy sets shapes, including convex fuzzy sets, so that the provided theoretical results can be applied to a wide range of fuzzy models. As a practical result, the paper provides a set of guidelines that can be followed for the design of optimal fuzzy interfaces.

1 Introduction

Fuzzy models are regarded as linguistic modeling structures with well-defined functional blocks of input and output interfaces along with a processing module (Figure 1). The central role of the input interface consists in the conversion of information coming from the environment in an internal format acceptable by the processing module. Symmetrically, the output interface provides a conversion procedure to transform information coming from the processing module into a suited external representation to be used in the environment [3].

The information transformation from the external to the internal representation can be carried out through a matching procedure employing a family of referential fuzzy sets that model some linguistic terms. Specifically, the input interface provides a mapping from real-valued data into the unit hypercube (fuzzy membership values), while the output interface transforms points in the hypercube into real numerical values. Although the roles of the input and output interfaces are quite different, both of them share the same framework as being based on a family of referential fuzzy sets. As a consequence, we will consider input and output interfaces indistinguishably in the rest of the paper.

As it is widely recognized that the impact of the performance of fuzzy model heavily depends on the input/output interfaces, a careful design of such functional blocks is crucial for the overall quality of the fuzzy model. With this purpose, several criteria have been proposed in order to guarantee well-designed interfaces in terms of two main factors: the semantic integrity of the modeled linguistic terms and the precise representation of uncertain input data. In particular, precise representation can be guaranteed by the so-called "Information Equivalence Criterion" [1], that is, an interface should conserve the information

V. Di Gesú, F. Masulli, and A. Petrosino (Eds.): WILF 2003, LNAI 2955, pp. 39–45, 2006.
© Springer-Verlag Berlin Heidelberg 2006

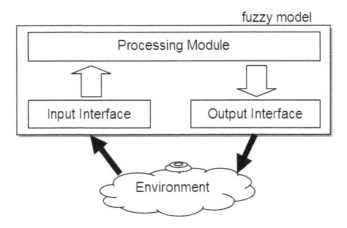

Fig. 1. The three functional blocks of a fuzzy model

inputted into (or being sent out from) the processing block. This is directly related to the necessity of ensuring that the overall system will process a legitimate representation of the inputted (resp. outputted) signal and not something else that may not represent it. An interface that satisfies the Information Equivalence Criterion is also called "optimal interface" [2]. Using optimal interfaces, it can be proved that each external datum has its own internal representation, and linguistic terms cover the entire universe of discourse, which is conversely completely defined by such linguistic terms.

Optimal interfaces have been extensively studied in the context of linguistic terms defined by triangular fuzzy sets [1, 2, 3, 7], but little attention has been paid to fuzzy sets of different shapes. On the other hand, many fuzzy models are derived by means of fuzzy sets of different shapes, such as trapezoidal, Gaussian, bell-shaped, etc., hence the issue of optimality of interfaces built with such kinds of fuzzy sets must be addressed. In this paper, we prove that interface optimality can be guaranteed for a wide class of fuzzy sets, provided that mild conditions are satisfied. In particular, after the definition of two main classes of fuzzy sets, namely strictly bi-monotonic fuzzy sets and loosely bi-monotonic fuzzy sets, two theorems are proved. The first theorem proves that optimal interfaces are always guaranteed for strictly bi-monotonic fuzzy sets (e.g. Gaussian fuzzy sets), provided that weak conditions hold, while optimality is guaranteed for loosely bi-monotonic fuzzy sets (e.g. triangular and convex fuzzy sets in general) if stronger conditions hold. The theorems provide sufficient condition for optimality for a wide class of fuzzy sets, including convex fuzzy sets, so that their result can be useful in a broad range of fuzzy modeling contexts. The paper is organized as follows. In the next Section, a fuzzy interfaces and optimality condition are formally defined. In Section 2, bi-monotonic fuzzy sets are introduced, while in Section 3 two theorems on optimality conditions for bi-monotonic fuzzy sets are presented and proved. Finally, a discussion and some conclusive remarks are drawn.

2   Fuzzy Interfaces

In this section, the notion of fuzzy interface and optimality condition are formally defined. Intuitively, a fuzzy interface is defined by a family of fuzzy sets defined on the same universe of discourse, which are properly ordered by an order relation. The availability of these two objects is necessary and sufficient to define a fuzzy interface.

Definition 1 (fuzzy interface). *Given a family of fuzzy sets*

$$\Phi = \{A_1, A_2, \ldots, A_n\} \tag{1}$$

defined over a universe of discourse $\mathbf{X}$, *and an ordering relation* $\prec$, *the fuzzy interface induced by* Φ *with ordering* $\prec$ *is defined as:*

$$\Lambda = \Lambda(\Phi, \prec) : \mathbf{X} \to [0, 1]^n \tag{2}$$

such that:

$$\forall x \in \mathbf{X} : \Lambda(x) = (A_1(x), A_2(x), \ldots, A_n(x)) \tag{3}$$

where $A_i(x)$ *is the membership function of* x *in fuzzy set* A_i *and assuming* $A_i \prec A_{i+1}, \forall i = 1, 2, \ldots, n - 1$.

The idea behind the concept of optimal interfaces states that an error-free conversion should exist when the values of a given numerical variable are successively transformed in the internal representation and vice-versa.

Definition 2 (optimality condition). *A fuzzy interface* $\Lambda = \Lambda(\Phi, \prec)$ *is optimal if there exists a function:*

$$\mathrm{N} : [0, 1]^n \to \mathbf{X} \tag{4}$$

such that:

$$\mathrm{N}(\Lambda(x)) = x \tag{5}$$

that is, Λ *is invertible.*

It has been proved [2] that using optimal interfaces, the following properties hold:

- Precise representation: $\forall x\prime, x\prime\prime \in \mathbf{X} : x\prime \neq x\prime\prime \to \Lambda(x\prime) \neq \Lambda(x\prime\prime)$
- Coverage: $\forall x \in \mathbf{X} \exists A \in \Phi$ s.t. $A(x) > 0$

3   Bi-monotonic Fuzzy Sets

The above mentioned properties are crucial for the design of interfaces that do not hamper the overall performance of the fuzzy model. As a consequence, an important issue concerns the study of the conditions that apply to families of fuzzy sets in order to induce optimal interfaces. In this section, we introduce two classes of fuzzy sets that cover most types of fuzzy sets, including convex fuzzy sets. These two classes play a central role in the formulation of optimality conditions.

Definition 3 (bi-monotonic fuzzy sets). *A one-dimensional fuzzy set A defined over universe of discourse $\mathbf{X} \subseteq \mathbb{R}$ is strictly bi-monotonic if there exists a prototype $p \in \mathbf{X}$ (i.e. $A(p) = 1$) such that the restrictions of the membership function $A : \mathbf{X} \to [0,1]$ to the sub-domains $\mathbf{X}_L = \mathbf{X} \cap]-\infty, p]$ and $\mathbf{X}_R = \mathbf{X} \cap [p, +\infty[$ are strictly monotone. The fuzzy set A is (loosely) bi-monotonic if such restrictions are loosely monotonic. Of course, strictly monotonic fuzzy sets are also loosely monotonic. We will call the two restrictions as A_L (left restriction) and A_R (right restriction).*

Lemma 1. *If A is strictly monotonic, then $\forall \pi \in [0,1] : \left| A^{-1}(\pi) \right| \leq 2$, where $A^{-1}(\pi) = \{x \in \mathbf{X} | A(x) = \pi\}$.*

Proof. If the range of the membership function of A is $\rho(A) \subseteq [0,1]$, then $\forall \pi \in [0,1[- \rho(A) : A^{-1}(\pi) = \emptyset$. Let p be a prototype of A. If $\pi \in \rho(A)$, let:

$$A_L^{-1}(\pi) = \{x \in \mathbf{X} \cap]-\infty, p] | A(x) = \pi\} \tag{6}$$

$$A_R^{-1}(\pi) = \{x \in \mathbf{X} \cap [p, +\infty[| A(x) = \pi\} \tag{7}$$

Then $\left| A_L^{-1}(\pi) \right| \leq 1$ because if $\exists x_1, x_2$ s.t. $x_1 < x_2 \wedge x_1 \in A_L^{-1}(\pi) \wedge x_2 \in A_L^{-1}(\pi)$, then $\exists x_1, x_2$ s.t. $x_1 < x_2 \wedge A_L(x_1) = A_L(x_2)$ that is, the left restriction A_L would not be strictly monotonic. The same is true for A_R. As a consequence, $A^{-1}(\pi) = A_L^{-1}(\pi) \cup A_R^{-1}(\pi) \Rightarrow \left| A^{-1}(\pi) \right| \leq \left| A_L^{-1}(\pi) \right| + \left| A_R^{-1}(\pi) \right| \leq 2$.   □

Corollary 1. *If p is a prototype of A, then $\left| A^{-1}(A(p)) \right| = 1$*

Proof. Note that $p \in A_L^{-1}(A(p)) \wedge p \in A_R^{-1}(A(p))$. If, ad absurdum, $\exists q$ s.t. $p \neq q \wedge q \in A^{-1}(A(p))$, then $q \in A_L^{-1}(A(p)) \vee A_R^{-1}(A(p))$, that is, $\left| A_L^{-1}(A(p)) \right| > 1 \vee \left| A_R^{-1}(A(p)) \right| > 1$. This is absurd.   □

Corollary 2. *The support of a strictly bi-monotonic fuzzy set A defined over $\mathbf{X}$ is $\mathbf{X} - O$, where O is a set with at most two elements, and can be eventually empty.*

Lemma 2. *Convex one-dimensional fuzzy sets are loosely bi-monotonic.*

Proof. Let A be a convex fuzzy set. Let $\alpha_1, \alpha_2 \in [0,1]$, $\alpha_1 < \alpha_2$ and $[A]_{\alpha_1}, [A]_{\alpha_2}$ the respective strict α-cuts ($[A]_\alpha = \{x \in \mathbf{X} | A(x) > \alpha\}$). Because of convexity, $[A]_{\alpha_1} \supseteq [A]_{\alpha_2}$. Let $m_k = \inf [A]_{\alpha_k}$ and $M_k = \sup [A]_{\alpha_k}$, for $k = 1, 2$. Then $m_1 \leq m_2 \wedge M_1 \geq M_2$. Let:

$$\forall x \in \mathbf{X} : A_L(x) = \alpha \Leftrightarrow \forall \beta > \alpha : \inf [A]_\beta > x \wedge \forall \beta < \alpha : \inf [A]_\beta < x \tag{8}$$

$$\forall x \in \mathbf{X} : A_R(x) = \alpha \Leftrightarrow \forall \beta > \alpha : \sup [A]_\beta < x \wedge \forall \beta < \alpha : \sup [A]_\beta > x \tag{9}$$

Then, by construction A_L, A_R are monotonic (not strictly in general), hence A is bi-monotonic.   □

Corollary 3. *Gaussian membership functions (and their complements) are strictly bi-monotonic. Triangular and trapezoidal membership functions (with their complements) are loosely bi-monotonic but, in general, not strictly bi-monotonic.*

Definition 4. *A multi-dimensional fuzzy set A is (strictly/loosely) bi-monotonic if it is the Cartesian product of one-dimensional (strictly/loosely) bi-monotonic fuzzy sets.*

4   Optimality Conditions

In this section, two sufficient conditions for interface optimality are provided, for the two classes of bi-monotonic fuzzy sets (strictly and loosely). Such conditions are fulfilled if some mild constraints are satisfied. As shown, while for strictly bi-monotonic fuzzy sets such constraints are easy to satisfy, for loosely bi-monotonic the constraints are more stringent and require careful design.

Theorem 1. *Let $\Phi = \{A_1, A_2, \ldots, A_n\}$ be a family of one-dimensional strictly bi-monotonic fuzzy sets, with respective distinct prototypes $p_1, p_2, \ldots, p_n$ such that $\forall x \in \mathbf{X} \exists p_i, p_j$ s.t. $p_i \leq x \leq p_j$. Let the following ordering relation be: $A_i \prec A_j \Leftrightarrow p_i < p_j$. Then, the fuzzy interface $\Lambda (\Phi, \prec)$ is optimal.*

Proof. We assume, without loss of generality, that $\forall i = 1, 2, \ldots, n - 1 : A_i \prec A_{i+1}$. Let $x \in \mathbf{X}$ and $\Lambda (x) = (\pi_1, \pi_2, \ldots, \pi_n)$. Let π_i, π_j be the values of $(\pi_1, \pi_2, \ldots, \pi_n)$ corresponding to two fuzzy sets $A_i, A_j \in \Phi$ with prototypes p_i, p_j such that $p_i \leq x \leq p_j$. Then, $A_i^{-1} (\pi_i) \cap A_j^{-1} (\pi_j) = \{x\}$. Indeed, suppose, ad absurdum, that $A_i^{-1} (\pi_i) \cap A_j^{-1} (\pi_j) = \{y, z\}$, with $y < z$ (note that $x = y \vee x = z$, since x will always compare in the intersection by construction of the defined sets). By Lemma 1, we have $y \in A_{iL}^{-1} (\pi_i) \wedge z \in A_{iR}^{-1} (\pi_i)$ and, symmetrically, $y \in A_{jL}^{-1} (\pi_j) \wedge z \in A_{jR}^{-1} (\pi_j)$. As a consequence, the prototypes p_i, p_j are such that $y \leq p_i < p_j \leq z$, that is $x \leq p_i < p_j \vee p_i < p_j \leq x$. This is absurd, since by hypotheses $p_i \leq x \leq p_j$ and if $x = p_i \vee x = p_j$ then $\left| A_i^{-1} (\pi_i) \right| = 1 \vee \left| A_j^{-1} (\pi_j) \right| = 1 \Rightarrow \left| A_i^{-1} (\pi_i) \cap A_j^{-1} (\pi_j) \right| = 1$. As a result, the function:

$$\mathrm{N} (\pi_1, \pi_2, \ldots, \pi_n) = x \Leftrightarrow A_1^{-1} (\pi_1) \cap A_n^{-1} (\pi_n) = \{x\} \tag{10}$$

is the inverse function of Λ, which is hence optimal.   □

Note that definition of N requires only the two extreme components π_1, π_n. This is theoretically acceptable, but in numerical simulations, more numerically robust solutions can be adopted, depending on the shape of the membership functions. As an example, if Gaussian membership functions are adopted, more robust numerical results can be obtained by selecting the two highest values of $(\pi_1, \pi_2, \ldots, \pi_n)$ and proceeding analytically to find the value of x.

Corollary 4. *Let a family of multi-dimensional strictly bi-monotonic fuzzy sets be $\Phi = \{\mathbf{A}_1, \mathbf{A}_2, \ldots, \mathbf{A}_n\}$ with $\mathbf{A}_i = A_{i1} \times A_{i2} \times \cdots \times A_{im}$ and $\forall \mathbf{x} = (x_1, x_2, \ldots, x_m) : \mathbf{A}_i (\mathbf{x}) = A_{i1} (x_1) \otimes A_{i2} (x_2) \otimes \cdots \otimes A_{im} (x_m)$ where $\otimes$ is any t-norm. If, for each $j = 1, 2, \ldots, m$, the fuzzy interface $\Lambda_j = \Lambda_j (\{A_{1j}, A_{2j}, \ldots, A_{nj}\}, \prec_j)$ is optimal (with $\prec_j$ properly defined as in theorem 1), then the fuzzy interface $\Lambda (\Phi, \prec)$ is optimal, for any choice of the ordering relation $\prec$.*

Proof. The inverse function of Λ can be derived by defining the inverse functions of each Λ_j, that is $N(\Lambda(\mathbf{x})) = (N_1(\Lambda_1(x_1)), N_2(\Lambda_2(x_2)), \ldots, N_n(\Lambda_n(x_n)))$.   □

Theorem 2. *Let $\Phi = \{A_1, A_2, \ldots, A_n\}$ be a family of one-dimensional loosely bi-monotonic fuzzy sets, such that*

$$\forall A \in \Phi, \forall \pi_A \in [0,1], \exists B \in \Phi, \exists \pi_B \in [0,1] \ s.t. \ \left| A^{-1}(\pi_A) \cap B^{-1}(\pi_B) \right| \leq 1$$

with respective distinct prototypes $p_1, p_2, \ldots, p_n$ such that $\forall x \in \mathbf{X} \exists p_i, p_j \ s.t. \ p_i \leq x \leq p_j$. Let the following ordering relation be: $A_i \prec A_j \Leftrightarrow p_i < p_j$. Then, the fuzzy interface $\Lambda(\Phi, \prec)$ is optimal.

Proof. The proof is similar to the previous theorem, where the condition $A_i^{-1}(\pi_i) \cap A_j^{-1}(\pi_j) = \{x\}$ is true by hypothesis.   □

5   Discussion

The theorems proved in the previous sections guarantee optimality of fuzzy interfaces provided that mild conditions hold. In the following, we briefly discuss the achieved results from a practical point of view, providing some guidelines for designing optimal fuzzy interfaces. For one-dimensional strictly bi-monotonic fuzzy sets (like Gaussian fuzzy sets), optimality of fuzzy interfaces can be easily guaranteed if the prototypes of fuzzy sets are distinct, with the leftmost and rightmost prototypes coinciding with minimum and maximum values of the universe of discourse. Moreover, if two fuzzy sets share the same prototype (e.g. one fuzzy set is the subset of the other) only one can be retained for the definition of the interface, thus preserving optimality. Finally, it is noteworthy that the derivation of the inverse function of the fuzzy interface requires - at least theoretically - only the two fuzzy sets corresponding to the leftmost and the rightmost prototypes. Such derivation is independent on the shape of the intermediate fuzzy sets. As a consequence, interface optimality becomes a trivial condition that is always held when strictly bi-monotonic fuzzy sets are used. For loosely bi-monotonic fuzzy sets, including all convex fuzzy sets in general, interface optimality is guaranteed provided that a stronger condition holds. In particular, it is required that for each fuzzy set there exists another fuzzy set which eliminates any possible ambiguity when a given level of membership is given. While such condition trivially holds for strictly bi-monotonic fuzzy sets, it can be violated for fuzzy sets with "flat" areas (i.e. areas where membership value is constant), like triangular or trapezoidal fuzzy sets (see Figure 2 for an example). As a consequence, this condition implies a careful design of the fuzzy interface, since it can be easily violated for particular choices of fuzzy sets' parameters.

For multi-dimensional bi-monotonic fuzzy sets, interface optimality heavily depends on interface optimality of one-dimensional projections. However, many techniques that automatically generate fuzzy interfaces, like clustering methods, do not assure the fulfillment of conditions that guarantee one-dimensional interface optimality. To overcome such drawback, interpretability-oriented clustering algorithms, like those in [4], [5] and [6], can be effectively applied.

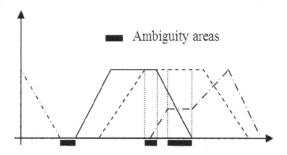

Fig. 2. A fuzzy interface with ambiguity areas

6   Conclusions

The formal approach introduced in the paper provides some guidelines in the design of fuzzy models, either if they are manually defined or automatically acquired from data. Specifically, the conditions for interface optimality of a wide range of fuzzy membership functions are outlined. As a key result, interface optimality can be checked for different types of membership functions, other than the most widely used triangular type, resulting particularly useful in fields like Fuzzy Control, where interface optimality is of fundamental importance.

References

1. W. Pedrycz, J.V. de Oliveira, "Optimization of Fuzzy Models", IEEE Trans. on Sys., Man and Cyb., vol. 26, no. 4, pp. 627-636, 1996
2. J.V. de Oliveira, "A Design Methodology for Fuzzy Systems Interfaces", IEEE Trans. on Fuzzy Systems, vol. 3, no. 4, pp. 404-414, 1995
3. J.V. de Oliveira, "On Optimal Fuzzy Systems I/O Interfaces", in Proc. 2nd IEEE Int. Conf. Fuzzy Syst., San Francisco, CA, pp. 851-856, 1993
4. G. Castellano, A.M. Fanelli, C. Mencar, "Generation of interpretable fuzzy granules by a double-clustering technique", Archives of Control Sciences, vol. 12 no. 4, pp. 397-410, 2002
5. T.W. Liao, A.K. Celmins, R.J. Hammel II, "A Fuzzy C-Means Variant for the Generation of Fuzzy Term Sets", Fuzzy Sets and Systems, vol. 135, pp. 241-257, 2003
6. J. Abonyi, R. Babuska, F. Szeifert, "Modified Gath-Geva fuzzy clustering for identification of Takagi-Sugeno fuzzy models", IEEE Trans. on Systems, Man and Cybernetics, Part B, Vol.32, No.5, pp. 612- 621, 2002
7. W. Pedrycz, "Why triangular membership functions?", Fuzzy Sets and Systems, Vol. 64, No. 1, pp. 21-30, 1994

Conversational Agent Model in Intelligent User Interface

Francesco Rago

MegaTris Comp. LLC,
113 Barksdale Professional Center Newark,
DE 19711, USA
Market.italy@megatris.com

Abstract. A Conversational Agent Model (CAM) adopts that aspect of the human interface that provides structure for the process of interpreting meaning. The goal of the model is to target those behaviors that regulate and represent information efficiently. The specific CAM is based on the Evolutionary Game Theory that considers an idealized scenario whereby a population of agents (possible behaviors) play an evolutionary game according to a pre-programmed behavior pattern and it is supposed that some evolutionary selection process operates over time on the distribution of behaviors. The selected behaviors interact with human using the interface.

1 Introduction

Actually there is a need to improve the access to web environment to support user in the use of the content. This is particularly true when the environment is a graphical three dimensions one where more sophisticated techniques for Human Computer Interfaces are required. As well know, Human-Computer Interaction (HCI) is a discipline concerned with the design, evaluation and implementation of interactive computing systems for human use and with the study of major phenomena surrounding them. The HCI approach we have used starts from Cassel's study of Conversational Agent Models (CAM). A CAM adopts those aspects of the human interface that provide structure for the process of interpreting meaning. The goal of the model is to target those behaviors that regulate and represent information efficiently. The CAM specific is based on the Evolutionary Game Theory that considers an idealized scenario whereby a population of agents (possible behaviors) play games according to a pre-programmed behavior pattern and it is supposed that some evolutionary selection process operates over time on the distribution of behaviors. A Fuzzy Cognitive Map (FCM) describes the evolution of the states and regulate possible behaviors (agents).). The FCM is the dynamic part of the model and describes the relationship between the events that input the interface of the Conversational Agent. An Evolutionary Game value the expected payoff earned by each agent. The expected payoff is earned by i-strategist and the payoff is calculated to support decision-making to select final behavior in the interface. The game is played over and over and the action of natural selection will result in the evolution of the fittest strategies.

V. Di Gesú, F. Masulli, and A. Petrosino (Eds.): WILF 2003, LNAI 2955, pp. 46–54, 2006.

2   A Conversational Model

Humans engage in complex representational activity involving speech and hand gesture, and they regulate this activity through social conversational protocols that include speech and eye gaze and head movements and hand gestures. In this context, we can view the human as providing structure for interlocutor that helps him navigate a complex description of the world. In building a conversational agent, our goal is to target those behaviors that regulate and facilitate the process of interaction and represent information efficiently and effectively. A conversational model has several key properties: the system internal representation of the world and information must be modality free but able to be conveyed by way of any one of several modalities; the functions of the system must be modality free but able to be realized in any one of a number of different surface behaviors in a number of different modalities; the representations of conversation cannot be all symbolic because cultural, social and technical conventions might not be able to be captured in logical form; and co-occurrences of surface-level behaviors carry meaning over that carried by each of the constituent behaviors. Cassell calls such a model as a multiplicity of representations.

2.1   Division Between Propositional and Interactional Functions

Contributions to the conversation are divided into propositional functions and interactional functions. The propositional function corresponds to the content of the conversation. The interactional function consists of cues that regulate the conversational process and includes a range of non-verbal behaviors. In short, the interactional discourse functions are responsible for creating and maintaining an open channel of communication between the participants, and propositional functions shape the actual content. Both functions can be fulfilled with the use of a number of available communication modalities.

2.2   Modality

Both verbal and non-verbal modalities are responsible for carrying out the interactional and propositional functions. It is not the case that the body behaviors are redundant. There are several different modalities of communications what allow us to pursue multiple goals in parallel, some of a propositional nature and some of an interactional nature. In fact 50 percent of gestures add non redundant information to the common ground of the conversation [9].

2.3   Behaviors Are Not Functions

The same communicative function does not always map onto the same observed behavior. The particular set of surface behaviors exhibited can change from person to person and from conversation to conversation. Therefore, to successfully build a model of how conversation works, one cannot refer to these behaviors, or surface features, alone. Instead, the emphasis has to be on identifying the high level structural elements or functions that make up a conversation. It is the understanding of these functions and how they work together to form a successful interaction that allows us to understand the behaviors in context.

3   Adaptive and Intelligent HCI-Methodology

Our methodology is quite general and derived from Duric model [11]. The main modules are behavioral processing, embodied cognition, and adaptive system interface. The user is interacting with an adaptive system interface, which changes as a function of the current task state and the cognitive state of the user. The non-verbal front end includes the perceptual and behavioral processing modules, and its input consists of raw sensory information about the user. The behavioral module processes information about actions done to the computer interface directly, such as keystroke choices and mouse gestures. The behavioral module provides streams of elementary features that are then grouped, parsed, tracked, and converted to representations of the information. In other words, one output of the behavioral processing module is a stream of states at each point in time. Signal and symbol integration and transformation is an old but difficult problem. It comes about because the world surrounding us is a mixture of continuous space-time functions with discontinuities. Recognition of these discontinuities in the world leads to representations of different states of the world, which in turn place demands on behavioral strategies. Similarly, an agent's (biological or artificial) closed-loop interactions with the world/environment can be modelled as a continuous process, whereas switching between behaviors is naturally discrete. Furthermore, the tasks that are either externally given to the agents or internally self-imposed prespecify and, hence, discretize an otherwise continuous behavior. Symbols not only provide nice abstractions for low-level strategies, but also allow us to move one level up the modelling hierarchy and observe the properties of the systems and their interactions among each other and their environment at a more macroscopic level. Symbolic representation mediates reasoning about the sequential and repetitive nature of various tasks". The adaptive and intelligent HCI methodology proposed by Duric addresses the problems raised above using embodied cognition to connect the apparent perceptual and behavioral sub symbolic representations and symbolic mental states, and in the process adaptively derive the summative sub symbolic states from raw signals and also adapt the user/system interface for enhanced performance and human satisfaction. These subsymbobs are fed into the embodied cognition module and mediate fusion and reasoning about possible cognitive states. While the subsymbols correspond to external manifestations of states, the cognitive states are hidden and not directly observable. The embodied cognition module generates hypotheses about possible task-relevant cognitive states, resolves any resulting ambiguity by drawing from contextual and temporal information, and optimally adapts the interface in order to enhance human performance. Knowledge of the user's state and the systems state are used to diagnose potential problems, and these diagnoses trigger adaptive and compensatory changes in the computer interface. The development of the behavioral processing and embodied cognition modules and their interactions is the key to making progress on constructing adaptive intelligent interfaces.

4   The Human-Computer Interface Modules

To satisfy Adaptive and Intelligent HCI requirements module has specific algo-
rithmic architecture: the behavior processing is performed by a fuzzy cognitive
map that track states (keystroke, command and mouse gestures of human).
States admit a multiplicity of representations and the behaviors provide streams
of elementary features that are then grouped, parsed, tracked, and converted to
representations of the information. These input to a FCM generates behavioral
hypothesis and such hypothesis (what-if) are input to an evolutionary game
where the different strategies are processed until decision about propositional
and interactional functions are accomplished.

5   Fuzzy Cognitive Map

The fuzzy cognitive map (FCM) is powerful tools for creating models of complex
systems. Like the fuzzy rule base, the FCM is a technology in which the application of Zadehan logic enhances an existing method. Political scientist Robert
Axelrod introduced the cognitive map in 1976, using it to represent knowledge
as an interconnected, directed, bilevel-logic graph. Nine years later, University
of Southern California-Los Angeles professor Bart Kosko expanded Axelrod's
maps to FCMs. An FCM is a graph, structured as a collection of nodes and
arcs. Nodes, called concepts, are system variables; their values change over time.
Connections among concepts, the arcs or edges of the graph represent causality.
An edge may connect any concept to any from other concept. An edge may
also connect a concept to itself, indicating that the future value of the concepts
depends on the concept's current value.

The runtime operation of an FCM consists of calculating the next value of
each concept in the FCM from the current concept and edge values. An FCM is a
sampled-data system, in which the collection of current concept values represents
the current overall system concept status. Depending on the number of concepts
and the number and complexity of connections, the system typically requires several steps to reach equilibrium, if, in fact, the system reaches equilibrium. Because
of feedback paths, a FCM can also be oscillatory or unstable. Several techniques
are available for calculating concept values of a system. The most common one is
a normalised sum of products. The first step is to take the product of each source
concept value and connecting edge value. You then sum these products and nor-
malise, or "squash," the result into the range of allowable concept values. A wide
selection of normalising functions is available. The purpose of these functions is to
cause sums greater than one (this can occur when several products are summed)
to be monotonically mapped into the 0 to 1 range. Appropriate normalising functions are those based on: the sigmoid function that is popular in neural networks,
linear functions of varying slopes, and a number of probability density functions.

6   Using Fuzzy Cognitive Map

We use the FCM to describe various external manifestations of state and this
sis a way to describe the behavior knowledge. The state vector C_i represents the

state. In other words, either a zero or a one in the state vector represents each event in the FCM, depending on whether the vector is turned off or on. FCM input states such as these fire all relationships in the FCM to some degree. This process shows how, in a fuzzy dynamic system, causal events affect each other as time goes by. To model the effect of the current state Ci (behavior) on the FCM we use the following technique to determine the new state (on or off) for each event C_i, each time t_{n+1} fires the FCM:

$$C_i(t_{n+1}) = S[\sum_{k=1}^{n} e_{ki}(t_n)C_k(t_n)], \tag{1}$$

S(x) is a bounded signal function indicating whether C, is turned off (0) or on (1)and e_{ki} is the connection strenght of the edges [15]. Based on the outcome of the what-if scenario, the agents control the likelihood of the behavior to exploit. The next step now is an algorithm to use the result of the what-if processing defying an engine to permit states evolution to embodied cognition.

7   Evolutionary Games (EG)

A central achievement of evolutionary game theory was the introduction of a method by which agents can play "optimal" strategies in the absence of ratio-nality. Evolutionary game theory considers an idealized scenario where by in a large population pairs of individuals (agent behaviors) are repeatedly drawn at random to play a symmetric two-player game. In contrast to traditional game theoretic models, players are not supposed to behave rationality or to have com-plete knowledge of the details of the game. They act instead according to a pre-programmed behavior pattern, or pure strategy, and it is supposed that some evolutionary selection process operates over time on the distribution of behaviors. We refer the reader to J. Hofbauer for excellent introductions to this field. Let

$$J = \{\ 1, ..., n\}\ . \tag{2}$$

be the set of available pure strategies. The states at a given instant is the vector $C = (C_1, ..., C_n)$. Clearly, population states are constrained to lie in a standard simplex Δ. For a $C \in \Delta$, we shall denote by $\sigma(x)$ the support of C, i.e., the set of nonextinct strategies:

$$\sigma(C) := \{i \in J : C_i > 0\}\ . \tag{3}$$

Let $A(a_{ij})$ be the n x n payoff matrix. Specifically, for each pair of strategies i, $i \in J$, represents the payoff of an individual playing strategy i against an opponent playing strategy ji. If the population is in state C, the expected payoff earned by an i-strategist is:

$$\pi_i(C) = \sum_{j=1}^{n} a_{ij}C_{ij} = (AC)_i \tag{4}$$

while the mean payoff over the entire state population is:

$$\pi(C) = \sum_{j=1}^{n} C_i \pi_i = C' A C \tag{5}$$

Evaluating the winning π_i we have identified a set of winning strategies relevant for the cognitive states. The EG is the embodied cognition module that generates hypothesis about possible task-relevant cognitive states. The interface applies them in the interactional system environment. In evolutionary game theory the assumption is made that the game is played over and over, generation after generation, and that the action of natural selection will result in the evolution of the fittest strategies. A general class of evolution equations is given by the following set of equations:

$$\dot{c} = c_i g_i(c) \tag{6}$$

where a dot signifies derivative (variations) with respect to time, and $g = (g_1, ..., g_n)$ is a function with open domain containing Δ. Here, the function g_i, $(i \in J)$ specifies the rate al which pure strategy i replicate. Payoff-monotonic game dynamics represent a wide class of regular selection dynamics for which useful properties hold. Intuitively, for a payoff-monotonic dynamics the strategies associated to higher payoffs will increase at a higher rate. Formally, a regular selection dynamics is said to be payoff-monotonic if:

$$g_i(C) > g_j(C) <=> \pi_i(C) > \pi_j(C) \tag{7}$$

for all $C \in \Delta$. In an unpublished paper, Hofbauer shows that the average population payoff is strictly increasing along the trajectories of any monotone game dynamics, provided that payoffs are symmetric. This result generalizes the celebrated fundamental theorem of natural selection. To each payoff is associated an operating strategy S_i.

8   Experimental Environment and Results

The experimental environment is a three dimensions interface where the human agent can navigate, views objects and dynamically modify the environments itself using appropriate options. The non-verbal front end includes the perceptual and behavioral processing modules, and its input consists of raw sensory information about the user. Knowledge of the user's state and the systems state are used to diagnose potential actions, and these diagnoses trigger adaptive and compensatory changes in the computer interface.The commands, mouse gestures, the virtual positions and paths in the three dimensions environment represents the human behaviors and it is processed performing operations on the states of the FCM. The EG engine determines the better operating strategy using the payoff matrix. The human agent is interacting with an adaptive system interface, which changes as a function of the current task and cognitive state. The performance of the interface increases if the evolution equation permits a payoff in line with the objective of the system. Intuitively, for a payoff-monotonic dynamics the strategies associated to higher payoffs will increase at a higher rate.

As explained above, the key contribution is the notion that Darwinian selection can replace the need for agent rationality. We have a large population of agents, each playing one of the game pure strategies. Once the payoff of each strategy is know, the next generation of the population of operating strategies, σ_{t+1}, can be created by applying Darwinian selection to the current population σ_t. This process is accomplished by the chosen difference equation that is suggested by Ficici and compliant with condition (6). According to this equation, each strategy reproduces in direct proportion to its fitness - evolutionary game theory assumes fitness proportionate selection.

$$\sigma_{t+1} = \sigma_t * \frac{\pi}{\sigma_t \bullet \pi} \tag{8}$$

where $\bullet$ is inner product.

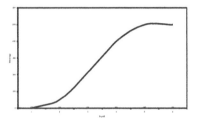

Fig. 1. Fitness Indicator

Experimentally the test of the system means to iterate until we arrive to a mix of payoff strategies that gives a fitness indicator considered stable (see Fig.1). Experts define a FCM and a strategies mix related to a interface environment with specific goals. During the interactions, users give answers to the task generated by strategies. After a set of iterations, it is reached an average payoff that has a sufficient performance in the target environment.

9   Conclusion

We have investigated properties of a specific CAM based on FCM theory and Evolutionary Game Theory. There is an evolutionary selection process that operates over time on the distribution of action strategies and the selected behaviors interact with human user. The FCM represents the knowledge of the systems and its states are used lo diagnose potential actions. The evolutionary game makes the choice about the best potential actions that are usable in the specific states context.

The advantage of the use of FCM is the possibility to operate with multiple uncertain states. The FCM permits to avoid a rule based system giving the advantage of a more simple and fast engine for the specific application, while the Evolutionary Game engine gives an evolutionary tool to support operational decisions.

References

1. Anderson, R., Boyle, C. E, Corbett,A. T.: Cognitive modelling and intelligent tutoring.' Artif Intell. vol. 42, pp. 7-49, 1-90.
2. Andre, E.,: Animated Interface Agents, Making Them Intelligent. Paper presented at the IJCAI'97 Workshop on Animated Interface Agents: Making Them Intelligent, 23-29 August, Nagoya, Japan.
3. Astington, J. W., Harris, P. L., and Qlson, D. R., eds.: Developing Theories of Mind. Cambridge, U.K.: Cambridge University Press.
4. Brooks, R., Brezeal, C., Breazeal, C., Lrie, R., Kemp, C., Majanovic, M., Scassellatati, B., and Williamson, M.:Alternative Essences of Intelligence. In Proceedings of the Fifteenth National Conference on Artificial Intelligence (1998) 961-967. Menlo Park, Calif.
5. Cassell, J., and Bickmore, T.: External Manifestations of Trustworthiness in the Interface. Communications of the ACM (2000)43(12): 50-56.
6. Cassell, J., and Thorisson, K. R.:The Power of a Nod and a Glance: Envelope versus Emotional Feedback in Animated Conversational Agents. Applied Artificial Intelligence (1999)13(4-5): 5 19-538.
7. Cassell, J., and Vilhjàlmsson, H.:Fully Embodied Conversational Avatars: Making Communicative Behaviours Autonomous. Autonomous Agents and Multi-Agent Systems (1999)2:45-64.
8. Cassell, J., McNeill, D., and McCullough, K.-E. Speech-Gesture Mismatches: Evidence for Qne Underlying Representation of Linguistic and Nonlinguistic Information. Pragmatics and Cognition (1999) 7(1): 1-33.
9. Cassell, J.; Stone, M.; and Yan, H.: Coordination and Context-Dependence in the Generation of Embodied Conversation. Paper presented at the First International Language Generation Conference (2000) 12-16 June, Mitzpe Ramon, Israel.
10. Cassell, J., Ananny, M., Basur, N., Bickmore, T., Chong, P., Mellis, D., Ryokai, K., Smith, J., Vilhjalmsson, H., and Yan, H. . Shared Reality: Physical Collaboration with a Virtual Peer. Paper presented at the ACM SIGCHI Conference on Human Factors in Computing Systems, (2000) 1-6 Aprii, The Hague, The Netherlands.
11. Duric, Z., et al.:Integrating perceptual and Cognitive Modelling for Adaptive and Intelligent HCI, Proceedings of the IEEE, Vol. 90, n. 7.
12. Elliott, C., Brzezinski, J.: Autonomous Agents as Synthetic Characters. AI Magazine (1998)19(2): 13-30.
13. Feiner, S., McKeown, K.: Automating the Generation of Coordinated Multimedia Explanations (1991) IEEE Computer 24(10): 33-41.
14. Ficici, S., et al.:A game-Thoric Investigation of Selection Method used in Evolutionary Algorithms, (1991) Demo Lab. Report.
15. Kosko, B.: Fuzzy Cognitive Maps, International Journal of Man-Machine Studies, 24 (1986)
16. Hofbauer,J., Sigmund,K.: Evolutionary and Population Dynamics, Cambridge, UK: Cambridge University Press, (1998).
17. Laurel, B.:The Art ofHuman-Computer Interface Design. Reading, Mass.: Addison-Wesley (1990).

18. Lester, J. C., Stone, B. A.: Increasing Believability in Animated Pedagogical Agents. Paper presented at Autonomous Agents 97, (1997), Marina Del Rey, California.
19. Maybury, M. T., Wahlster, W., : Introduction. In Readings in Intelligent User Interfaces, (1998) 1-38. San Francisco, Calif.: Morgan Kaufmann.
20. Rickel, J., Johnson, W. L.: Animated Agents for Procedural Traning in Virtual Reality: Perception, Cognition, and Motor Control. Applied Artificial Intelligence (1998) 13(4-5): 343-382.
21. Rosenschein, S., and Kaelbling, L.:The Synthesis of Machines with Provable Epistemic Properties. In Proceedings of the Conference on Theoretical Aspects of Reasoning about Knowledge, (1986) 83-98. San Francisco, Calif.: Morgan Kaufmann.
22. Samuelson, L. : Evolutionary Games and Equilibrium Selection, (1997) MIT Press.
23. Weibull, J.W. Evolutionary Game Theory. Cambridge, Mass.: MIT Press, 1995.

A Fuzzy Frame-Based
Knowledge Representation Formalism

Andrea G.B. Tettamanzi

Università degli Studi di Milano,
Dipartimento di Tecnologie dell'Informazione,
Via Bramante 65, I-26013 Crema (CR), Italy
andrea.tettamanzi@unimi.it

Abstract. This paper describes a formalism for representing imprecise knowledge which combines traditional frame-based formalisms with fuzzy logic and fuzzy IF-THEN rules. Inference in this formalism is based on unification and the calculus of fuzzy IF-THEN rules, and lends itself to an efficient implementation.

1 Introduction

This paper describes a frame-based formalism for representing imprecise knowledge, developed within a large research project on knowledge management.

The formalism is frame-based, but frames are considerably simplified to achieve an elegant algebraic description, which is heavily inspired by the unification-based grammar formalisms [4] developed in the last two decades by the natural language processing community. Unification, indeed, plays a central role in this formalism as the main inference rule, which implements multiple inheritance.

The frame-based formalism is extended to accommodate uncertainty and imprecision by combining it with fuzzy logic [5], in a way analogous to other proposals whose aim was to combine frame-based knowledge representation formalisms with Bayesian networks [2]. Furthermore, the formalism incorporates procedural information in the form of fuzzy IF-THEN rules.

According to this formalism, knowledge consists of three basic types of objects:

- knowledge *elements*, which can be either atomic (*atoms*) or complex (*frames*);
- fuzzy sets, or *linguistic values*;
- *relations*, which can be fuzzy rules or subsumption relations.

2 Knowledge Elements

A knowledge element captures the intuitive notion of a *concept*. The set of all knowledge elements will be denoted by $\mathcal{E}$. An element can be either atomic or complex.

2.1 Atomic Elements

An atomic element or, simply, an *atom*, is a concept which cannot be (or is not) analyzed as an aggregate of simpler components. In an application which takes

V. Di Gesú, F. Masulli, and A. Petrosino (Eds.): WILF 2003, LNAI 2955, pp. 55–62, 2006.
© Springer-Verlag Berlin Heidelberg 2006

for granted the nature of numbers, this might be the case of numerical values like 1, 4/5, 193,439,499, or π; another general example of atomic elements might be the two opposites *yes* : *no*, or *present* : *absent*, or $+$: $-$, used to specify whether a given feature is possessed or not by a concept.

This is what is sometimes called an *individual* in description logics [1]. The set of all atomic elements will be denoted by $\mathcal{C}$.

2.2   Complex Elements

A complex element, on the contrary, is a concept which can (and actually is) broken down into more basic components, or features. A complex element can be thought of as a logic type or sort, or, using the terminology of object-oriented systems, a *class*.

We represent such an element as a *frame* [3], i.e., an aggregate of *slots*, where a slot is an attribute-value pair. However, we depart from conventional frames in dispensing with *facets*, and in treating type, value restriction, and values uniformly. The set of all complex elements will be denoted by $\mathcal{F}$.

Each slot predicates a given feature of the element, identified by its attribute, from the set $\mathcal{A}$. This predication is obtained by making a restriction on the values (other elements) that attribute may take up. In order to capture the (possibly) uncertain nature of knowledge, this value restriction is regarded as a *possibility distribution* over $\mathcal{E}$. In other words, the set of values of an attribute may take up is fuzzy: classical sets are thus provided for as a special case[1].

Therefore, a slot is an association between an attribute and a fuzzy set of knowledge elements, which must be regarded as its possible (or admissible) values.

Given a frame $x \in \mathcal{F}$, the (possibly fuzzy) value of its slot identified by attribute $a \in \mathcal{A}$ will be denoted by $x.a$. Therefore, $x.a$ is the fuzzy set of possible values (a possibility distribution) for attribute a that an individual of class x might have. So, in a sense, we can regard $x.a$ both as a restriction on the values of attribute a, or as an assignment of a set of values to attribute a. The most specific case is when $x.a$ is the singleton set $\{e\}$, with $e \in \mathcal{E}$, which we may read "the a of x is e", as in "the *elevation* of *Mount Everest* is *8,850 m*".

We say attribute $a \in \mathcal{A}$ in frame $x \in \mathcal{F}$ is unrestricted if and only if $x.a = \mathcal{E}$. The frame for which all attributes are unrestricted is a representation of the most general element, the one that subsumes all other knowledge elements, atomic or complex: we call it the *top* element, and denote it by the symbol $\top$.

---

[1] In general, one would expect frames defining types with a high level of abstraction to have crisp sets as the values of their slots, and low level class frames and instance frames to show more and more fuzziness. The intuitive motivation for this is simple: we may have a very clear abstract idea of what *white* and *yellow* are: these are our conceptual categories, our ontology. Things become more complicated when we want to describe what we know about the color of a real, actual object, say an old sheet of paper. Then we might find its color to fit into the white type only to a degree, and into the yellow type to another degree. This agrees very well with our everyday experience: abstractions are clean-cut and simple (because they abstract away from unimportant details), whereas reality is fuzzy and complex.

Dual to this element is the *bottom* element $\perp$, subsumed by all other elements, which, in intuitive terms, is the equivalence class of those frames that cannot correspond to any "actual" concept, just because at least one of their slots has the empty set as the set of admissible values. We might also refer to this element as the *inadmissible* element. The $\perp$ element is something we would never want to have in our knowledge base, since it would be the index of a logical contradiction or inconsistency.

It is clear that the definition of a complex element is recursive, since we do not restrict the elements in the fuzzy set of admissible values of attributes to be atomic. In principle, there is no limit to the level of nesting of complex elements.

3   Fuzzy Sets of Elements

We will use min as the t-norm and max as the t-conorm, and represent a fuzzy set S of knowledge elements as a mapping $S : \mathcal{E} \rightarrow [0, 1]$, thus writing $S(e)$, for all $e \in \mathcal{E}$, to denote the membership degree of e in S. We will also adopt Zimmermann's [7] notation of fuzzy sets as formal summations (or integrals).

Accordingly, given two fuzzy sets of elements S and T:

- $S \subseteq T$ if and only if, for all $e \in \mathcal{E}$, $S(e) \leq T(e)$;
- $[S \cup T](e) = \max\{S(e), T(e)\}$ for all $e \in \mathcal{E}$;
- $[S \cap T](e) = \min\{S(e), T(e)\}$ for all $e \in \mathcal{E}$;
- $\bar{S}(e) = 1 - S(e)$ for all $e \in \mathcal{E}$.

Given a fuzzy set S, its *support*, denoted by $\mathrm{supp}(S)$, is the crisp set of all $e \in \mathcal{E}$ such that $S(e) > 0$.

A slot mapping attribute $a \in \mathcal{A}$ into a fuzzy set of elements S will be denoted as $a : S$, and a frame will be denoted as a column vector of slots.

Actually, a complex knowledge element is a bipartite graph, whose nodes are of two types: knowledge elements and fuzzy sets; arcs from an element to a set are labeled by an attribute, whereas arcs from a set to an element are labeled by a membership degree. To represent such structures on paper, when more than one attribute share the same set of values or the same frame is a member of more than one set, a label (the name of a variable) enclosed in parentheses will be put at the left of the first mention of the referred object and will be used to stand for the same object, like in

$$
\begin{bmatrix}
\text{grandparent: (x)} \dfrac{1}{\left[\text{name: }\frac{1}{\text{John}}\right]} \\[2ex]
\text{parent: } \dfrac{1}{\begin{bmatrix}\text{parent: (x)} \\ \text{name: }\frac{1}{\text{Peter}}\end{bmatrix}} \\[2ex]
\text{name: }\dfrac{1}{\text{George}}
\end{bmatrix} . \tag{1}
$$

4   Interpretation

The semantics of this formalism is given by a fuzzy interpretation, consisting of a non-empty domain $\mathcal{U}$, the universe of discourse, and an assignment $\cdot^{\mathcal{I}}$, which maps every knowledge element e into a fuzzy subset $e^{\mathcal{I}}$ of $\mathcal{U}$. We extend this assignment to map fuzzy sets of knowledge elements into fuzzy subsets of $\mathcal{U}$. In particular, it is useful to define

$$\mathcal{E}^{\mathcal{I}} \equiv \bigcup_{e \in \mathcal{E}} e^{\mathcal{I}}, \quad \mathcal{C}^{\mathcal{I}} \equiv \bigcup_{c \in \mathcal{C}} c^{\mathcal{I}}, \text{ and } \quad \mathcal{F}^{\mathcal{I}} \equiv \bigcup_{x \in \mathcal{F}} x^{\mathcal{I}}.$$

In general, given a fuzzy set S of knowledge elements, for all $u \in \mathcal{U}$,

$$S^{\mathcal{I}}(u) = \max_{e \in \mathcal{E}} \min\{S(e), e^{\mathcal{I}}(u)\}.$$

This is the fuzzy equivalent of saying that $u \in S^{\mathcal{I}}$ iff there exists a knowledge element e such that $e \in S$ and $u \in e^{\mathcal{I}}$.

Individual objects of the application domain (individuals for short) are the elements of $\mathcal{U}$; they will be denoted by u, v, etc.

Therefore, for all $e \in \mathcal{E}$ and $a \in \mathcal{A}$, and for all individuals $u, v \in \mathcal{U}$,

1. $0 \le e^{\mathcal{I}}(u) \le 1$;
2. $0 \le a^{\mathcal{I}}(u, v) \le 1$;
3. $\top^{\mathcal{I}}(u) = \mathcal{E}^{\mathcal{I}}(u) = 1$;
4. $\bot^{\mathcal{I}}(u) = 0$.

A fuzzy set S of knowledge elements might be equivalent, in terms of the interpretation, to a single knowledge element x: we use precisely this property to define equality between a fuzzy set of knowledge elements and knowledge elements, as in the case of $\top$ and $\mathcal{E}$. We define $x = S$ if and only if, for all $u \in \mathcal{U}$, $x^{\mathcal{I}}(u) = S^{\mathcal{I}}(u)$.

Furthermore, the interpretation maps every attribute a into a fuzzy binary relation $a^{\mathcal{I}} \subseteq \mathcal{F}^{\mathcal{I}} \times \mathcal{U}$, whereby, for all $u, v \in \mathcal{U}$,

$$a^{\mathcal{I}}(u, v) = \max_{x \in \mathcal{F}} \min\{x^{\mathcal{I}}(u), (x.a)^{\mathcal{I}}(v)\}$$
$$= \max_{x \in \mathcal{F}} \min\{x^{\mathcal{I}}(u), \max_{e \in \mathcal{E}} \min\{x.a(e), e^{\mathcal{I}}(v)\}\}$$

as it is intuitive, i.e., for all the frames x by which individual u is described (to a certain degree), we say that the possibility that v is a value of attribute a for u is in fact the possibility that $u \in x^{\mathcal{I}}$ and $v \in (x.a)^{\mathcal{I}}$; of all the possible frames describing u, we take the one that yields the maximum degree of membership.

Atomic knowledge elements are all mutually disjoint, and, as a whole, they are disjoint from complex knowledge elements[2].

---

[2] Therefore, one might assume that atomic knowledge elements represent individual elements in the universe of discourse, and nothing would change. As a matter of fact, if the interpretation of an atom contains more than one element, those elements are virtually indistinguishable for the formalism.

5   Subsumption

Given $x, y \in \mathcal{F}$, x subsumes y ($x \sqsupseteq y$), iff, for all $u \in \mathcal{U}$, $y^{\mathcal{I}}(u) \leq x^{\mathcal{I}}(u)$. Subsumption can also be extended to fuzzy sets of elements: given $S, T \subseteq \mathcal{E}$, $S \sqsupseteq T$ iff $(S \cap \mathcal{C}) \supseteq (T \cap \mathcal{C})$ and, for all $a \in \mathcal{A}$,

$$\bigcup_{x \in S \cap \mathcal{F}} x.a \sqsupseteq \bigcup_{y \in T \cap \mathcal{F}} y.a. \tag{2}$$

By their very nature, atomic elements cannot subsume each other or any other element than $\bot$, and be subsumed by any other element than $\top$.

Frames, on the other hand, can subsume and be subsumed by other frames. However, in order to precisely define subsumption over $\mathcal{F}$, we need to extend the definition of subsumption to the fuzzy sets of elements.

A natural extension in terms of the sementics defined in Section 4 is the following: given $S, T \subseteq \mathcal{E}$, $S \sqsupseteq T$ if and only if

$$(S \cap \mathcal{C}) \supseteq (T \cap \mathcal{C}). \tag{3}$$

In other words, Equation 3 requires the set of atoms in fuzzy set S to include the set of atoms in fuzzy set T, whereas Equation 2 requires the union of the values of attribute a for all frames in S to subsume the union of the values of the same attribute for all the frames in T.

Given this definition, subsumption between frames can be defined as follows: Given $x, y \in \mathcal{F}$, $x \sqsupseteq y$ if and only if, for all $a \in \mathcal{A}$, $x.a \sqsupseteq y.a$. This definition is recursive just like frames are recursive; however, recursion ends as soon as atomic values are reached, and Equation 3 is applied, or an unrestricted attribute appears on the left-hand side of Equation 2, whose value $\mathcal{E} = \top$ subsumes everything.

Subsumption defines a partial ordering of elements, and it is easy to verify that $\mathcal{E}$ forms a complete lattice with respect to the subsumption ordering relationship.

6   Unification

The *meet* operation on this lattice is called *unification*: the unification of two elements $x, y \in \mathcal{E}$ is the element $z = x \sqcap y$ such that, for all $\hat{z} \in \mathcal{E}$, $x \sqsupseteq \hat{z}$ and $y \sqsupseteq \hat{z}$ implies $z \sqsupseteq \hat{z}$, i.e., the most general element subsumed by both x and y.

It is easy to derive a more operational definition, leading to a unification algorithm whose time complexity is $O(nm)$, where n and m are the "size" of the two frames or fuzzy sets that are to be unified: for all $x \in \mathcal{E}$, $c, d \in \mathcal{C}$,

- $x \sqcap x = x$;
- $\top \sqcap x = x \sqcap \top = x$;
- $\bot \sqcap x = x \sqcap \bot = \bot$.
- $c \neq d$ implies $c \sqcap d = \bot$.
- $x \in \mathcal{F}$, $\top \neq x \neq \bot$, implies $c \sqcap x = x \sqcap c = \bot$.

For all $x, y \in \mathcal{F}$, and for all $a \in \mathcal{A}$,

$$(x \sqcap y).a = x.a \sqcap y.a; \tag{4}$$

furthermore, for all fuzzy sets of elements $S, T \subseteq \mathcal{E}$,

$$S \sqcap T = \sum_{e \in \mathcal{E} \backslash \perp} \frac{\min_{x \in S, y \in T : x \sqcap y = e}\{S(x), T(y)\}}{e}, \tag{5}$$

or, equivalently, for all $x \in S$ and $y \in T$,

$$[S \sqcap T](e) = \begin{cases} \min_{x \in S, y \in T : x \sqcap y = e}\{S(x), T(y)\}, & \text{if } e \neq \perp; \\ 0 & \text{otherwise.} \end{cases} \tag{6}$$

Translated into a simple algorithm, Equation 6 says that, in order to unify two fuzzy sets S and T, one must:

1. try to unify every member of S with every member of T, obtaining a collection of elements;
2. discard all $\perp$ results;
3. associate with each resulting element a degree of membership that is the minimum between those of the two operands in their respective set;
4. merge multiple copies of the resulting elements while taking as their degree of membership the minimum;
5. build the unified set $S \sqcap T$ from all the remaining results.

It is clear that the number of intermediate elements $x \sqcap y$ to be calculated is $\|\text{supp}(S)\| \cdot \|\text{supp}(T)\|$; therefore, if n is the typical cardinality of the supports of the fuzzy sets involved in unification operations, the computational complexity of calculating unification between sets is $O(n^2)$ frame unifications. Frame unification, in turn, is linear in the number of slots. Since some of the unifications $x \sqcap y$, with $x \in S$ and $y \in T$ might fail, $\|\text{supp}(S \sqcap T)\| \leq \|\text{supp}(S)\| \cdot \|\text{supp}(T)\|$.

In the special case where $x.a \subseteq \mathcal{C}$ and $y.a \subseteq \mathcal{C}$, i.e, when attribute a can take only atomic values, Equations 4 and 6 combine to give

$$(x \sqcap y).a = x.a \cap y.a. \tag{7}$$

7 Fuzzy Rules

Whereas frames and elements provide the descriptive devices of the representation formalism, relations, in the form of subsumption relations and fuzzy rules, provide the main mechanisms for inference.

A fuzzy IF-THEN rule has the form

$$\text{IF } S_1 \text{ is } T_1 \text{ AND } \ldots \text{ AND } S_{n-1} \text{ is } T_{n-1} \text{ THEN } S_n \text{ is } T_n, \tag{8}$$

where $S_i, T_i \subseteq \mathcal{E}$, $i = 1, \ldots, n$.

The degree of truth of an antecedent clause "S_i is T_i" is given by the maximum degree of membership of the members of $S_i \sqcap T_i$, or

$$\tau(S_i \text{ is } T_i) = \sup_{e \in \mathcal{E}}\{(S_i \sqcap T_i)(e)\}. \tag{9}$$

The degree of truth of the consequent clause equals the smallest degree of truth of its antecedents:

$$\tau(S_n \text{ is } T_n) = \min_{i=1,\ldots,n-1}\{\tau(S_i \text{ is } T_i)\}. \tag{10}$$

8   Inference

When a knowledge engineer models a domain, she constructs an ontology, say $\mathcal{O}$, by defining knowledge elements and connecting them by means of

1. subsumption axioms, of the form $x \sqsupseteq y$, where $x, y \in \mathcal{F}$,
2. slot-value axioms of the form $x.a(e) = \alpha$, where $x \in \mathcal{F}$, $e \in \mathcal{E}$, and $0 \leq \alpha \leq 1$ is a membership degree of e in $x.a$,
3. fuzzy IF-THEN rules, defined in Section 7.

During this process, it is important to find out whether a newly defined knowledge element makes sense or whether it is contradictory. From a logical point of view, a knowledge element makes sense if there is some interpretation that satisfies the axioms of $\mathcal{O}$ (that is, a model of $\mathcal{O}$) such that the concept denotes a nonempty fuzzy set in that interpretation. A knowledge element with this property is said to be *satisfiable* with respect to $\mathcal{O}$ and *unsatisfiable* otherwise.

Afterwards, when the knowledge contained in $\mathcal{O}$ is used, it is important to be able to calculate logical consequences of the above three types of axioms. Both tasks require a system to perform some kind of inference.

Two basic mechanisms for inference are provided for within this knowledge representation formalism:

- *inheritance* according to the subsumption relation;
- *mapping*, i.e., functional dependence, according to the calculus of the fuzzy IF-THEN rules [6].

The two mechanisms are strictly combined and operate at the same time, in the sense that the value of every slot is the unification of all the slots subsuming it (inheritance) and of all the values of the consequent clauses referring to it.

Inheritance and mapping combine as follows:

$$x.a = \left(\coprod_r T_r \cap \tau(x.a \text{ is } T_r) \right) \sqcap \prod_{y \sqsupseteq x} y.a. \tag{11}$$

where the T_r's are the values predicated by the consequents of the rules

$$\text{IF} \dots \text{THEN } x.a \text{ is } T_r.$$

It should be noted that in Equation 11 the inherited value of an attribute is given by the unification of all its values in the subsuming frames, *including* the frame itself. Therefore, the semantics of the explicitly defined value of a slot is to be understood "modulo" any more restrictive definition inherited from superclasses. Furthermore, the contribution of fuzzy rules, as dictated by the calculus of fuzzy rules, is disjunctive. This allows us to exploit the interpolative behavior of fuzzy rules.

9 Conclusions

A knowledge representation formalism has been described which is based on the combination of three concepts:

- frame-based knowledge representation formalisms;
- unification, as found in unification-based grammar formalisms;
- fuzzy set theory.

The resulting formalism has been specially developed for and used in an innovative technological framework for knowledge management, whose main feature is the ability to semantically index documents by representing the (uncertain) knowledge about their content and relating it to an ontology. That framework is currently being validated by means of three vertical applications in the domains of banking regulations, insurance, and IT service outsourcing.

Acknowledgements

The work described in this paper was carried out in the framework of the Eureka "Information and Knowledge Fusion (IKF)" Project (E! 2235).

References

1. Franz Baader, Diego Calvanese, Deborah McGuinness, Daniele Nardi, and Peter Patel-Schneider, editors. *The Description Logic Handbook: Theory, implementation and applications.* Cambridge, 2003.
2. Daphne Koller and Avi Pfeffer. Probabilistic frame-based systems. In *Proceedings of AAAI '98*, pages 580–587, 1998.
3. Marvin Minsky. A framework for representing knowledge. In Patrick H. Winston, editor, *The Psychology of Computer Vision.* 1975.
4. Stuart M. Shieber. *An Introduction to Unification-based Approaches to Grammar.* CSLI, Lecture Notes Number 4. Chicago University Press, Chicago, IL, 1986.
5. L. A. Zadeh. Fuzzy sets. *Information and Control*, 8:338–353, 1965.
6. L. A. Zadeh. The calculus of fuzzy if-then rules. *AI Expert*, 7(3):22–27, March 1992.
7. H.-J. Zimmermann. *Fuzzy Set Theory and its Applications.* International series in management science/operations research. Kluwer, Boston, 1985.

Statistical Analysis of the Different Operator Involved in the Fuzzy Inference Process

O. Valenzuela[1], I. Rojas[2], and F. Rojas[2]

[1] Department of Mathematics
[2] Department of Computer Architecture and Computer Technology,
University of Granada, E. 18071 Granada, Spain

Abstract. The main architectures, learning abilities and applications of fuzzy systems are well documented. However, to the best of our knowledge, no in-depth analyses have been carried out into the influence on the behaviour of the fuzzy system arising from the use of different alternatives for the design of the fuzzy inference process (mainly, different implication operators and T-norm). Thus, as a complement to the existing intuitive knowledge, it is necessary to have a more precise understanding of the significance of the different alternatives. In the present contribution, the relevance and relative importance of the parameters involved in such a design are investigated by using a statistical tool, the ANalysis Of the VAriance (ANOVA).

1 Introduction and Motivation

Since Zadeh introduced the theory of fuzzy sets, and the Minimum, the Maximum and the Complement as the operators on fuzzy sets, many alternative operators have been proposed in the specialized literature. Thus, providing a set of logical connectives for fuzzy sets constitutes a central issue in theoretical research and in the development of practical applications. There exist many possibilities to select the set of basic operations in the fuzzy inference process. As there are many possibilities to select the set of basic operators used in the fuzzy inference process, the search for the fuzzy operators that are most suitable for the different steps of a fuzzy system, their characterization and evaluation, can be included among the most important topics in the field of fuzzy logic. A better insight into the performances of the alternative operators would make it easier to develop a fuzzy application. Examining the specialized literature, it is clear that the selection of the best fuzzy implication operator has become one of the main question in the design of a fuzzy system, being occasionally contradictory (at presently there are more than 72 fuzzy implication proposed and investigated). An approach to the problem from a different perspective is given. The question is to determine whether the selection of the fuzzy implication operator is more important with respect to the behaviour of the fuzzy system than the operators (mainly T-norm) involved in the definition of the implication function and in the rest of the inference process. Also, which implication operators have similar behaviour?

The structure of a fuzzy system comprises a set of IF-THEN fuzzy rules, Ψ, composed of r rules, R_p $(p = 1, ..., r) : \Psi = \{R_p; p = 1, ..., r\}$. Each rule has the form:

V. Di Gesú, F. Masulli, and A. Petrosino (Eds.): WILF 2003, LNAI 2955, pp. 63–71, 2006.
© Springer-Verlag Berlin Heidelberg 2006

IF X is A THEN Y is B, where A and B are fuzzy variables (linguistic variables such as old, small, high, etc.) described by membership functions in universes of discourse U and V, respectively, where the variables X and Y take their values. A fuzzy rule is represented by means of a fuzzy relation R from set U to set V (or between U and V), that represents the correlation between A and B as follows:

$$R : U \times V \to [0,1] : (u,v) \to I(\mu_A(u), \mu_B(v)), \quad (u,v) \in U \times V \qquad (1)$$

where μ_A and μ_B are the membership functions of A and B, and I is the implication operator which is defined in terms of the so called T-norm and T-conorm operators. When the fuzzy rules have more than one input variable in the antecedent part (rules in the form IF X_1 is A_1 AND ... X_m is A_m THEN Y is B_1), the membership value $\mu_A(X^t)$ is calculated by:

$$\mu_A(X^t) = T\left(\mu_{A_1}(X_1), ..., \mu_{A_m}(X_m)\right) \qquad (2)$$

where $X^t = (X_1(t), ..., X_m(t))$ is the vector of the input crisp signals fed to the fuzzy system in the time t, and T represents a T-norm operator. In this way, the most important elements in the fuzzy inference process are the fuzzy implication operator, I, the T-norm and T-conorm operators. In the literature there are many possibilities for the selection of the fuzzy operators that determine how each individual rule is evaluated and how to obtain a final conclusion of all the rules in conjunction. The proper definition of connectives (conjunction, disjunction, negation, implication, etc.) constitutes a central issue in the theoretical and applied studies of the area [4]. This paper analyzes the performance of some fuzzy implications proposed in the bibliography together with the operators needed for their definition and for the fuzzy inference process. To do this, an appropriate statistical tool has been used: the multifactorial analysis of the variance ANOVA [1, 3], which consists of a set of statistical techniques that allow the analysis and comparison of experiments, by describing the interactions and interrelations between either the quantitative or qualitative variables (called factors in this context) of the system.

2   Application of ANOVA in the Design of a Fuzzy System

The ANalysis Of the VAriance (commonly referred to as ANOVA) is one of the most widely used statistical techniques. The theory and methodology of ANOVA was developed mainly by R. A. Fisher during the 1920s [3]. ANOVA belies its name in that it is not concerned with analyzing variances but rather with analyzing the variation in means. ANOVA examines the effects of one, two or more quantitative or qualitative variables (termed factors) on one quantitative response. ANOVA is useful in a range of disciplines when it is suspected that one or more factors affect a response. ANOVA is essentially a method of analyzing the variance to which a response is subject into its various components, corresponding to the sources of variation which can be identified.

Suppose the easy case that the number of factors affecting the outcome of the experiment is two. We denote by $X_{i,j}$ $(i = 1, ...n_1; j = 1, ..., n_2)$ the value observed when the first factor is at the i-th level and the second at the j-th level. It is assumed that the two factors do not act independently and therefore that there exists an interaction between them. In this case, the observations fit the following equation:

$$X_{i,j,k} = \mu + \alpha_i + \beta_j + (\alpha\beta)_{i,j} + \varepsilon_{i,j,k} \tag{3}$$

where μ is the fixed effect that is common to all the populations, α_i is the effect associated with the i-th level of the first factor and β_j is the effect associated with the j-th level of the second factor. The term $(\alpha\beta)_{i,j}$ denotes the joint effect of the presence of level i of the first factor and level j of the second one; this, therefore, is denominated the interaction term. The term $\varepsilon_{i,j,k}$ is the influence on the result of everything that could not be assigned of random factors. The null hypothesis is proposed that each term of the above equation is independent of the levels involved; in other words, on the one hand we have the two equality hypotheses for the levels of each factor:

$$H_{01} : \alpha_1 = \ldots = \alpha_i = \ldots = \alpha_{n_1}$$
$$H_{02} : \beta_1 = \ldots = \beta_j = \ldots = \beta_{n_2} \tag{4}$$

and on the other, the hypothesis associated with interaction, which can be expressed in an abbreviated way as:

$$H_{03} : (\alpha\beta)_{i,j} = 0 \quad \forall i, j \tag{5}$$

The hypothesis of the equality of several means arises when a number of different treatments or levels of the main factors are to be compared. Frequently one is interested in studying the effects of more than one factor, or the effects of one factor when certain other conditions of the experiment vary, which then play the role of additional factors. With ANOVA, we test a null hypothesis that all of the population means are equal against an alternative hypothesis that there is at least one mean that is not equal to the others. We find the sample mean and variance for each level of the main factor. Using these values, we obtain two different estimates of the population variance. The first one is obtained by finding the sample variance of the n_k sample means from the overall mean. This variance is referred to as the *variance between the means*. The second estimate of the population variance is found by using a weighted average of the sample variances. This variance is called the *variance within the means*. Therefore, ANOVA allows us to determine whether a change in the measure of a given variable is caused by a change in the level of a factor or is just originated by a random effect. In this way, it allows us to distinguish between the components which cause the variations appearing in a set of statistical data and to determine whether the discrepancies *between* the means of the factors are greater than would reasonably be expected according to the variations *within* these factors.

The two estimates of the population variance are then compared using the F-**ratio** test statistic. Calculating the sum of the squares of the observations extended to the levels of all the factors (S_T) and the sum of squares within each level (S_R), and dividing S_T and S_R by the appropriate number of degrees of freedom (**D.F.**), obtaining s_T and s_R respectively, the F-ratio is computed as s_T/s_R. This calculated value of the F-ratio for each factor is then compared to a critical value of F of Snedecor with the appropriate degrees of freedom to determine whether we should reject the null hypothesis. When there is no treatment effect, the ratio should be close to 1. If a level of a main effect has a significant influence on the output variable (observed variable, in our case the Error Index), the observed value of F will be greater than the F-Snedecor distribution, with a sufficiently high confidence level (usually 95%). In this case the null hypothesis is rejected and it is argued that at least one of the levels of the analyzed factor must affect the response of the system in a different way. The F-ratio test assumes normal populations with equal variance and independent samples. The analysis is sensitive to inequality of variance (heteroscedasticity) when the sample sizes are small and unequal and care should be taken in interpreting the results.

The comparison between the F-ratio and the F-Snedecor distribution is expressed through the significance level (**Sig. Level**). If this significance level is lower than 0.05 then the corresponding levels of the factor are statistically significant with a confidence level of 95%. Thus, this is the main statistical parameter that will be considered in next sections in order to derive conclusions about the different factors influencing the design of a fuzzy system.

As a first step, ANOVA determines whether or not the null hypothesis is true, indicating whether all the effects of the different levels of each factor are mutually equivalent and whether the interactions of a certain order are null. From this point, the goal is to verify which factors produce meaningful alterations in the output when their levels change. In the case of the null hypothesis being rejected, a more profound study must be carried out to classify the levels of the most significant factors, taking into account the size of their effects and seeking differences in the output response produced when using a given level of those factors [3]. The levels of a factor that are not statistically different form a homogeneous group and therefore the choice between the various levels belonging to a given homogeneous group has no significant repercussion on the response. Thus, once we discover that some of the factors involved in the design of an fuzzy system do not fulfil the null hypothesis, a study is carried out of the levels of this factor that may be considered statistically non-significant, using Multiple Range Test tables for this purpose; these tables describe the homogeneous groups possible for each of the levels of the factor being analyzed.

Table 1. Levels of each factor considered in the statistical analysis

	Fuzzy implication op.	T-norm	T-conorm	Defuzzifier
Level 1	**Mamdani (R_m)**	**Minimum**	**Maximum**	**Middle of Maxima**
Level 2	Stochastic (R_{st})	Product	Goguen	First of Maxima
Level 3	Kleene-Dienes (R_b)	Einstein	Einstein	Last of Maxima
Level 4	Lukasiewicz (R_a)	Giles	Giles	Height Defuz.
Level 5	Cao (R_{Cao})	Dombi ($\gamma = 0.5$)	Dombi ($\gamma = 0.5$)	Center of Area
Level 6	Early-Zadeh (R_z)	Dombi ($\gamma = 1$)	Dombi ($\gamma = 3$)	ξ-Quality ($\xi = 1$)
Level 7	Gödel (R_g)	Hamacher ($\lambda = 0.5$)	Hamacher	ξ-Quality ($\xi = 2$)
Level 8	Gaines (R_{Gaines})	Yager ($\beta = 2$)	Yager ($\beta = 2$)	Slide Defuz. ($\delta = 0.1$)
Level 9	Wu (R_W)	Yager ($\beta = 4$)	Yager ($\beta = 4$)	Slide Defuz. ($\delta = 0.9$)

In the statistical study performed in next sections, the factors considered are the implication operators, T-norm and T-conorm and the type of defuzzifier. Table 1 gives the different levels considered in each factor when carrying out multifactorial ANOVA (this is not a one-way ANOVA, because we considered all the factors simultaneously). Each of these factors has different levels. For example minimum, product, Einstein, Giles, Dombi, Hamacher and Yager are the levels considered for the type of T-norm. The response variable used to perform the statistical analysis is the mean square error in the output transfer function of a fuzzy system, when some of the levels of the factor considered vary with respect to a reference design. The changes in the response variable are produced when a new combination of T-norm, T-conorm, fuzzy implication function or defuzzification method is considered, thus changing the structure of the fuzzy system.

3 Functional Blocks in Fuzzy Inference Process

As commented above, many authors have been and continue to be interested in investigating the applicability of fuzzy implication operators. The fuzzy implication functions can be classified as follows: 1) Strong Implications (S-Implications). This family corresponds to the definition of implications in fuzzy logic based on classical Boolean logic. Examples belonging to this family are the Diene, Dubois-Prade and Mizumoto implications. 2) Quantum Logic Implications (QL-Implications). These type of implications have the form $I(a, b) = S(N(a), T(a, b))$, where T is a T-norm. An example of this type of operator is the Zadeh implication. 3) Residual Implications (R-Implications). The functions belonging to this family reflect a partial ordering on propositions, and are obtained by residuation of a T-norm in the form $I(a, b) = \sup\{\beta \in [0, 1]/T(a, \beta) \leq b\}$. Examples of this class of functions are the Gödel, Lukasiewicz and Sharp fuzzy implications. 4) Interpretation of the implication as a conjunction. The form of this function is $I(a, b) = T(a, b)$, which is clearly not an operator that fulfils the condition to be considered as a fuzzy implication. However, in the fuzzy control field, implications which are represented by a T-norm, such as the minimum (Mamdani) or product (Larsen), are usually used for the design of the inference process [5, 6].

With respect to the T-norm and T-conorm operators, many studies on the mathematical properties of these functions and their influence on the fuzzy inference process have been made [8]. Dozens of mathematical functions, each more complex and difficult to implement than the last, have been proposed [2, 7, 8, 9]. Moreover, parametrical operators [2, 9] have been frequently used. Because of the great variety of proposed T-norms, it might be thought that some of them should be able to combine fuzzy sets as human beings aggregate information. In practice the minimum and product operators are used for the conjunction of fuzzy sets because of their simplicity of implementation. However, there are empirical studies [2] that have pointed out that these classical operators do not represent the way human beings aggregate information.

During the last few years a great deal of research work has focused on the use of different types of defuzzifier and on the analysis of the properties of new defuzzification methods [2]. For example [10] introduces a parameterized family of defuzzification operators, called Semi LInear DEfuzzification (SLIDE). To carry out the statistical study, a selection is made of a set of alternatives representative of each of the factors to be considered. As previously remarked, the response variable used to perform the statistical analysis is the mean square error in the output transfer function of a fuzzy controller, when the factors considered change with respect to a reference. This reference is the combination of implication function, T-norm, T-conorm and defuzzifier shown in bold print in Table 1, that give the different levels considered in each factor to carry out the multifactorial ANOVA.

4   Results of the ANOVA Statistical Study

For the statistical study, a total of 40 fuzzy controllers were examined using systems found in the bibliography, with different numbers and types of membership functions and rules, in order to obtain wide-ranging results. Therefore, all the possible configurations of factors used (T-norm, T-conorm, fuzzy implication and defuzzification method) are evaluated for each of the 40 different knowledge bases. Table 2 gives the four-way variance analysis for whole set of examples of fuzzy systems studied. The analysis of variance table containing the sum of squares, degrees of freedom, mean square, test statistics, etc., represents the initial analysis in a compact form. This kind of tabular representation is customarily used to set out the results of ANOVA calculations. As can be seen from Table 2, the defuzzification method and the type of T-norm present the greatest statistical relevance because the higher the F-Ratio or the smaller the significance level, the greater the relevance of the corresponding factor. The fuzzy implication operator and the T-conorm selected are not so significant. These conclusions are also confirmed by the multiple range tables for the different factors (Table 3). Analyzing the different levels of each of these main factors, it is possible to understand their influence on the characteristics of the inference process and on the fuzzy implication, enabling levels with the same response repercussion to be grouped homogeneously. From Table 3, it is clear that there are two homogeneous groups of implication operators that are not disjoint, thus there exists fuzzy implication which can be classified within the two groups. One group includes the R_m, R_g, R_a, R_{st}, R_{Gaines}, R_W, and R_{Cao} implication operators and the other contains R_g, R_a, R_{st}, R_{Gaines}, R_W, R_{Cao}, R_b, and R_z. The biggest difference in the mean appears between the Mamdani operator (which, indeed, should be considered as a T-norm operator and not an implication one)

Table 2. ANOVA table for the analysis of the main variables in fuzzy inference process

Main Factors	Sum of Squares	D. F.	F-Ratio	Sig. level
Fuzzy implication operator	3.3	8	1.22	0.2960
T-norm	5.9	8	2.15	0.0296
T-conorm	2.9	8	1.07	0.3830
Defuzzifier	15.9	8	5.83	0.0000

Table 3. Multiple Range test for the variables analized

Levels of variable *Fuzzy Implication operator*	Mean	Homogeneous Groups	
1: Mamdani (R_m)	0.32	X	
7: Gödel (R_g)	0.71	X	X
4: Lukasiewicz (R_a)	1.18	X	X
2: Stochastic (R_{st})	1.21	X	X
8: Gaines (R_{Gaines})	1.37	X	X
9: Wu (R_W)	1.51	X	X
5: Cao (R_{Cao})	1.60	X	X
3: Kleene-Dienes (R_b)	1.90		X
6: Early-Zadeh (R_z)	2.16		X

Limit to establish significant differences: ± 1.35

Levels of variable *T-norm operator*	Mean	Homogeneous Groups	
1: Minimum	0.15	X	
9: Yager $(\beta = 4)$	0.64	X	X
6: Dombi $(\gamma = 1)$	1.13	X	X
2: Product	1.61		X
8: Yager $(\beta = 2)$	1.71		X
7: Hamacher $(\lambda = 0.5)$	1.95	X	X
3: Einstein	2.34	X	X
5: Dombi $(\gamma = 0.5)$	3.13		X
4: Giles	3.25		X

Limit to establish significant differences: ± 1.35

Levels of variable *T-conorm operator*	Mean	Homogeneous Groups	
1: Maximum	0.12	X	
6: Dombi $(\gamma = 3)$	0.22	X	
9: Yager $(\beta = 4)$	0.35	X	X
7: Hamacher	0.50	X	X
8: Yager $(\beta = 2)$	0.72	X	X
2: Goguen	0.81	X	X
3: Einstein	1.04	X	X
5: Dombi $(\gamma = 0.5)$	1.18	X	X
4: Giles	1.67		X

Limit to establish significant differences: ± 1.35

Levels of variable *Defuzzifier method*	Mean	Homogeneous Groups	
1: Middle of Maxima	0.13	X	
9: Slide Defuzzification $(\delta = 0.9)$	0.54	X	X
7: ξ-Quality Defuzzification $(\xi = 2)$	0.84	X	X
2: First of Maxima	1.49		X
3: Last of Maxima	1.54		X
4: Height Defuzzification	2.92		X
8: Slide Defuzzification $(\delta = 0.1)$	3.17		X
6: ξ-Quality Defuzzification $(\xi = 1)$	3.41		X
5: Center of Area	3.64		X

Limit to establish significant differences: ± 1.35

and the Zadeh operator. Table 3 shows the results for the T-norm operators, giving three homogeneous groups. The analysis for the T-conorm factor, there are two not disjoint homogeneous groups, with similar behaviour on the design of a fuzzy system. It is important to point out that the ANOVA analysis is capable of ordering the T-norms and T-conorms from more to less restrictive. In Table 3 the levels of the defuzzifier have been grouped into three groups (the last ones with empty intersections, which means that there are no similarities between them). The first group is composed by the Middle of Maxima, Slide and ξ-Quality Defuzzification with $\delta = 0.9$ and $\xi = 2$, respectively. The second group is composed by the Slide ($\delta = 0.9$), ξ-Quality ($\xi = 2$), First Maximum, and the Last Maximum. Finally, the third group includes the Height defuzzification, Slide ($\delta = 0.1$), ξ-Quality ($\xi = 1$) and the Center of Area.

5   Conclusion

The goal of this paper is to get a better insight into determining the factor that have the most relevant influence on the design and performance of a fuzzy system, in order to establish the main factor to be carefully studied when a real application is developed. To do this, an appropriate statistical tool has been used: multifactorial analysis of the variance, that allow the analysis and comparison of experiments, by describing the interactions and interrelations between either the quantitative or qualitative variables (called factors in this context) of the system. The selection of an appropriate implication operator is unfortunately one of the most confusing tasks a designer must face. Choosing an implication operator from the many viable options is a hard task, not just because there is a chance of selecting the wrong one, but because it is difficult to justify the choice. Furthermore, we have to consider that the final output is not only determined by the implication operator but also by the accompanying aggregation operator (mainly T-norm and T-conorm) and the defuzzification method. This quadruple yields more than a hundred combinations to be examined when considering the different methods found in the literature. The present statistical study was motivated by the great variety of alternatives that a designer has to take into account when developing a fuzzy system. Thus, instead of the existing intuitive knowledge, it is necessary to have a more precise understanding of the significance of the different alternatives.

Acknowledgements

This work has been partially supported by the Spanish CICYT Project DPI2001-3219.

References

1. G. Casella and R. L. Berger. *Statistical Inference*. Duxbury Advanced Series. Brooks Cole, 2nd edition, 2001.
2. D. Driankov, H. Hellendoorn, and M. Reinfrank. *An Introduction to Fuzzy Control*. Springer Verlag, 2nd edition, 1996.

3. R. A. Fisher. The Comparison of Samples with Possibly Unequal Variances. *Annals of Eugenics*, 9:174–180, 1939.
   http://www.library.adelaide.edu.au/digitised/fisher/162.pdf.
4. J. C. Fodor and T. Keresztfalvi. Nonstandard Conjunctions and Implications in Fuzzy Logic. *International Journal of Approximate Reasoning*, 12(2):69–84, Feb. 1995.
5. J. B. Kiszka, M. E. Kochaska, and D. S. Sliwiska. The Influence of Some Fuzzy Implication Operators on the Accuracy of a Fuzzy Model – Part I. *Fuzzy Sets and Systems*, 15(2):111–128, Feb. 1985.
6. J. B. Kiszka, M. E. Kochaska, and D. S. Sliwiska. The Influence of Some Fuzzy Implication Operators on the Accuracy of a Fuzzy Model – Part II. *Fuzzy Sets and Systems*, 15(3):223–240, Apr. 1985.
7. E. Trillas, S. Cubillo, and C. del Campo. A few Remarks on Some T-conditional Functions. In *Proceedings of the Sixth IEEE International Conference on Fuzzy Systems*, volume 1, pages 153–156, 1997.
8. I. B. Turksen. Interval-valued Fuzzy Sets and 'Compensatory AND'. *Fuzzy Sets and Systems*, 51(3):249–370, Nov. 1992.
9. R. R. Yager. Criteria Importances in OWA Aggregation: An application of Fuzzy Modeling. In *Proceedings of the Sixth IEEE International Conference on Fuzzy Systems*, volume 3, pages 1677–1682, 1997.
10. R. R. Yager and D. P. Filev. SLIDE: A Simple Adaptive Defuzzification Method. *IEEE Transactions on Fuzzy Systems*, 1(1):69–78, Feb. 1993.

Concepts and Fuzzy Models for Behavior-Based Robotics

Andrea Bonarini, Matteo Matteucci, and Marcello Restelli

Politecnico di Milano Artificial Intelligence and Robotics Lab,
Department of Electronics and Information,
Politecnico di Milano, Milan, Italy
Phone: +39 02 2399 3525 – Fax: +39 02 2399 3411
{bonarini, matteucc, restelli}@elet.polimi.it

Abstract. In this paper, we propose a modeling paradigm that uses fuzzy sets to represent concepts on which control modules of a behavior-based autonomous robot operate. The primitives defined in the modeling paradigm are expressive enough to represent the knowledge needed by planning, coordination, and reactive control of a multi-robot control system. At the same time, it provides a well-founded tool to represent in a compact way the data interpretations, needed to reason effectively about what is happening in the world and what is desired to happen. This modeling paradigm makes the design of behavior, planning, and coordination modules easy, since its primitives are simple and expressive.

1 Introduction

Since some years, the most common architectures of autonomous robots integrate the planning activity, which provides goals for the robot, with behavior-based reactivity, which implements simple and fast control modules. In designing this kind of hybrid architectures, most of the issues arise from the connection between the conceptual and physical level representations used respectively in the deliberative and reactive components of the system. Although this practice is now common, only few efforts have been done to formalize, unify, and optimize the knowledge representation model in order to seamless integrate the components in the hybrid architecture.

In this paper, we present our approach to knowledge modelling for autonomous robots, aimed at providing a common framework to represent all the knowledge needed by the modules that participate in control and coordination. We define the conceptual aspects needed to represent this type of knowledge and we introduce fuzzy sets as a tool to support this representation. This fuzzy conceptual representation is used by all the modules of our control architecture: *MAP* (*Map Anchors Percepts*) [4] that integrates data from sensors and other data sources building an internal representation of the world, *BRIAN* (*Brian Reacts by Inferential ActioNs*) [3] that manages the behaviors and implements all the reactive functionalities of our system, and *SCARE* (*Scare Coordinates Agents in Robotic Environments*) [5] that coordinates the agent's behaviors and plans its activity. In fact, a uniform knowledge representation makes it possible a coordinated design of the modules, and an efficient exchange of information.

V. Di Gesú, F. Masulli, and A. Petrosino (Eds.): WILF 2003, LNAI 2955, pp. 72–79, 2006.
© Springer-Verlag Berlin Heidelberg 2006

2   Concepts and the Fuzzy Model

In a robotic environment, agents have to interact with several *physical objects* and this interaction is typically implemented as a perception-action loop. Robots are equipped with sensors perceiving physical characteristics of the environment and they use these *percepts* to build an internal representation of the environment. Once this internal representation is formed, it is possible to use it for deliberative or reactive processing which produces actions to be executed in the environment. In this paper, we do not go into the theoretical details related to the problem of matching percepts with the corresponding semantic meaning of the physical objects. Instead, we focus on the knowledge representation we use to face the problem of creating, and maintaining in time, the connection between symbol-level and signal-level representations of the same physical object [4].

We propose to use a two stages process for creating the agent internal representation of the environment: first of all percepts are used to instantiate a real-valued conceptual model of the environment and then this conceptual model is interpreted in terms of fuzzy predicates to be used in coordination and control.

Percepts are processed by sensing modules (i.e., smart sensors) to produce high level features. Features referring to a specific physical object are collected around the same internal representation, referred to as its *perceptual image* and it can be seen as the instance of a *concept*. In a formal way, a concept C is described by a set of properties defined as tuples in the form $p \triangleq < label, \mathbb{D}, \rho >$, where *label* denotes the property name, $\mathbb{D}$ is the set of all the possible values for that property given a specific representation code (e.g. for the colors we can use the set $\{red, green, blue, \ldots\}$, or the RGB space $\mathbb{N}^3_{[0,255]}$, or a fuzzy classification of this) and ρ represents a restriction of the domain $\mathbb{D}$ for the property in the specific concept.

According to this concept-based knowledge representation, a property can be either directly perceived, and thus related to a set of high level features coming from sensors, or it can be derived from other properties through inference or computation. This approach allows properties specific to the concept to provide additional information about the perceptual image, or to infer unsensed characteristics.

Depending on the concept and on the specific application domain, a property can be classified as *substantial* or *accidental*. Substantial properties characterize the immutable part of a concept: for a given object, their values do not change over time, and they can be used for object recognition since they explain the essence of the object they represent. Accidental properties do not characterize a concept: their values are specific to each conceptual instance, and they can vary over time. They cannot be used for object recognition, but are the basis of instance formation, tracking and model validation. During robot activity, data coming from sensors are matched against concepts in the conceptual model, and, when enough evidence is collected, a concept instance is generated, which inherits by default property values eventually not detected by sensors [4].

Using concepts it is possible to describe both domain specific and general knowledge used by an agent during its activity. To explain how this knowledge is used, we introduce the notion of model $\mathcal{M}$: given D as the set of the known domains, a model $\mathcal{M}_d$ is the set of all the concepts known by the agent referring to the specific domain $d \in D$, linked by relationships – structural (e.g., generalization, and specialization) and domain specific (e.g., colors and landmark in structured environments).

The definition of concepts at different levels of abstraction is important to support the classification of percepts, and the instantiation of concepts. Concepts are organized in *ontologies*, which may be partially defined independently from the specific application, at least up to a certain abstraction level. For instance, it is possible to give general properties of *movable objects*, as a concept specializing the more general concept *objects*, and in turn specialize it in *mobile robots* and *human beings*. Such general concepts may also participate in general inferential processes, which allow, for instance, to infer that people and mobile robots usually stay on the ground, information useful to compute distances from images. When facing a specific application, it is then possible to complement the general ontology with application-specific information; for instance, we may already know that balls are spherical, but in a Robocup [2] robot soccer application we also know that the ball is red and has a given dimension. In case of uncertainty, it is often more reliable to instantiate a more general perceptual image. For instance, again in a Robocup application, robots belonging to different teams wear different markers, which may be detected with some uncertainty; therefore, a set of features may be aggregated more reliably as an instance of *robot*, than as an instance of *opponent robot*.

From the design point of view, the presence of a reference model makes it possible a modular design, with people having different competence interacting on the same knowledge. People working on sensors would know that they should produce certain information in a given format, and people working on control could rely on that. Once the conceptual model $\mathcal{M}$ relative to the agent's established knowledge has been instantiated, we have an internal representation of the environment on which it is possible to evaluate logical predicates, apply inference, or execute behavior control modules. We call this internal representation *domain* and we will denote it with $\mathcal{D}$.

Fuzzy predicates may represent concept instances related to aspects of the world, goals, and information coming from other agents. They are represented by a *label* λ, its *truth value* μ_λ, computed by fuzzy evaluation of the concept instance properties, and a *reliability value* ξ_λ to take into account the quality of the instance. For instance, we may have a predicate represented as $< ObstacleInFront, 0.8, 0.9 >$, which can be interpreted as: "It is quite true ($\mu_\lambda = 0.8$, coming from the fuzzyfication of real-valued properties) that there is an obstacle in front of the robot, and this statement has a reliability quite high ($\xi_\lambda = 0.9$, due to the reliability of the sensing conditions)"

We consider ground and complex fuzzy predicates. *Ground fuzzy predicates* range on concept properties directly available to the agent through $\mathcal{D}$, and have a truth value corresponding to the degree of membership of instance properties to labeled fuzzy sets. The reliability of sensorial data is provided by the anchoring process basing on percept analysis, and goal reliability is stated by the planner. A *complex fuzzy predicate* is a composition of fuzzy predicates obtained by fuzzy logic operators. Complex fuzzy predicates organize the basic information contained in ground predicates into a more abstract model. In Robocup, for instance, we can model the concept of ball possession by the *BallOwner* predicate, defined by the conjunction of the ground predicates *BallNorth* and *BallInKick*, respectively deriving from the fuzzyfication of the direction and distance properties of the ball concept instance in $\mathcal{D}$.

Some of the most important properties that can be obtained by basing the robot control architecture on the model using the knowledge model are below summarized.

- *noise filtering*: using a conceptual model of the environment it is possible to eliminate out–layers in percepts and filter in a proper way noisy data coming from sensors; this produces more reliable information for the other modules effectively controlling the agent
- *sensor fusion*: percepts coming from different sensors, and referring to the same objects, can be fused enhancing fault tolerance and enabling on–line diagnosis
- *virtual sensing*: a model of the environment can be used to infer new features, not perceived by physical sensors
- *time consistency*: the instances in the conceptual model represent a state of the environment; it is possible to maintain and monitor its consistency in real–time; this activity can be used to learn and check models
- *abstraction*: the use of fuzzy predicates instead of raw data, or features, in the behavior definition gives more abstraction in designing robot behaviors, and robustness to noisy data; it also facilitates design, since gives the designer the possibility to reason in symbolic terms. Moreover, exchanging this information is more effective for agents of a Multi-Agent System (MAS) sharing the same semantics for symbols.

3   SCARE, the Coordination System

Cooperation holds a very important role in multi-agent system applications. To face the typical issues of these applications, we have implemented *SCARE* [5] a general architecture for coordination in multi-robot domains. SCARE is able to deal with:

- *heterogeneity*: when a MAS is made up of agents with different skills, our architecture exploits these differences in order to improve the overall performance
- *communication*: coordination policy may change according to the amount of information that can be exchanged among agents and according to network connectivity
- *adaptation*: in order to grant the autonomy of the system, the coordination mechanism is able to adapt its parameters in reaction to environment changes

Using SCARE, the MAS application developer has to identify the macro-activities that the agents can carry out. To cope with uncertainty of the perception and approximate definitions, we adopt the *fuzzy predicates* approach introduced in Section 1. In this way, the states of the model belong to a situation with a certain degree. By introducing a threshold $\bar{t}$ it is possible to define a situation with a fuzzy predicate: $\sigma = \{m \in \mathcal{M} | \mu(m) > \bar{t}\}$ $\bar{t} \in [0, 1]$. Fuzzy predicates give the possibility to obtain a measure of the matching between a predefined situation σ and the current state of the model. In the job assignment process, in order to establish how much each activity is suited for the agent, we use several parameters implemented by fuzzy predicates, which operate on the domain $\mathcal{D}$:

- *cando*: define when the activity can take part in the assignment process;
- *attitude*: define how much the skills of the agent are useful for the activity;
- *chance*: define the situation where the agent has good chances to succeed;
- *utility*: define the situation where the activity is useful for the agent team;

- *success*: define the goal achievement situation for the activity;
- *failure*: define the situation where the activity should be stopped because of unrecoverable failure.

An activity terminates when the success or failure conditions are verified. If an agent is idle, a job assignement process starts. For each activity, the cando predicates are evaluated in order to reject those activities that cannot take place. For each remaining activity, utility and chance predicates, and the agent's attitude are considered, thus obtaining indicators to take the decision. Through the application of some multi-objective technique (e.g., weighted sums, goal programming, normal-boundary intersection, multilevel programming, or others), each agent gets an ordered list of activities (*agenda*). Once all the agendas are produced they must be compared in order to achieve a coordinated assignment of jobs (for details see [5]).

4   BRIAN: The Behavior Management System

Especially in dynamic environments, the main approach to robot control design is the so called behavior-based architecture [1]. In such approach, the robot controller is obtained by the implicit cooperative activity of behavioral modules. Each module operates on a small subset of the input space implementing a relatively simple mapping from sensorial input to actions; the global behavior of the robot arises from the interaction among all these modules. One of the major problems in behavior-based robotics is the design of this interaction, usually pre–defined in terms of inhibitory relationships or vectorial composition of the module output.

In our behavior management system *BRIAN*, integration and coordination among behavior modules is achieved using two sets of fuzzy predicates associated to each of them: *CANDO* and *WANT* conditions. In BRIAN we face the issue of controlling the interaction among modules by decoupling them with context conditions described in terms of fuzzy predicates evaluated over internal state and environmental situation present in $\mathcal{D}$, goals generated by *SCARE*, and communications with other agents.

CANDO conditions are used to decide whether a behavior module is appropriate to the specific situation: if they are not verified, the behavior module activation does not make sense. The designer has to put in this set all the fuzzy predicates which have to be true, at least to a significant extent, to give sense to the behavior activation. For instance, in order to consider to kick a ball into the opponent goal, the agent should have the ball control, and it should be oriented towards the goal. This set of conditions has a twofold result: decoupling behavior design and increasing the computational efficiency of the behavior management system.

WANT conditions represent the motivation for an agent to execute a behavior. They may be related either to the environmental context (e.g., *BallInFront*, "the ball is in front of me"), or from strategic goals (e.g., *CollectDocuments*, "I have to collect the documents to be delivered"). Composition of the actions proposed by behaviors modules active at the same time is implemented by the WANT conditions, which represent the opportunity of executing them in the specific context.

The use of these two different sets of conditions allows the designer to design a dynamic network of behavior modules defined by means of context predicates. This is

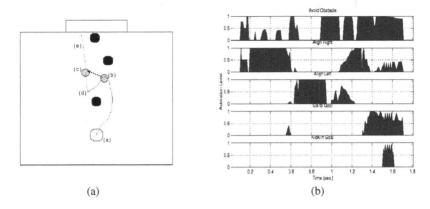

(a)   (b)

Fig. 1. The trace of robot trajectory during the test and the activation level of the behaviors

a sensible improvement with respect to usual behavior-based architectures; we do not have a complex predefined interaction schema that has to take into account all possible execution contexts. In fact, at any instant, the agent knows that it could play only a restricted set of behavior modules (i.e., those enabled by the CANDO conditions), and it has to select/merge the behaviors consistent with its present motivations.

In BRIAN, each behavioral module receives data in input and provides output commands to be issued to the environment. This is obtained through fuzzy logic controllers where a set of fuzzy rules match a description of the situation given in terms of fuzzy predicates, and produces actions for the actuators by composing the output proposed by each rule by a T-conorm.

5   Experimental Results

In this section we present in details the results obtained in a particular experiment where the robot executes a standard Robocup challenge used in this case to test the composition of behavioral modules.

In figure 1(a) you can see the experimental setting of the test. The black objects are static obstacles the grey one is the ball to catch and kick in the goal. The track in the plot is taken from real data: the trajectory is projected on the field using the odometry of the robot. The robot starts in position (a), after 0.5 sec the robot, incidentally touching the ball (position (b)), moves it to the position (c). So it has to dynamically change its behavior to face this unforeseen situation. The trajectory executed by the robot is obtained by selecting and blending different actions proposed by different behavioral units and reacting to changes in the environment (e.g., the variation of ball position as shown in figure $1(b)$). In this experiment, we use only five simplified basic behaviors to show the effectiveness of our approach (see Table 1).

The predicates appearing in the fuzzy conditions are computed by evaluating fuzzy sets on data in the domain $\mathcal{D}$, and composing them. In figure 2, you may see the definition of some of the fuzzy sets involved in the definition of the above mentioned

Table 1. CANDO and WANT conditions for each behavior

Behavior	CANDO	WANT
Avoid Obstacle	`(ObstaclePresent)`	

Align Right	`(AND (AND (BallSeeing)`
	`          (NOT (RigthAligned)))`
	`     (NOT (AND (BallOwner)`
	`               (Aligned))))`
		`(AND (OR (AlonePlayer)(ForwardRole))`
		`     (AND (NOT (ObstacleAvoiding))`
		`          (NOT (GoalNear))))`

Align Left	`(AND (AND (BallSeeing)`
	`          (NOT (LeftAligned)))`
	`     (NOT (AND (BallOwner)`
	`               (Aligned))))`
		`(AND (OR (AlonePlayer)(ForwardRole))`
		`     (AND (NOT (ObstacleAvoiding))`
		`          (NOT (GoalNear))))`

Go to Goal	`(AND (BallOwner)(Aligned))`	`(AND (NOT (AbstacleAvoiding))` `     (NOT (GoalNear)))`
Kick in Goal	`(AND (BallOwner)(Aligned))`	`(GoalNear)`

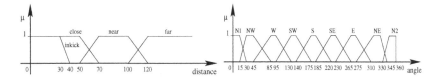

Fig. 2. The definition of some of the fuzzy sets used to compute the predicates involved in CANDO and WANT conditions of the behavior modules developed for Robocup

predicates. In particular, we have reported the frame of cognition the distance to the ball, and the direction of the ball.

Complex predicates are computed by composing basic ones. For instance, the `BallOwner` predicate is computed as (`AND BallNord BallInKick`), where `BallNord` comes from (`OR N1 N2`) computed from the second frame of cognition reported in figure 2, and `BallInKick` comes from the value of `InKick` from the distance frame of cognition. Analogous computations bring to the evaluation of all the needed predicates.

During the experiment we are presenting, we have logged the activation level of CANDO and WANT for each behavior module (figure 3(a) and (b)) and the final behavior activation level coming from the combination of CANDO and WANT (figure 1(b)). From figure 3(b) you may notice that, during this experiment, the WANT conditions for *Align Left*, *AlignRight* and *GoToGoal* have the same activation level, since the robot is playing alone so the predicate (`AlonePlayer`) is always verified and the other conditions are the same for all the behaviors.

As you may notice from the definitions of the WANT conditions of *AlignLeft* and *AlignRight* in Table 1, it is possible to include in them also context description predicates like the actual role of the teammate (i.e., `ForwardRole`) or the explicit reference to other behaviors (i.e., `ObstacleAvoiding`). In the example, the value of `ForwardRole` has been set by the user to be always TRUE; in a real sistuation SCARE sets this value according to the evaluation of current situation and the planning strategy. This is just an example of how our formalism can be used both for modeling the context and controlling the behaviors blending.

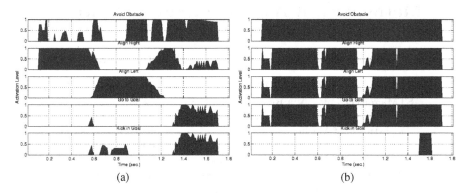

Fig. 3. The activation level of CANDO (a) and WANT (b) conditions during the test

6   Conclusion

In this paper we have presented the fuzzy cognitive model we use to integrate in a uniform framework the deliberative and reactive components of multi-agent systems. The cognitive model we propose, integrates coordination, planning and reactive behaviors providing a common cognitive substratum for a team of robots where behavioral modules are used as high-level macro-actions that compose structured plans defined by a flexible multi-agent coordination system.

All the elements in the knowledge processing level are based on simple fuzzy predicates that can be easily managed, designed and adapted. Doing it this way, the control model can be easily designed to be tuned and adapted on-line so that the team strategies and the role of robots in the control schemata can be automatically modified to face different opponent teams, and changes in robot performances [5].

References

1. R. C. Arkin. *Behavior-Based Robotics*. MIT Press, Cambridge, MA, 1998.
2. M. Asada, H. Kitano, I. Noda, and M. Veloso. Robocup: today and tomorrow – what we have learned. *Artificial Intelligence Journal*, 110:193–214, 1999.
3. A. Bonarini, G. Invernizzi, T. Labella, and M. Matteucci. An architecture to co-ordinate fuzzy behaviors to control an autonomous robot. *Fuzzy Sets and Systems*, 134(1):101–115, 2002.
4. A. Bonarini, M. Matteucci, and M. Restelli. Anchoring: do we need new solutions to an old problem or do we have old solutions for a new problem? In *Proceedings of the AAAI Fall Symposium on Anchoring Symbols to Sensor Data in Single and Multiple Robot Systems*, page In press, Menlo Park, CA, 2001. AAAI Press.
5. A. Bonarini and M. Restelli. An architecture to implement agents co-operating in dynamic environments. In *Proc. of AAMAS 2002 - Autonomous Agents and Multi-Agent Systems*, pages 1143–1144, New York, NY, 2002. ACM Press.

Mathematical Aspects of Fuzzy Control

Paolo Amato[1], Antonio Di Nola[2], and Mirko Navara[3]

[1] Soft Computing, Si-Optics and Post Silicon Technologies Corporate R&D
STMicroelectronics, Via Remo De Feo 1, 80022 Arzano, NA, Italy
paolo.amato@st.com
[2] Department of Mathematics and Informatics, University of Salerno
via S. Allende, 84081 Baronissi, Salerno, Italy
adinola@unisa.it
[3] Center for Machine Perception, Department of Cybernetics,
Faculty of Electrical Engineering, Czech Technical University,
Technická 2, 166 27 Praha, Czech Republic
navara@cmp.felk.cvut.cz

Abstract. In recent decades, fuzzy controllers were successfully applied
to many tasks. Their use was based more on engineering intuition than
on deep mathematical treatment. Here we collect several criteria that a
fuzzy controller should satisfy in order to represent the meaning of the
rule base. Surprisingly, these conditions are often ignored and violated.
Sometimes this is caused only by wrong design, but there are cases when
the principle of the controller does not admit to satisfy these criteria.
We discuss them in more detail and formulate conclusions for selection
of an appropriate type of fuzzy controller.

1 Introduction

At present, Mamdani–Assilian controllers form the basis of numerous applications in automatic control. They allow for representing a multidimensional function (control surface) in a very transparent form of if-then rules. This makes the design and tuning of fuzzy controllers relatively easy and fast.

A detailed analysis of the properties of Mamdani–Assilian (and similar) fuzzy controllers lead to some criticism; the rule base is represented only roughly, with some distortion. This drawback was compensated by other advantageous properties in applications. One of them is computational efficiency which is better than that of other fuzzy controllers based on a compositional rule of inference, see [13]. Mathematical study of properties of fuzzy controllers may lead to recommendations that improve the results, see [14]. Here we continue this research by discussion of several (both mathematical and practical) problems concerning rule bases and inference mechanism of fuzzy controllers.

Our treatment applies to rule bases which are designed either by experts or automatically (by a fuzzy neural network, genetic algorithm, etc.). The aspects discussed here seem to be particularly significant in the case of automatic design when the proper interpretation of rules may be crucial for convergence of tuning.

V. Di Gesú, F. Masulli, and A. Petrosino (Eds.): WILF 2003, LNAI 2955, pp. 80–88, 2006.
© Springer-Verlag Berlin Heidelberg 2006

2   Theoretical Analysis of Fuzzy Controllers

Let X and Y denote the input and the output space of a controller, respectively. They are supposed to be convex subsets of finite-dimensional real vector spaces. For a set Z, we denote by $\mathcal{F}(Z)$ the set of all fuzzy subsets of Z. The expert's knowledge may be expressed by a base of rules of the form

$$\text{if } x \in X_i \text{ then } y \in Y_i \,,$$

where $X_i \in \mathcal{F}(X)$ are *antecedents* and $Y_i \in \mathcal{F}(Y)$ are *consequents*, $i \in \{1, \ldots, n\}$ (see [6]). Following [20], the knowledge from the rule base should be represented by a fuzzy relation $R \in \mathcal{F}(X \times Y)$. We apply it in the *compositional rule of inference* which assigns to a fuzzy input $X^* \in \mathcal{F}(X)$ a fuzzy output $Y^* \in \mathcal{F}(Y)$ by $Y^* = X^* \underset{T}{\circ} R$, i.e.,

$$Y^*(y) = \sup_{x \in X} T(X^*(x), R(x, y)) \,, \tag{1}$$

where T is a fixed t-norm modelling a fuzzy conjunction [7].

Here we discuss three types of fuzzy controllers:

1. The **residuum-based controller** uses the compositional rule of inference (1) with the fuzzy relation R of the form

$$R(x, y) = \min_{i \leq n} I_T(X_i(x), Y_i(y)) \,, \tag{2}$$

where

$$I_T(a, b) = \sup\{c \in [0, 1] : T(a, c) \leq b\}$$

is the *residuum* (or *R-implication*) induced by T. This form reflects exactly the meaning of the rule base as a conjunction of implications. Nevertheless, it is rarely used. One reason is that the residuum is noncontinuous for any t-norm without zero divisors (e.g., for the minimum or the algebraic product). This may (but does not have to) cause undesirable behaviour (discontinuity) of the controller. Another disadvantage of the residuum-based controller is its higher computational complexity in comparison with other approaches which will be discussed later.

2. The **Mamdani–Assilian controller** [10] uses (1) with

$$R(x, y) = \max_{i \leq n} T(X_i(x), Y_i(y)) \tag{3}$$

i.e.,

$$
\begin{aligned}
Y^*(y) &= \sup_{x \in X} T\left(X^*(x), \max_{i \leq n} T(X_i(x), Y_i(y))\right) \\
&= \max_i T\left(\underbrace{\sup_{x \in X} T(X^*(x), X_i(x))}_{\mathcal{D}(X^*, X_i)}, Y_i(y)\right).
\end{aligned}
\tag{4}
$$

The latter form allows for an effective calculation using the values

$$\mathcal{D}(X^*, X_i) = \sup_{x \in X} T(X^*(x), X_i(x)), \tag{5}$$

called the *degrees of overlapping* of X^*, X_i. Their use allows to avoid nested cycles over spaces X, Y. Notice that the simplification is possible due to the associativity of T; among others, it requires that the same t-norm T is used in (3) and (1).

3. The **controller with conditionally firing rules** [13] is a generalization of Mamdani–Assilian controller (see [14] for its detailed description). It uses rescalings of membership degrees in both the input and the output space and the degree of overlapping $\mathcal{D}(X^*, X_i)$ in (4) is replaced by the *degree of conditional firing* of the ith rule defined as

$$\mathcal{C}_i = \frac{\mathcal{D}\big(\varrho(X^*), \varrho(X_i)\big)}{\max_j \mathcal{D}\big(\varrho(X^*), \varrho(X_j)\big)} \tag{6}$$

(using the rescaled membership functions $\varrho(X^*), \varrho(X_j)$).

We concentrate on the following questions:

1. Why (and how) to avoid nonsignificant outputs?
2. Restrictions on the shape of antecedents.
3. Do the antecedents have to cover the whole input space?
4. What happens if we add a new rule?

3   Analysis of Fuzzy Controllers

To formulate mathematically the desirable properties of a fuzzy controller, we have to introduce several basic notions from fuzzy set theory. For a fuzzy set $A \in \mathcal{F}(Z)$, we define its *support* $\text{Supp}\, A = \{z \in Z : A(z) > 0\}$ and the *core* of A, $\text{core}\, A = \{z \in Z : A(z) = 1\}$, and we call A *normal* iff $\text{core}\, A \neq \emptyset$. A fuzzy set is called *convex* if all its α-cuts are convex sets. For fuzzy subsets $A_1, \dots, A_n$ of the same universe, Z, their *convex hull* is the smallest (w.r.t. the pointwise ordering) convex fuzzy set $C \in \mathcal{F}(Z)$ satisfying $A_i(z) \leq C(z)$ for all $z \in Z$, $i = 1, \dots, n$.

3.1   General Conditions on a Fuzzy Controller

The following (rather natural) requirements on a fuzzy controller are imposed in [13]:

[Int1] If the input coincides with an antecedent, then the output coincides with the respective consequent.

[Int2] Let $Y_{\mathbf{zero}}$ be the output corresponding to the zero input (i.e., without input information). For each normal input, $X^* \in \mathcal{F}(X)$, the corresponding output Y^* is strictly greater than $Y_{\mathbf{zero}}$ (i.e., it carries information about the input).

[Int3] The output Y^* belongs to the convex hull of the consequents of all firing rules (i.e., all rules satisfying $\operatorname{Supp} X_i \cap \operatorname{Supp} X^* \neq \emptyset$).

[Int4] If a crisp input belongs to the core of an antecedent (i.e., one rule fires totally), then the output coincides with the respective consequent.

Condition [Int1] interprets the rule base so that an antecedent—considered as a typical input for firing of the rule—should result in the corresponding consequent as an output. Thus the membership function of the consequent says to which extent an output value y is desirable in the situation described by the antecedent. This is not the only possible interpretation: Sometimes the consequents are interpreted as *bounds* of outputs and only an inequality is considered. (We consider upper bounds in case of a residuum-based controller and lower bounds for the remaining two controllers studied here.) This means that one rule gives a (lower or upper) bound of membership degree ("relevance of the output value") and we do not exclude the possibility that the final membership degree may be effected by another rule. This generalization leads to a system of fuzzy relational *inequalities* instead of equalities which were studied in [4], [5], [15], [18], etc. As far as we know, the generalization to fuzzy relational inequalities has not been mathematically treated yet and it remains a subject of future research.

Condition [Int2] is discussed in detail in the following sections.

Condition [Int3] says that the output does not exceed the convex hull of outputs corresponding to all firing rules, so the controller performs an interpolation of given data. In fact, [Int3] is a rather weak formulation of this requirement and it should be strengthened, but it is difficult to formulate a better condition in the space of multidimensional fuzzy vectors. (The space of fuzzy vectors—considered as a subspace of a linear space of functions—has an infinite dimension.) There seems to be no problem in satisfaction of [Int3] in fuzzy controllers.

Condition [Int4] ensures that a fully firing rule determines the output independently of other rules. It is not a special instance of [Int1] for crisp inputs. It refers to the rather rare case when the degree of firing is 1. Thus [Int4] represents the principle: "If we have an entirely good solution (rule), we do not need the others." Although it may be discussed whether this is exactly what we want in a fuzzy controller, this condition has a very important consequence: without it, extreme output values (consequents of a single rule) may disappear, inducing a tendency to middle (average) output values and "weak" action of the controller.[1]

3.2 Significance of Outputs

Condition [Int2] guarantees the significance of the output. Each admitted input (normality is a common assumption here) should give nontrivial information about output values. Otherwise, the controller does not have effect and the output does not reflect any properties of the input.

What causes difficult problems is the interplay of conditions [Int1] and [Int2]. To satisfy [Int2], the supports of antecedents must overlap. Unless we use a

---

[1] In fact, this condition was obtained as a side effect of the effort to satisfy the preceding three conditions.

nilpotent t-norm T, this implies that the degrees of overlapping of antecedents must be nonzero. On the other hand, solvability of the system of fuzzy relational equations resulting from condition [Int1] gives an upper bound of the degrees of overlapping of different antecedents, $\mathcal{D}(X_i, X_j)$ (see [4, 15] for more details). Taking a nilpotent t-norm for T would help to satisfy [Int2], but it makes [Int1] more restrictive, so this does not help to satisfy both conditions simultaneously [12]. Following [13], neither a residuum-based, nor a Mamdani–Assilian controller admit to satisfy [Int1] and [Int2] simultaneously in rather typical situations. This is the principal motivation of the controller with conditionally firing rules. According to [13], it satisfies requirements [Int1]–[Int4] for each rule base such that:

[C1] Each antecedent is normal.
[C2] Each point of the input space belongs to the support of some antecedent.
[C3] No consequent is covered by the maximum all other consequents.
[C4] "Weak disjointness of antecedents": $\mathcal{D}(X_i, X_j) \leq 1$ whenever $i \neq j$.

Condition [C4] does not admit two totally firing rules for a crisp input; thus no contradiction occurs in [Int4]. We admit that [C4] might be too restrictive for some rule bases encountered in applications. The other conditions seem to be rather weak.

A practical experiment verifying the advantageous properties of the controller with conditionally firing rules was described in [14, 19].

The controller with conditionally firing rules is ready for tests on software-implemented tasks. However, many contemporaneous applications use a specialized fuzzy hardware which admits a cheap and fast technical solution. For this, special chips were developed which perform the operations of a Mamdani–Assilian controller. Paper [1] describes a method of implementation of the controller with conditionally firing rules using this fuzzy hardware and a modified rule base. This method works properly only for crisp inputs, but this constraint does not seem to be too restrictive; in fact, current fuzzy hardware handles only crisp inputs [9].

3.3   Shapes and Number of Rules

In our mathematical study, we did not impose any restrictions on the shape of antecedents; they could be arbitrary fuzzy subsets of the input space. Usually the hardware devices that implement fuzzy logic compute the antecedents in $X \subseteq R^k$ as fuzzy intersections of k one-dimensional fuzzy sets, i.e.,

$$X_i = T(X_{i1}, \ldots, X_{ik}),\tag{7}$$

where $X_{ij} \in \mathcal{F}(R)$ is a fuzzy set describing the jth input in the ith rule. In particular, if $T = \min$, then X_i becomes the cylindric extension (cartesian product) of fuzzy sets $X_{i1}, \ldots, X_{ik}$.

It is a rather common case that each antecedent can be expressed in the form (7). (Often some inputs are not used and can be omitted.) Then this limitation causes no restrictions on the design of the controller.

However, more complex shapes of antecedents are also encountered. We can approximate each of them by several fuzzy sets of the form (7). This partition leads to more rules (possibly with the same consequent). An increased number of rules might be compensated by more efficient hardware. This approach causes no problem in Mamdani–Assilian or residuum-based controllers. In contrast to this, a controller with conditionally firing rules does not work the same way if we cover one antecedent by several fuzzy sets. The new degrees of conditional firing are smaller in general. (No problem of this kind arises if the partition of an antecedent is crisp, but this is usually not the case.) This may make the use of standard fuzzy hardware impossible, because we cannot build up the degree of conditional firing from one-dimensional fuzzy sets. For this reason, a controller with conditionally firing rules can be implemented by the standard fuzzy hardware only for special forms of antecedents and their rescaling ρ.

3.4 Covering of the Input Space by Antecedents

As a trivial consequence of [Int2], the input space X has to be covered by (the supports of) antecedents, $X = \bigcup_{i \leq n} \operatorname{Supp} A_i$ (condition [C2]). Surprisingly, this condition is violated in many fuzzy controllers. See, e.g., the example of the control of inverted pendulum (cartpole problem, balancing a pole) in [8–Chapter 4]. Table 1 there (Table 4.1 in the German editions) shows a rule base where only 19 from 49 possible antecedents are used and they do not cover the input space. As an example of a recent application, we may mention fuzzy controller-based prediction of consumption of electricity described in detail in [21]. If the input space is not covered by the antecedents, there exists a normal input (at least some crisp value) which produces the same output as the zero input. This situation seems highly undesirable and should be avoided.

There are several reasons why some fuzzy controllers admit a rule base in which antecedents do not cover the input space:

1. The uncovered inputs are considered impossible. In this case they should not be included in the input space X at all. This may be easily done, unless it contradicts the convexity of X.
2. The inputs are fuzzified so that they always overlap with an antecedent. In this case the fuzzification (or rejection of some input sets) must be explicitly mentioned as a substantial part of the design of the controller.
3. Some situations do not require any action of the controller. E.g., in the cartpole problem [8–Chapter 4] the contoller may sometimes stop, "relax", and wait until a new situation activates a rule and a negative feedback. This approach substantially decreases the number of rules. Numerous controllers work on this principle.

    From our point of view, this reduction of rules causes a problem. This discrepancy may be resolved by considering formally a new, implicit, *"else-rule"*, which may be roughly expressed as: "Unless another rule fires, do not do anything." This assumes that there is an implicit output meaning "no action" or "wait". This may mean, e.g., zero outputs or keeping the outputs constant. The implicit output is strongly application-dependent. Very often it is defined by the hardware, because it appears as an output value of the controller disconnected from the input.

Trying to include the else-rule in our formalism, we may describe it as an if-then rule (number 0) with consequent Y_0 causing the implicit output and antecedent X_0 covering the "else" case. While the meaning of X_0 is clear in the case of crisp antecedents, the usual case of fuzzy antecedents represents a problem. In order to cover the input space by antecedents (see above), X_0 must overlap with other antecedents (at least for continuous membership functions, which is usually the case). One possibility is to take

$$X_0(x) = \max\left(0, 1 - \sum_{i=1}^{n} X_i(x)\right). \tag{8}$$

Nevertheless, the else-rule has a special role. For instance, it may be discussed whether condition [Int1] should be imposed on the else-rule, too. Condition [Int2] may be considered unimportant if the intersection of all consequents produces exactly the required implicit output. The restrictions on the shape of antecedents do not apply to the else-rule. In contrast to this, [Int4] is essential for the else-rule. (It is always satisfied if we use (8); then the else-rule fires totally iff all the other rules do not fire at all.)

4. Although we suggest to fuzzify the antecedents (and not the inputs) to satisfy [Int2], other approaches are studied in the literature. In particular, much effort has been invested in methods of *interpolation* of the rules when the rule base is sparse, see e.g. [3]. This may be interpreted as a metarule saying "these rules may be interpolated". As far as we know, it remains an open problem whether the same effect can be achieved by merely changing the antecedents. We conjecture that this is not the case, but problems arise due to high complexity of control tasks to which this method is applied. Also this question should be a subject of further study.

3.5   Adding a New Rule

Tuning a fuzzy controller, we may encounter a new situation which is not properly solved by any of the rules. Then it becomes necessary to add a new rule determining the output in similar states. Although it is possible to modify the whole rule base after this change, usually the new rule is merely added to those already used (which were found successful in other situations). As shown by H. Prade, this approach may have an undesirable side effect, especially if it is used repeatedly and many new rules are added. (This may happen in automatic design of the rule base, see e.g. [2].)

If we add a new rule to a residuum-based controller, the control surface, as well as the output, decreases. Thus the output membership degrees become closer to 0 and they may carry less information.

In the Mamdani–Assilian controller, the opposite situation occurs: The control surface and the output increase. This monotonic development may result in output membership degrees closer to 1 and carrying less information.

In contrast to the above two cases, the controller with conditionally firing rules behaves differently. Although the newly added rule does not change the *form* of other rules, it modifies their *effect* through the formula determining the degrees of conditional firing (6). When the new rule fires, the others are attenuated proportionally. This increases the membership degrees in points of the new consequent (provided that the degree of firing of the new rule is sufficiently high) and decreases the membership degrees of other points. The corresponding fuzzy output respects the new rule and may carry more relevant information. Thus the controller with conditionally firing rules may be recommended in systems where we expect many new rules added during the phase of tuning.

Recently a new experiment was done by D. Peri [16]. Using the method of automatic generation of fuzzy rules for approximation according to [17], he implemented a system for medical diagnostics based on numerous parameters of different nature. Several methods (incl. Mamdani–Assilian approximation and its modification with conditionally firing rules) were tested on three data sets— one with artificial data, two with real data (one which enabled relatively easy and precise classification, one which was much more difficult). Our approach with conditionally firing rules was worse in two of these three tasks, but it was the best in the most important case—real data with difficult classification. In all cases it resulted in an approximation with the least number of rules. Until a more detailed analysis of the advantages and drawbacks of this approach is complete, it may be at least considered as an alternative to other methods, giving sometimes very perspective results.

4   Conclusion

We compared three types of fuzzy controllers and analyzed several natural conditions that should be satisfied. Although well motivated by mathematical arguments, these conditions sometimes cause problems or are violated in the design of fuzzy controllers. We discuss the reasons (separately for each condition) and show possible solutions with regard to each type of controller.

Acknowledgements. This research was supported by the Czech Ministry of Education under Research Programme MSM 212300013 "Decision Making and Control in Manufacturing", grant 201/02/1540 of the Grant Agency of the Czech Republic, and grant INDAM. The authors thank to numerous experts whose remarks contributed to this subject, particularly to E.P. Klement, T. Lund, R. Mesiar, V. Novák, I. Perfilieva, I. Petružela, and H. Prade.

References

1. P. Amato, A. Di Nola, and M. Navara: Reformulation of fuzzy controller with conditionally firing rules, In: M. Mohammadian (ed.) *Proc. Int. Conf. Computational Intelligence for Modelling, Control and Automation*, Vienna, Austria, 2003, 140–151.
2. P. Amato and C. Manara: Relating the theory of partitions in MV-logic to the design of interpretable fuzzy systems, In: *Trade-off between Accuracy and Interpretability in Fuzzy Rule-Based Modeling*, J. Casillas, O. Cordón, F. Herrera, and L. Magdalena (Eds), Springer Verlag, Berlin, 2002.

3. P. Baranyi, I. Bavelaar, L. Kóczy, and A. Titli: Inverse rule base of various fuzzy interpolation techniques, In: *Proc. Congress IFSA 97*, Vol. II, Praha, 121–126, 1997.
4. B. De Baets: A note on Mamdani controllers, In: D. Ruan, P. D'hondt, P. Govaerts, and E. Kerre (Eds), *Intelligent Systems and Soft Computing for Nuclear Science and Industry*, World Scientific Publishing, Singapore, 22–28, 1996.
5. A. Di Nola, S. Sessa, W. Pedrycz, and E. Sanchez: *Fuzzy Relation Equations and Their Applications to Knowledge Engineering*, Kluwer, Dordrecht, 1989.
6. D. Driankov, H. Hellendoorn, and M. Reinfrank: *An Introduction to Fuzzy Control*, Springer, Heidelberg, 1993.
7. S. Gottwald: *Fuzzy Sets and Fuzzy Logic*, Vieweg, Braunschweig, 1993.
8. R. Kruse, J. Gebhardt, and F. Klawon: *Foundations of Fuzzy Systems.* J. Wiley, 1994.
9. T. Lund, A. Torralba, R.G. Carvajal, and J. Ramirez-Angulo: A Comparison of Architectures for a Programmable Fuzzy Logic Chip, *International Symposium on Circuits and Systems (ISCAS)*, Orlando, Florida, Vol. V, 623–626, May 1999.
10. E. H. Mamdani and S. Assilian: An experiment in linguistic synthesis of fuzzy controllers, *Int. J. Man-Mach. Stud.*, Vol. 7, 1–13, 1975.
11. B. Moser and M. Navara: Conditionally firing rules extend the possibilities of fuzzy controllers, *Proc. CIMCA '99*, M. Mohammadian (Ed), IOS Press, Amsterdam, 242–245, 1999.
12. B. Moser and M. Navara: Which triangular norms are convenient for fuzzy controllers? *Proc. EUSFLAT-ESTYLF Joint Conf. 99*, Universitat de les Illes Balears, Palma (Mallorca), 75–78, 1999.
13. B. Moser and M. Navara: Fuzzy controllers with conditionally firing rules, *IEEE Trans. Fuzzy Systems*, Vol. 10, No. 3, 340–348, 2002.
14. M. Navara and J. Šťastný: Properties of fuzzy controller with conditionally firing rules, In: P. Sinčák, J. Vaščák, V. Kvasnička, J. Pospíchal (Eds), *Intelligent Technologies — Theory and Applications*, IOS Press, Amsterdam, 2002, 111–116.
15. I. Perfilieva and A. Tonis: Criterion of solvability of fuzzy relational equations system, *Proc. Congress IFSA 97*, Praha, 1997, 90–95.
16. D. Peri: *Fuzzy Rules Induction in Medical Diagnosis.* Technical Report, CTU, Praha, 2003.
17. R. Rozich, T. Ioerger, R. Yager: FURL – A Theory Revision Approach to Learning Fuzzy Rules. Proc. IEEE Int. Conf. Fuzzy Systems, 2002, 791–796.
18. E. Sanchez: Resolution of composite fuzzy relation equations, *Information and Control* 30 (1976), 38–48.
19. J. Šťastný: *Comparison of Mamdani and CFR Controller* (in Czech), Research Report CTU–CMP–2001–04, Center for Machine Perception, Czech Technical University, Prague, 2001,
ftp://cmp.felk.cvut.cz/pub/cmp/articles/navara/TR_Stastny.ps.gz.
20. L.A. Zadeh: Outline of a new approach to the analysis of complex systems and decision processes, *IEEE Trans. Syst. Man Cybern.*, Vol. 3, No. 1, 28–44, 1973.
21. L. Žák: Estimation of the effect of weather on the electric energy consumption by means of a fuzzy controller (in Czech), *Automation* **45** (2002), 326–330.

Piecewise Linear Fuzzy Sliding Mode Control

Mariagrazia Dotoli and Biagio Turchiano

Dipartimento di Elettrotecnica ed Elettronica, Politecnico di Bari,
Via Re David 200, 70125 Bari, Italy
{dotoli, turchiano}@poliba.it

Abstract. We present a novel fuzzy sliding mode control technique for a class of second order dynamical systems based on a piecewise linear sliding manifold. The proposed approach benefits from a reduction in the control action magnitude with respect to classical sliding mode control strategies, enhancing the effectiveness of such strategies under a saturated control input. In addition, employing the proposed fuzzy rule based algorithm results in smooth dynamics when the trajectory is in the vicinities of the sliding manifold.

1 Introduction

Fuzzy Sliding Mode Control (FSMC) techniques are hybrid methodologies combining the effectiveness of Sliding Mode Control (SMC) with the immediacy of fuzzy control algorithms [3]. FSMC approximates the input/output map of SMC by applying a fuzzy inference mechanism to a linguistic rule base [1, 2]. The resulting benefits include smooth dynamics, as opposed to the typical SMC chattering, and a restriction of the fuzzy rule table dimension with respect to classical fuzzy controllers [3]. In this paper we introduce a novel FSMC technique for a class of dynamical systems based on a piecewise linear sliding manifold. We discuss the effectiveness of the technique under a saturated control input with respect to SMC and classical FSMC. Moreover, we illustrate the proposed technique on a design example.

2 Sliding Mode Control

Consider the following dynamical system [4]:

$$\dot{x}_1 = x_2$$
$$\dot{x}_2 = f(\mathbf{x}) + b(\mathbf{x})u \tag{1}$$

where $\mathbf{x}=[x_1 \ x_2]^T$ is the state vector, u is the control input, $f(\mathbf{x})$ and $b(\mathbf{x})$ are nonlinear functions. Consider a given trajectory $x_{1d}(t)$ and the error $e=x_1-x_{1d}$. SMC forces the system, after a reaching phase, to a sliding line containing the operating point:

$$s(x) = \dot{e} + \lambda e = x_2 - x_{2d} + \lambda(x_1 - x_{1d}) = 0 \ , \tag{2}$$

where $x_{2d}(t) = \dot{x}_{1d}(t)$ and the sliding constant λ is strictly positive. At steady state the system follows the desired trajectory once $s(\mathbf{x}(t_{reach}))=0$, with t_{reach} representing the

V. Di Gesú, F. Masulli, and A. Petrosino (Eds.): WILF 2003, LNAI 2955, pp. 89–96, 2006.

reaching time [4]. Hence, a suitable control action is to be designed for the system to hit the sliding surface (2). We select the Lyapunov function [4]

$$V = \frac{1}{2}s^2(\mathbf{x}) ,$$ (3)

with the following control action

$$u = b^{-1}(\mathbf{x}) \cdot (\hat{u} - K \text{sign}(s(\mathbf{x}))), \quad K > 0 ,$$ (4)

where K is a design parameter or a function of $\mathbf{x}(t)$ such that $K = K(\mathbf{x})$, 'sign' represents the sign function, and it holds [4]

$$\hat{u} = -(f(\mathbf{x}) - \ddot{x}_{1d} + \lambda \dot{e}) .$$ (5)

By derivation of the Lyapunov function (3) we get:

$$\dot{V} = s(\mathbf{x})\dot{s}(\mathbf{x}) = -Ks(\mathbf{x})\text{sign}(s(\mathbf{x})) + ds \le -\eta \,|\, s(\mathbf{x}) \,| .$$ (6)

with $K \ge \eta$. Hence, $\dot{V}$ is negative definite in the switching line, which is attractive and, if $e(t=0) \ne 0$, will be reached in a finite time t_{reach} [4]. We remark that, due to the sign function in (4), the SMC exhibits chattering, i.e., high frequency switching.

3 Fuzzy Sliding Mode Control (FSMC)

A popular solution to the drawbacks of SMC is to combine it with fuzzy logic [2]. The benefits of the resulting FSMC strategies are the reduction of chattering and of the computational effort with respect to SMC techniques.

Generally speaking, FSMC is characterized by a heuristic rule table. The typical FSMC for system (1) is governed by the following control law [3]:

$$u = b^{-1}(\mathbf{x}) \cdot \left(\hat{u} + u_{fuzz}(e, \dot{e}, \lambda) \right) ,$$ (7)

where $\hat{u}$ is defined according to (5) and the fuzzy contribution lies in the term:

$$u_{fuzz}(e, \dot{e}, \lambda) = u_{fuzz}(s(\mathbf{x})) = -K_{fuzz}(s(\mathbf{x})) \cdot \text{sign}(s(\mathbf{x})) ,$$ (8)

where $K_{fuzz}(s(\mathbf{x})) \ge 0$.

It has been shown that a SMC with boundary layer is mimicked by a FSMC (7)-(8) with the rule base [3]: R1) If s is Negative, then u_{fuzz} is Positive; R2) If s is Zero, then u_{fuzz} is Zero; R3) If s is Positive, then u_{fuzz} is Negative.

4 FSMC with Piecewise Linear Switching Manifold

We propose a novel FSMC, based on a piecewise linear switching manifold, to enhance the effectiveness of FSMC under a saturated control input.

4.1   A Novel FSMC Methodology

Consider system (1) and define the following variable:

$$s^*(\mathbf{x}) = \begin{cases} \dot{e} + \lambda e & \text{if } |e| < e_H \\ \dot{e} + \lambda e_H \cdot \text{sign}(e) & \text{if } |e| \geq e_H \end{cases},\tag{9}$$

where the sliding constant λ and the design parameter e_H are strictly positive. Now, consider the modified piecewise linear sliding surface (see Fig. 1):

$$s^*(\mathbf{x}) = 0.\tag{10}$$

By (2) and (10), we distinguish the following regions in the phase plane: Zone 1) $|e| < e_H$, $s = s^*$ (e.g. A in Fig. 1); Zone 2) $|e| \geq e_H$, $|s^*| \leq |s|$ and $s, s^* \geq 0$ (e.g. B in Fig. 1); Zone 3) $|e| \geq e_H$, $|s^*| \leq |s|$ and $s, s^* \leq 0$ (e.g. C in Fig. 1); Zone 4) $|e| \geq e_H$, $|s^*| \geq |s|$ and $s, s^* \leq 0$ (e.g. D in Fig. 1); Zone 5) $|e| \geq e_H$, $|s^*| \geq |s|$ and $s, s^* \geq 0$ (e.g. E in Fig. 1): Zone 6) $|e| \geq e_H$ and $s^* \geq 0$, $s \leq 0$ (e.g. F in Fig. 1); Zone 7) $|e| \geq e_H$ and $s^* \leq 0$, $s \geq 0$ (e.g. G in Fig. 1).

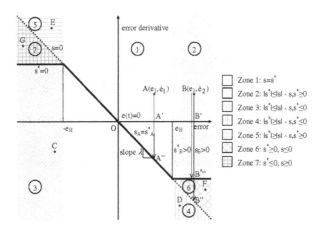

Fig. 1. Linear ($s=0$, *dotted line*) and piecewise linear ($s^*=0$, *solid line*) sliding surfaces

Now, consider a FSMC

$$u = b^{-1}(\mathbf{x}) \cdot \left(\hat{u}^* + u^*_{\text{fuzz}}(e, \dot{e}, \lambda) \right),\tag{11}$$

$$\hat{u}^* = \begin{cases} -(f(\mathbf{x}) - \ddot{x}_{1d} + \lambda \dot{e}) & \text{if } |e| < e_H \\ -(f(\mathbf{x}) - \ddot{x}_{1d}) & \text{if } |e| \geq e_H \end{cases},\tag{12}$$

$$u^*_{\text{fuzz}}(e, \dot{e}, \lambda) = u^*_{\text{fuzz}}(s^*(\mathbf{x})) = -K_{\text{fuzz}}(s^*(\mathbf{x})) \cdot \text{sign}(s^*(\mathbf{x})).\tag{13}$$

The FSMC rule table in Sect. 3 is maintained, by substituting s with s^* and u_{fuzz} with u^*_{fuzz}. We show that (1) is stable under (11)-(12)-(13), and $s^*(\mathbf{x})=0$ is attractive.

Proposition 1. The sliding line (10) is attractive for the trajectory of system (1) under the FSMC with piecewise linear sliding manifold (11)-(12)-(13).

Proof. Consider the Lyapunov function

$$V = \frac{1}{2}s^{*2}(\mathbf{x}) \ . \tag{14}$$

By (1), (11), (12) and (13), for all the operating points $\mathbf{x}(t)$ such that $|e| < e_H$ it holds:

$$\ddot{e} = -\lambda\dot{e} - K_{fuzz}(s^*(\mathbf{x})) \cdot sign(s^*(\mathbf{x})) + d \ . \tag{15}$$

Hence, for all $\mathbf{x}(t)$ such that $|e| < e_H$, by (14) and (15) we get:

$$\dot{V} = s^*(\mathbf{x}) \cdot \dot{s}^*(\mathbf{x}) = s^*(\mathbf{x}) \cdot (\ddot{e} + \lambda e) = -K_{fuzz}(s^*(\mathbf{x})) \cdot |s^*(\mathbf{x})| + d \cdot s^*(\mathbf{x}) \le -\eta^* |s^*(\mathbf{x})| , \tag{16}$$

where η^* is a strictly positive design constant such that the upper bound of $K_{fuzz}(s^*(\mathbf{x}))$ is $K^*_{fuzzmax} \ge \eta^*$. On the other hand, for all $\mathbf{x}(t)$ such that $|e| \ge e_H$, by (9) $\dot{s}^*(\mathbf{x}) = \ddot{e}$. Now, reasoning as above, we get:

$$\ddot{e} = -K_{fuzz}(s^*(\mathbf{x})) \cdot sign(s^*(\mathbf{x})) + d \ . \tag{17}$$

Hence, for all $\mathbf{x}(t)$ such that $|e| \ge e_H$, it holds:

$$\dot{V} = s^*(\mathbf{x}) \cdot \dot{s}^*(\mathbf{x}) = s^*(\mathbf{x}) \cdot \ddot{e} = -K_{fuzz}(s^*(\mathbf{x})) \cdot |s^*(\mathbf{x})| + d \cdot s^*(\mathbf{x}) \le -\eta^* |s^*(\mathbf{x})|$$

and we get (16) again. Therefore, $\dot{V}$ is definite negative in the piecewise linear switching manifold, and (10) is attractive for the FSMC (11)-(12)-(13).

Proposition 2. If $x_1(t=0) \ne x_{1d}(t=0)$ and the trajectory is off the piecewise linear sliding line (10), then the surface $s^*(\mathbf{x})=0$ will be reached in a finite time t_{reach} such that:

$$t_{reach} \le \frac{|s^*(\mathbf{x}(t=0))|}{\eta^*} \ . \tag{18}$$

Proof. The proposition may be easily derived integrating the modified sliding condition (16) between $t=0$ and $t=t_{reach}$. The detailed proof is omitted for lack of space.

We have proven that after a finite time reaching phase the system trajectory hits the modified sliding surface (10). Now, to prove that (1) is stable under (11)-(12)-(13), we demonstrate that once the system enters the sliding mode it keeps sliding along the switching manifold to the origin (0,0) of the error phase plane.

Proposition 3. Once system (1) under (11)-(12)-(13) hits the piecewise linear switching manifold (10), its trajectory converges to the origin of the error phase plane.

Proof. Let $s^*(\mathbf{x}(t=0))=0$. If $\mathbf{x}(t=0)$ is such that $|e| < e_H$, then $s^*(\mathbf{x}(t=0))=s(\mathbf{x}(t=0)$ and the proposition follows from the integration of (3). On the other hand, if $|e| \ge e_H$ and s*($\mathbf{x}(t=0)$)=0, the proposition may be easily derived integrating (10). The detailed proof is omitted for lack of space.

4.2 Comparison of the Proposed FSMC with Classical FSMC

In numerous applications the modified FSMC reduces the initial sliding variable magnitude (and ultimately the control action magnitude) with respect to the traditional FSMC. If the actuator saturates, implementing (7) results in the control law:

$$u = sat\left(\frac{u_i}{U}\right) \cdot U \ , \tag{19}$$

where u and u_i are the actual and ideal control law, U is the maximum control magnitude and by (11) it holds

$$u_i = b^{-1}(\mathbf{x}) \cdot \left(\hat{u} - K_{fuzz}(s(\mathbf{x})) \cdot sign(s(\mathbf{x}))\right) \ . \tag{20}$$

Now, suppose that saturation occurs at a time instant t. By (19) it holds:

$$u(t) = \pm U \ , \tag{21}$$

$$u = u_i - sign(u_i) \cdot \Delta(\mathbf{x}) \ , \tag{22}$$

where $\Delta(\mathbf{x}(t))$ is the positive residual control action and we neglected the time dependencies for sake of simplicity. It can be shown that under the saturated control input (22) the switching manifold is attractive for system (1) under a FSMC with linear sliding surface and saturated input if one of the following conditions holds:

$$sign(s(\mathbf{x}) \cdot b(\mathbf{x}) \cdot u_i) \geq 0 \ . \tag{23}$$

$$\Delta(\mathbf{x}) < \frac{\eta}{|b(\mathbf{x})|} \ , \ sign(s(\mathbf{x}) \cdot b(\mathbf{x}) \cdot u_i) = -1 \ . \tag{24}$$

Now, consider a modified FSMC (11) sharing the parameters of (20). The control action is (19), where u_i is now:

$$u_i = b^{-1}(\mathbf{x}) \cdot \left(\hat{u}^* - K_{fuzz}(s^*(\mathbf{x})) \cdot sign(s^*(\mathbf{x}))\right) \tag{25}$$

and $\hat{u}^*$ is expressed by (12). Reasoning as above, we infer that the switching manifold is attractive for (1) under (19)-(25) if one of the following conditions holds:

$$sign(s^*(\mathbf{x}) \cdot b(\mathbf{x}) \cdot u_i) \geq 0 \ . \tag{26}$$

$$\Delta^*(\mathbf{x}) < \frac{\eta^*}{|b(\mathbf{x})|} \ , \ sign(s^*(\mathbf{x}) \cdot b(\mathbf{x}) \cdot u_i) = -1 \ . \tag{27}$$

It is reasonable to suppose that, if e_H has been properly selected, the initial operating point belongs to zones 2 or 3 in Fig. 1 and $|s^*(\mathbf{x})| \leq |s(\mathbf{x})|$ holds (e.g. if x_2 represents the plant speed, $x_{2d}(t) = 0$ is required and the initial velocity is equal to zero). Hence, consider an initial position $\mathbf{x}(t)$ and a design parameter e_H such that $|e(t)| \geq e_H$ and $(e(t), \dot{e}(t))$ belongs to zones 2 or 3 in Fig. 1, i.e., $|s^*(\mathbf{x}(t))| \leq |s(\mathbf{x}(t))|$. Consider two FSMCs defined by (19)-(20) and (19)-(25), identical for all their design parameters but for the switching manifold. Suppose that the initial condition is such that both FSMCs produce a saturated control input. It can be shown that it holds:

$$\Delta(\mathbf{x}) - \Delta^*(\mathbf{x}) = |\,b^{-1}(\mathbf{x})\,| \cdot \lambda \dot{e} \cdot \text{sign}(s(\mathbf{x})) + |\,b^{-1}(\mathbf{x})\,| \cdot (K_{\text{fuzz}}(s(\mathbf{x})) - K^*_{\text{fuzz}}(s^*(\mathbf{x}))) \qquad (28)$$

Now, since $|s^*(\mathbf{x}(t))| \le |s(\mathbf{x}(t))|$ we get (see the rule table in Sect. 3):

$$0 \le K_{\text{fuzz}}(s^*(\mathbf{x})) \le K_{\text{fuzz}}(s(\mathbf{x})) \ . \qquad (29)$$

Hence, if the FSMC with piecewise linear switching manifold is designed such that:

$$\alpha(\mathbf{x}) = K_{\text{fuzz}}(s(\mathbf{x})) - K^*_{\text{fuzz}}(s^*(\mathbf{x})) + \lambda |\,\dot{e}\,| \cdot \text{sign}(s(\mathbf{x}) \cdot \dot{e}) \ge 0 \ , \qquad (30)$$

we get $\Delta(\mathbf{x}) \ge \Delta^*(\mathbf{x})$ and we infer that condition (27) is less restrictive than (24). Hence, the fuzzy contribution in the modified FSMC is smaller than the corresponding one required in a classical FSMC. We conclude that under suitable design of the piecewise linear switching manifold the proposed technique represents an effective alternative to the classical FSMC for systems of type (1) with saturated control input.

5   Illustrated Design Example

We now illustrate the proposed FSMC on a design example. Consider the simplified model of the motion of an underwater vehicle [4]:

$$\begin{aligned} \dot{x}_1 &= x_2 \\ \dot{x}_2 &= -\frac{1}{5}|\,x_2\,|\,x_2 + \frac{1}{5}u \end{aligned} \ , \qquad (31)$$

where x_1 and x_2 respectively define the vehicle position and u is the control input [4]. Suppose that the desired trajectory is $x_{1d}(t) = x_{2d}(t) = 0$ and that the initial condition is $x_1(0) = 1$, $x_2(0) = 0$. Now, choose $\lambda = 1$, so the sliding line is as follows [4]:

$$s(\mathbf{x}) = x_1 + x_2 \ . \qquad (32)$$

Then, choose $\eta = 0.1$, $K = 5$ and an SMC as follows [4]:

$$u = 5\left(\frac{1}{5}|\,x_2\,|\,x_2 - x_2 - 5 \cdot \text{sign}(s(\mathbf{x}))\right) , \qquad (33)$$

Now, consider a FSMC with sliding line (32) and the following control law:

$$u = 5\left(\frac{1}{5}|\,x_2\,|\,x_2 - x_2 + u_{\text{fuzz}}(s(\mathbf{x}))\right) , \qquad (34)$$

where u_{fuzz} is defined according to the rule base introduced in Sect. 3. In addition, let us adopt triangular membership functions with completeness equal to 1, the sup-min rule of inference and the center of area defuzzification method [2]. Moreover, the input (output) scaling gain is $Gs^* = 2$ ($GK_{\text{fuzz}} = 10$).

Consider a modified FSMC (11) with $b^{-1}(\mathbf{x}) = 5$ in accordance with (31) and the same parameters as the previous FSMC. The sliding line, with $\lambda = 1$ and $e_H = 0.45$, is:

$$s^*(\mathbf{x}) = \begin{cases} x_1 + x_2 & \text{if} \quad |x_1| < 0.45 \\ x_2 + 0.45 \cdot \text{sign}(x_1) & \text{if} \quad |x_1| \geq 0.45 \end{cases}. \tag{35}$$

Moreover, according to (12) we define:

$$\hat{u}^* = \begin{cases} \dfrac{1}{5}|x_2|x_2 - x_2 & \text{if} \quad |x_1| < 0.45 \\ \dfrac{1}{5}|x_2|x_2 & \text{if} \quad |x_1| \geq 0.45 \end{cases}. \tag{36}$$

In Fig. 2 we report the simulation results for the SMC, the linear sliding manifold FSMC and the modified FSMC for an initial condition $x_1(0)=2$ and $x_2(0)=1$. All controllers are effective in tracking the desired trajectory, but the SMC displays chattering (see Fig. 2c). Moreover, the modified FSMC is about 1.5 seconds slower than the other controllers (see Fig. 2a). Now, we repeat the simulations under the three control laws when the maximum control input magnitude equals U=1. Results are reported in Fig. 3: it is apparent that the modified FSMC is several seconds faster than the other two control laws (see Fig. 3a), and that it is less prone to saturation (see Fig. 3c).

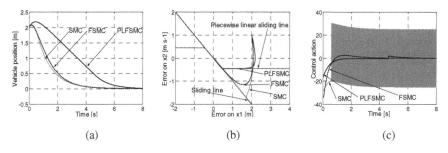

Fig. 2. Example dynamics (a), trajectory (b) and control input (c) under SMC (*grey*), FSMC (*black dashed*) and FSMC with piecewise linear switching line (*black solid*)

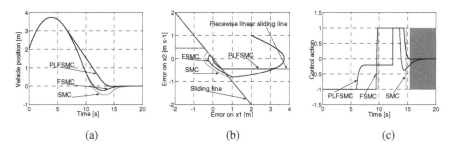

Fig. 3. Example dynamics (a), trajectory (b) and control input (c) under SMC (*grey*), FSMC (*black dashed*) and FSMC with piecewise linear switching line (*black solid*) with saturation

6 Conclusions

We introduced a novel FSMC technique for a class of second order dynamical systems based on a piecewise linear sliding manifold. We demonstrated that a second order nonlinear system in canonical form is stable under the proposed FSMC. We showed that the advantage of the approach lies in the decrease of the control action with respect to SMC and FSMC techniques employing a linear sliding surface, thus enhancing the effectiveness of SMC in the presence of a saturated control input. In addition, we showed that the fuzzy rule based algorithms smooth the system dynamics in the vicinities of the switching manifold with respect to the adoption of classical SMC strategies. We illustrated the proposed technique on a design example.

References

1. Dotoli, M., Maione, B., Naso, D.: Fuzzy Sliding Mode Controllers Synthesis Through Genetic Optimization. In: Zimmermann, H.-J., Tselentis, G., van Someren, M., Dounias, G. (eds.): Advances in Computational Intelligence and Learning, Methods and Applications. Kluwer Academic Publishers, Boston (2002) 331-341
2. Jantzen, J.: Linear Design Approach to a Fuzzy Controller. In: Verbruggen, H.B., Babuska, R. (eds.): Fuzzy logic Control: Advances in Applications. World Scientific, Singapore (1999) 313-329
3. Palm, R., Driankov, D., Hellendoorn, H.: Model Based Fuzzy Control. Springer-Verlag, Berlin (1997)
4. Slotine, J.-J., Weiping, L.: Applied Non Linear Control. Prentice Hall, Englewood Cliffs, NJ (1991)

Application of Fuzzy Logic Controllers for Laser Tracking with Autonomous Robot System

Jia Lu and Yunxia Hu

Computer Science and Information System, University of Phoenix,
5050 NW 125 Avenue, Coral Springs, Florida, FL 33076, USA
clujia@email.uophx.edu

Abstract. This paper presented an application of fuzzy logic controller for high accuracy laser tracking with autonomous robot system. A main point of a laser tracking system design was to integrate electrical, optical and fuzzy logic theory. The research was conducted for laser tracking system in fuzzy logic control from the observations. The parameters of the input were obtained by measuring a large number throughout the measuring procedure. The measurement accuracy was 0.1 mm over the measurement workspace. The measurement accuracy of the laser beam was about 120 μm for a workspace of a 3x3x3 m^3. The system obtained satisfactory transient responses. The overshoot was 5.0% and steady-state error was 4.5% to satisfy the steady state error requirements. Simulation results have shown the advantage of fuzzy logic controller in respect of its transient response, steady-state response, and tracking performance.

1 Introduction

The laser tracking system are well established and widely accepted in industrial and medical fields, but suffer from limitations such as high cost and low measurement speed [1]. Since then, we have enhanced the automated most steps of the calibration procedure and developed a new method to solve the correspondence problems [2]. Laser tracking has the similar measurement accuracy, which is close to most commercial robots. Laser tracking system is used to measure the position of the robot to analyze the reflection of a laser beam [3]. Data processing was used to count the fringes in the reflected beam, which gave a very accuracy estimate of the distance between the tool and the laser tracking [4]. It measured both position and precision to track the robot from a small servo-controller unit mounted on a tripod. The position error was changed proportionally to the equivalent force error in the working space [5]. In order to achieve high accuracy we needed good hardware equipment and the processing methods. Based on the experiences with a previous system, a detailed analysis of the performance was carried out. The system adapted automatically to different objects without user interaction. A basic requirement of the laser tracking measurement system was that during the tracking measurement process, the outgoing laser beam from the laser transducer system and returned laser beam from the target would have interference at any moment. The analysis of the error sources existing in the laser transducer system and development of effectiveness of the controller in the laser tracking system application were also the objective of this research.

V. Di Gesú, F. Masulli, and A. Petrosino (Eds.): WILF 2003, LNAI 2955, pp. 97–102, 2006.

2 Tracking with Robot System

2.1 Measurements

It was designed with a high accuracy, high speed of tracking laser interferometer, and high precision angular encoders. The measurement volume of 70 m diameter and a measurement rate of up to 1000 points per second were used for the research systems. The flexible application was setup for the determination of large objects. The tracking of the maximum target speed was laser beam > 6.0 m/s at right angles to laser beam >4.0 m/s. The range of measurement was: horizontal $\pm 235°$; vertical $\pm 45°$; distance 0-35 m. The accuracy was: 20m for slow moving; 40 m for fast moving. The measurement accuracy of the laser beam was about 120 μm for a workspace of a 3x3x3 m^3. It had a laser beam with tracking gimbals. The tracking gimbals could work depending on different measurement requirements. The laser tracking system consisted of the three parts: laser transducer systems, gimbals tracking system, and computer control system.

2.2 Components

In the laser tracking, there were three sets of laser transducer systems. Each of them included a beam interferometer, beam splitters, a tracking mirror, tracking gimbals and detector. Optical laser transducer is an elementary device, which was able to transform a non-electrical physical measured input value into an electrical output within a given measuring range. It relied on the photo-electric effect with laser diodes and photodiodes that was used for detectors. For this tracking system, it provided rotation about two orthogonal axes. Each axis had an encoder for angle measurement and a direct motor to allow remote controlled movement. The upper part of the tube contained laser interferometer to measure distance differences. The laser beam also functioned as the collimation axis of the instrument and was sent to a reflector via a mirror attached to the transit axis. The photodetector beside the interferometer received a portion of the reflected beam and was responsible for the tracking. The tracker supported a reflected that provided offset distance from the tracking head that could be used to set the interferometer's initial distance. The controller was connected to the detection by two cables of 5 m length, contained the tracker's main electronics. The signal from the photodetector needed no further amplification before transmission to the tracker processor via the controller. The accurate laser interferometer measurement was accomplished by the laser transducer system. The tracking of the target motion was accomplished by the tracking gimbals system and the computer control system controls. It coordinated the operations to realize a smooth tracking and accurate target positions. Applying the measurement principle of laser tracking system, we could obtain accurate the relative distance between the target and interferometers. The detector detected the error signal from the returning laser beam. This error signal was proportional to the error signal on the retroreflector mounted on the moving target. It was sent to the input of the controller, which used this error signal to achieve the closed-loop control for the tracking gimbals to track the movement of the target during the process of the measurement.

2.3 Moving Target

There were three tracking gimbals should be mounted as far as possible from one to another in order to obtain high quality measurement data. A laser transducer system was utilized to obtain the position offset of the target that was installed on the middle-effector of the robot. Applying the measurement principle of laser transducer system, one could obtain accurately the relative levels between the target and three interferometers. The optical part emitted a laser beam to the gimbal. The gimbal directed this beam to a mirror mounted on the target. The mirror reflected the beam back to the optical section. Once the target moved, laser spot would generate an offset from the quadrant detector's surface center. It would provide the error during moving. This error would be sent out from the quadrant detector in the form of an analog electrical signal that was converted into digital before it entered the computer. Then the computer produced an output signal by using the control algorithm. The output signal forced the machine to turn a certain angle accordingly in order to catch up the moving target. As the target kept moving, a sequence of error signals would force the machine to turn consecutively. In this case, it would track the target wherever it went. The control task of the laser tracking system was to track a moving target in workspace using the tracker positions and the laser beam positions as feedback signals. The dynamic model of the motor gimbals system was important to develop a fuzzy logic controller for the laser tracking system. For the laser tracking system, it was necessary to estimate the precision for the global picture of the control system.

2.4 Encoded Signals

The personal computer (PC) was mounted with two interface boards. One of the boards was the control board that received encoded signals from the gimbal and sent out control signal back to the gimbal. The second board was the converter that received and amplified signals from the quadrant detector. The control system was Compaq Pentium III, Presario 2700 with the MATLAB Fuzzy Logic ToolBox 2.1 and Simulink for designing and simulating systems based on fuzzy logic. The purpose was to test a fuzzy logic controller on the laser tracking system. The PC communicates with the gimbal subsystem. It went through a control board plugged in one of the slots. It would receive the signal coming from the quadrant detector in the optical part via conversion board. The gimbal control system played a role as an inner loop PID controller in the system. This inner loop controller consisted of the control board mounted in the personal computer and decoded. The measurement accuracy must use the special tool, which it was attached at the robot. It required sufficient room for the cables to be set up around the robot.

The orientation error was measured by the deflection of a laser beam returned from a mirror attached at the robot. The displacement error was measured by the deflection the beam as it passed through a lens. This measuring accuracy was better than the 0.05 mm quoted for the laser tracking units and the robot. There might also be a plant model to have a sufficiently accurate model for us how to build an optimal controller. In general, the plant would be a dynamical system by a set of differential equations. The input represented a desired response, and the output was the actual response. The input represented what the desired output should be after the signal had stopped. A feedback controller was desired to generate an output that caused some corrective effort to be applied to a process so as to drive a measurable process variable. The controller used an actuator to affect the process and a detector to measure the results. A Simulink graphics model took the analog values of the gains. It simulated the system step response. The actual setup of the models consisted of a step input signal fed to a summation block. The constant values to be used in the fuzzy block were calculated using a separate code. These values calculated the analog gains for the various digital gains.

3   Fuzzy Logic Controllers

The laser tracking system for this research was controlled by a simplified version of a fuzzy proportional-integrate-derivative (PID) controller. This control derived its name from the fact that the total control actuation was the sum of the three parts. These parts were based on the error derived from the difference between the desired input and the actual measured output fed back. The proportional part was a component that is directly proportional to the error, and the integral and derivative parts were proportional to the integral and derivative of the error, respectively.

The error was pointed out as the digital signal that converted from the analog output, which represented the offset of the laser spot from the control point. This error signal also represented the displacement in the mirror by the target moving in the target. Error change equals the previous error minus the error from the last sampling. To control the gimbal as precisely as possible, we needed to use different fuzzy sets for each variable: error, change in error, and control input in this research. In traditional set theory, membership of an object belonging to a set can be one of the two values: 0 or 1. The FLC was based on the controller's response. To establish the structure of the FLC, the triangle shapes of membership function were used in this research. It was supposed that the error is "zero" in an imprecise way. If the error was zero and the change in error was small positive, then the control input was small negative. If the error was small positive and the error change was small positive, then the control input was small medium positive. Thus, if the error was actually 0.1, its membership in Z would be 0.5, and the value of the triangular function was at that point. These rules were reasonable and straightforward so that it was like human reasoning. In this research, we collected all the IF-THEN rules together and formed a lookup table for the fuzzy controller that was much more concise and easier to manipulate. Continuing with the research, the linguistic values of the error were taken to be negative (N), zero(Z) and positive with the membership functions. The fuzzy set, or membership functions, and control rule were combined together to form the lookup table, and the outcome of the step was a fuzzy variable. The output could be obtained from the lookup table directly, and the outcome of the step was a crisp variable again. From the research, the method was used to obtain the lookup table. The method was to use the input error and change in error, combined with the membership function, to calculate the output in real time. This method was accurate and smooth for the control output.

4   Simulation

There was a good correspondence in regard to larger amplitudes although some of the modeled controls were clipped. The output of the system was connected to the arm of a robot. The arm was attached mechanically to the controller. As the robot's arm moved, the output signals were supplied by the computer. Since a computer's output signal was digital, the A/D converter changed the value and produced the signals. The computer outputs a series of numbers that increment until a value was reached that represented the desired position. The system tried to correct the overshoot error by reversing the direction of the arm. The arm oscillated above the below the position before it stopped.

The offset was low gain with wide band of the controller. The integral control was used to develop a control signal on the value of the offset. It was used along with the control model in the controller of the closed-loop system. When an error signal first appeared, the controller was tuned so that the control signal returned the process to the desired control point. The control signal was fast acting. As the arm nears the desired position, the error signal stopped changing and approached zero. The result was that the outputs went to zero. Since the set point and measured variable were not exactly equal, it caused the arm to move remaining distance. The gain adjustments were performed by automatically controllers. For the linear movement of the robot for the laser tracking, both PI control and fuzzy control could guide the target to move along the desired trajectory. Performance of the fuzzy control was even better. Results of the robot guiding a target in a linear movement with constant velocity were acceptable. During the measurement process with the laser tracking system, the optical interference between the outgoing laser beam and returning laser beam must occur at all the time. The overshoot was the less 5%, steady-state error was less 4.5% to satisfy the steady state error requirements.

The simulated closed-loop step responded of the fuzzy logic controllers. The setting time was about 0.024 second for the control system. It could be found that it was a non-steady static error system. The tracking requirement was satisfied without broken point during the tracking process. The output of the system was very smooth for various directions of target motion. The laser head output was in the range. The error signals were measured by the detector, which the errors rated about 4.5% of the measurement range. The average value of the measured signal was taken to greatly reduce the noise effect. The steady-state error of the control system was enabled in the state.

Although a great number of conventional manually calibration techniques have found their ways into practice and provided satisfactory solutions to the spectrum of complex processes, but suffer from limitations such as high cost and low measurement speed. There is no doubt that the fuzzy logic controllers have their remarkable advantage in coping with systems whose mathematical models in nonlinear. We choose the fuzzy logic controllers for laser tracking system because they are more simplicity, efficiency, and precision than the traditional calibration techniques. From the figure 5, it was very clear that the steady-state error was satisfied for the accurate measurement in the fuzzy logic controllers for the laser tracking system. They are in respect of its transient response, steady-state response, and tracking performance.

5 Conclusion

Laser tracking is an excellent technique to deal with dynamic measurement problems. The application requires high frequency coordinate determination to control robot system manipulating the object. The laser tracking gimbal can measure the distance between the gimbal and target. A fuzzy logic controller was applied to the laser track-ing system to measure the coordinate of the target. The laser beam was utilized to track and measure the positions of the end-effector of the robot in a working space in real time. Both position and orientation of the end-effector of the robot realized the objective movement effectively during the initialization process. The results showed that the robot could successfully guide the target through linear and circular move-ments. The performance of control strategy was confirmed by the results. It was satis-fied for both transient and steady state responses. A good dynamic model was neces-sary to design a satisfied digital controller in the accurate tracking measurement. Simulations were made for fuzzy control in order to make the process move objective. The laser tracking performance of the controller was also verified through the re-search. Laser tracking system will also be able to many of the measuring tasks per-formance for industrial and the medical fields.

References

1. Bohm. J.: Data Processing and Calibrations of a Cross-Pattern Stripe Projector. IAPRS, Vol. XXXIII, Amsterdam. (2000).
2. James, D. and Chen, X.: A laser Range Scanner Designed for Minimum Calibration Com-plexity. IEEE Proceedings of the Third International Conference on 3D Digital Imaging and *Modeling, 3DIM*.(2001).
3. Bai, Y.: Design and Implementation of a Control System for a Laser Tracking Measurement System. Proc. 1995 Conf. on Recent Advances in Robotics, Orlando. Florida. (1995).
4. Gilby, J. and Parker, G.: Laser Tracking System to Measure Robot Arm Performance. *Uni-versity of Surrey, Guildford, UK,* pp. 180-182. (1982).
5. Ju, M. S and Lin, Dong-Huang.: Application of Fuzzy Control Theory in Development of a Robot for Neuro-Rehabilitation of Elbow. *BED-Vol. 50, Bioengineering Conference ASME* (2001).

Fuzzy Relational Neural Network for Data Analysis

Angelo Ciaramella[1,2], Roberto Tagliaferri[1,2],
Witold Pedrycz[3], and Antonio Di Nola[1]

[1] DMI University of Salerno,
via S. Allende 84081 Baronissi (SA), Italy
{ciaram, robtag, adinola}@unisa.it
[2] INFM unit of Salerno,
via S. Allende 84081 Baronissi (SA), Italy
[3] Dept. of Electrical an Computer Engineering,
University of Alberta, T6G 2V4 Edmonton, Alberta, Canada
pedrycz@ee.ualberta.ca

Abstract. In this paper, a Fuzzy Neural Network based on a fuzzy relational "IF-THEN" reasoning scheme (FRNN) is described. Different experiments on benchmark data from the UCI repository of Machine learning database are proposed for classification and approximation tasks. The model is compared with some other methods known in literature pointing out the fundamental features of the model.

1 Introduction

A Fuzzy Relational Model (FRM) is essentially a rule-based model consisting of all the possible rules that can be defined for a system, but with the additional feature that the rules can have variable degrees of truth [4]. In this paper, we design a Fuzzy Neural Network based on a fuzzy relational "IF-THEN" reasoning scheme (FRNN). We show the main features of the model and its power in function approximation and classification tasks. We have to mark that considering a sum of product inference system and using the Stone-Weierstrass Theorem the FRNN model can approximate any function on a compact set [3, 4]. Starting from this main result we also proved that the FRNN model reaches better results in function approximation with respect to known algorithms [3, 4]. We have to note that the FRNN model permits to obtain better results, also with few input membership functions, than the models known in literature citePhd. Moreover, studying the model from a probabilistic (or possibilistic) point of view, we can conclude that using the relations we can directly describe the conditional probability (or possibility) between input-output.

2 Fuzzy Relational Neural Network

Since a fuzzy relation expresses the dynamic features of a system described by a fuzzy model, it is natural to design a fuzzy neural network (FRNN) based on the

V. Di Gesú, F. Masulli, and A. Petrosino (Eds.): WILF 2003, LNAI 2955, pp. 103–109, 2006.

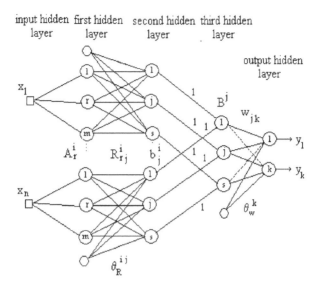

Fig. 1. Fuzzy Neural Network model: detailed model

fuzzy relation [3, 4, 10, 12]. It should be pointed out that the weights of the net between the two layers as well as the input and output values are truth values, i.e. elements of some complete residuated lattice (the structure of truth values) [3, 4, 12]. Now, we detail the architecture of the FRNN system in figure 1. If we consider n inputs which are discretized into m_i input levels by a fuzzifier and k output which are obtained by the defuzzification of M discretized levels then using different t-norms and s-norms the outputs of the layers are

$$f_k(\overline{x}) = \frac{\sum_{j=1}^{M} \overline{y}_k^j \left[\mathbf{T}_{i=1}^n \left[\mathbf{S}_{r=1}^{m_i} (\mu_{A_r^i}(x_i) \mathbf{t} \mu_{R_{rj}^i}) \mathbf{s} \theta_{R^j}^i \right] \right]}{\sum_{j=1}^{M} \left[\mathbf{T}_{i=1}^n \left[\mathbf{S}_{r=1}^{m_i} (\mu_{A_r^i}(x_i) \mathbf{t} \mu_{R_{rj}^i}) \mathbf{s} \theta_{R^j}^i \right] \right]} \tag{1}$$

where $f : U \subset \mathcal{R}^n \to \mathcal{R}$, $\overline{x} = (x_1, x_2, \dots, x_n) \in U$, where M is the number of fuzzy rules, n the number of relation matrices, m_i the number of input membership functions of the i-th relation, $\mu_{A_r^i}$ is the membership function on the input space, $\overline{y}_k^j$ is the apex on the output space and $\mu_{R_{rj}^i}$ is the weight from the r-th input to j-th output of the j-th relation matrix [3, 4].

The fuzzy sets of the input space are described by a Gaussian function or by a generalized-bell function [5].

2.1   FRNN Learning

To apply the BP method to the model we consider the total error E due to the outputs of the network as $E = \sum_{l=1}^{p} E^l$ where $E^l = \frac{1}{2} \sum_{k=1}^{c} (y_k^l - t_k^l)^2$. In the case of classification we use a cross-entropy error function [1]. Once the partial derivatives of the error function E^l with respect to the parameters have been computed, we obtain the learning rules for the parameters of the three layers [3, 4]. Now we have to remark that the output vector **y** of the model is a linear function of the weights **w** of the defuzzification level. Therefore we can calculate the weights of this level applying a pseudoinverse technique [1, 3, 4]. We mark that the problem of the fuzzification is solved using unsupervised clustering techniques as, for example, the Kohonen's learning rule or the Fuzzy C-Means algorithm [6, 3, 4].

3   Classification

In the first experiment we apply the FRNN model to data classification of IRIS data set [7]. In figure 2 we plot the contour plot of the fuzzy sets B^1, B^2 and B^3 estimated after the learning. We obtain a 96% of correct classification on the training set, a 97.3% of correct classification on the test set and a correct classification of 96.67% on all the data set. The fuzzy sets B^1, B^2 and B^3 are well determined and in this way we can describe in a simple way the fuzzy rules [3, 4]. These results are comparable with those obtained by the model proposed by Nauck [7]. However, we note that using the NEFCLASS approach we obtain some fuzzy sets that cover all the input space and then it is difficult to extract the IF-THEN rules. In the second experiment we consider two benchmark data

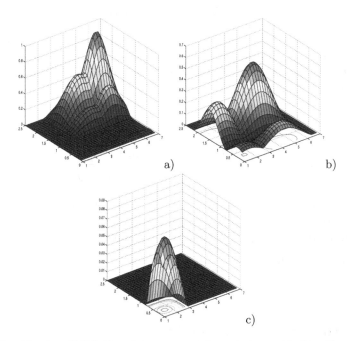

Fig. 2. Classification (IRIS): Pseudoinverse matrix technique with $\mathbf{T} = \odot$ = algebraic product, $\mathbf{S} = \bigvee$ = union and $\mathbf{t} = \otimes$ = bounded product; a) b) c) plot of the fuzzy sets B^1, B^2 and B^3 estimated after the learning, respectively

Table 1. Classification percentages considering the Cancer data set (cancer1)

	Training	Validation	Test
FRNN	95.1429	97.7143	98.2759
MLP	98.2857	98.8571	98.2759
RBF	96	97.1429	97.1264

Table 2. Classification percentages considering the Diabetes data set (diabetes1)

	Training	Validation	Test
FRNN	71.6146	75	71.3542
MLP	81.25	77.6042	70.4375
RBF	69.2708	70.83	67.1875

of the UCI machine learning databases repository [11], that are Cancer and Diabetes, respectively. To compare the performance of the FRNN method we use a RBF neural network (4 Gaussian functions for each input) and a MLP neural network (4 hidden units) [9]. In table 1 we compare the performance of the models using the Cancer data set. In table 2 we compare the performance of the models using the Diabetes data set. We note that in all the experiments the FRNN model presents the best generalization features.

4   FRNN for Function Approximation

In this section we design the FRNN with a sum of product relational model, product inference, centroid defuzzification, and Gaussian functions. In [3, 4] it is demonstrated that with these features the FRNN model is capable to approximate any real continuous function on a compact set to arbitrary accuracy and has better performance than known methods. In details the output of the model (multi-input-one-output) is the following

$$f(\overline{\mathbf{x}}) = \frac{\sum_{i=1}^{M} \overline{z}^i \left[\mu_{B^{(i)}} \prod_{j=1}^{n} \left(\sum_{k=1}^{m_j} r_{ki}^{(j)} \mu_{A_k^{(j)}}(x_j) \right) \right]}{\sum_{i=1}^{n} \left[\mu_{B^{(i)}} \prod_{j=1}^{m} \left(\sum_{k=1}^{m_j} r_{ki}^{(j)} \mu_{A_k^{(j)}}(x_j) \right) \right]} \tag{2}$$

where $f : U \subset R^n \to R$, $\overline{\mathbf{x}} = (x_1, x_2, \ldots, x_m) \in U$, M is the number of fuzzy rules in the fuzzy rule bases, n the number of relations, m_j the number of input membership functions for the j-th relation, $\mu_{A_k^{(j)}}$ and $\mu_{B^{(i)}}$ are the membership functions on the input and output spaces respectively, $\overline{z}^i$ is the apex on the output space and $r_{ki}^{(j)}$ is the weight from the k-th input to i-th output of the j-th relation matrix.

5   Performance in Function Approximation

In the first experiment we consider a chaotic time series given by the Mackey-Glass differential equation [5]. The NEFPROX system [7], used to approximate time series, has four input and one output variables. To measure the performance we use a Root Mean Square Error (RMSE) [1, 5]. The NEFPROX model after the learning achieves a Sum-of-Square error (RMSE in [8]) on the training set of 0.0315 and on the validation set of 0.0332. Using the ANFIS model [5] a better approximation can be obtained (Sum-of-Square error of 0.0016 and of 0.0015; RMSE of $6.331 \cdot 10^{-5}$ and of $6.148 \cdot 10^{-5}$)(fig. 3a). In figure 3b we plot the residuum between the output of the ANFIS model (y) and the target data (t) both for training and validation sets. In the FRNN model we set 2 membership functions for the input and output spaces. In this case we consider a 75% overlap of the membership functions. If we use the technique introduced in [4] to determine the fuzzy rules then we have 2 rules of this type:

$$R_1 : \text{if } x_1 \text{ is } \widetilde{A}_{11} \text{ and } x_2 \text{ is } \widetilde{A}_{12} \text{ and } x_3 \text{ is } \widetilde{A}_{13} \text{ and } x_4 \text{ is } \widetilde{A}_{14} \text{ then } y \text{ is } B_1 \quad (3)$$

$$R_2 : \text{if } x_1 \text{ is } \widetilde{A}_{21} \text{ and } x_2 \text{ is } \widetilde{A}_{22} \text{ and } x_3 \text{ is } \widetilde{A}_{23} \text{ and } x_4 \text{ is } \widetilde{A}_{24} \text{ then } y \text{ is } B_2 \quad (4)$$

where $\widetilde{A}_{ij}$ is described by

$$\widetilde{A}_{ij} = [A_{1j} \text{ and } R_{1i}^j] \text{ or } [A_{2j} \text{ and } R_{2i}^j] \quad (5)$$

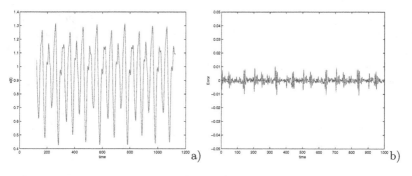

Fig. 3. Approximation and prediction of the Mackey-Glass chaotic time series (ANFIS model): a) approximation-prediction; b) residuum

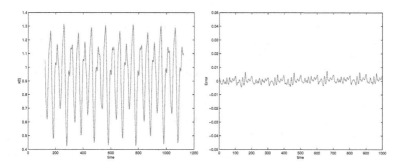

Fig. 4. Approximation and prediction of the Mackey-Glass chaotic time series (FRNN model): approximation-prediction and residuum (75% overlapping)

Table 3. Squared Error Percentage considering the Building data set (building1)

	Training	Validation	Test
FRNN	0.0267	0.2155	0.0746
MLP	0.0766	0.5313	0.3936
RBF	0.3738	2.3622	0.8915

Table 4. Squared Error Percentage considering the Flare data set (flare1)

	Training	Validation	Test
FRNN	0.0261	0.0337	0.0463
MLP	0.4081	0.2575	0.5807
RBF	0.2814	0.2633	0.5760

with $j = 1, \ldots, 4$, where 4 is the number of input variables, and $i = 1, \ldots, 2$, where 2 is the number of rules. After the learning, the FRNN model achieves a Sum-of-Square error of 0.0011374 on the training set and of 0.00090622 on the validation set. Moreover, the RMSE is of $4.4665 \cdot 10^{-5}$ and of $3.5304 \cdot 10^{-5}$, respectively (fig. 4).

In the second experiment we consider two benchmark data of the UCI machine learning databases repository [11], that are Building and Flare, respectively. In the FRNN model we use a sum of product inference system, two memberships on the input space for each variable. For the MLP model we use 4 hidden units with logistic functions. For the RBF model we use 4 Gaussian functions for each input. To evaluate the error we use a squared error percentage [11]. In table 3, we compare the performance of the models on the Building data set. In table 4 we compare the performance of the models on the Flare data sets. We note that in all the experiments the FRNN model presents the best features.

6   Conclusion

We showed the main features of a novel neuro-fuzzy system. The FRNN model that we described is based on a fuzzy relational "IF-THEN" reasoning scheme. A main result is obtained using the model to classify the IRIS data set. The results are compared with the NEFCLASS method and the performance is very good. An interesting result is also obtained using the Cancer and Diabetes data sets from UCI databases repository. In function approximation the model is compared with the ANFIS model and the NEFPROX system for approximation and for the prediction of a Mackey-Glass chaotic time series. Also in this case, it presents a good performance and can extract rules in a simple way. Very interesting results results are also obtained using the Building and Flare data sets of the UCI databases repository. Finally, we can conclude that the model presents good performance both for classification and function approximation. Concluding, the neuro-fuzzy model could be used for complex systems identification in real world applications.

References

1. C.M. Bishop, Neural Networks for Pattern recognition, *Oxford University Press*, 1995
2. A. Ciaramella, R. Tagliaferri, W. Pedrycz, Fuzzy Relations Neural Network, *Proceedings of the 10th IEEE International Conference on Fuzzy Systems*, December 2001, paper P287
3. A. Ciaramella, R. Tagliaferri, W. Pedrycz, A. Di Nola, Fuzzy Relational Neural Networks, submitted to IEEE Tran. on Neural Networks
4. A. Ciaramella, Soft Computing Methodologies for Data Analysis, PhD Thesis, DMI - University of Salerno, Italy, 2002
5. J.S.R. Jang, C.-T. Sun, E. Mizutani, Neuro-Fuzzy and Soft Computing (A Computational Approach to Learning and Machine Intelligence), Prentice Hall, Upper Saddle River, NJ 07458, 1997
6. C.T. Lin, C.S.G. Lee, Neural Fuzzy Systems: a Neuro-fuzzy Synergism to Intelligent Systems, Upper Saddle River-NJ: Prentice Hall, 1996
7. D. Nauck, R. Kruse, NEFCLASS - a Neuro-Fuzzy Approach for the Classification of Data, K.M. George, Janice H. Carrol, Ed Deaton, Dave Oppenheim, and Jim Hightower, Editors, Applied Computing 1995, *Proc. of the 1995 ACM Symposium on Applied Compurintg*, Nashville, Feb. 26-28, pp. 461-465, ACM Press, New York, February 1995
8. D. Nauck, U. Nauck, R. Kruse, Generating Classification Rules with the Neuro-Fuzzy System NEFCLASS, *Proc. Biennal. Conf. of the North America Fuzzy Information Processing Society (NAFIPS'96)*, Berkeley, CA, 1996
9. I. T. Nabney, Netlab Algorithms for Pattern Recognition, Springer-Verlag, 2002
10. W. Pedrycz, Fuzzy Control and Fuzzy Systems (second, extended, edition), New York: John Wiley and Sons, New York, 1993
11. L. Prechelt, PROBEN 1 - A Set of Neural Network Benchmark Problems and Benchmarking Rules, Technical Report, 21/94, September 30, 1994
12. R. Tagliaferri, A. Ciaramella, A. Di Nola, Radim Bělohlávek, Fuzzy Neural Networks Based on Fuzzy Logic Algebras Valued Relations, accepted for publication

A Neuro-fuzzy System for the Prediction of the Vehicle Traffic Flow

Massimo Panella[1], Antonello Rizzi[1],
Fabio Massimo Frattale Mascioli[1], and Giuseppe Martinelli[1]

INFO-COM Dpt., University of Rome "La Sapienza",
Via Eudossiana 18, I-00184 Rome, Italy
panella@infocom.uniroma1.it
http://infocom.uniroma1.it/~panella

Abstract. In this paper, we propose a fuzzy system to control vehicle traffic flows on a street network. At a given point of the street network, data are collected by a peripheral unit equipped with infrared sensors. Row data are sent by the GSM/GPRS network to a centralized data processing server, where a simple set of fuzzy rules is employed to classify the row data samples into three flow states corresponding to flowing, intense and congested conditions. The core of the system is constituted by a neuro-fuzzy system, which is used to predict the time series constituted by the fuzzy membership of traffic measures to the three predefined flow states. We report the results concerning the comparison tests we carried out using an ANFIS network synthesized by a hyperplane clustering procedure and some well-known prediction techniques used as benchmarks.

1 Introduction

The growth of vehicular traffic besides the limits of street networks, the low availability of economic resources to be employed in mobility improvements and the pollution problem make the optimal management of the existing logistic infrastructures a fundamental challenge for human health and quality of life.

During the last decades, the constant growth of vehicular transportation has increased the traffic congestion. A vehicular congestion state means a greater number of accidents, besides increased travel times. In presence of congestion, the frequency of vehicular accidents is at least the double with respect to normal flow conditions. The growth of the capacity of the street network is not always feasible, and often it is preferable to consider other approaches, such as the flow control, by which it is possible to reduce the congestion level and the estimated number of possible accidents, together with a better use of the existing infrastructures. The modern research on this field is dealing with flow control, reduction of flow instability, traffic routing on alternative paths and systems which are able to communicate to the users (drivers) in real time.

In general, a control system for vehicular flow is composed mainly of three components: the monitoring system, the control logic, and the set of actuators

V. Di Gesú, F. Masulli, and A. Petrosino (Eds.): WILF 2003, LNAI 2955, pp. 110–118, 2006.
© Springer-Verlag Berlin Heidelberg 2006

which makes the control itself feasible. In this paper, we illustrate a traffic control system based on the prediction of vehicle flows by a neuro-fuzzy network. The system has been designed upon the assumption that the capability to predict the intensity of traffic flows can significantly enhance the effectiveness of control; it has been already realized as an industrial prototype, with some pilot installations throughout the Italian territory. The whole system is structured as illustrated in Fig. 1. For instance, the monitoring system is constituted by a set of peripheral units (PUs); each of them includes an infrared sensor, a simple processing unit and a GSM communication unit. A PU sends the data at predefined time intervals or when a significant event is rose (for example, when the vehicle flow evidences a substantial change). Collected data are sent to a radio communication hub through the GSM/GPRS network. The hub is connected by an Ethernet LAN to a data processing and storage server (where the prediction software runs), a gateway (by which the local traffic control system communicate with other higher geographic level control systems) and a set of clients computers used by control operators to interact with the system. The set of actuators is composed by LED array screens, arranged near a predefined set of important network nodes, by which it is possible to communicate in real time useful information to the drivers.

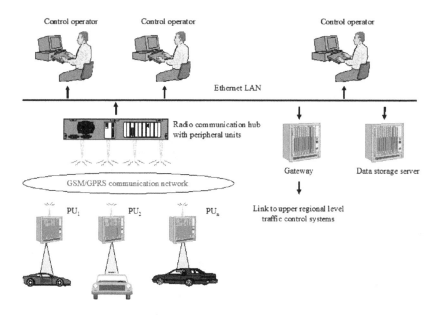

Fig. 1. The vehicle flow control system

The control logic takes the form of a prediction software, running on the main server; its description will be illustrated in Sect. 2, while in Sect. 3 we will briefly depict the prediction systems employed in the tests discussed in Sect. 4. Our conclusion will be drawn in Sect. 5.

2   The Vehicle Flow Monitoring Problem

The fuzzy system proposed in this paper will be applied in the following by using data collected from the control system illustrated in the previous section. For instance, we will consider the vehicular flow of a urban street in the downtown of Rome (Italy). The information coming from sensors can be well represented by two time series: the number of vehicles flowing through the street and the mean time they spend to go across it (i.e. the mean cross-time). More precisely, each sample of these time series is related to a specific observation interval of 15 minutes; thus, we will have 96 samples per day. A representative daily behavior of the number of vehicles and of the mean cross-time is illustrated in Fig. 2. Data are normalized between 0 and 1 by using the extreme values of each sequence; the first sample corresponds to the observation interval between 00:00 and 00:15, the last sample corresponds to the observation interval between 23:45 and 00:00 (next day).

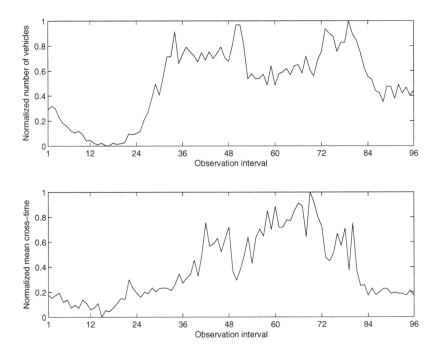

Fig. 2. Basic data collected by the monitoring system

A reasonable interpretation of traffic in the street can be based on three different situations: *flowing*, *intense*, and *congested*. The proposed fuzzy system is intended to forecast which situation will occur in the future, so that suitable decisions can be operated to manage the traffic in the surrounding areas. The major hypothesis we are making in this approach is to determine each of the previous traffic states by using data collected from the monitoring system. For instance, this can be obtained through a two-dimensional scatter plot where each point corresponds to an observation interval and where its coordinates are obtained by a sample of the vehicle number time series (abscissa) and by the corresponding sample of the mean cross-time (ordinate). A typical scatter plot, corresponding to data of Fig. 2 is illustrated in Fig. 3.

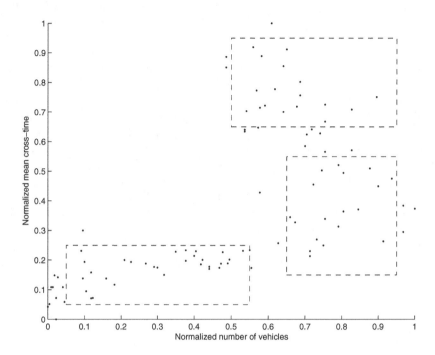

Fig. 3. Scatter plot of data in Fig. 2

There are several considerations that can be made about this kind of scatter plots. The major one concerns the areas that can be associated with the traffic states previously mentioned. We applied in this case to experts of traffic management as, for example, transport engineers. Such areas are evidenced in Fig. 3 as dashed rectangles: the one on the left side is associated with a flowing traffic; the lowermost on the right side is associated with an intense traffic; the uppermost on the right side is associated with a congested traffic.

It is important to note that some points can lie outside such areas; in this regard, the use of fuzzy logic can evidently improve the robustness of the inductive process leading to the identification of the traffic state. The use of the Simpson's Min-Max strategy is straightforward in this sense [1]. In fact, it consists in covering the patterns with hyperboxes (HBs) with boundary hyperplanes parallel to the co-ordinate axes of the data reference system. Consequently, each hyperbox H_r can be associated with a rectangle identifying a particular traffic state and is completely defined by two points in the data space, i.e. its 'min' and 'max' vertices $\underline{v}_r$ and $\underline{w}_r$, respectively. The HB can be considered as a crisp frame on which different types of membership functions (MFs) can be adapted. In the following, we will adopt the original Simpson's MF, in which the slope outside the HB is established by the fuzziness parameter γ [1]. The default value $\gamma = 5$ will be used in the following.

Therefore, the fuzzy approach characterizing the proposed system can be summarized as follows: for each observation interval (i.e. a sample) we measure the number of vehicles and the mean cross-time; this will correspond to a point in the said scatter plot; the MF value of this point is evaluated for each of the three considered HBs. In conclusion, we will obtain three time series, each representing the fuzzy degree of uncertainty in assuming a particular traffic state (i.e. flowing, intense, congested) in that observation interval.

The MFs obtained from the scatter plot of Fig. 3 by using the Simpson's MF are illustrated in Fig. 4. The behavior of MFs evidenced in this figure allows a qualitative assessment of the validity of the proposed approach. In particular, there are slots of time where the MFs assume well different values, thus evidencing precise traffic situations. Nevertheless, as will be discussed in the following, the use of fuzzy logic is essential for a robust management of transient or unexpected situations between the considered traffic states.

The typical evolutions of the MFs in Fig. 4 also prove the feasibility to make prediction: there is a characteristic information that is related to the transition between different traffic states and that can be exploited by a predictor in order to forecast future situations. In fact, points in Fig. 3 lie in a local region during

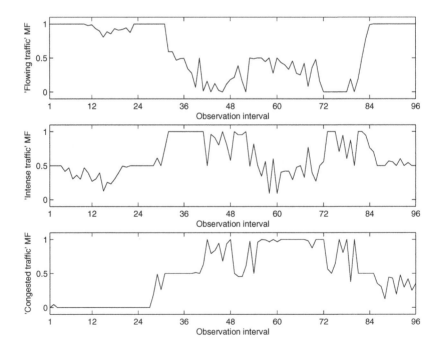

Fig. 4. MFs to different traffic states for the scatter plot of Fig. 3

a slot of time and then sharply move toward a different region, thus indicating a change in the traffic state. This is similar to the evolution of the attractor of a chaotic system (i.e. the whole traffic system in this case), which can be eventually corrupted by noise (i.e. random events during the vehicular flow). For this reason, we will use prediction techniques suited to chaotic time series.

The structure of the vehicle flow prediction system is evidently based on the previous data preprocessing system, which determines the sequences of MFs by using data obtained from the monitoring system. The information contained in the MF sequences can be processed to obtain a prediction of traffic states in future observation intervals. Several alternatives are possible in this regard, essentially based on cross and multi-prediction techniques. We propose in this paper to train a neuro-fuzzy predictor for each MF sequence, so that we will obtain for each future observation interval the prediction of the MF value to each traffic state. This gives to the prediction system the maximum degree of flexibility. In fact, a soft decision on the traffic management can be taken by a human expert based on the predicted fuzzy values. Alternatively, an automatic process can be used based on a 'winner takes all' (WTA) strategy, which classifies the traffic state based on the MF scoring the maximum value for that observation interval. For the sake of simplicity, we will consider the latter approach in order to evaluate and to compare the performance of the proposed fuzzy prediction system. In other word, we will consider the traffic classification accuracy, by applying the WTA strategy to the predicted MF sequences and to the corresponding ones that are used as test sets.

3   The Neuro-fuzzy Prediction of MF Sequences

As will be proved in the following, the MF sequences to be predicted are characterized by a chaotic behavior. In this case, a generic chaotic sequence $S(n)$ can be considered as the output of a chaotic system that is observable only through $S(n)$. Consequently, the sequence $S(n)$ should be embedded in order to reconstruct the state-space evolution of this system. The usual embedding technique, which is useful for chaotic sequences, is based on the determination of both the embedding dimension D of the reconstructed state-space attractor and the time lag T between the embedded past samples of $S(n)$; i.e.:

$$\underline{x}_n = \begin{bmatrix} S(n) & S(n-T) & S(n-2T) & S(n-(D-1)T) \end{bmatrix}, \qquad (1)$$

where $\underline{x}_n$ is the reconstructed state at time n. Both the values of D and T will be determined in the following by applying the methods suggested in [2]. In particular, D will be obtained by using the False Nearest Neighbors (FNN) method, whereas T will be obtained by using the Average Mutual Information (AMI) method. The prediction of $S(n)$ can be obtained by using the relationship between the (reconstructed) state and the system output. In fact, the embedding of $S(n)$ is intended to obtain an 'unfolded' version of the actual system attractor, so that the difficulty of the prediction task can be reduced. Therefore, the prediction of a chaotic sequence $S(n)$ can be stated as the determination of the function $f(\cdot)$, which approximates the link between the reconstructed state $\underline{x}_n$ and the output sample at the prediction distance q, i.e. $S(n + q) = f(\underline{x}_n)$, $q > 0$. In the following we will use the default value $q = 1$.

Because of the intrinsic non-linearity and non-stationarity of a chaotic system, $f(\cdot)$ should be a non-linear function, which can be determined only by using data driven techniques [3]. In other words, the prediction of $S(n)$ can be solved through the solution of the function approximation problem of $f(\underline{x})$. We propose in this regard the use of neuro-fuzzy networks, which in general are particularly suited to the solution of function approximation problems by using a training set of samples.

In this paper, we will use Adaptive Neuro-Fuzzy Inference Systems (ANFIS), which are constituted by a set of R rules of Sugeno first-order type [4]. The k-th rule, $k = 1 \ldots R$, has the following form:

$$\text{If } x_1 \text{ is } B_1^{(k)}, \text{ and} \ldots, \text{ and } x_m \text{ is } B_m^{(k)} \text{ then } y^{(k)} = \sum_{j=1}^{m} a_j^{(k)} x_j + a_0^{(k)}, \quad (2)$$

where $\underline{x} = [x_1 \ x_2 \ldots x_m]$ is the input pattern and $y^{(k)}$ is the output associated with the rule. The latter is characterized by the MFs $\mu_{B_j^{(k)}}(x_j)$ of the fuzzy input variables $B_j^{(k)}$, $j = 1 \ldots m$, and by the coefficients $a_j^{(k)}$, $j = 0 \ldots m$, of the crisp output. Several alternatives are possible for the fuzzification of crisp inputs, the composition of input MFs, and the way rule outputs are combined [5]. Usually, these choices lead to the following structure of the fuzzy inference system:

$$\tilde{y} = \frac{\sum_{k=1}^{R} \mu_{\underline{B}^{(k)}}(\underline{x}) \, y^{(k)}}{\sum_{k=1}^{R} \mu_{\underline{B}^{(k)}}(\underline{x})}, \quad (3)$$

where $\underline{B}^{(k)}$ is the overall fuzzy input variable, $\mu_{\underline{B}^{(k)}}(\underline{x})$ the corresponding MF, and $\tilde{y}$ the prediction, for a given input $\underline{x}_n$, of the actual value $S(n + q)$.

As previously discussed, the process $f(\underline{x})$ to be estimated is known by means of numerical examples, i.e. by a training set of P input-output pairs related to the reconstructed state $\underline{x}_n$ and to the value to be predicted $S(n + q)$. In this case, a useful approach to the synthesis of ANFIS networks is based on a clustering procedure of the training set [5], [6]. In this regard, we will use the Optimized Hyperplane Clustering Synthesis (OHCS) approach proposed in [7], which is able to achieve a better generalization capability of the resulting ANFIS network. The OHCS technique is based on a clustering procedure in the joint input-output data space, so that the linear consequent of Sugeno rules (i.e. the hyperplanes) are directly determined. Successively, the MFs of the rule antecedents are determined by considering a suitable classification problem in the input space, where each pattern $\underline{x}_n$ is labeled with an integer representing the hyperplane to which it has been assigned. Any fuzzy classification algorithm can be used in this regard; we used in OHCS the Adaptive Resolution Classifier (ARC) [8], belonging to the class of Simpons's Min-Max models. Furthermore, the generalization capability of the ANFIS network is maximized only if the latter consists of a suitable number of rules. However, the determination of the optimal number is a very critical problem to be solved, since the neural network might be easily overfitted in the case of noisy or ill-conditioned data. In order to alleviate these problems, we proposed in OHCS a constructive procedure for the automatic determination of the ANFIS rules; it aims to a regularization of the network architecture based on learning theory [9].

4   Illustrative Tests

In order to validate the OHCS prediction technique, we will consider in this section the ANFIS networks generated by applying the Subtractive Clustering (SUBCL) method, the Radial Basis Function (RBF) neural networks, and simple linear predictors determined by the least-squares technique. All these systems have been trained by using the 'Neural Network' toolbox of the Matlab^{TM} software package.

Data considered in the following tests have been collected by the monitoring system in a street of the downtown of Rome for eight consecutive days in the month of June 2002. Thus, we have sequences constituted by 768 samples: the first 576 (six days) are used as training set and the last 192 (two days) as test set. The training set of each MF sequence is used to compute the embedding dimension D and the time lag T by the AMI and FNN methods. The level of chaos present in the sequences is evaluated by means of the Spatio-Temporal Entropy (STE), which is defined and measured using the 'VRA' software package [10]. The STE index takes on values close to 50% in the case of chaotic signals and tends to 100% in the case of noise.

The prediction results for the considered MF sequences are illustrated in the first three rows of Table 1. The first two columns show the embedding parameters used for each sequence, while the third column refers to the relevant STE. The latter evidences the predominant chaotic behavior of the MF sequences, which score STE values around 50%. The successive four columns show the prediction performances obtained by using the predictors under investigation. The performances are measured on the test set by the Normalized Mean Squared Error (NMSE), i.e. the ratio between the mean squared prediction error and the variance of the sequence to be predicted. The overall performance of the traffic control system is measured by using the WTA defuzzification strategy discussed

Table 1. Performance results of the proposed control system using different predictors

Data	D	T	STE	OHCS	SUBCL	RBF	Linear
'Flowing' traffic MF	4	13	31%	0.167	0.221	0.180	0.205
'Intense' traffic MF	4	13	50%	0.120	0.129	0.138	0.146
'Congested' traffic MF	3	12	40%	0.117	0.123	0.122	0.110
Overall control system			—	3.09%	4.17%	3.64%	5.21%

in Sect. 2. The classification errors are reported in the last row of Table 1 as the percentage of samples of the test set not correctly classified.

5   Conclusions

In this paper, we have proposed a control system for the prediction of the vehicle traffic flow; the system has been realized by considering some pilot installations in the downtown of Rome. Row data are classified into three significant flow states, by using fuzzy rules manually determined by a human expert. The core of the control system is a prediction technique suited for chaotic time series and based on ANFIS neuro-fuzzy networks as function approximation models. The neuro-fuzzy networks are trained by a constructive algorithm (OHCS) which performs a particular type of joint input-output space clustering (i.e. the hyperplane clustering technique). This algorithm is characterized by a high automation degree, since its constructive nature allows us to train a suited neuro-fuzzy model, and hence a predictor, without any need of human expertise. The performances shown in Sect. 4 establish the superiority of the OHCS algorithm with respect to other prediction systems presented in the technical literature. Such results encourage us to improve the system in its most critical part, i.e. the manual determination of the fuzzy rules used to obtain the time series to be predicted.

References

1. Simpson, P.K.: Fuzzy Min-Max Neural Networks Part 1: Classification. IEEE Transactions on Neural Networks **3** (1992) 776–786
2. Abarbanel, H.D.I.: Analysis of Observed Chaotic Data. Springer-Verlag Inc., New York (1996)
3. Panella, M., Rizzi, A., Martinelli, G.: Refining accuracy of environmental data prediction by MoG neural networks. Neurocomputing (2003) *in press*
4. Jang, J.-S.R.: ANFIS: Adaptive-Network-Based Fuzzy Inference System. IEEE Transactions on Systems, Man, and Cybernetics **23** (1993) 665–685
5. Jang, J.-S.R., Sun, C.T., Mizutani, E.: Neuro-Fuzzy and Soft Computing: a Computational Approach to Learning and Machine Intelligence. Prentice Hall, Upper Saddle River, NJ, USA (1997)
6. Guillaume, S.: Designing Fuzzy Inference Systems from Data: an Interpretability Oriented Review. IEEE Transactions on Fuzzy Systems **9** (2001) 426–443
7. Panella, M., Rizzi, A., Frattale Mascioli, F.M., Martinelli, G.: ANFIS Synthesis by Hyperplane Clustering. In: Proceedings of IFSA/NAFIPS 2001, Vancouver, Canada, **1** (2001) 340–345
8. Rizzi, A., Panella, M., Frattale Mascioli, F.M.: Adaptive Resolution Min-Max Classifiers. IEEE Transactions on Fuzzy Systems **13** (2002) 402–414
9. Haykin, S.: Neural Networks, a Comprehensive Foundation, 2nd ed. Prentice Hall, Upper Saddle River, NJ, USA (1999)
10. Kononov, E.: Visual Recurrence Analysis (VRA). Available at http://pw1.netcom.com/~eugenek, Version 4.2, November 15 (1999)

On the Use of Neuro-fuzzy Techniques for Analyzing Experimental Surface Electromyographic Data

Domenico Costantino, Francesco Carlo Morabito, and Mario Versaci

University *"Mediterranea"* of Reggio Calabria,
Faculty of Engineering, DIMET, Reggio Calabria, Italy
Phone: +39 0965 875224; Fax: +39 0965 875220
morabito@unirc.it, versaci@ing.unirc.it

Abstract. In this paper, the electrical signals coming from muscles in activity through experimental electromyogram interference patterns measured on human subjects are investigated. The experiments make use of surface ElectroMyoGraphic (sEMG). The use of Independent Component Analysis (ICA) is suggested as a method for processing raw sEMG data by reducing the "cross-talk" effect. ICA also allows us to remove artefacts and to separate the different sources of muscle activity. The main ICs are used to reconstruct the original signal by using a neuro-fuzzy network. An auto-associative Neural Network that exploits wavelet coefficients as an input vector is also used as simple detector of non-stationarity based on a measure of reconstruction error.

1 Introduction to the Problem

Electrical signals detected on the human body form the starting point of diagnostic procedures in most medical protocols. They are commonly inspected but they are analyzed in some automatic ways. Data gathered from these diagnostic tests, commonly collected in database, such as the Electroencephalogram (EEG), the Electromyogram (EMG), the Electrocardiogram (ECG) and, more recently, functional Magnetic Resonance Imaging (fMRI), tend to be complex, large and high-dimensional. The trend towards digitization of the traditionally analog EEG, EMG and ECG signals has coincided with the development of computing power and multivariate signal processing techniques capable of manipulating and analyzing such large data sets ([1]). The use of Independent Component Analysis (ICA), an unsupervised learning technique which generalizes Principal Component Analysis (PCA), commonly implemented through Neural Network (NN) schemes, is proposed in this study to process experimental biomedical data. Applied to sEMG (surface ElectroMyoGraphy) data, ICA results in numerous spatially-independent patterns, each associated with a unique time-course, providing a way to separate different electrical signals coming from different muscle activities ([2]). In contrast to the variable nature of the surface EMG recorded from a single muscle in isolation, ICA of the sEMG from several muscles simultaneously allows the detection of highly reproducible components

V. Di Gesú, F. Masulli, and A. Petrosino (Eds.): WILF 2003, LNAI 2955, pp. 119–126, 2006.
© Springer-Verlag Berlin Heidelberg 2006

for example in the sEMG of the face and the throat during swallowing and in the sEMG of arm muscles during reaching movements. This paper is organized as follows. In Section 2 the type of data coming from electrical activity of muscles will be discussed. In Section 3 we shall propose the idea of motion through integration of sub-movements and the computational model incorporating sub-movements will be presented. Section 4 is devoted to the proposal of NN schemes to implement ICA. Section 5 will report the results achieved and the assumption of stationarity of the signals, where the wavelet approach will be proposed. Finally, some conclusions are drawn.

2   The Experimental ElectroMyographic (EMG) Signals

When skeletal muscle fibers contract, they conduct electrical activity (APs) that can be measured by electrodes affixed to the surface of the skin above muscles ([3]). As the APs pass by the electrodes, spikes of electrical activity are observed and pulses of muscle fiber contractions are produced. Small functional groups of muscle fibers, termed motor units (MUs), contract synchronously, resulting in a motor unit action potential (MUAP). To sustain force, an MU is repeatedly activated by the central nervous system several times per second. The repetition, or average, firing rate is often between 5 and 30 times per second (or faster). The amplitude of the signal varies in the range 20 - 2000 μV. The EMG signal is widely used as a suitable means to have access to physiological processes involved in producing joint movements. The sEMG measures the electrical potential resulting from the superposition of single muscle fibers action potentials. The use of sEMG simplifies the acquisition of the signals not only due to the non-invasiveness of the procedure but also because the acquisition can be done during the execution of functional exercises. In the latter case, two sensors are placed on the muscle under analysis. The experimental data here analyzed come from non-invasive surface EMG sensors, which present the cross-talk effect, i.e., they detect electrical activities from several muscles simultaneously in action. Furthermore, there are various sources of "noise" that affects the registration. The movement of muscles, the modifications of the contact impedance of the electrodes, and the slight variation of the electrode locations suggests the use of suitable techniques of filtering of the raw sEMG data.

3   Computational Models Incorporating Sub-movements

A growing body of evidence suggests movements which appear smooth to the naked eye are actually composed of the temporal and spatial superposition of discrete sub-movements precisely recruited and coordinated by the central nervous system ([4]). However, the spatial and temporal overlap of sub-movements has generally made it impossible, with the common computational tools available to the neuroscientist, to isolate the effects of individual sub-movements. Detection of non-stationarity in the sEMG and kinematic variables is necessary to detect the onset of temporally overlapping sub-movements. We investigate the information-theoretic considerations of channel capacity and bandwidth as important determinants in the selection and sensorimotor integration of individual sub-movements. Some computational approaches have attempted to model reaching movements as incorporating sub-movements; however, they have not addressed many of the unanswered questions regarding the characteristics of sub-movements. Others have attempted to model reaching movements without considering sub-movements at all. Smoothness, an empirical observation of motor movements, has often used as a cost function to optimize the models. Intuitively, sub-movements are groups of muscles that have the tendency to activate together following a common neural input. We assert that a sub-movements is "hard-wired" by adulthood, in the sense that it may be encoded in the spinal cord as part of a Central Pattern Generator (CPG), and also partly reflect the anatomical distribution across several muscles of a single nerve root exiting the spinal cord. To suggest a computational model of sub-movements, we initially make the stationarity assumption. Since the EMG is an indirect measure of the neural command to the muscle, the Mutual Information (MI) can be used as a metric to infer the recordings from two EMG electrodes contain common neural input. The ICA model can be used to provide a useful starting point for the rigorous definition of a sub-movement upon which more elaborate models can be created. If we model the sEMGs recorded from each electrode to be the linear superposition of activity from different group of muscles (possibly encoded with CPGs) that tend to co-activate, the, the goal is to estimate the cortical modulation of the commonly influenced muscles. A single sub-movement is defined as $m(t) = UC(t)$, $t = t_0 \longrightarrow t_n$, where m is a column vector, with m_j representing the muscle electrical activity contributing to the jth electrode as a function of time, U is a stationary column vector representing the relative weighting that a given cortical command gives to the different muscle areas, and $C(t)$ is the unknown scalar neural command over time. If several, e.g. p, sub-movements during a complex movement are temporally (and spatially) overlapping, the linear combination of $m_k(t_k)$ outputs $M(t)$, the total muscle electrical activity over the duration of the whole movement and M_j is the electrical activity recorded from the jth electrode, C_k represents the relative activation of the kth sub-movement by an independent cortical command, and the matrix $U_{j,k}$ has as its columns, U_k, the vectors defining the different sub-movements. If we assume that for a given time-period, say T, a constant number of sub-movements, c, are simultaneously active, thus, we have $M = UC$, where M is the matrix of the electrical activity, C is the matrix of presumed independent cortical commands, and U is a matrix defining the sub-movements. The goal is then, given the recordings from the electrodes, and not knowing U, to estimate the different cortical influences, C. If the C_k are assumed to be independent, this is possible through the ICA.

4   Independent Component Analysis (ICA)

ICA is a method for finding a linear non-orthogonal co-ordinate system in any multivariate data. The directions of the axes of this co-ordinate system are determined by both the second and higher order statistics of data. The goal is to perform a linear transformation that makes the resulting variables as statistically independent from each other as possible. Blind source separation by ICA has received attention because of its potential applications in signal processing. Here, the goal is to recover independent sources given only sensor observation that are unknown linear mixtures of the latent source signals. To blind source separation researches, the ICA emerged within the framework of unsupervised learning. In particular([5]) proposed an algorithm based on information theory that was then used to maximize the mutual information between the inputs and the outputs of a NN. Each neuron of an "output" layer should be able to encode features that are as statistically independent as possible from other neurons over another ensemble of "inputs". The statistical independence of the outputs implies that the multivariate probability density function (pdf) of the outputs can be factorized as a product of marginal pdf's. ([6]), derived stochastic gradient learning rules for achieving the prescribed maximization. The same Authors put the problem in terms of an information-theoretic framework and demonstrated the separation and deconvolution of linearly mixed sources ([7]). Among the various approaches proposed in the literature to implement the ICA, the approach used in ([8]) is the algorithm developed by in ([6]) which is based on an Infomax NN, where a self-organizing algorithm is used to maximize the information transferred in a network of non-linear units. The general framework of ICA is now simply described as the blind separation problem, typically introduced by the "cocktail party problem": we have n different sources $\underline{s}_j$ (that is, the speakers $i = 1,...,n$) and m different linear mixtures x_j (that is, the microphones $j = 1,...,m$). By referring to $\underline{x}$ as the matrix of the observed signals, and as s the matrix of the independent components, the matrix $\underline{W}$, called unmixing matrix, satisfies the following property: $\underline{s} = \underline{W} \cdot \underline{x}$ or, by defining the mixing matrix $\underline{A}$ as: $\underline{x} = \underline{A} \cdot \underline{s}$ then the mixing and unmixing matrixes are related by the following equation: $\underline{W}^{-1} = \underline{A}$. Bell and Sejnowski derived a self-organizing learning algorithm to maximize the information transferred to a NN of non-linear units. By defining the differential entropy for a continuous random variable x as:$H(x) = - \int_{-\infty}^{+\infty} f_x(x) \cdot \ln[f_x(x)] \cdot dx$ when $f_x(x)$ is the probability density function of the considered variable. The conditional differential entropy is defined as follows: $H(y|x) = - \int_{-\infty}^{+\infty} f_x(x) \int_{-\infty}^{+\infty} f_y(y|x) \cdot \ln[f_y(y|x)] \cdot dx \cdot dy$ It represents to the variations that occur in the information carried by y when x is observed. Finally the mutual information between two variables x and y is given by: $MI(x,y) = H(x) - H(x|y) = H(y) - H(y|x)$. This quantity measures the information that is added to x when y is observed, or to y when x is observed. The Bell-Sejnowski approach is based on the use of a NN able to minimize the mutual information between the input $\underline{x}$ and the output $\underline{y}$ of the neural network where $\underline{y}$ are the independent components. If we suppose to have noise-free input data, $\underline{y}$ can be obtained from $\underline{x}$ by a deterministic manner: in this case, $H(y|x)$ assumes its lowest value $(-\infty)$. The problem in this case is that the density functions of the unknown components cannot be computed, and therefore the

$H(y|\underline{x})$ is difficult to be estimated. This drawback can be overcame by taking into account that, if y can be computed from $\underline{x}$ by an invertible continuous deterministic mapping, the maximization of $MI(\underline{x}|y)$ corresponds to maximize the entropy of the outputs. In the NN case, we have to maximize the $H(y)$ with respect to the network parameters $\underline{w}$. If we have just one input x and one output y, if the mapping from x to y is defined as $y = g(x)$, and if $g(\bullet)$ has a unique inverse, then the probability density function of y can be computed as: $f_y(y) = \left|\dfrac{\partial y}{\partial x}\right| \cdot f_x(x)$. The differential entropy of y is given by: $H(y) =$

$-E[\ln(f_y)] = -\displaystyle\int_{-\infty}^{+\infty} f_y(y) \cdot \ln[f_y(y)] \cdot dy = E\left[\ln\left|\dfrac{\partial y}{\partial x}\right|\right] - E[\ln(f_x(x))]$. To max-

imize the differential entropy, we need to maximize just the first term. This maximization is carried out by a stochastic gradient ascent learning. The update step can be computed as: $\Delta w \propto \dfrac{\partial H}{\partial w} = \dfrac{\partial}{\partial w}\left(\ln\left|\dfrac{\partial y}{\partial x}\right|\right) = \left(\dfrac{\partial x}{\partial y}\right)^{-1} \cdot \dfrac{\partial}{\partial w}\left(\dfrac{\partial y}{\partial x}\right)$.

If $g(\bullet)$ becomes the logistic transfer function, of the scaled and translated input: $y = \dfrac{1}{1+\exp{-[(w \cdot x + w_0)]}}$, the update term can be rewritten as the update step for the weight w: $\Delta w \propto \dfrac{1}{w} + x \cdot (1 - 2y)$ and the update step for the bias weight can be computed as: $\Delta w_0 \propto 1 - 2y$. In the most general multivariate case, we have: $f_{y_1,y_2,...,y_N}(y_1, y_2, ..., y_N) = |\underline{J}|^{-1} \cdot f_{x_1,x_2,...,x_N}(x_1, x_2, ..., x_N)$, where $\underline{J}$ is the transformation Jacobian. The update step for the matrix weight becomes: $\underline{\Delta w} \propto \underline{\Delta w}^{-T} + (\underline{1} - 2\underline{y}) \cdot \underline{x}^T$, where $\underline{1}$ is a unit column vector and the update step for the bias weight vector can be computed as: $\underline{\Delta w_0} \propto \underline{1} - 2\underline{y}$. The input data are measurements of N different input sources, and, therefore, they can be referred to as a matrix $\underline{x}$, where the ith column represents the ith sample of the each source. The inputs of the neural network are $\underline{h} = \underline{W} \cdot \underline{x}_s$ and $\underline{x}_s$ are called sphered data. The sphered data are computed by zero-meaning the input data $\underline{x}$ by sphering these data with the following matrix operation: $\underline{x}_s = \underline{S} \cdot \underline{x}_0$; $\underline{x}_0 = \underline{x} - E[\underline{x}]$; $\underline{S} = 2\left(\sqrt{E[\underline{x}_0 \cdot \underline{x}_0^T]}\right)$; where $\underline{S}$ is called sphering matrix, and it is used to speed the convergence. The infomax NN estimate the matrix $\underline{y}$, where the ith column represents the ith sample of the each independent component.

5   Neuro-fuzzy Inference for Representing sEMG Signal

The signal is firstly decomposed in non-orthogonal components whose statistical independence is maximized. Through a ranking procedure, we select a subset of components that mostly characterize the raw signal. The fuzzy curve technique ([9]) is here proposed as a ranking technique. To understand how a fuzzy curve works, let us consider a Multi-Input Single-Output system (MISO) for which we possess a data base of input-output pairs with possible not relevant inputs. In our problem, the inputs of the model are the ICs, x_i ($i = 1, ..., 16$) and the considered output, y, is the sEMG signal. We wish determine which ICs are the most important among 16 possible candidates. We assume that m training data are available, thus xik ($k = 1, ..., m$) are the ith co-ordinate of each of m training patterns. The fuzzy curve is defined as: $c_i(x_i) = \frac{\sum_k \Phi_{i,k}(x_i)y_k}{\sum_k \Phi_{i,k}(x_i)}, k = 1, ..., m$ where $\Phi_{ik} = \exp{-[\frac{x_{ik}-x_i}{\sigma}]^2}$ is a Gaussian function.

The method exploits the flatness of the fuzzy curve, since the output is scarcely influenced by the input value if the related fuzzy curve is nearly flat. The importance of the input is determined on the basis of a figure of merit which is defined as the range of the fuzzy curve, $(c_{i-max} - c_{i-min})$. If the output variable is independent of x_i , that is $y(x_i) = cost$, the fuzzy curve c_i is also independent of x_i and then $(c_{i-max} - c_{i-min}) = 0$. The selected ICs are used as the input vector of a neuro-fuzzy scheme to approximate the original signal, commonly referred to as Adaptive Neuro-Fuzzy Inference System (AN-FIS) ([10]). In particular, we extract a set of rules that is able to model the data behavior. The method determines the number of rules and the antecedent Fuzzy Membership Functions (FMFs) and uses linear least squares estimation to determine each rule's consequent. The Toolbox to extract a Fuzzy Inference System (FIS) that can be tuned in various respects. ANFIS routine is indeed about taking a FIS and tuning it with a learning algorithm based on some collections of input-output data. The network structure facilitates the computation of the gradient vector for computing parameter corrections in a FIS. Once the gradient vector is carried out, we can apply a number of optimization routines to reduce an error measure (sum of the squared difference between actual and desired output). We found that each channel can be well recovered with 3-4 ICs. For reconstructing channel #4, we use three ICs (in order #1, #2 and #6 ICs), extracted by means of fuzzy curves approach. The inference data bank includes 15 rules with three antecedents and connective AND. After defuzzification, we are able to reproduce the non-linear mapping among three inputs and the output with a very low RMS reconstruction error (in the order of %5 full scale).

6   Experimental Results and Treatment of Non-stationary

The experiment treated in this work refers to a subject who is asked to execute the following task : 1) pointing of the left/right side (alternatively) of a monitor with the hand: the action is repeated 50 times; 2) each pointing event is alternate by a rest. The data are acquired with 16 channels with unipolar electrodes (there is a reference electrode). Each signal is hypothesized being the superposition of fundamental building blocks, namely, the Independent Components (ICs). The ICA-NN scheme proposed has been used to extract ICs from sEMG recordings. In what follows, we will report some results that have been achieved in this study. The following Table reports the correspondence between the placements of sEMG electrodes and the related muscles. Each ICs consists of a temporally independent waveform and a spatial distribution over the electrodes. Measuring the ICs of sEMG will provide a more reliable and robust measure of motor performance than interpreting the activity of each individual muscles in isolation. There are advantages of separating the sEMG signals into temporally ICs, namely, the ICs are less susceptible to changes in position of the electrodes, and therefore more suitable for serially monitoring performance; the

ICs are more likely to correspond to brain activations, by looking for common cortical influences in the muscle activity. The extraction of ICs is based on the assumption of stationarity among different trials of the same experiment. In the practice, for such sEMG data, this is a hardly acceptable assumption. We would like now to propose a time-frequency approach to the analysis of sEMG data (or their ICs counterparts) that allows to cope with signal non-stationarity. The sEMG is indeed non-stationary as its statistical properties change over time. The Motor Unit Action Potentials (MUAPs) are transients that exist for a short period of time: for that reason, time-frequency methods are useful to character-ize the localized frequency content of each MUAP. The use of a time-frequency representation also allows, in principle, to detect the onset of sub-movements, according to what we explained in the previous Sections. We have carried out the wavelet analysis in both the time domain of sEMG and of the ICs, in order to show that this kind of analysis should be carried out on the original space (the IC space is generated by already making a stationarity assumption). The wavelet transform also guarantees to possibility of not specifying in advance the key signal features and the optimal basis functions needed to project the signal in order to highlight the features. An orthogonal wavelet transform is charac-terized by two functions: 1)the scaling function $\phi(x) = \sqrt{2} \sum_{x \in Z} \phi(2x - k)$ and 2)its associated wavelet $\psi(x) = \sqrt{2} \sum_{x \in Z} g(k)\phi(2x - k)$ where $g(k)$ is a suit-able weighting sequence. The sequence $h(k)$ is the so-called refinement filter. The wavelet basis functions are constructed by dyadic dilation (index j) and transla-tion (index k) of the mother wavelet: $\psi_{jk} = 2^{j/2}\psi(x/2^{-j} - k)$. The sequences h and g can be selected such that $\{\psi_{jk}\}_{jk} \in Z^2$ constitutes an orthonormal basis of L2, the space of finite energy functions. This orthogonality permits the wavelet coefficients $d_j(k) = \langle f, \psi_{jk} \rangle$ and the approximation coefficients $c_j(k) = \langle f, \phi_{jk} \rangle$ of any function $f(x)$ to be obtained by inner product with the corresponding basis functions. In practice, the decomposition is only carried out over a finite number of scales J. The wavelet transform with a depth J is then given by:

$$f(x) = \sum_{j=1}^{J}\sum_{k \in Z} d_j(k)\psi_{jk} + \sum_{k \in Z} c_J(k)\phi_{Jk}.$$ We shall use the WT to derive a set

of features that can reveal singularity and to detect the precursors of the non-stationarity. A set of features derived from the inspection of the scale-dilation plane have been used as input vector of an auto-associative NN that is able to alarm the user about modification of the energy content of the spectrum. The features are extracted by considering the correspondence between singularities of a function and local maxima of its wavelet transform. A singularity corresponds to pairs of modulus maxima across several scales. Feature extraction is accom-plished by the computation of the singularity degree (peakiness), i.e., the local Lipschitz regularity, which is estimated from the wavelet coefficients decay. The modulus maxima plots have been drawn and a thresholding operator is used in order to reduce the number of effective wavelet coefficients needed to represent the original functions. Once the features have been extracted by inspecting the modulus maxima plot, we can use the corresponding nonzero coefficients in or-der to predict the raising of nonstationarity. A MLP NN with an input layer of corresponding size acts as a bottleneck network. The NN fed by the wavelet coefficients computes the estimation of the corresponding wavelet coefficients at the output: a reconstruction error is computed. If the error overcomes a prescribed threshold level, the non-stationarity signal is activated and the following trials are used to compute a novel matrix weights.

7 Conclusions

The paper proposed the use of some NNs to process experimental electrical data derived from non-invasive sEMG experiments. The raw data have been analyzed by a neural IC processor aiming to obtain signals that can be easily correlated to cortical activity. The assumption of stationarity is then relaxed in order to cope with time-varying mixing systems, more adherent to the biophysical problem at hand. An auto-associative NN exploits the features obtained by wavelet transforming the raw data for making a quick and efficient prediction of non-stationarity.

References

1. M. Akay, *Time-frequency and Wavelets in Biomedical Signal Processing*, Piscataway, NJ, IEEE Press, 1997
2. Jung T. P., S. Makeig, T. W. Lee, M. J. McKeown, G. Brown, A. J. Bell and T. J. Sejnowski, Independent Component Analysis of Biomedical Signals - The 2nd Int'l Workshop on Independent Component Analysis and Signal Separation, 2000.
3. M.J. McKeown, Cortical activation related to arm movement combinations, Muscle Nerve, Vol 9, Suppl. 9.4, 2000.
4. C.M. Harris, On the optimal control of behaviour: A stochastic perspective, J. Neurosci. Meth, Vol. 83, pp. 73-88, 1998.
5. R. Linsker, An Application of the Principle of Maximum Information Preserving to Linear Systems, In Advances in Neural Information Processing Systems 1.
6. A.J. Bell and T.J. Sejnowski, An Information-Maximization Approach to Blind Separation and Blind Deconvolution, Neural Computation, Vol.7, pp.1129-1159, 1995.
7. A.J. Bell, T.J. Sejnowski, Learning the higher-order structure of a natural sound, Network Computation in Neural Systems, Vol.7, 1996.
8. T.-W. Lee, M. Girolami, and T. J. Sejnowski, Independent component analysis using an extended infomax algorithm for mixed sub-gaussian and super-gaussian sources, Neural Computation, Vol. 11, N.2, pp. 417-441, 1999.
9. Y. Lin, et al., Non Linear System Input Structure Identification: Two Stage Fuzzy Curves and Surfaces, IEEE Transactions on Systems, Man, and Cybernetics, Vol. 26, N.5, 1998, pp. 678-684.
10. R. Jang, ANFIS: Adaptive-Network based Fuzzy Inference System, IEEE Transactions on Systems, Man, and Cybernetics, Vol. 23, N. 3, 1993.

Linear Regression Model-Guided Clustering for Training RBF Networks for Regression Problems

Antonino Staiano[1,2], Roberto Tagliaferri[1,2], and Witold Pedrycz[3]

[1] DMI, Università di Salerno, 84081 Baronissi (Sa), Italy
{astaiano, robtag}@unisa.it
[2] INFM Unità di Salerno,
[3] ECERF - University of Alberta, Edmonton, Canada
pedrycz@ee.ualberta.ca

Abstract. In this paper, we describe a novel approach to fuzzy clustering which organizes the data in clusters on the basis of the input data and builds a 'prototype' regression function as a summation of linear local regression models to guide the clustering process. This methodology is shown to be effective in the training of RBFNN's. It is shown that the performance of such networks is better than other types of networks.

1 Introduction

Objective function-based clustering algorithms [1] are often used in the determination of the prototypes of the Radial Basis Functions Neural Networks (RBFNN's)[2]. One drawback that is commonly encountered when using clustering methods for RBFNN's is that all of them are regarded as completely unsupervised, i.e. the target output set Y is simply ignored during training. However, the clustering mechanism needs to determine groups within the data that are relatively homogeneous with regard to the output variables. There are many works where the information on the output space to guide the clustering process is exploited and, most of them are referred as input-output clustering. One of a particular interest is proposed by Gonzales et al. [3], where a new technique, called Clustering for Function Approximation (CFA), analyzes the output variability of the target function during the clustering process and augments the number of prototypes in those input zones where the target function is more variable. Our starting point is the Conditional Fuzzy c-means (CFC) described in [6] where the process of revealing the structure in the input space (input variables) is conditioned upon some linguistic landmarks defined in the output space: it reveals a structure in the input data in a context established in the output space. This context is treated as a fuzzy set. Our goal is to overcome some limitations of [6]: 1) the building of linguistic landmarks in the form of membership functions (made by the experts); 2) their definition in the case of input space dimensions greater than 2.

V. Di Gesú, F. Masulli, and A. Petrosino (Eds.): WILF 2003, LNAI 2955, pp. 127–132, 2006.

2   The Proposed Clustering Procedure

2.1   Theoretical Framework

We extend the original FCM objective function [1] used by the clustering method. Let $\{\mathbf{x}_1, ..., \mathbf{x}_N\} \subset R^n$ be the patterns to cluster and $y_k \in R, k = 1, ..., N$ be the corresponding desired output values.

Let us suppose to organize the data in c clusters, we can associate a local linear regression model for each cluster, i.e.

$$\hat{y}^i - z_i = \mathbf{a}_i^T(\mathbf{x} - \mathbf{v}_i), \ i = 1, ..., c, \tag{1}$$

where $\mathbf{a}_i^T \in \mathbb{R}^\kappa$ are the parameters of the $i - th$ local model. The $\{\mathbf{v}_1, ..., \mathbf{v}_c\}$ and $z_i \in \mathbb{R}, i = 1, ..., c$ are the cluster centers, in the input and output space, respectively. Note that the $z_i \in \mathbb{R}, i = 1, ..., c$ play the role of biases in each local model. At this point we build an overall linear regression model given by the sum of the c local models:

$$\hat{y}_k = \sum_{i=1}^{c} \hat{y}_k^i = \sum_{i=1}^{c} \mathbf{a}_i^T(\mathbf{x}_k - \mathbf{v}_i) + z_i. \tag{2}$$

This models are switched by the values of the partition matrix u_{ik} associated to the clusters:

$$\hat{y}_k = \sum_{i=1}^{c} u_{ik}[\mathbf{a}_i^T(\mathbf{x}_k - \mathbf{v}_i) + z_i] \tag{3}$$

Note that (1) assumes a direct interpretation: at $\mathbf{x} = \mathbf{v}_i$, $\hat{y}^i = z_i$. In other words, if $\mathbf{x}_k = \mathbf{v}_i$ then $\hat{y}_k = z_i$. This means that (2) switches between regions of the clusters in the input space.

Now, rather than defining J based on $\mathbf{x}_k \in R^n$ only, we supply it with information on the output space by defining a new objective function which assumes the following form:

$$J = \sum_{i=1}^{c} \sum_{k=1}^{N} u_{ik}^m(\|\mathbf{x}_k - \mathbf{v}_i\|^2 + \alpha(y_k - \hat{y}_k)^2). \tag{4}$$

The parameter $\alpha > 0$ is a weighting factor used to control the influence of the information about the output space during the clustering process, in particular α decreases in time to allow a fine tuning in the solutions found by the clustering algorithm. Now, by applying the Lagrange multipliers technique to J in (4) we derive the necessary conditions for the partition matrix and the prototypes, namely

$$u_{ik} = \frac{1}{\sum_{j=1}^{c} \left(\frac{\|\mathbf{X}_k - \mathbf{V}_i\|^2 + \alpha(\hat{y}_k - y_k)^2}{\|\mathbf{X}_k - \mathbf{V}_j\|^2 + \alpha(\hat{y}_k - y_k)^2} \right)^{1/m-1}}, \tag{5}$$

$$1 \le i \le c; \ 1 \le k \le N.$$

and

$$\mathbf{v}_i = \frac{\sum_{k=1}^{N} u_{ik}^m \mathbf{x}_k}{\sum_{k=1}^{N} u_{ik}^m}, \ 1 \le i \le c. \tag{6}$$

2.2 The Regression Parameters

In order to calculate the regression parameters $\mathbf{a}_i^T \in \mathbb{R}^n$, $i = 1, ..., c$ we solve c least square problems, that is, one for each local model:

$$min \;\; V = \frac{1}{2} \sum_{k=1}^{N} \{u_{ik}[\mathbf{a}_i^T(\mathbf{x}_k - \mathbf{v}_i) + z_i] - y_k\}^2 \tag{7}$$

and we can rewrite this expression in the form

$$min \;\; V = \frac{1}{2} \sum_{k=1}^{N} \{\mathbf{a}_i^T \phi_i(\mathbf{x}_k) - b_i\}^2 \tag{8}$$

where

$$\phi_i(\mathbf{x}_k) = u_{ik}(\mathbf{x}_k - \mathbf{v}_i)$$

and

$$b_i = y_k - u_{ik} z_i, \;\; i = 1, ..., c.$$

Differentiating (8) with respect to the parameters $\mathbf{a}_i^T$ and setting the derivative to zero we obtain (in matrix notation and following the pseudo-inverse approach) the solution for the regression parameters

$$A^T = \Phi^\dagger B \tag{9}$$

where $\Phi^\dagger$ denote the pseudo-inverse of Φ. We will call our clustering method Linear Regression Clustering (LRC). At the end of the clustering process, the set of prototypes obtained by the algorithm are used in the RBFNN architecture and then the pseudo-inverse approach is performed to optimize the hidden to output weights.

3 RBF Neural Network

The main topology of the RBFNN is shown in (Fig. 1).

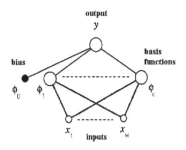

Fig. 1. RBFNN's general architecture

Each hidden node evaluates a kernel function (receptive field) $\Phi(\mathbf{x})$ on the incoming input, and the output $y(\mathbf{x})$ is simply a weighted linear summation of the output of the kernel functions:

$$y(\mathbf{x}) = \sum_{i=0}^{c} w_i \Phi_i(\mathbf{x}) \tag{10}$$

Each kernel function gives its higher output when the input is closer to its center, and the value decreases monotonically as the distance from the center increases. We propose in the next section a particular form of the kernel function. The distance can be defined in different ways, but the Euclidean distance is the most popular one, and is also used by us. Of course, this topology may be generalized with the output layer consisting of more neurons.

3.1   Learning Procedure

The training phase of RBFNN's is accomplished in two separated steps: (1) training of the first layer weights (i.e. the kernel function centers) by means of a clustering procedure and (2) calculation of the hidden to output weights. Let us suppose to have already determined the kernel function centers by LRC, $\mathbf{v}_1, ..., \mathbf{v}_c$, the RBF units determine the level of matching of the current pattern $\mathbf{x} \in R^n$ with the given prototypes $\mathbf{v}_1, ..., \mathbf{v}_c$. Each of these prototypes is associated to its corresponding RBF unit. Let us denote the obtained levels of matching by $z_1, z_2, ..., z_c$. The matching level z_i is inversely proportional to the distance between $\mathbf{x}$ and the prototype of the i-th RBF unit, $\mathbf{v}_i$. More specifically, the activation level z_i of the i-th receptive field is based upon the similarity between $\mathbf{x}$ and the prototype of the field, weighted by the partition matrix coming from the clustering procedure. Since these levels sum up to one (for proper normalization), this leads us to the optimization problem

$$min_{z_1,...,z_c} \left\{ \sum_{i=1}^{c} z_i^2 \|\mathbf{x}_k - \mathbf{v}_i\|^2 u_{ik} \right\}, \quad k = 1, ..., N, \tag{11}$$

subject to

$$\sum_{i=1}^{c} z_i = 1 \tag{12}$$

By applying the Lagrange multipliers technique we obtain the following equation for the basis function activations:

$$z_i = \Phi_i(\mathbf{x}_k) = \frac{1}{\sum_{j=1}^{c} \left(\frac{\|\mathbf{x}_k - \mathbf{v}_i\|^2 u_{ik}}{\|\mathbf{x}_k - \mathbf{v}_j\|^2 u_{jk}} \right)}, \quad k = 1, ..., N. \tag{13}$$

The neuron situated in the output layer carries out a linear combination of the matching levels, yielding

$$y = \sum_{i=1}^{c} w_i z_i \tag{14}$$

where $w_1, w_2, ..., w_c$ are the hidden-to-output weights. This expression can be formulated in a matrix notation as follows

$$\mathbf{y}(\mathbf{x}) = WZ \qquad (15)$$

where $W = (w_j)$ and $Z = (Z_i)$. We can optimize the weights by the minimization of a suitable error function. It is particularly convenient to consider a sum-of-squares error function. In this case the formal solution for the weights is given by [2]

$$W^T = Z^\dagger T \qquad (16)$$

where the notation $Z\dagger$ denotes the pseudo-inverse of Z. When a new input pattern $\mathbf{x}$ is presented to the system, the RBFNN computes the activation level $z_i, i = 1, ..., c$ through (13) and then these values are then combined together to compute the output value using (14).

4   Experimental Results

The proposed algorithm is performed on synthetic data, and compared to CFA [3] and CFC [6]. Furthermore, the proposed system is compared with the standard RBFNN architecture available under Netlab [5].

The function to approximate is

$$y = f(x_1, x_2) = \frac{(x_1 - 2)(2x_1 + 1)}{1 + x_1^2} \frac{(x_2 - 2)(2x_2 + 1)}{1 + x_2^2}$$

defined over $[-5, 5] \times [-5, 5]$. For comparison aim the error criterion adopted is the normalized root mean squared error (NRMSE). The function was approximated using two different training sets, a limited one of 26 examples (see figure 2) and a complete training set of 441 examples obtained from a grid of 21×21 points equidistributed in the input interval defined for the function. LRC was run 25 times. The results obtained are reported in table 1 where the results reported in [3] for the CFA and CFC for the limited and complete data sets, respectively and the standard Netlab RBFNN are also shown. The results highlight better results for the LRC for both limited and complete data sets. Figure 2 depicts the target function and the RBFNN output on the test set in the best case result ($c = 10$ clusters) for the limited data set.

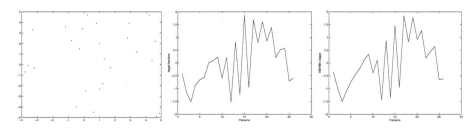

Fig. 2. Form left to right: Training set, synthetic two-variable function to approximate (limited data set) and RBFNN output ($c = 10$ clusters)

Table 1. RBFNN approximation errors (mean NRMSE). Limited two-variable function data set (up) and complete data set (down) (25 run).

Number of clusters	LRC	CFC	CFA	Netlab RBFNN
6	0.512	0.756	0.779	0.781
8	0.401		0.672	0.655
9	0.271	0.709	0.593	0.586
10	0.161		0.575	0.558
Number of clusters	LRC	CFC	CFA	Netlab RBFNN
6	0.613	0.838	0.812	0.838
8	0.491		0.713	0.799
9	0.277	0.812	0.708	0.782
10	0.185		0.705	0.762

5   Conclusions

We have presented a novel clustering algorithm to search for the centroids of the hidden units of the RBFNN's. Our model overcomes the limitations in [6] and further reduce the error rates with respect to [3] by developing an automated system in which a "prototype regression function" is built and inserted in the fuzzy c-means functional in order to adjust the prototypes according to both the input variables distribution and the regression function in the output space. The prototype regression function is built as a linear combination of local linear regression models [4], one for each cluster. The obtained results show clearly that our system outperforms RBFNN's trained with CFC and CFA.

References

1. Bezdek, J.C., Keller, J., Krisnapuram, R., Pal, N.R: Fuzzy Models and Algorithms for Pattern Recognition and Image Processing. Kluwer Academic Publisher, (1999).
2. Bishop, C.M.: Neural Networks for Pattern Recognition. Oxford University Press, New York, U.S.A., (1995).
3. Gonzales, J., Rojas, I., Pomares, H., Ortega,J., Prieto, A.: A New Clustering Technique for Function Approximation. IEEE Transaction On Neural Networks, **13**, NO. 1, (2002) pp. 132-142.
4. Hastie, T., Tibshirami, R., Friedman, J.: The Elements of Statistical Learning: Data Mining, Inference and Prediction. Springer-Verlag, (2001).
5. Nabney, I.: NETLAB: algorithms for pattern recognition.-(Advances in pattern recognition). Springer, (2001).
6. Pedrycz, W.: Conditional Fuzzy Clustering in the Design of Radial Basis Function Neural Networks. IEEE Transaction on Neural Networks, **9**, NO. 4, (1998) pp. 601-612.

An Iterative Algorithm for Fuzzy Quadratic Programming Problems

Silvio Giove

Department of Applied Mathematics, University Ca' Foscari of Venice,
Dorsoduro n. 3825/E - 30125 Venice, Italy
sgiove@unive.it

Abstract. This paper describes an interactive algorithm for fuzzy non linear programming problems. Based on some general results, an iterative algorithm is proposed, which modifies the admissible region in such a way as to increase at each step the global performance. The algorithm can be applied if a crisp sub-problem obtained by the original fuzzy one is solvable. This is the case of quadratic-linear target function with linear constraints. In this case, the numerical simulation showed good convergence property of the proposed procedure.

1 Introduction

Fuzzy mathematical programming problems (FMP for brevity) were quite studied in the specialized literature, see among other ones, [1], [8], [9], [14], [16], [21], [22]. In this paper, a particular FMP problem is considered. Some general properties are established, and an iterative algorithm is proposed, under the hypothesis that a solution exists for a particular parametric crisp problem obtained by the original fuzzy one. This algorithm is then applied to the quadratic-linear case. Finally a test simulation is proposed to a simple quadratic FMP.

2 Fuzzy Programming Problems

Let us consider the following FMP problem[1]:

$$\begin{cases} \widetilde{min}_x f(x) \\ g_i(x) \widetilde{\geq} 0 \\ x \in X \end{cases} \tag{1}$$

with $x \in R^n, i = 1, .., m, X \subseteq R^n$. The optimizing solution satisfies as best as possible both the target and the constraints, usually implying the maximization of the aggregated membership degrees of both the target function and the constraints. Let U be the admissible region of the crisp version of the problem (1).

---

[1] For a fuzzy approach to mathematical programming problem see, among other ones, [19], [21], [22].

V. Di Gesú, F. Masulli, and A. Petrosino (Eds.): WILF 2003, LNAI 2955, pp. 133–139, 2006.

Some suitable defined membership functions represent the satisfaction degrees of the target function, $\mu_0(f(x))$ and the ones of each constraint, $\mu_0(g_i(x))$. The FMP (1) can be converted into the following crisp non linear problem:

$$\max_{x \in X} C(x) \qquad (2)$$

where $C(x)$ represents the global satisfaction degree:

$$C(x) = \min\{\nu_0(x), \nu_1(x), ..., \nu_m(x)\} \qquad (3)$$

and $\nu_0(x) = \mu_0(f(x))$, $\nu_i(x) = \mu_i(g(x))$, for $i = 1, .., m$. This problem is equivalent to the following one, in the space R^{n+1}, see [19]:

$$\begin{cases} \max_{x,\lambda} \lambda \\ \nu_i(x) \geq \lambda, & i = 0, ..., m \\ x \in X \\ \lambda \in [0,1] \end{cases} \qquad (4)$$

The satisfaction degree assigned to each constraint and to the target function is usually represented by continuous and almost everywhere differentiable monotonic fuzzy numbers. In particular, $\mu_i(x)$ are increasing fuzzy numbers and $\mu_0(x)$ is a decreasing fuzzy number. The following piecewise linear is one of the most commonly used for monotonic membership functions[2]:

$$\mu_0(z) = \begin{cases} 1, & z \leq p_0 \\ \frac{z - c_0}{p_0 - c_0}, & p_0 < z \leq c_0 \\ 0, & z > c_0 \end{cases} \qquad (5)$$

$$\mu_0(z) = \begin{cases} 0, & z \leq p_i \\ \frac{z - p_i}{c_i - p_i}, & p_i < z \leq c_i \\ 1, & z > c_i \end{cases} \qquad (6)$$

with $p_i \leq c_i, i = 1, .., m$. Depending on the type of the target function and the constraints, many methods were proposed to solve the problem (4), see the quoted references. Here a new approach is proposed, based on an iterative algorithm. The following Section 3 describes the algorithm in the general case, while the Section 4 particularizes the procedure to the quadratic-linear case. Finally in the Section 5 a numerical example is described.

3   An Interactive Algorithm for Fuzzy Programming Problems

Usually, the non linear problem (4) is a difficult problem, sometimes impossible to be solved. In what follows, an iterative approach method is proposed, under

---

[2] The fuzzy numbers (5), are sometimes called S-type while the (6) are called Z-type, see [18].

the hypothesis that an associated (and usually easier) sub-problem can be solved. First of all, let us now consider the following crisp parametric problem P_λ, $\forall \lambda \in [0, 1], i = 1, .., m$:

$$P_\lambda = \begin{cases} \min_x f(x) \\ \nu_i(x) \geq \lambda \\ x \in X \end{cases} \tag{7}$$

Let Ω_λ be the admissible region of the problem (7), and x_λ the solution of the problem P_λ. If the free problem $\min_x f(x)$ admits the solution x_f with $\nu_0(x_f) \leq \min_i \{\nu_i(x_f)\}$, it is immediate to verify that such solution cannot be ameliorated, and $C(x_f) = \nu(x_f)$. Moreover, in what follows we shall suppose that such free problem admits a global minimum; the converse is clearly of poor interest.

The iterative optimization algorithm is based on the two following Propositions, that can be easily verified.

Proposition 1. If Ω_λ is a convex set, then $\lambda_1 \geq \lambda_2$ implies $\Omega_{\lambda_1} \subseteq \Omega_{\lambda_2}$.

Proposition 2. Let us suppose that the free crisp problem, $\min_{x \in X} f(x)$, admits a global minimum in correspondence of the point x_f with $\nu_0(x_f) > \min_i \{\nu_i(x_f)\}$. If Ω_λ is a convex set, $\forall \lambda \in [0, 1]$, and if $f(x)$ is a differentiable convex function, then the problem (4) admits a global optimal solution x^*, corresponding to a particular value $\lambda^* \in [0, 1]$. Furthermore $\nu_i(x^*) \geq \lambda^*$, $\forall i = 0, 1, ..., m$, and $\exists i \in \{0, 1, ..., m\} : \nu_i(x^*) = \nu_0(x^*) = \lambda^*$.

The optimization algorithm is based on the Proposition 1 and 2. Suppose that an algorithm exist to solve the parametric sub-problem $P_\lambda, \forall \lambda \in [0, 1]$. Let x_λ be the solution of the sub-problem P_λ. Then, if the hypotheses of the Proposition 2 are satisfied, the following iterative algorithm solves the FMP in a finite number of steps:

a) solve the free problem: $x_f = \operatorname{argmin}_x f(x)$; compute the values $\nu_0(x_f)$ and $\overline{\nu}(x_f) = \min\{\nu_1(x_f), .., \nu_m(x_f)\}$. If $\nu_0(x_f) \leq \overline{\nu}(x_f)$ then stop, the solution is optimal with satisfaction degree $C(x_0) = \nu_0(x_f)$, and cannot be ameliorated. Otherwise $(\nu_0(x_f) > \overline{\nu}(x_f))$, set $\lambda = 0, t = 0$,
b) solve the parametric problem P_λ, and compute the values

$$\nu_0(x_\lambda), \overline{\nu}(x_\lambda) = \min\{\nu_1(x_\lambda), \ldots, \nu_m(x_\lambda)\}$$

c) if $\nu_0(x_\lambda) > \overline{\nu}(x_\lambda)$ then reduce the admissible region, increasing suitably the value of λ (see the Proposition 1), and goto b),
d) if $\nu_0(x_\lambda) < \overline{\nu}(x_\lambda)$ then enlarge the admissible region, decreasing suitably the value of λ, and goto b),
e) if $\nu_0(x_\lambda) = \overline{\nu}(x_\lambda)$ then stop; the optimal solution is reached, with $x^* = x_\lambda$ and satisfaction degree $C(x^*) = \nu_0(x^*) = \overline{\nu}(x^*)$.

In the steps c) and d) the value of λ can be computed using a dichotomic method, for instance $\lambda \leftarrow \frac{(\nu_0(x_\lambda) + \overline{\nu}(x_\lambda))}{2}$. The condition $\nu_0(x_\lambda) = \overline{\nu}(x_\lambda)$ is supposed verified, as usual, when the inequality: $\mid \nu_0(x_\lambda) - \overline{\nu}(x_\lambda) \mid \leq \epsilon$ is satisfied, being ϵ a pre-fixed positive threshold. Moreover, the Propositions 1, 2 guarantee that the algorithm converges in a finite number of steps.

4   Application to the Fuzzy Quadratic-Linear Optimization Problem

Even if the proposed algorithm[3] could be used to solve a linear programming problem, its usefulness is emphasized in the non linear case. To this purpose, let us consider a particular non linear FMP, namely, a quadratic problem with linear constraints. In this case, the problem (1) is:

$$\begin{cases} \widetilde{\min}_x x'Qx + Dx \\ Ax - b \widetilde{\geq} 0 \\ x \geq 0 \end{cases} \tag{8}$$

Let us supposed satisfied the conditions for the convexity and for the existence of the global minimum for the crisp case problem. The region U is obviously a convex set. Furthermore, let the membership functions μ_0, μ_i be continuous and differentiable almost everywhere. Then from the Propositions 1 and 2 an optimal solution exists, and the proposed algorithm can be used. In fact, the crisp parametric problem is a quadratic-linear problem with linear constraints, and can be easily solved using standard techniques, for instance the *penalty* function approach [4], [10]. As a matter of fact, the sub-problem (7) becomes:

$$P_\lambda = \begin{cases} \min_x x'Qx + Dx \\ \nu_i(x) \geq \lambda \\ x \geq 0 \end{cases} \tag{9}$$

where $\nu_i(x) = \mu_i(A_i x - b_i)$, being A the i-th row of the matrix A and b_i the i-th element of the vector b. Let $I_\lambda(\mu_i)$ be the *level set* of the function $\mu_i(z)$:

$$I_\lambda(\mu_i) = \{z \in R^n : \mu_i(z) \geq \lambda\} \tag{10}$$

Then, since $\mu_i(z)$ is an increasing S-type fuzzy number, from (10) the constraint $\nu_i(x) = \mu_i(A_i x - b_i)$ can be written as $A_i x - b_i \geq \inf I_\lambda(\mu_i)$, so that (9) becomes:

$$P_\lambda = \begin{cases} \min_x x'Qx + Dx \\ A_i x - b_i \geq \inf I_\lambda(\mu_i) \\ x \geq 0 \end{cases} \tag{11}$$

that is a quadratic-linear problem with linear constraints. In the next Section the optimization algorithm will be applied to a simple instance of two-dimensional quadratic problem.

5   A Numerical Test

Let us consider the following quadratic-linear optimization problem:

---

[3] For the solution of fuzzy linear programming problems, see for instance [3], [12], [17] and the references therein. A different approach is the based on the *possibilistic* theory, see [2], [5], [8], [15].

$$\begin{cases} \widetilde{min}_{x,y}(x^2 + y^2) \\ x + y \underset{\sim}{\geq} 2 \\ x, y \geq 0 \end{cases} \tag{12}$$

The target function is differentiable and convex. Let the membership functions of the target function, $\mu_0(z)$, and of the (sole) constraints, $\mu_1(z)$ given by:

$$\mu_0(z) = e^{-0.5z^2} \tag{13}$$

$$\mu_1(z) = \begin{cases} 0, & z \leq 0 \\ 0.5z, & 0 < z \leq 2 \\ 1, & z > 2 \end{cases} \tag{14}$$

that is:

$$\nu_0(x, y) = e^{-0.5(x^2+y^2)} \tag{15}$$

$$\nu_1(x, y) = \begin{cases} 0, & x + y \leq 0 \\ 0.5(x + y), & 0 < x + y \leq 2 \\ 1, & x + y > 2 \end{cases} \tag{16}$$

Applying the iterative algorithm, the fuzzy problem (12) can be rapidly solved. With $\epsilon = 0.0001$ we obtain the results in the following Table 1, where each rows corresponds to a complete iteration of the procedure. The first column reports the iteration counter t, the second and the third ones contains the value of the minimizing solution, x_λ, y_λ[4]. The fourth column reports the value of the target function at the t-th iteration, while in the fifth, in the sixth and in the seventh columns appear the membership degrees of the objective function and of the constraint, together with their absolute difference. Finally, the last column reports the value of the parameter λ to be applied in the next iteration, λ_{t+1} .

Table 1. Results of the iterative algorithm

t	x_λ	y_λ	$f_\lambda = f(x_\lambda, y_\lambda)$	μ_o	μ_1	$\mid \mu_o - \mu_1 \mid$	λ_{t+1}
1	0	0	0	1	0	1	0.5
2	0.5	0.5	0.5	0.8825	0.5	0.3825	0.6912
3	0.6912	0.6912	0.9556	0.6334	0.6912	0.0578	0.6623
4	0.6623	0.6623	0.8773	0.6805	0.6623	0.0182	0.6714
5	0.6714	0.6714	0.9016	0.6660	0.6714	0.0054	0.6687
6	0.6687	0.6687	0.8943	0.6703	0.6687	0.0016	0.6695
7	0.6695	0.6695	0.8965	0.6690	0.6695	0.0005	0.6692
8	0.6692	0.6692	0.8958	0.6694	0.6692	0.0001	0.6693
9	0.6693	0.6693	0.8960	0.6693	0.6693	0.00005	-

The optimal solution is reached in 9 steps. Even if this example is rather simple, nevertheless a so rapid convergence is quite satisfactory. Let us observe that the optimal solution of the crisp problem is given by $(x = 1, y =$

---

[4] Note that $x_\lambda = y_\lambda$ since the associated parametric sub-problem (11) has the solution $(x_\lambda = \lambda, y_\lambda = \lambda), \forall \lambda \in [0, 1]$.

1), with optimal value equal to 2. In the fuzzy case, the solution is $(x^* = 0.6693, y^* = 0.6693)$ with optimal value $f^* = f(x^*, y^*) = 0.8960$, better than in the crisp case (for a minimization problem), despite an acceptable violation of the constraint.

6   Conclusion

In this paper a fuzzy programming problem is considered, where the satisfaction degrees of the target function and the constraints are computed by means of suitable fuzzy numbers. An iterative algorithm is proposed, under the hypothesis that a solution exists for a correspondent crisp sub-problem. Based on some natural hypotheses on the membership functions, on the target and on the constraints, the convergence of the algorithm is assured in a finite number of steps. The algorithm is then applied to the case of a fuzzy quadratic-linear problem with linear constraints, showing good numerical performances. Possible future extensions will consider other type of target function, like quasi-convex functions and the linear-fractional case [6], together with the application of the algorithm to fuzzy dynamic programming problems, for which some interesting suggestions can be found in [7], [11].

Acknowledgements

The author expresses his thanks to anonymous referees for the helpful comments and suggestions.

References

1. BELLMAN R.E., ZADEH L.A., Decision making in a fuzzy environment, *Management Sci.*, Ser. B 17, 141-164, 1970.
2. BUCKLEY J.J., FEURING T., HAYASHI Y., Possibilistic linear programming with triangular fuzzy numbers, *Fuzzy Sets and Systems*, 26, 135-138, 1988.
3. BUCKLEY J.J., FEURING T., HAYASHI Y., Multi-objective fuzzy fuzzified linear programming, *International Journal of Uncertainty, Fuzziness and Knowledge-Based Systems*, 9, 5, 605-621, 2001.
4. CANESTRELLI E., GIOVE S., Optimizing a quadratic function with linear coefficients, *Control and Cybernetics*, 20, 3, 25-36, 1991.
5. CANESTRELLI E., FULLER R., GIOVE S., Sensitivity analysis in possibilistic quadratic programming, *Fuzzy Sets and Systems*, 82, 51-56, 1996.
6. DUTTA D., TIWARI R.N., RAO J.R., Multiple objective linear fractional programming - A fuzzy set theoretic approach, *Fuzzy Sets and Systems*, 52, 39-45, 1992.
7. FILEV D., ANGELOV P., Fuzzy optimal control, *Fuzzy Sets and Systems*, 47, 151-156, 1992.
8. INUIGUCHI M., RAMIK J., Possibilistic linear programming: a brief review of fuzzy mathematical programming and a comparison with stochastic programming in portfolio selection problem, *Fuzzy Sets and Systems*, 111, 3-28, 2000.

9. INUIGUCHI M., ICHIHASHI H., TANAKA H., SLOWINSKI, R., TEGHEM, J. (EDS.), Fuzzy programming: a survey of recent developments, in: *Stochastic versus Fuzzy Approaches to Multiobjective Mathematical Programming under Uncertainty*, Kluwer Academic Publishers, 45-68, 1990.

10. JAMISON K.D., LODWICK W.A., Fuzzy linear programming using a penalty method, *Fuzzy Sets and Systems*, 119, 97-110, 2001.

11. KACPRZYK J., ESOGBUE A.O., Fuzzy dynamic programming: main developments and applications, *Fuzzy Sets and Systems*, 81, 31-45, 1996.

12. KUWANO H., On the fuzzy multi-objective linear programming problem: goal programming approach, *Fuzzy Sets and Systems*, 82, 57-64, 1996.

13. LEVARY R.R., Optimal control problems with multiple goal objectives, *Optimal Control Applications & Methods*, 7, 201-207, 1986.

14. LI H.-L., YU C.-S., A fuzzy multiobjective program with quasi-concave membership functions and fuzzy coefficients, *Fuzzy Sets and Systems*, 109, 59-81, 2000.

15. LUHANDJULA M.K., On possibilistic programming, *Fuzzy Sets and Systems*, 18, 15-30, 1986.

16. MALECKI H.R., TATA M.,MASHINCHI M., Linear programming with fuzzy variables, *Fuzzy Sets and Systems*, 109, 21-33, 2000.

17. TANAKA H., ICHIHASHI H., ASAI K., A formulation of fuzzy linear programming problem based on comparison of fuzzy numbers, *Control and Cybernetics*, 13, 3, 185-194, 1984.

18. VON ALTROCK C., *Fuzzy logic and neurofuzzy applications explained*, Prentice Hall, New York, 1995.

19. YAGER R.R., ZADEH L.A (EDS.), *An introduction to fuzzy logic applications in intelligence systems*, Kluwer Academic Publishers, Boston, 1992.

20. ZADEH L.A., Fuzzy sets, *Inform. Control*, 8, 338-353, 1965.

21. ZIMMERMANN H. J., Fuzzy programming and linear programming with several objective functions, *Fuzzy Sets and Systems*, 1, 45-55, 1978.

22. ZIMMERMANN H. J., Fuzzy set theory and mathematical programming, in: *Fuzzy Sets Theory and Applications*, A. Jones et al. Eds., Reidel, Dortrecht, 99-114, 1986.

A General Defuzzification Method for Fuzzy Total Cost in an Inventory Without Backorder Case

Gisella Facchinetti[1] and Nicoletta Pacchiarotti[2]

[1] Department of Economics,
University of Modena and Reggio Emilia, Italy
[2] Department of Pure and Applied Mathematics,
University of Modena and Reggio Emilia, Italy

Abstract. We hereby consider the total cost in an inventory without backorder model, where the cost of storing and the total demand over the planning time period are triangular fuzzy numbers: therefore the total cost is a triangular fuzzy number too. In order to obtain a crisp optimal solution, we use a defuzzification method called Weighted Average Value (WAV), which is more general than others presented by several authors. Such a solution coincides with the usual one, if coefficients collapse to real numbers.

1   Introduction

Many authors face problems related to economic models, studying models where well-known optimisation methods are involved. Very often real problems require a trade off between representations which are very precise and accurate, such as the ones stemming from numerical evaluations, and others which are meaningful to humans, even if not numerical, but given in a vague way. These two kinds of representations are so to say antagonist, because the more accurate they are, the less understandable they are. Actually, variables and parameters, involved in the model, may be given in an imprecise way, hence it is suitable to deal with them in a fuzzy sense. In order to solve the optimisation problem in a fuzzy context, generally the extension principle can be widely used [5, 13, 17]. The procedure is much more direct if the function to be optimised is linear with respect to the parameters to be fuzzified [16, 18].

Most papers dealing with this case proceed as follows: if the optimisation problem they face is the minimization of a cost function, they study the total cost in the crisp case and find the optimal solution which minimizes the cost. Then, some variables, or parameters, may be fuzzified using triangular or trapezoidal fuzzy numbers; this renders the function to be minimized a fuzzy number too. At this step this fuzzy number is defuzzified by "centroid" or "signed distance" and the crisp function obtained is finally optimised. Moreover, the optimal point and the optimal value are compared with the solution obtained in the crisp case. This kind of procedure is possible as, if fuzzy numbers are of triangular type, either

V. Di Gesú, F. Masulli, and A. Petrosino (Eds.): WILF 2003, LNAI 2955, pp. 140–147, 2006.
© Springer-Verlag Berlin Heidelberg 2006

the "centroid" and the "signed distance" method are linear and the derivative is a linear operator too.

Following Yao and Chiang [18], we study the problem of inventory without backorder in a fuzzy sense and present a defuzzification method which generalizes the "centroid" and the "signed distance" they use: the problem is linear w.r.to the parameters we fuzzify. In particular, the total cost is a function of the order quantity per cycle q, and the inventory without backorder context produces that it depends on several parameters, like the cost of storing a and the total demand s over the planning time period T. In practice, the total demand s may often be approximately estimated only and if we consider it like a random variable, it seems difficult to know its probability distribution. Therefore, the total demand may lie in an interval and the estimate value s belongs to it; moreover, the cost of storing a may fluctuate in a perfect competitive market. Hence the fuzzy total cost is linear in a and s and is a triangular fuzzy number. We hereby study the same crisp problem, but we use a more general defuzzification method, which allows us to map a fuzzy number on a real value inside its support. This method, called Weighted Average Value (WAV), was introduced by Campos-Gonzales ([3, 4, 11]) as a ranking function and then it was presented in a systematic way by Facchinetti ([7]). The WAV depends on two real parameters, λ and r : λ is connected with the pessimistic or optimistic point of view of the decision maker, r depends on the preference of the decision maker to give more or less weight to different subsets of the support. The choice may depend on subjective elements, on the nature of the problem and on the sensitivity of the decision-maker. It is easy to demonstrate that the "centroid" and the "signed distance" are particular cases of WAV.

Even in this more general scenario, we find the optimal solution of the fuzzy case and prove that the crisp solution may be seen as a particular case of the fuzzy one.

Finally, we study the behaviour of WAV solution with respect to parameters λ and r and we present a numerical example.

2   Total Cost in an Inventory Without Backorder Case

Yao and Chiang ([18]) consider the following problem :

In a crisp context a total cost function for an inventory without backorder problem is defined as follows:

$$F(q) = \left(at_q \frac{q}{2} + c\right) \frac{s}{q} \qquad q > 0 \qquad (1)$$

where: T is the length of the plan, a is the cost of storing one unit per day, c is the cost of placing an order, s is the total demand over the planning time T, t_q is the length of a cycle, q is the order quantity per cycle.

As $\frac{q}{t_q} = \frac{s}{T}$, the total cost function becomes

$$F(q) = aT\frac{q}{2} + c\frac{s}{q} \qquad q > 0 \qquad (2)$$

It is easy to see that the quantity which minimizes the total cost is

$$q^\star = \sqrt{\frac{2cs}{aT}} \qquad (3)$$

and the minimum cost is:

$$F(q^\star) = \sqrt{2cTas} \qquad (4)$$

3   Weighted Average Value (WAV)

We remember that a fuzzy set $\tilde{u}$ is defined by a generalized characteristic function $\mu_{\tilde{u}}(.)$, called membership function, defined on a universe X, which assumes values in $[0, 1]$. In the following, X denotes a non empty subset of R.

Definition 1. The fuzzy set $\tilde{u}$ is a fuzzy number iff:
1) $\forall \alpha \in [0,1]$ the set $u^\alpha = \{x \in R \ : \ \mu_{\tilde{u}}(x) \geq \alpha\} = [u_1^\alpha, u_2^\alpha]$, which is called α -cut of $\tilde{u}$, is a convex set.
2) $\mu_{\tilde{u}}(.)$ is an upper-semicontinuous function.
3) $Supp(\tilde{u}) = \{x \in R : \mu_{\tilde{u}}(x) > 0\}$ is a bounded set in R.
4) $\exists x \in Supp(\tilde{u})$ such that $\mu_{\tilde{u}}(x) = 1$

Definition 2. A triangular fuzzy number, $\tilde{u} = (u_1 - \Delta_1, u_1, u_1 + \Delta_2)$, $\Delta_1 > 0$, $\Delta_2 > 0, 0 \leq u_1 - \Delta_1$ is represented by the membership function

$$\mu_{\tilde{u}}(x) = \begin{cases} 0 & x \leq u_1 - \Delta_1 \\ 1 + \dfrac{x - u_1}{\Delta_1} & u_1 - \Delta_1 < x \leq u_1 \\ 1 + \dfrac{u_1 - x}{\Delta_2} & u_1 < x \leq u_1 + \Delta_2 \\ 0 & x > u_1 + \Delta_2 \end{cases}$$

We denote the set of fuzzy numbers by FN, and triangular fuzzy numbers by TFN.

Definition 3. We call " I- evaluation function" a real function $\phi : I \to R$, where I is the set of all closed bounded intervals A of R, i.e. $A = [a_1, a_2], a_1, a_2 \in R, a_1 \leq a_2$.
    In the following, we'll write $\phi(A) = \phi([a_1, a_2]) = \phi(a_1, a_2)$.
    In general, it is not possible to request a priori any property on $\phi(.)$, but it seems reasonable to consider functions which are increasing in both variables and have some regularity properties (i.e., $\phi \in C^{(1)}$). For instance, we can consider the family $\{\phi_\lambda\}_{\lambda \in [0,1]}$ of linear functions

$$\phi_\lambda(A) = \lambda a_2 + (1 - \lambda) a_1, \lambda \in [0, 1]. \qquad (5)$$

In a decisional context, the decision maker may choose the parameter λ, according to his point of view be optimistic or pessimistic.

Definition 4. We call Weighted Average Value (WAV) of $\tilde{u} \in FN$, with respect to the additive measure S on $[0, 1]$ and the parameter $\lambda \in [0, 1]$,   the value

$$M_\lambda(S, \tilde{u}) = \int_0^1 \phi_\lambda(u^\alpha) \, dS \tag{6}$$

where $\phi_\lambda(.)$ is the I-evaluation function (5) on the α-cut of $\tilde{u}$. Notice that

$$M_\lambda(S, \tilde{u}) = \lambda M^\star(S, \tilde{u}) + (1 - \lambda) M_\star(S, \tilde{u}) \tag{7}$$

where

$$M_\star(S, \tilde{u}) = \int_0^1 \phi(u_1^\alpha) \, dS \quad \text{and} \quad M^\star(S, \tilde{u}) \int_0^1 \phi(u_2^\alpha) \, dS \tag{8}$$

As additive measure, we can use a Stieltjes measure S defined through the function $s(\alpha) = \alpha^r, \forall r > 0,$ then $S([a, b]) = b^r - a^r$, $\forall a, b \in [0, 1]$; in this case, WAV depends on two parameters λ and r and has the following expression

$$M_\lambda(r, \tilde{u}) = r \int_0^1 \alpha^{r-1} \phi_\lambda(u^\alpha) \, d\alpha = M_\lambda(S, \tilde{u}) = \lambda M^\star(r, \tilde{u}) + (1-\lambda) M_\star(r, \tilde{u}) \tag{9}$$

where

$$M_\star(r, \tilde{u}) = r \int_0^1 \alpha^{r-1} u_1^\alpha \, d\alpha \quad \text{and} \quad M^\star(r, \tilde{u}) = r \int_0^1 \alpha^{r-1} u_2^\alpha \, d\alpha \tag{10}$$

The choice of r is connected with these types of preferences: with $r > 1$, S gives more weight to the high values of $\alpha \in [0, 1]$; with $r < 1$, S gives more weight to the low values of $\alpha \in [0, 1]$ and with $r = 1$ we obtain a linear preference and S gives the same weight to all the values $\alpha \in [0, 1]$.

In the last case we have a particular measure, which is the Lebesgue measure $L(]a, b[) = b - a \; \forall a, b \in [0, 1]$. It is easy to see that for particular choices of λ and S (10) coincides with known comparison indexes (see [1], [2], [3], [4], [6], [10], [14], [15]). For more details see [7]. In particular, if $\lambda = 1/2$ and $r = 1$, WAV coincides with the "signed distance" ; if $\lambda = r = 1/2$, and $\tilde{u} \in TFN$, WAV coincides with the "centroid". Both these defuzzificators are used by Yao and Chiang in [18]. As already said, the decision maker chooses particular values of r according to his preference towards particular subsets of the support. In fact, there is an immediate connection between $[M_\star(r, \tilde{u}), M^\star(r, \tilde{u})]$ and $\tilde{u}$: denote by $\tilde{u}^r$ the fuzzy number with membership function $\mu_{\tilde{u}^r} = x^r \circ \mu_{\tilde{u}}$. We have $[M_\star(r, \tilde{u}), M^\star(r, \tilde{u})] = [M_\star(1, \tilde{u}^r), M^\star(1, \tilde{u}^r)]$. If $\tilde{u} \in$ TFN, the previous interval is a subset of $Supp \; \tilde{u}$, which is the projection on the real axe of the segment we obtain cutting $\tilde{u}$ at the level $\bar{\alpha} = 1 - \int_0^1 \alpha^r \, d\alpha = \dfrac{r}{r + 1}$. A consequence of this choice is that the defuzzified value lies in a subset of the support; such a subset becomes as much narrow as the value of r increases.

4   Main Properties of WAV

Theorem 1. $M_\lambda(r, \tilde{u})$ *is a linear function, positively homogeneous on the space of the fuzzy number TFN. (see [7])*

If $\tilde{u} = (u_1 - \Delta_1, u_1, u_1 + \Delta_2) \in TFN$ it easy to see that WAV is

$$M_\lambda(r, \tilde{u}) = \lambda M^\star(r, \tilde{u}) + (1 - \lambda)M_\star(r, \tilde{u}) = u_1 + \frac{\lambda \Delta_2 - (1 - \lambda)\Delta_1}{r + 1} \qquad (11)$$

In this case we can, in natural way, extend $M_\lambda(r, \tilde{u})$ and define it in $r = 0$ as $M_\lambda(0, \tilde{u})$.
For any $\tilde{u} \in TFN$, we can consider $M_\lambda(r, \tilde{u})$ just as a function $g_{\tilde{u}}(\lambda, r)$ defined on $D = [0, 1] \times [0, +\infty[$.

Property 1. $g_{\tilde{u}}(\lambda, r)$ is continuous on D, increasing with respect to the parameter $\lambda \in [0, 1], \forall \tilde{u} \in TFN$.

Property 2. $g_{\tilde{u}}(\lambda, r)$ is

i)increasing with respect to the parameter $r \geq 0$ if $\lambda < \dfrac{\Delta_1}{\Delta_1 + \Delta_2}$,

ii)decreasing with respect to the parameter $r \geq 0$ if $\lambda > \dfrac{\Delta_1}{\Delta_1 + \Delta_2}$,

iii) if $\lambda = \dfrac{\Delta_1}{\Delta_1 + \Delta_2}$, then, $g_{\tilde{u}}(\lambda, r) = u_1$.

These properties lead us to the conclusion that $M_\lambda(r, \tilde{u})$ attains its minimum for $\lambda = 0$, for every $r \geq 0$ fixed, and if $\lambda = 0$, we have $\lambda = 0 < \frac{\Delta_1}{\Delta_1 + \Delta_2}$. That is the minimum value of $M_\lambda(r, \tilde{u})$ w.r.to (λ, r) is $M_0(0, \tilde{u}) = u_1 - \Delta_1$.
Moreover, the "centroid" can be obtained as $M_{0.5}(0.5, \tilde{u})$ and the "signed distance" as $M_{0.5}(1, \tilde{u})$. Since $\lambda = 0.5$ is fixed, if we wish compare their values, we may observe that if $\Delta_2 < \Delta_1$, then $\lambda = 0.5 < \frac{\Delta_1}{\Delta_1 + \Delta_2}$ and $M_{0.5}(r, \tilde{u})$ is increasing w.r.to r ; consequently the "centroid" method $M_{0.5}(0.5, \tilde{u})$ gives a smaller value than the "signed distance", $M_{0.5}(1, \tilde{u})$. On the contrary if $\Delta_2 > \Delta_1$, we have that $M_{0.5}(1, \tilde{u}) < M_{0.5}(0.5, \tilde{u})$. If $\Delta_1 = \Delta_2$, then $M_{0.5}(0.5, \tilde{u}) = M_{0.5}(1, \tilde{u}), \forall \tilde{u} \in TFN$.

5   Fuzzy Total Cost and Optimal Solution

In a real problem it is difficult to specify exactly the total demand s in a plan period T; on the contrary, the decision maker can quite easily place this value in an interval $[s - \Delta_1, s + \Delta_2]$, where $0 \leq \Delta_1 \leq s, \Delta_2 \geq 0$.
For this reason, following Yao-Chiang, we consider the total demand as a triangular fuzzy number (t.f.n.)

$$\tilde{s} = (s - \Delta_1, s, s + \Delta_2), 0 \leq \Delta_1 \leq s, \Delta_2 \geq 0 \qquad (12)$$

Similarly, we consider that the cost of storing one unit per day a in a plan period T may fluctuate in an analogous interval and we fuzzify it as follows :

$$\tilde{a} = (a - \Delta_3, a, a + \Delta_4), 0 \leq \Delta_3 \leq a, \Delta_4 \geq 0 \qquad (13)$$

Let $\otimes$ be the usual product of a $\tilde{u} \in TFN$ and a positive number and $\oplus$ the usual sum on TFN; then the fuzzy total cost in an inventory without backorder model is :

$$F_q(\tilde{a}, \tilde{s}) = \left(\frac{Tq}{2} \otimes \tilde{a}\right) \oplus \left(\frac{c}{q} \otimes \tilde{s}\right) = \tilde{F}(q) = (F_1, F_2, F_3) \tag{14}$$

where

$$F_1 = \frac{Tq}{2}(a - \Delta_3) + \frac{c}{q}(s - \Delta_1) \;;\; F_2 = \frac{Tq}{2}a + \frac{c}{q}s \;;\; F_3 = \frac{Tq}{2}(a + \Delta_4) + \frac{c}{q}(s + \Delta_2), \tag{15}$$

The linearity in $\tilde{a}$ and $\tilde{s}$ of $F_q(\tilde{a}, \tilde{s})$, and the linearity of $M_\lambda(r, \tilde{u})$ produce that:

$$M_\lambda(r, \tilde{F}(q)) = \frac{Tq}{2} M_\lambda(r, \tilde{a}) + \frac{c}{q} M_\lambda(r, \tilde{s}) \tag{16}$$

It is easy to check that equation (16) has exactly the same shape than the characteristic equation (2) of the crisp case, provided that we change each crisp coefficient with the WAV of the corresponding fuzzy coefficient. Consequently, we can proceed through the same path and observe that $M_\lambda(r, \tilde{F}(q))$ is a crisp function of q parameterized by λ and r, so we can derive it and compute its point of minimum and the minimum cost

$$\hat{q}_{\lambda,r} = \sqrt{\frac{2cM_\lambda(r, \tilde{s})}{TM_\lambda(r, \tilde{a})}} \;;\; M_\lambda(r, \tilde{F}(\hat{q}_{\lambda,r})) = \sqrt{2cT} \sqrt{M_\lambda(r, \tilde{s})M_\lambda(r, \tilde{a})} \tag{17}$$

which have once again the same shape than the crisp solution $q^\star$ and the crisp minimum total cost $F(q^\star)$, (see (3) and (4)); if a and s are crisp, $\hat{q}_{\lambda,r} = q^\star$ and $F(q^\star) = M_\lambda(r, \tilde{F}(\hat{q}_{\lambda,r}))$.

Remark 1. In order to compare the crisp result with the defuzzified one, we may compute the difference

$$M_\lambda(r, \tilde{F}(q)) - F(q) = \frac{\frac{Tq}{2}(\lambda\Delta_4 - (1-\lambda)\Delta_3) + \frac{c}{q}(\lambda\Delta_2 - (1-\lambda)\Delta_1)}{r+1} \tag{18}$$

$$= \frac{\lambda(\frac{Tq}{2}\Delta_4 + \frac{c}{q}\Delta_2) - (1-\lambda)(\frac{Tq}{2}\Delta_3 + \frac{c}{q}\Delta_1)}{r+1} = \frac{\lambda\Theta_2 - (1-\lambda)\Theta_1}{r+1}$$

where $\Theta_1 = (\frac{Tq}{2}\Delta_3 + \frac{c}{q}\Delta_1)$ and $\Theta_2 = (\frac{Tq}{2}\Delta_4 + \frac{c}{q}\Delta_2)$. Therefore the last equality states that $\forall r \geq 0$ the difference $M_\lambda(r, \tilde{F}(q)) - F(q)$ lies in the interval $[-\Theta_1, \Theta_2]$ and this difference is zero if and only if the convex combination with parameter λ of the two values $-\Theta_1$ and Θ_2 is zero.

In the general case, it is not easy to find a simple evaluation for this difference. On the contrary, if $\lambda = 0.5$, then $M_\lambda(r, \tilde{F}(q))$ is close to $F(q)$ when $|\Delta_2 - \Delta_1| \to 0$ and $|\Delta_4 - \Delta_3| \to 0$; moreover they coincide if the t.f.n. are isosceles.

Remark 2. If we are interested in finding the minimum of $M_\lambda(r, \tilde{F}(\hat{q}_{\lambda,r}))$ as a function of parameters λ and r, we may proceed as follows.

Property 1 states that $M_\lambda(r, \tilde{u})$ attains its minimum for $\lambda = 0$, for every fixed $r \geq 0$; applying Property 2 to the case $\lambda = 0$, we obtain that the minimum value of $M_0(r, \tilde{u})$ with respect to r is $M_0(0, \tilde{u})$. Finally, as $h(t) = \sqrt{t}$ is an increasing function, the minimum of $M_\lambda(r, \tilde{F}(\hat{q}_{\lambda,r}))$ is

$$M_0(0, \tilde{F}(\hat{q}_{0,0})) = \sqrt{2cT}\sqrt{(a - \Delta_1)(s - \Delta_3)}. \tag{19}$$

6 A Numerical Example

We consider in the total cost function (2) the same numerical values considered in [18]: $a = 3$, $c = 4$, $s = 30$ $T = 5$; then $q^\star = 4$ and $F(q^\star) = 60$.

Let us change the crisp total demand s in the t.f.n. $\tilde{s} = (s - \Delta_1, s, s + \Delta_2)$ and the crisp cost of storing a in the t.f.n. $a = (a - \Delta_3, a, a + \Delta_4)$ and examine how the point of minimum and the minimum cost depend on the spreads.

If $\lambda = r = \dfrac{1}{2}$ or $\lambda = \dfrac{1}{2}$ and $r = 1$, the WAV coincides respectively with the centroid or with the signed distance and the corresponding minimum values can be read in [18], Table 1. If $\lambda = \dfrac{1}{3}$ and $r = 2$ the values varies according Table (20).

Δ_1	Δ_2	Δ_3	Δ_4	$\hat{q}_{\lambda,r}$	$M_\lambda(r, \tilde{F}(\hat{q}_{\lambda,r}))$	
1	1.5	1	1.5	4.03	59.3868	
1	2	1	2	4.00	60.0000	
1	2.5	1	2.5	3.97	60.6090	
2	1	1	2	3.98	59.6657	
2	1.5	1.5	2	4.06	58.6052	(20)
2	2.5	2.5	3	4.15	57.5744	
1	1.5	1.5	1	4.15	57.6815	
1	2	2	1	4.24	56.5685	
1	2.5	2.5	1	4.34	55.4287	
2	3	1.5	1.5	4.11	58.2014	

7 Conclusions

In this paper we illustrate two different topics: at first, that WAV contains as particular cases "centroid" and "signed distance" and many other defuzzificators known in literature. Secondly, this more general defuzzification method, used in a fuzzy problem of inventory without backorder, generalizes the results obtained by Yao and Chiang [18] and presents some more general information. These results are due to the linearity of the cost function with respect the variables to fuzzify and to the "linearity" of the WAV. Every linear defuzzification process applied to linear functions will produce analogous results. So many other papers can be generalized following this idea. In order to obtain innovative results in this field, we think it is suitable to work either with functions which are not linear in the fuzzy variable (see [5], [8], [13], [16]), or (and) with not linear defuzzificators (see [9]). We are still studying these two topics.

References

1. Adamo, J.M. : "Fuzzy decision trees". Fuzzy Sets and Systems. **4** (1980), 207-219.
2. Bortolan, G., Degani, R. : "A review of some methods for ranking fuzzy numbers". Fuzzy Set and Systems **15** (1985), 1-19.
3. Campos L.M., Gonzalez, A. : "A subjective approach for ranking fuzzy numbers". Fuzzy Set and Systems **29** (1989), 145-153
4. Campos, L.M., Gonzalez, A. : "Further contributions to the study of the Average Value for ranking Fuzzy Numbers". Int. Journal of Approximate reasoning **10** (1994), 135-153.
5. Chang S.C., Yao J.S. : " Economic reorder point for fuzzy backorder quantity". European Journal of Operational Research **109** (1998), 183-202.
6. Facchinetti, G., Ghiselli Ricci, R., Muzzioli S.: "Note on ranking fuzzy triangular numbers". International Journal of Intelligent Systems.**13** (1998), 613-622.
7. Facchinetti, G. : "Ranking functions induced by weighted average of fuzzy numbers". Fuzzy Optimisation and Decision Making, **1** (2002), n.3 313-327. Kluwer Accademic Publishers,
8. Facchinetti, G., Giove, S., Pacchiarotti, N. :" Optimisation of a non linear fuzzy function". Soft Computing **6** (2001), Iss.6 (2002), 476-480.
9. Facchinetti, G., Ghiselli Ricci, R. : "A characterization of a general class of ranking functions on triangular fuzzy numbers". Fuzzy Set and Systems, (2003) to appear.
10. Fortemps, P., Roubens, M., : "Ranking and defuzzification methods based on area compensation". Fuzzy sets and Systems **82** (1996), 319-330.
11. Gonzalez, A. : " A study of the ranking function approach through mean values". Fuzzy Set and Systems **35** (1990), 29-41.
12. Kaufmann, A., Gupta, M.M.: "Introduction to fuzzy arithmetic". Van Nostrand Reinhold Company, 1985.
13. Lee, H.M., Yao, J.S. : "Economic order quantity in fuzzy sense for inventory without backorder model". Fuzzy sets and Systems **111** (1998), 465-495.
14. Tsumura, Y., Terano, T. and Sugeno, M. : "Fuzzy fault tree analysis, Summary of papers on general fuzzy problems". Report n7 (1981). 21-25.
15. Yager, R.R : "A procedure for Ordering Fuzzy Subsets over the unit interval". Information Sciences **24** (1981), 143-161.
16. Yao, J.S. and Chang, S.C. : "Economic principle on profit in the fuzzy sense". Fuzzy Set and Systems **117** (2001), 113-127.
17. Yao, J.S., Lee, H.M.: "Fuzzy inventory with or without backorder quantity with trapezoidal fuzzy number". Fuzzy Set and Systems **105** (2000), 311-337.
18. Yao, J.S., Chiang, J. : " Inventory without backorder with fuzzy total cost and fuzzy storing defuzzified by centroid and signed distance". European Journal of Operational Research **148** (2003), 401-409.

Fuzzy Rough Sets and
Multiple-Premise Gradual Decision Rules

Salvatore Greco[1], Masahiro Inuiguchi[2], and Roman Slowinski[3]

[1] Faculty of Economics, University of Catania, Corso Italia, 55,
95129 Catania, Italy
salgreco@unict.it
[2] Graduate School of Engineering Science, Osaka University, 1-3, Machikaneyama,
Toyonaka, Osaka 560-8531, Japan
inuiguti@sys.es.osaka-u.ac.jp
[3] Institute of Computing Science, Poznan University of Technology, 60-965 Poznan, and
Institute for Systems Research, Polish Academy of Sciences, 01-447 Warsaw, Poland
roman.slowinski@cs.put.poznan.pl

Abstract. We propose a new fuzzy rough set approach which, differently from most known fuzzy set extensions of rough set theory, does not use any fuzzy logical connectives (t-norm, t-conorm, fuzzy implication). As there is no rationale for a particular choice of these connectives, avoiding this choice permits to reduce the part of arbitrary in the fuzzy rough approximation. Another advantage of the new approach is that it is based on the ordinal properties of fuzzy membership degrees only. The concepts of fuzzy lower and upper approximations are thus proposed, creating a base for induction of fuzzy decision rules having syntax and semantics of gradual rules. The proposed approach to rule induction is also interesting from the viewpoint of philosophy supporting data mining and knowledge discovery, because it is concordant with the method of concomitant variations by John Stuart Mill. The decision rules are induced from lower and upper approximations defined for positive and negative relationships between credibility degrees of multiple premises, on one hand, and conclusion, on the other hand.

1 Introduction

It has been acknowledged by different studies that fuzzy set theory and rough set theory are complementary because of handling different kinds of uncertainty. Fuzzy sets deal with possibilistic uncertainty, connected with imprecision of states, perceptions and preferences (Dubois, Prade, Yager 1997). Rough sets deal, in turn, with uncertainty following from ambiguity of information (Pawlak 1991). The two types of uncertainty can be encountered together in real-life problems. For this reason, many approaches have been proposed to combine fuzzy sets with rough sets (see for example Dubois, Prade 1992).

Let us remember that fuzzy sets (Zadeh 1965) are based on the idea that, given a universe U, the membership of $y \in U$ in a set X from U admits a graduality represented by means of function $\mu_X : U \to [0,1]$ such that $\mu_X(y)=0$ means non-membership, $\mu_X(y)=1$ means full membership, and for all intermediate values the greater $\mu_X(y)$, the more

V. Di Gesú, F. Masulli, and A. Petrosino (Eds.): WILF 2003, LNAI 2955, pp. 148–163, 2006.

credible the membership of y in X. An analogous idea of graduality is introduced in fuzzy logic with respect to the truth value $v(p)$ of a proposition p such that $v(p)=0$ means that p is definitely false, $v(p)=1$ that p is definitely true and for all intermediate values the greater $v(p)$, the more credible the truth of p. In the context of fuzzy sets, fuzzy connectives, being functions from $[0,1]\times[0,1]$ to $[0,1]$, represent conjunction (t-norm), disjunction (t-conorm) or implication (fuzzy implications such as S-implication or R-implication) (see, e.g., (Klement, Mesiar, Pap 2000)).

Let us also remember that rough set theory (Pawlak 1982, 1991) is based on the idea that some knowledge (data, information) is available about elements of a set. For example, knowledge about patients suffering from a certain disease may contain information about body temperature, blood pressure, etc. All patients described by the same information are indiscernible in view of the available knowledge and form groups of similar cases. These groups are called elementary sets and can be considered as elementary building blocks of the available knowledge about patients. Elementary sets can be combined into compound concepts. Any union of elementary sets is called crisp set, while other sets are referred to as rough set. Each rough set has boundary line cases, i.e. objects which, in view of the available knowledge, cannot be classified with certainty as members of the set or of its complement. Therefore, in the rough set approach, any set is associated with a pair of crisp sets called the lower and the upper approximation. Intuitively, the lower approximation consists of all objects which certainly belong to the set and the upper approximation contains all objects which possibly belong to the set. The difference between the upper and the lower approximation constitutes the boundary region of the rough set.

The main preoccupation in almost all the studies conjugating rough sets with fuzzy sets was related to a fuzzy extension of Pawlak's definition of lower and upper approximations using fuzzy connectives. In fact, there is no rule for the choice of the "right" connective, so this choice is always arbitrary to some extent.

Another drawback of fuzzy extensions of rough sets involving fuzzy connectives is that they are based on cardinal properties of membership degrees. In consequence, the result of these extensions is sensitive to order preserving transformation of membership degrees. For example, consider the t-conorm of Lukasiewicz as fuzzy connective; it may be used in the definition of both fuzzy lower approximation (to build fuzzy implication) and fuzzy upper approximation (as a fuzzy counterpart of a union). The t-conorm of Lukasiewicz is defined as:

$$T^*(\alpha,\beta) = \min\{\alpha+\beta, 1\}$$

$T^*(\alpha,\beta)$ can be interpreted as follows. If $\alpha=\mu_X(z)$ represents the membership of $z \in U$ in set X and $\beta=\mu_Y(z)$ represents the membership of z in set Y, then $T^*(\alpha,\beta)$ expresses the membership of z in set $X \cup Y$. Given two fuzzy propositions p and q, putting $v(p)=\alpha$ and $v(q)=\beta$, $T^*(\alpha,\beta)$ can be interpreted also as $v(p \vee q)$, the truth value of the proposition $p \vee q$.

Let us consider the following values of arguments:

$$\alpha=0.5,\ \beta=0.3,\ \gamma=0.2,\ \delta=0.1$$

and their order preserving transformation:

$$\alpha'=0.4,\ \beta'=0.3,\ \gamma'=0.2,\ \delta'=0.05.$$

The values of the t-conorm are in the two cases as follows:

$$T^*(\alpha,\delta) = 0.6, \qquad T^*(\beta,\gamma) = 0.5, \qquad T^*(\alpha',\delta') = 0.45, \qquad T^*(\beta',\gamma') = 0.5.$$

One can see that the order of the results has changed after the order preserving transformation of the arguments. This means that the Lukasiewicz t-conorm takes into account not only the ordinal properties of the membership degrees, but also their cardinal properties. A natural question arises: is it reasonable to expect from membership degree a cardinal content instead of ordinal only? Or, in other words, is it realistic to claim that a human is able to say in a meaningful way not only that

a)   "object x belongs to fuzzy set X more likely than object y" (or "proposition p is more credible than proposition q")

but even something like

b)   "object x belongs to fuzzy set X two times more likely than object y" (or "proposition p is two times more credible than proposition q")?

We claim that it is safer to consider information of type a), because information of type b) is rather meaningless for a human (see Marchant 2004).

The above doubt about the cardinal content of the fuzzy membership degree shows the need for methodologies which consider the imprecision in perception typical for fuzzy sets but avoid as much as possible meaningless transformation of information through fuzzy connectives.

The approach we propose for fuzzy extension of rough sets takes into account the above request. It avoids arbitrary choice of fuzzy connectives and not meaningful operations on membership degrees. Our approach belongs to the minority of fuzzy extensions of the rough set concept that do not involve fuzzy connectives and cardinal interpretation of membership degrees. Within this minority, it is related to the approach of Nakamura and Gao (1991) using α-cuts on fuzzy similarity relation between objects.

We propose a methodology of fuzzy rough approximation that infers the most cautious conclusion from available imprecise information. In particular, we observe that any approximation of knowledge about Y using knowledge about X is based on positive or negative relationships between premises and conclusions, i.e:

i)   "the more x is X, the more it is Y" (positive relationship),
ii) "the more x is X, the less it is Y" (negative relationship).

The following simple relationships illustrate i) and ii): "the larger the market share of a company, the greater its profit" (positive relationship) and "the greater the debt of a company, the smaller its profit" (negative relationship). These relationships have been already considered within fuzzy set theory under the name of *gradual decision rules* (Dubois, Prade 1992). Recently, Greco, Inuiguchi and Slowinski (2003, 2004) proposed an approach for induction of gradual decision rules relating knowledge about X and knowledge about Y, represented by a single premise and a single conclusion, respectively. It handles ambiguity of information through fuzzy rough approximations. In this paper, we want to extend this approach to induction of gradual decision rules having multiple premises representing knowledge about X. Examples of these decision rules are: "if a car is speedy with credibility at least 0.8 and it has high fuel consumption with credibility at most 0.7, then it is a good car with a credibility at least 0.9" and "if a car is speedy with credibility at most 0.5 and it has high fuel consumption with credibility at least 0.8, then it is a good car with a credibility at most 0.6".

Remark that the syntax of gradual decision rules is based on monotonic relationship that can also be found in dominance-based decision rules induced from preference-ordered data. From this point of view, the fuzzy rough approximation proposed in this article is related to the dominance-based rough set approach (Greco, Matarazzo, Slowinski 1999, 2001, 2005).

For the reason of greater generality, one could eventually drop the assumption of the monotonic relationship between premise and conclusion in gradual rules. For example, the gradual rule "the greater the temperature the better the weather" is true in some range of temperature only (say, up to 25 degrees C). In such cases, however, one can split the domain of the premise into sub-intervals, in which the monotonicity still holds, and represents the regularities observed in these sub-intervals by gradual rules. For example, we can split the range of the temperature into two open subintervals, under 25 degrees C and over 25 degrees C, obtaining the two gradual rules: "the greater the temperature the better the weather", which is valid in the first interval, and "the smaller the temperature the better the weather", which is valid in the second interval. Therefore, the concept of monotonicity in gradual rules is intrinsic to the idea of induction whose aim is to represent regularities according to the simplest law (see, Proposition 6.363 of Wittgenstein (1922): *"The process of induction is the process of assuming the simplest law that can be made to harmonize with our experience"*). We claim that this simplest law is the monotonicity.

The above Proposition of Wittgenstein is borrowed from the paper by Aragones, Gilboa, Postelwaite and Schmeidler (2002) on a similar subject. Remark, however, that these authors consider rules with non-monotonic relationships between premise and conclusion, and, moreover, their rule induction procedure is based on a cardinal concept of the credibility of information.

The model of rule induction proposed in this paper is interesting also from the viewpoint of data mining, knowledge discovery, machine learning and their philosophical background (Cornish, Elliman 1995, Bensusan 2000, Williamson 2004). In fact, applications of data mining, knowledge discovery and machine learning requires a proper theory related to such questions as:

- Can the whole process of knowledge discovery be automated or reduced to pure logics?
- In what degree pieces of evidence found in data support a hypothesis? (Greco, Pawlak, Slowinski 2004)
- How to choose an inductive strategy appropriate for the task one is facing?
- What is the relationship between machine learning and philosophy of science?
- "Is machine learning experimental Philosophy of science?" (Bensusan 2000)

In this paper, we focus on the kind of discoveries permitted by our methodology. The rule induction approach we are proposing is concordant with the method of concomitant variation proposed by John Stuart Mill. The general formulation of this method is the following: *"Whatever phenomenon varies in any manner whenever another phenomenon varies in some particular manner, is either a cause or an effect of that phenomenon, or it is connected with it through some causation"* (Mill 1843). In simpler words, the method of concomitant variation searches for positive or negative relations between magnitudes of considered variables. Mill's example concerned the tides and the position of the moon. In the above example of decision rules concerning evaluation of a car, the variations in evaluation of the car are positively related with variations in its speed and negatively related with variations in its fuel consumption. Cornish and Elliman (1995) note that within current practice of data mining, the method of concomitant variation is the one which receives the least attention among the other methods proposed by Mill (method of agreement, method of difference, method of indirect difference and method of residues). However Cornish and Elliman (1995) observe also that the method of concomitant variation "*is believed to have the greatest potential for the discovery of knowledge, in such areas as biology and bio-medicine, as it addresses parameters which are forever present and inseparable*".

The plan of the article is the following. In the next section, we are defining the syntax and the semantics of considered gradual decision rules; we also show how they represent positive and negative relationships between fuzzy sets corresponding to multiple premises and to conclusion of a decision rule. In section 3, we are introducing fuzzy rough approximations consistent with the considered gradual decision rules. Section 4 deals with rule induction based on rough approximations. In section 5 we introduce fuzzy rough modus ponens and fuzzy rough modus tollens based on gradual decision rules. Section 6 is grouping conclusions and remarks on further research directions.

2 Gradual Decision Rules with Positively or Negatively Related Premises and Conclusion

Let us consider condition attributes $X_1,\ldots,X_n$, related with decision attribute Y. More precisely, we shall denote by $X_i^\uparrow$ a fuzzy value of attribute X_i positively related with decision attribute Y, and by $X_i^\downarrow$, a fuzzy value of attribute X_i negatively related with decision attribute Y. We aim to obtain gradual decision rules of the following types:

- *lower-approximation rules* (L-rule): "if
    - $x \in X_{i1}^\uparrow$ with credibility $C(X_{i1}^\uparrow) \geq \alpha_{i1}$, and $x \in X_{i2}^\uparrow$ with credibility $C(X_{i2}^\uparrow) \geq \alpha_{i2}$ ..., and $x \in X_{ir}^\uparrow$ with credibility $C(X_{ir}^\uparrow) \geq \alpha_{ir}$, and
    - $x \in X_{j1}^\downarrow$ with credibility $C(X_{j1}^\downarrow) \leq \alpha_{j1}$, and $x \in X_{j2}^\downarrow$ with credibility $C(X_{j2}^\downarrow) \leq \alpha_{j2}$ ... , and $x \in X_{js}^\downarrow$ with credibility $C(X_{js}^\downarrow) \leq \alpha_{js}$,

    then decision $x \in Y$ has credibility $C(Y) \geq \beta$",

- *upper-approximation rule* (U-rule): "if
    - $x \in X_{i1}^\uparrow$ with credibility $C(X_{i1}^\uparrow) \leq \alpha_{i1}$, and $x \in X_{i2}^\uparrow$ with credibility $C(X_{i2}^\uparrow) \leq \alpha_{i2}$ ..., and $x \in X_{ir}^\uparrow$ with credibility $C(X_{ir}^\uparrow) \leq \alpha_{ir}$, and
    - $x \in X_{j1}^\downarrow$ with credibility $C(X_{j1}^\downarrow) \geq \alpha_{j1}$, and $x \in X_{j2}^\downarrow$ with credibility $C(X_{j2}^\downarrow) \geq \alpha_{j2}$ ..., and $x \in X_{js}^\downarrow$ with credibility $C(X_{js}^\downarrow) \geq \alpha_{js}$,

    then decision $x \in Y$ has credibility $C(Y) \leq \beta$".

The above decision rules will be represented by $(r+s+2)$-tuples $< X_{i1}^{\uparrow},...,X_{ir}^{\uparrow},X_{j1}^{\downarrow},...,X_{js}^{\downarrow},Y\!,f>$ and $< X_{i1}^{\uparrow},...,X_{ir}^{\uparrow},X_{j1}^{\downarrow},...,X_{js}^{\downarrow},Y\!,g>$, respectively, where $f\!:\![0,1]^{r+s}\!\rightarrow\![0,1]$ and $g\!:\![0,1]^{r+s}\!\rightarrow\![0,1]$ are functions relating the credibility of membership in $X_{i1}^{\uparrow},...,X_{ir}^{\uparrow},X_{j1}^{\downarrow},...,X_{js}^{\downarrow}$ with the credibility of membership in Y in lower- and upper-approximation rules, respectively. More precisely, functions f, and g permit to rewrite the conclusion part of above decision rules as follows:

- L-rule: "then decision $x\in Y$ has credibility $C(Y)\geq\beta=f(\alpha_{i1},...,\alpha_{ir},\alpha_{j1},...,\alpha_{js})$";
- U-rule: "then decision $x\in Y$ has credibility $C(Y)\leq\beta=g(\alpha_{i1},...,\alpha_{ir},\alpha_{j1},...,\alpha_{js})$".

If we have sufficient information about the lower boundary and upper boundary of credibility $C(Y)$, functions f and g would be obtained as functions which are monotonically non decreasing with $\alpha_{i1},...,\alpha_{ir}$ and monotonically non increasing with $\alpha_{j1},...,\alpha_{js}$. Otherwise, we cannot expect such monotonicity properties of functions f and g. Namely, under some partial information about those boundaries, functions f and g cannot be monotonically non decreasing with $\alpha_{i1},...,\alpha_{ir}$ and monotonically non increasing with $\alpha_{j1},...,\alpha_{js}$. In what follows, we assume only some partial information about the lower boundary and upper boundary of credibility $C(Y)$ so that functions f and g are not always monotonically non decreasing with $\alpha_{i1},...,\alpha_{ir}$ and monotonically non increasing with $\alpha_{j1},...,\alpha_{js}$.

Given an L-rule $LR=< X_{i1}^{\uparrow},...,X_{ir}^{\uparrow},X_{j1}^{\downarrow},...,X_{js}^{\downarrow},Y\!,f>$ and an object z, taking into account that function f is not necessarily monotonic, we define the lower boundary of membership of z in Y with respect to LR, denoted by $C(z,LR,Y)$, as follows:

$$C(z,LR,Y)= \inf_{\alpha\in E^{+}(z)} f\left(\alpha_{i1},...,\alpha_{ir},\alpha_{j1}...,\alpha_{js}\right)$$

where

$$E^{+}(z)=\{\alpha=(\alpha_{i1},...,\alpha_{ir},\alpha_{j1},...,\alpha_{js})\in [0,1]^{r+s}:$$

$\alpha_h\geq\mu_{X_h}(z)$ for each $X_h\in \{ X_{i1}^{\uparrow},...,X_{ir}^{\uparrow} \}$, and $\alpha_h\leq\mu_{X_h}(z)$ for each

$$X_h\in \{ X_{j1}^{\downarrow},...,X_{js}^{\downarrow} \}\}.$$

Namely, with $f(\alpha_{i1},...,\alpha_{ir},\alpha_{j1},...,\alpha_{js})$, we revise the lower boundary by using the knowledge that credibility $C(Y)$ is monotonically nondecreasing with credibilities $C(X_{i1}^{\uparrow}),...,C(X_{ir}^{\uparrow})$ and monotonically non increasing with credibilities $C(X_{j1}^{\downarrow}),...,$ $C(X_{js}^{\downarrow})$. Note that this modification does not change the conclusion, i.e. $C(z,LR,Y)=f(\alpha_{i1},...,\alpha_{ir},\alpha_{j1},...,\alpha_{js})$, when function f is monotonically non decreasing with $\alpha_{i1},...,\alpha_{ir}$ and monotonically non increasing with $\alpha_{j1},...,\alpha_{js}$.

Intuitively, the lower boundary represents the lowest credibility we can assign to membership of object z in Y on the basis of an L-rule LR, given the hypothesis about the positive relationships with respect to membership in $X_{i1}^{\uparrow},...,X_{ir}^{\uparrow}$ and the negative relationship with respect to membership in $X_{j1}^{\downarrow},...,X_{js}^{\downarrow}$. Analogously, given an U-rule $UR=< X_{i1}^{\uparrow},\ldots, X_{ir}^{\uparrow}, X_{j1}^{\downarrow},\ldots, X_{js}^{\downarrow}, Y, g>$ and an object z, we define the upper boundary of membership of z to Y with respect to UR, denoted by $C(z,UR,Y)$, as follows:

$$C(z,UR,Y)= \sup_{\alpha \in E^{-}(z)} g(\alpha_{i1},\ldots,\alpha_{ir},\alpha_{j1},\ldots,\alpha_{js})$$

where

$$\bar{E}^{-}(z)=\{\alpha=(\alpha_{i1},\ldots,\alpha_{ir},\alpha_{j1},\ldots,\alpha_{js})\in [0,1]^{r+s}:$$

$\alpha_h \leq \mu_{X_h}(z)$ for each $X_h \in \{ X_{i1}^{\uparrow},\ldots, X_{ir}^{\uparrow} \}$, and $\alpha_h \geq \mu_{X_h}(z)$ for each

$$X_h \in \{ X_{j1}^{\downarrow},\ldots, X_{js}^{\downarrow} \}\}.$$

Namely, from $g(\alpha_{i1},\ldots,\alpha_{ir},\alpha_{j1},\ldots,\alpha_{js})$, we modify the upper boundary by using the knowledge that credibility $C(Y)$ is monotonically non decreasing with credibilities $C(X_{i1}^{\uparrow}),\ldots, C(X_{ir}^{\uparrow})$ and monotonically non increasing with credibilities $C(X_{j1}^{\downarrow}),\ldots,$ $C(X_{js}^{\downarrow})$. Note that this modification does not change the conclusion, i.e., $C(z,UR,Y)=g(\alpha_{i1},\ldots,\alpha_{ir},\alpha_{j1},\ldots,\alpha_{js})$ when function g is monotonically non decreasing with $\alpha_{i1},\ldots,\alpha_{ir}$ and monotonically non increasing with $\alpha_{j1},\ldots,\alpha_{js}$.

Intuitively, the upper boundary represents the highest credibility we can assign to membership of object z in Y on the basis of an U-rule UR, given the hypothesis about the positive relationships with respect to membership in $X_{i1}^{\uparrow},\ldots, X_{ir}^{\uparrow}$ and the negative relationship with respect to membership in $X_{j1}^{\downarrow},\ldots, X_{js}^{\downarrow}$.

Two L-rules $LR=< X_{i1}^{\uparrow},\ldots, X_{ir}^{\uparrow}, X_{j1}^{\downarrow},\ldots, X_{js}^{\downarrow}, Y, f>$ and $LR'=< X_{i1}^{\uparrow},\ldots, X_{ir}^{\uparrow}, X_{j1}^{\downarrow},\ldots,$ $X_{js}^{\downarrow}, Y, f'>$ are equivalent if for all possible objects z we have that $C(z,LR,Y)=$ $C(z,LR',Y)$.

Two U-rules $UR=< X_{i1}^{\uparrow},\ldots, X_{ir}^{\uparrow}, X_{j1}^{\downarrow},\ldots, X_{js}^{\downarrow}, Y, g>$ and $UR'=< X_{i1}^{\uparrow},\ldots, X_{ir}^{\uparrow}, X_{j1}^{\downarrow},$ $\ldots, X_{js}^{\downarrow}, Y, g'>$ are equivalent if for all possible objects z we have that $C(z,UR,Y)=$ $C(z,UR',Y)$.

Theorem 1. For each L-rule $LR=< X_{i1}^{\uparrow},\ldots, X_{ir}^{\uparrow}, X_{j1}^{\downarrow},\ldots, X_{js}^{\downarrow}, Y, f>$ there exists an equivalent L-rule $LR'=< X_{i1}^{\uparrow},\ldots, X_{ir}^{\uparrow}, X_{j1}^{\downarrow},\ldots, X_{js}^{\downarrow}, Y, f'>$ with functions $f'(\alpha_{i1},\ldots,\alpha_{ir},$ $\alpha_{j1},\ldots,\alpha_{js})$ non-decreasing in each of its first r arguments and non-increasing in its last s arguments.

For each U-rule $UR=< X_{i1}^{\uparrow},\ldots, X_{ir}^{\uparrow}, X_{j1}^{\downarrow},\ldots, X_{js}^{\downarrow}, Y, g>$ there exists an equivalent U-rule $UR'=< X_{i1}^{\uparrow},\ldots, X_{ir}^{\uparrow}, X_{j1}^{\downarrow},\ldots, X_{js}^{\downarrow}, Y, g'>$ with functions $g'(\alpha_{i1},\ldots,\alpha_{ir},\alpha_{j1},\ldots,\alpha_{js})$ non-decreasing in each of its first r arguments and non-increasing in its last s arguments.   ◆

An L-rule can be regarded as a gradual rule (Dubois, Prade 1992]); indeed, it can be interpreted as:

"the more object x is $X_{i1},\ldots,X_{ir}$ and the less object x is $X_{j1},\ldots,X_{js}$, the more it is Y".

Analogously, the U-rule can be interpreted as:

"the less object x is $X_{i1},\ldots,X_{ir}$ and the more object x is $X_{j1},\ldots,X_{js}$, the less it is Y".

On the other hand, the syntax of L- and U-rules is more general than that of usual gradual rules introduced in (Dubois, Prade 1992). Indeed, while the usual gradual rules are statements of the type "if $\mu_X(x) \geq \alpha$, then $\mu_Y(x) \geq \alpha$", the simplest L-rule states "if $\mu_{X_i^\uparrow}(x) \geq \alpha_i$, then $\mu_Y(x) \geq \beta$" or "if $\mu_{X_j^\downarrow}(x) \leq \alpha_j$, then $\mu_Y(x) \geq \beta$". Therefore, the L- and U-rules permit to consider different degrees of credibility in premises and conclusion, which is not the case of the gradual rules.

Let us also remark that the syntax of L- and U-rules is similar to the syntax of "at least" and "at most" decision rules induced from dominance-based rough approximations of preference-ordered decision classes (Greco, Matarazzo, Slowinski 1999, 2001, 2005).

3 Fuzzy Rough Approximations

The functions f and g introduced in the previous section are related to specific definitions of lower and upper approximations considered within rough set theory (Pawlak 1991). Let us consider a universe of discourse U and $r+s+1$ fuzzy sets, $X_{i1}^\uparrow,\ldots,X_{ir}^\uparrow$, $X_{j1}^\downarrow,\ldots,X_{js}^\downarrow$ and Y, defined on U by means of membership functions $\mu_{X_h}:U{\to}[0,1]$, $h \in \{i1,\ldots,ir,j1,\ldots,js\}$ and $\mu_Y:U{\to}[0,1]$. Suppose that we want to approximate knowledge contained in Y using knowledge about $X_{i1}^\uparrow,\ldots,X_{ir}^\uparrow$, $X_{j1}^\downarrow,\ldots,X_{js}^\downarrow$, under the hypothesis that $X_{i1}^\uparrow,\ldots,X_{ir}^\uparrow$ are positively related with Y and $X_{j1}^\downarrow,\ldots,X_{js}^\downarrow$ are negatively related with Y.

Then, the lower approximation of Y given the information on $X_{i1}^\uparrow,\ldots,X_{ir}^\uparrow$, $X_{j1}^\downarrow,\ldots,X_{js}^\downarrow$ is a fuzzy set $\underline{App}(X_{i1}^\uparrow,\ldots,X_{ir}^\uparrow,X_{j1}^\downarrow,\ldots,X_{js}^\downarrow,Y)$, whose membership function for each $x \in U$, denoted by $\mu[\underline{App}(X_{i1}^\uparrow,\ldots,X_{ir}^\uparrow,X_{j1}^\downarrow,\ldots,X_{js}^\downarrow,Y),x]$, is defined as follows:

$$\mu[\underline{App}(X_{i1}^\uparrow,\ldots,X_{ir}^\uparrow,X_{j1}^\downarrow,\ldots,X_{js}^\downarrow,Y),x] = \inf_{z \in D\uparrow(x)}\{\mu_Y(z)\} \tag{1}$$

where for each $x \in U$, $D\uparrow(x)$ is a non-empty set defined by

and $\mu_{X_h}(z) \leq \mu_{X_h}(x)$ for each $X_h = X_{j1}^\downarrow,\ldots,X_{js}^\downarrow$ }.

Lower approximation $\mu[\underline{App}(X_{i1}^\uparrow,\ldots,X_{ir}^\uparrow,X_{j1}^\downarrow,\ldots,X_{js}^\downarrow,Y),x]$ can be interpreted as follows: in the universe U the following implication holds:

"If $\mu_{X_h}(z) \geq \mu_{X_h}(x)$ for each $X_h = X_{i1}^\uparrow,\ldots,X_{ir}^\uparrow$, and $\mu_{X_h}(z) \leq \mu_{X_h}(x)$ for each $X_h = X_{j1}^\downarrow,\ldots,X_{js}^\downarrow$, then $\mu_Y(z) \geq \mu[\underline{App}(X_{i1}^\uparrow,\ldots,X_{ir}^\uparrow,X_{j1}^\downarrow,\ldots,X_{js}^\downarrow,Y),x]$."

Interpretation of lower approximation (1) is based on a specific meaning of the concept of ambiguity. According to knowledge about $X_{i1}^{\uparrow},\dots, X_{ir}^{\uparrow}$, $X_{j1}^{\downarrow},\dots, X_{js}^{\downarrow}$, the membership of object $x \in U$ to fuzzy set Y is ambiguous if there exists an object $z \in U$ such that $\mu_{X_h}(z) \geq \mu_{X_h}(x)$ for each $X_h = X_{i1}^{\uparrow},\dots, X_{ir}^{\uparrow}$, and $\mu_{X_h}(z) \leq \mu_{X_h}(x)$ for each $X_h = X_{j1}^{\downarrow},\dots, X_{js}^{\downarrow}$, however, $\mu_Y(x) > \mu_Y(z)$.

Remark that the above meaning of ambiguity is concordant with the dominance principle introduced in rough set theory in order to deal with preference-ordered data (Greco, Matarazzo, Slowinski 1999, 2001, 2005). In this case, the dominance principle says that, having an object with some membership degrees in X and Y, its modification consisting in an increase of its membership in X should not decrease its membership in Y; otherwise, the original object and the modified object are ambiguous.

Analogously, the upper approximation of Y given the information on $X_{i1}^{\uparrow},\dots, X_{ir}^{\uparrow}$, $X_{j1}^{\downarrow},\dots, X_{js}^{\downarrow}$ is a fuzzy set $\overline{App}\,(X_{i1}^{\uparrow},\dots, X_{ir}^{\uparrow}, X_{j1}^{\downarrow},\dots, X_{js}^{\downarrow},Y)$, whose membership function for each $x \in U$, denoted by $\mu[\,\overline{App}\,(X_{i1}^{\uparrow},\dots, X_{ir}^{\uparrow}, X_{j1}^{\downarrow},\dots, X_{js}^{\downarrow},Y), x]$, is defined as follows:

$$\mu[\,\overline{App}\,(X_{i1}^{\uparrow},\dots, X_{ir}^{\uparrow}, X_{j1}^{\downarrow},\dots, X_{js}^{\downarrow},Y), x] = \sup_{z \in D\downarrow(x)} \{\mu_Y(z)\} \qquad (2)$$

where for each $x \in U$, $D\downarrow(x)$ is a non-empty set defined by

$$D\downarrow(x) = \{z \in U: \ \mu_{X_h}(z) \leq \mu_{X_h}(x) \text{ for each } X_h = X_{i1}^{\uparrow},\dots, X_{ir}^{\uparrow},$$
$$\text{and } \mu_{X_h}(z) \geq \mu_{X_h}(x) \text{ for each } X_h = X_{j1}^{\downarrow},\dots, X_{js}^{\downarrow}\}.$$

Upper approximation $\mu[\,\overline{App}\,(X_{i1}^{\uparrow},\dots, X_{ir}^{\uparrow}, X_{j1}^{\downarrow},\dots, X_{js}^{\downarrow},Y), x]$ can be interpreted as follows: in the universe U the following implication holds:

"If $\mu_{X_h}(z) \leq \mu_{X_h}(x)$ for each $X_h = X_{i1}^{\uparrow},\dots, X_{ir}^{\uparrow}$, and $\mu_{X_h}(z) \geq \mu_{X_h}(x)$ for each $X_h = X_{j1}^{\downarrow},\dots, X_{js}^{\downarrow}$, then $\mu_Y(z) \leq \mu[\,\overline{App}\,(X_{i1}^{\uparrow},\dots, X_{ir}^{\uparrow}, X_{j1}^{\downarrow},\dots, X_{js}^{\downarrow},Y), x]$."

Theorem 2. Let us consider fuzzy sets $X_{i1}^{\uparrow},\dots, X_{ir}^{\uparrow}$, $X_{j1}^{\downarrow},\dots, X_{js}^{\downarrow}$ and Y defined on U. The following properties are satisfied:

1) for each $x \in U$

$$\mu[\underline{App}(X_{i1}^{\uparrow},\dots, X_{ir}^{\uparrow}, X_{j1}^{\downarrow},\dots, X_{js}^{\downarrow},Y), x] \leq \mu_Y(x) \leq$$
$$\mu[\,\overline{App}\,(X_{i1}^{\uparrow},\dots, X_{ir}^{\uparrow}, X_{j1}^{\downarrow},\dots, X_{js}^{\downarrow},Y), x]$$

2) for any negation $N(\cdot)$, being a strictly decreasing function $N:[0,1] \to [0,1]$ such that $N(1)=0$ and $N(0)=1$, for each fuzzy set $X_h = X_{i1}^{\uparrow},\dots, X_{ir}^{\uparrow}, X_{j1}^{\downarrow},\dots, X_{js}^{\downarrow}$ and Y defined on U, and for each $x \in U$

$2.1) \mu[\underline{App}(X_{i1}^{\uparrow},...,X_{ir}^{\uparrow},X_{j1}^{\downarrow},...,X_{js}^{\downarrow},Y^c),x]=$

$=N(\mu[\overline{App}(X_{i1}^{c\uparrow},...,X_{ir}^{c\uparrow},X_{j1}^{c\downarrow},...,X_{js}^{c\downarrow},Y),x]),$

$2.2) \mu[\overline{App}(X_{i1}^{\uparrow},...,X_{ir}^{\uparrow},X_{j1}^{\downarrow},...,X_{js}^{\downarrow},Y^c),x]=$

$=N(\mu[\underline{App}(X_{i1}^{c\uparrow},...,X_{ir}^{c\uparrow},X_{j1}^{c\downarrow},...,X_{js}^{c\downarrow},Y),x]),$

$2.3) N(\mu[\overline{App}(X_{i1}^{\uparrow},...,X_{ir}^{\uparrow},X_{j1}^{\downarrow},...,X_{js}^{\downarrow},Y),x])=$

$=\mu[\underline{App}(X_{i1}^{c\uparrow},...,X_{ir}^{c\uparrow},X_{j1}^{c\downarrow},...,X_{js}^{c\downarrow},Y^c),x],$

$2.4) N(\mu[\underline{App}(X_{i1}^{\uparrow},...,X_{ir}^{\uparrow},X_{j1}^{\downarrow},...,X_{js}^{\downarrow},Y),x])=$

$=\mu[\overline{App}(X_{i1}^{c\uparrow},...,X_{ir}^{c\uparrow},X_{j1}^{c\downarrow},...,X_{js}^{c\downarrow},Y^c),x],$

where for a given fuzzy set W, the fuzzy set W^c is its complement defined by $\mu_{W^c}(x)=N(\mu_W(x))$.

3)   for each $\{X_{h1}^{\uparrow},...,X_{hv}^{\uparrow}\}\subseteq\{X_{i1}^{\uparrow},...,X_{ir}^{\uparrow}\}$ and $\{X_{k1}^{\downarrow},...,X_{kw}^{\downarrow}\}\subseteq\{X_{j1}^{\downarrow},...,X_{js}^{\downarrow}\}$

$3.1)\ \mu[\underline{App}(X_{i1}^{\uparrow},...,X_{ir}^{\uparrow},X_{j1}^{\downarrow},...,X_{js}^{\downarrow},Y),x]\geq$

$\geq\mu[\underline{App}(X_{h1}^{\uparrow},...,X_{hv}^{\uparrow},X_{k1}^{\downarrow},...,X_{kw}^{\downarrow},Y),x],$

$3.2)\ \mu[\overline{App}(X_{i1}^{\uparrow},...,X_{ir}^{\uparrow},X_{j1}^{\downarrow},...,X_{js}^{\downarrow},Y),x]\leq$

$\leq\mu[\overline{App}(X_{h1}^{\uparrow},...,X_{hv}^{\uparrow},X_{k1}^{\downarrow},...,X_{kw}^{\downarrow},Y),x].$

4)   for each $x,y\in U$, such that $\mu_{X_h}(x)\geq\mu_{X_h}(y)$ for each $X_h\in\{X_{i1}^{\uparrow},...,X_{ir}^{\uparrow}\}$, and $\mu_{X_h}(x)\leq\mu_{X_h}(y)$ for each $X_h\in\{X_{j1}^{\downarrow},...,X_{js}^{\downarrow}\}$, we have

$4.1)\mu[\underline{App}(X_{i1}^{\uparrow},...,X_{ir}^{\uparrow},X_{j1}^{\downarrow},...,X_{js}^{\downarrow},Y),x]\geq$

$\geq\mu[\underline{App}(X_{i1}^{\uparrow},...,X_{ir}^{\uparrow},X_{j1}^{\downarrow},...,X_{js}^{\downarrow},Y),y],$

$4.2)\mu[\overline{App}(X_{i1}^{\uparrow},...,X_{ir}^{\uparrow},X_{j1}^{\downarrow},...,X_{js}^{\downarrow},Y),x]\geq$

$\geq\mu[\overline{App}(X_{i1}^{\uparrow},...,X_{ir}^{\uparrow},X_{j1}^{\downarrow},...,X_{js}^{\downarrow},Y),y].$ ♦

Results 1), 2) and 3) of Theorem 2 can be read as fuzzy counterparts of results well-known within the classical rough set theory. More precisely, 1) says that fuzzy set Y includes its lower approximation and is included in its upper approximation; 2) represents complementarity properties of the proposed fuzzy rough approximations; 3) expresses the fact that when we approximate Y, if we pass from a set of attributes to its subset, for any $x \in U$, the membership to the lower approximation of Y does not increase while the membership to the upper approximation of Y does not decrease. Result 4) is more related with the specific context in which we are defining rough approximation: it says that lower and upper approximations respect monotonicity with respect to fuzzy membership functions $\mu_{X_h}(x)$, and more precisely, that they are non-decreasing operators with respect to $\mu_{X_h}(x)$ for $X_h \in \{ X_{i1}^{\uparrow}, \ldots, X_{ir}^{\uparrow} \}$ and non-increasing operators with respect to $\mu_{X_h}(x)$ for $X_h \in \{ X_{j1}^{\downarrow}, \ldots, X_{js}^{\downarrow} \}$.

4 Decision Rule Induction from Fuzzy Rough Approximations

The lower and upper approximations defined above can serve to induce L-rules and U-rules respectively. Let us remark that inferring L-rules $< X_{i1}^{\uparrow}, \ldots, X_{ir}^{\uparrow}, X_{j1}^{\downarrow}, \ldots, X_{js}^{\downarrow}, Y, f>$ and U-rules $< X_{i1}^{\uparrow}, \ldots, X_{ir}^{\uparrow}, X_{j1}^{\downarrow}, \ldots, X_{js}^{\downarrow}, Y, g>$ is equivalent to find functions $f(\cdot)$ and $g(\cdot)$. Since we want to induce decision rules representing the considered universe U, the following conditions of correct representation must be satisfied by the L-rule $< X_{i1}^{\uparrow}, \ldots, X_{ir}^{\uparrow}, X_{j1}^{\downarrow}, \ldots, X_{js}^{\downarrow}, Y, f>$ and U-rule $< X_{i1}^{\uparrow}, \ldots, X_{ir}^{\uparrow}, X_{j1}^{\downarrow}, \ldots, X_{js}^{\downarrow}, Y, g>$ searched for:

- correct representation with respect to the lower approximation: for all $x \in U$ and for each $\alpha \in [0,1]^{r+s}$,

$$[\mu_{X_h}(x) \leq \alpha_h \text{ for each } X_h \in \{ X_{i1}^{\uparrow}, \ldots, X_{ir}^{\uparrow} \},$$

$$\text{and } \mu_{X_h}(x) \geq \alpha_h \text{ for each } X_h \in \{ X_{j1}^{\downarrow}, \ldots, X_{js}^{\downarrow} \}]$$

$$\Rightarrow$$

$$f(\alpha) \geq \mu[\underline{App}(X_{i1}^{\uparrow}, \ldots, X_{ir}^{\uparrow}, X_{j1}^{\downarrow}, \ldots, X_{js}^{\downarrow}, Y), x]$$

- correct representation with respect to the upper approximation: for all $x \in U$ and for each $\alpha \in [0,1]^{r+s}$,

$$[\mu_{X_h}(x) \geq \alpha_h \text{ for each } X_h \in \{ X_{i1}^{\uparrow}, \ldots, X_{ir}^{\uparrow} \},$$

$$\text{and } \mu_{X_h}(x) \leq \alpha_h \text{ for each } X_h \in \{ X_{j1}^{\downarrow}, \ldots, X_{js}^{\downarrow} \}]$$

$$\Rightarrow$$

$$g(\alpha) \leq \mu[\overline{App}(X_{i1}^{\uparrow}, \ldots, X_{ir}^{\uparrow}, X_{j1}^{\downarrow}, \ldots, X_{js}^{\downarrow}, Y), x]$$

These conditions of correct representation are concordant with the idea that lower and upper approximation are reference values for a cautious lower and upper evaluation of membership in set Y on the basis of the membership in $X_{i1}^{\uparrow}, \ldots, X_{ir}^{\uparrow}, X_{j1}^{\downarrow}, \ldots$ and $X_{js}^{\downarrow}$.

In general there are more than one L-rule $< X_{i1}^{\uparrow},..., X_{ir}^{\uparrow}, X_{j1}^{\downarrow},..., X_{js}^{\downarrow},Y,f>$ and more than one U-rule $< X_{i1}^{\uparrow},..., X_{ir}^{\uparrow}, X_{j1}^{\downarrow},..., X_{js}^{\downarrow},Y,g>$ satisfying the correct representation condition. Thus, how to choose "the best L-rule and the best U-rule"? To answer this question, we propose the following conditions of prudence:

- given two L-rules $LR=< X_{i1}^{\uparrow},..., X_{ir}^{\uparrow}, X_{j1}^{\downarrow},..., X_{js}^{\downarrow},Y,f>$ and $LR'=< X_{i1}^{\uparrow},..., X_{ir}^{\uparrow}, X_{j1}^{\downarrow},..., X_{js}^{\downarrow},Y,f'>$ we say that LR is more prudent than LR' if for all $\alpha \in [0,1]^{r+s}$, $f(\alpha) \leq f'(\alpha)$,

- given two U-rules $UR=< X_{i1}^{\uparrow},..., X_{ir}^{\uparrow}, X_{j1}^{\downarrow},..., X_{js}^{\downarrow},Y,g>$ and $UR'=< X_{i1}^{\uparrow},..., X_{ir}^{\uparrow}, X_{j1}^{\downarrow},..., X_{js}^{\downarrow},Y,g'>$ we say that UR is more prudent than UR' if for all $\alpha \in [0,1]^{r+s}$, $g(\alpha) \geq g'(\alpha)$.

These conditions of prudence are concordant with the idea of presenting the most cautious evaluation of membership in set Y on the base of the membership in $X_{i1}^{\uparrow},..., X_{ir}^{\uparrow}, X_{j1}^{\downarrow},...$ and $X_{js}^{\downarrow}$. In this sense the "lower evaluation" of the membership in set Y should be the smallest possible while the "upper evaluation" should be the largest possible.

Let CLR be the set of all the L-rules $LR=< X_{i1}^{\uparrow},..., X_{ir}^{\uparrow}, X_{j1}^{\downarrow},..., X_{js}^{\downarrow},Y,f>$ satisfying the condition of correct representation. We say that the L-rule $LR^{\#}=< X_{i1}^{\uparrow},..., X_{ir}^{\uparrow}, X_{j1}^{\downarrow},..., X_{js}^{\downarrow},Y,f^{\#}>$ is maximally prudent if $LR^{\#}$ is more prudent than all other LR rules in CLR.

Let also CUR be the set of all the U-rules $UR=< X_{i1}^{\uparrow},..., X_{ir}^{\uparrow}, X_{j1}^{\downarrow},..., X_{js}^{\downarrow},Y,g>$ satisfying the condition of correct representation. We say that the U-rule $UR^{\#}=< X_{i1}^{\uparrow},..., X_{ir}^{\uparrow}, X_{j1}^{\downarrow},..., X_{js}^{\downarrow},Y,g^{\#}>$ is maximally prudent if $UR^{\#}$ is more prudent than all other UR rules in CUR.

Theorem 3. If $LR^{\#}=< X_{i1}^{\uparrow},..., X_{ir}^{\uparrow}, X_{j1}^{\downarrow},..., X_{js}^{\downarrow},Y,f^{\#}>$ is an L-rule maximally prudent and $UR^{\#}=< X_{i1}^{\uparrow},..., X_{ir}^{\uparrow}, X_{j1}^{\downarrow},..., X_{js}^{\downarrow},Y,g>$ is an U-rule maximally prudent, then:

for each $\alpha \in [0,1]^{r+s}$,

$$f^{\#}(\alpha) = \inf_{LR \in CLR} f(\alpha) = \begin{cases} \sup_{x \in A^{-}(\alpha)} \left\{ \mu \left[App\left(X_{i1}^{\uparrow},..., X_{ir}^{\uparrow}, X_{j1}^{\downarrow},..., X_{js}^{\downarrow}, Y \right), x \right] \right\} & \text{if } A^{-}(\alpha) \neq \varnothing \\ 0 & \text{if } A^{-}(\alpha) = \varnothing \end{cases}$$

and

$$g^{\#}(\alpha) = \sup_{UR \in CUR} g(\alpha) = \begin{cases} \inf_{x \in A^{+}(\alpha)} \left\{ \mu \left[\overline{App}\left(X_{i1}^{\uparrow},..., X_{ir}^{\uparrow}, X_{j1}^{\downarrow},..., X_{js}^{\downarrow}, Y \right), x \right] \right\} & \text{if } A^{+}(\alpha) \neq \varnothing \\ 1 & \text{if } A^{+}(\alpha) = \varnothing \end{cases}$$

where

$$A^-(\alpha)=\left\{x\in U:\ \mu_{X_h}(x)\le\alpha_h\ \text{for each}\ X_h\in\{\ X_{i1}^{\uparrow},\dots,X_{ir}^{\uparrow}\ \},\ \text{and}\ \mu_{X_h}(x)\ge\alpha_h\ \text{for each}\right.$$

$$\left. X_h\in\{\ X_{j1}^{\downarrow},\dots,X_{js}^{\downarrow}\ \}\right\},$$

$$A^+(\alpha)=\left\{x\in U:\ \mu_{X_h}(x)\ge\alpha_h\ \text{for each}\ X_h\in\{\ X_{i1}^{\uparrow},\dots,X_{ir}^{\uparrow}\ \},\ \text{and}\ \mu_{X_h}(x)\le\alpha_h\ \text{for each}\right.$$

$$\left. X_h\in\{\ X_{j1}^{\downarrow},\dots,X_{js}^{\downarrow}\ \}\right\}.$$

Moreover, for any $z\in U$

$$f^{\#}\left(\mu_{X_{i1}^{\uparrow}}(z),\dots,\mu_{X_{ir}^{\uparrow}}(z),\mu_{X_{j1}^{\downarrow}}(z),\dots,\mu_{X_{js}^{\downarrow}}(z)\right)=\mu[\underline{App}(\ X_{i1}^{\uparrow},\dots,X_{ir}^{\uparrow},X_{j1}^{\downarrow},\dots,X_{js}^{\downarrow},Y),z],$$

$$g^{\#}\left(\mu_{X_{i1}^{\uparrow}}(z),\dots,\mu_{X_{ir}^{\uparrow}}(z),\mu_{X_{j1}^{\downarrow}}(z),\dots,\mu_{X_{js}^{\downarrow}}(z)\right)=\mu[\overline{App}(\ X_{i1}^{\uparrow},\dots,X_{ir}^{\uparrow},X_{j1}^{\downarrow},\dots,X_{js}^{\downarrow},Y),z].\ \blacklozenge$$

Theorem 3 is a characterization of the decision rules obtained through our fuzzy rough approach: there is only one L-rule and one U-rule maximally prudent in the set of L-rules and U-rules satisfying the property of correct representation and these are the L-rule *LR#* and the U-rule *UR#*. Let us also remark the importance of lower and upper approximations obtained through our fuzzy rough approach for the definition of L-rule *LR#* and the U-rule *UR#*. The last part of Theorem 3 says that the L-rule *LR#* and the U-rule *UR#* permit an exact reclassification of any object $z\in U$. More precisely, function $f^{\#}$ reassigns z its lower approximation, i.e.

$$f^{\#}\left(\mu_{X_{i1}^{\uparrow}}(z),\dots,\mu_{X_{ir}^{\uparrow}}(z),\mu_{X_{j1}^{\downarrow}}(z),\dots,\mu_{X_{js}^{\downarrow}}(z)\right)=\mu[\underline{App}(\ X_{i1}^{\uparrow},\dots,X_{ir}^{\uparrow},X_{j1}^{\downarrow},\dots,X_{js}^{\downarrow},Y),z],$$

while function $g^{\#}$ reassigns z its upper approximation, i.e.

$$g^{\#}\left(\mu_{X_{i1}^{\uparrow}}(z),\dots,\mu_{X_{ir}^{\uparrow}}(z),\mu_{X_{j1}^{\downarrow}}(z),\dots,\mu_{X_{js}^{\downarrow}}(z)\right)=\mu[\overline{App}(\ X_{i1}^{\uparrow},\dots,X_{ir}^{\uparrow},X_{j1}^{\downarrow},\dots,X_{js}^{\downarrow},Y),z].$$

5 Fuzzy Rough Modus-Ponens and Fuzzy Rough Modus Tollens

The L-rule and the U-rule can be used to evaluate objects, possibly not belonging to U, by means of a proper generalization of *modus ponens* (MP) and *modus tollens* (MT) in order to infer a conclusion from gradual rules. Classically, the MP has the following form:

if	$X \rightarrow Y$	is true
and	X	is true
then	Y	is true

MP has the following interpretation: assuming an implication $X \rightarrow Y$ (decision rule) and a fact X (premise), we obtain another fact Y (conclusion). If we replace the classical decision rule above by our L-rules and U-rules, then we obtain the following two generalized fuzzy-rough MP:

if $\mu_{X_h}(x) \geq \alpha_h$ for each $X_h \in \{ X_{i1}^{\uparrow},\dots, X_{ir}^{\uparrow} \}$, and $\mu_{X_h}(x) \leq \alpha_h$ for each

$X_h \in \{ X_{j1}^{\downarrow},\dots, X_{js}^{\downarrow} \}$ $\rightarrow \mu_Y(x) \geq f(\alpha)$ $[\alpha=(\alpha_{i1},\dots,\alpha_{ir},\alpha_{j1},\dots,\alpha_{js})]$

and $\mu_{X_h}(x) \geq \alpha'_h$ for each $X_h \in \{ X_{i1}^{\uparrow},\dots, X_{ir}^{\uparrow} \}$, and $\mu_{X_h}(x) \leq \alpha'_h$ for each

$X_h \in \{ X_{j1}^{\downarrow},\dots, X_{js}^{\downarrow} \}$

---

then $\mu_Y(x) \geq f(\alpha')$ $[\alpha'=(\alpha'_{i1},\dots,\alpha'_{ir},\alpha'_{j1},\dots,\alpha'_{js})]$

if $\mu_{X_h}(x) \leq \alpha_h$ for each $X_h \in \{ X_{i1}^{\uparrow},\dots, X_{ir}^{\uparrow} \}$, and $\mu_{X_h}(x) \geq \alpha_h$ for each

$X_h \in \{ X_{j1}^{\downarrow},\dots, X_{js}^{\downarrow} \} \rightarrow \mu_Y(x) \leq g(\alpha)$ $[\alpha=(\alpha_{i1},\dots,\alpha_{ir},\alpha_{j1},\dots,\alpha_{js})]$

and $\mu_{X_h}(x) \leq \alpha'_h$ for each $X_h \in \{ X_{i1}^{\uparrow},\dots, X_{ir}^{\uparrow} \}$, and $\mu_{X_h}(x) \geq \alpha'_h$ for each

$X_h \in \{ X_{j1}^{\downarrow},\dots, X_{js}^{\downarrow} \}$

---

then $\mu_Y(x) \leq g(\alpha')$ $[\alpha'=(\alpha'_{i1},\dots,\alpha'_{ir},\alpha'_{j1},\dots,\alpha'_{js})]$

Classically, the MT has the following form:

if	$X \rightarrow Y$	is true
and	Y	is false

| then | X | is false |

MT has the following interpretation: assuming an implication $X \rightarrow Y$ (decision rule) and a fact *not Y* (premise), we obtain another fact *not X* (conclusion). If we replace the classical decision rule above by our L-rules and U-rules, then we obtain the following two generalized fuzzy-rough MT:

if $\mu_{X_h}(x) \geq \alpha_h$ for each $X_h \in \{ X_{i1}^{\uparrow},\dots, X_{ir}^{\uparrow} \}$, and $\mu_{X_h}(x) \leq \alpha_h$ for each

$X_h \in \{ X_{j1}^{\downarrow},\dots, X_{js}^{\downarrow} \} \rightarrow \mu_Y(x) \geq f(\alpha)$ $[\alpha=(\alpha_{i1},\dots,\alpha_{ir},\alpha_{j1},\dots,\alpha_{js})]$

and $\mu_Y(x) < f(\alpha')$ $[\alpha'=(\alpha'_{i1},\dots,\alpha'_{ir},\alpha'_{j1},\dots,\alpha'_{js})]$

---

then $\mu_{X_h}(x) < \alpha'_h$ for at least one $X_h \in \{ X_{i1}^{\uparrow},\dots, X_{ir}^{\uparrow} \}$, or $\mu_{X_h}(x) > \alpha'_h$ for at leat one

$X_h \in \{ X_{j1}^{\downarrow},\dots, X_{js}^{\downarrow} \}$

if $\mu_{X_h}(x) \leq \alpha_h$ for each $X_h \in \{ X_{i1}^{\uparrow},\dots, X_{ir}^{\uparrow} \}$, and $\mu_{X_h}(x) \geq \alpha_h$ for each

$X_h \in \{ X_{j1}^{\downarrow},\dots, X_{js}^{\downarrow} \} \rightarrow \mu_Y(x) \leq g(\alpha)$ $[\alpha=(\alpha_{i1},\dots,\alpha_{ir},\alpha_{j1},\dots,\alpha_{js})]$

and $\mu_Y(x) > g(\alpha')$ $[\alpha'=(\alpha'_{i1},\dots,\alpha'_{ir},\alpha'_{j1},\dots,\alpha'_{js})]$

---

then $\mu_{X_h}(x) > \alpha'_h$ for at least one $X_h \in \{ X_{i1}^{\uparrow},\dots, X_{ir}^{\uparrow} \}$, or $\mu_{X_h}(x) < \alpha'_h$ for at least one

$X_h \in \{ X_{j1}^{\downarrow},\dots, X_{js}^{\downarrow} \}$

6 Conclusions and Further Research Directions

In this paper we presented a new fuzzy rough set approach. The main advantage of this new approach is that it infers the most cautious conclusions from available imprecise information, without using neither fuzzy connectives nor specific parameters, whose choice are always subjective to some extent. Another advantage of our approach is that it uses only ordinal properties of membership degrees. We noticed that our approach is related to:

- gradual rules, with respect to syntax and semantics of considered decision rules,
- dominance-based rough set approach, with respect to the idea of monotonic relationship between credibility degrees of multiple premises and conclusion,
- Mill's method of concomitant variation with respect to the philosophy of data mining and knowledge discovery.

We think that this approach gives a new prospect for applications of fuzzy rough approximations in real-world decision problems. More precisely, we envisage the following two extensions of this methodology:

1) Variable precision fuzzy rough approximation: in this paper we propose to calculate the degree of membership to the fuzzy lower approximation on the basis of non-ambiguous objects only, however, it might be useful in practical applications to allow a limited number of ambiguous objects as well; in this way we may get less specific rules of the type: *"the larger the market share of a company, the greater its profit, in l% of the cases"*, where l is a parameter controlling the proportion of ambiguous objects in the definition of the lower approximation.
2) Imprecise input data represented by fuzzy numbers and missing values: the evaluation of the object in the universe U from which the rough approximations and the gradual decision rules are induced may include imprecise values, represented by fuzzy numbers, or missing values.

Acknowledgements. The research of the first author has been supported by the Italian Ministry of Education, University and Scientific Research (MIUR). The second author acknowledges financial support by the Grant-in-Aid for Scientific Research (B) No. 17310098.The third author wishes to acknowledge financial support from the the Ministry of Scientific Research and Information Technology.

References

1. Aragones, E., Gilboa, I., Postlewaite, A., Schmeidler, D., *Accuracy vs. simplicity: A complex trade-off*, PIER working paper 02-027, 2002
2. Bensusan, H., Is machine learning experimental philosophy of science?, In A. Aliseda, D. Pearce (eds.), *ECAI2000 Workshop notes on Scientific Reasoning in Artificial Intelligence and the Philosophy of Science*, 2000, pp. 9-14
3. Cornish T.A.O., Elliman, A.D., What has Mill to say about Data Mining? *Proc. 11th Conference for AI Applications*, LA, February 20-22, 1995, Pubs. IEEE Computer Society Press, pp. 347–353

4. Dubois, D., Prade, H., Yager, R., *Information Engineering*, J.Wiley, New York, 1997
5. Dubois, D., Prade, H., Gradual inference rules in approximate reasoning, *Information Sciences*, 61 (1992) 103-122
6. Greco, S. Inuiguchi, M., Slowinski, R., Rough Sets and Gradual Decision Rules, [in] G. Wang, O. Lin Y. Yao, A Skowron (Eds.): *Rough Sets, Fuzzy Sets, Data Mining, and Granular Computing*, Lecture Notes in Computer Science, vol. 2639, Springer-Verlag, Berlin, 2003, pp. 156-164
7. Greco, S. Inuiguchi, M., Slowinski, R., A new proposal for rough fuzzy approximations and decision rule representation, [in] D. Dubois, J. Grzymala-Busse, M. Inuiguchi and L. Polkowski (eds.), *Transation on Rough Sets II: Rough Sets and Fuzzy Sets*, Lecture Notes in Computer Science, vol. 3135, Springer-Verlag, Berlin, 2004, pp. 156-164
8. Greco, S., Matarazzo, B., Slowinski R., The use of rough sets and fuzzy sets in MCDM. Chapter 14 [in] T.Gal, T.Stewart, T.Hanne (eds.), *Advances in Multiple Criteria Decision Making*, Kluwer Academic Publishers, Boston, 1999, pp. 14.1-14.59
9. Greco, S., Matarazzo, B., Slowinski R., Rough sets theory for multicriteria decision analysis, *Europena Journal of Operational Research*, 129 (2001) no.1, 1-47
10. Greco, S., Matarazzo, B., Slowinski R., Decision rule approach. [in] J. Figueira, S. Greco, M. Ehrgott (eds.), *Multiple Criteria Decision Analysis, State of the art Surveys*, Springer, 2005, 507-561 (Chapter 13)
11. Greco, S., Pawlak, Z., Slowinski R., Can Bayesian confirmation measures be useful for rough set decision rules?, *Engineering Applications of Artificial Intelligence* 17 (2004) 345–361
12. Klement, E. P., Mesiar, R., Pap, E., *Triangular Norms*, Kluwer Academic Publishers, Dordrecht, 2000
13. Marchant, T., The measurement of membership by comparisons, *Fuzzy Sets and Systems*, 148, 157-177, 2004
14. Mill, J.S., *A System of Logic, Ratiocinative and Inductive: Being a connected View of the Principles of Evidence and the Methods of Scientific Investigation*, [in] Collected Works, Volume VII, Books l-m, J.M. Robson (ed.) University of Toronto Press, RKP, 1843/1973.
15. Nakamura, A., Gao, J.M., A logic for fuzzy data analysis, *Fuzzy Sets and Systems*, 39, 1991, 127-132
16. Pawlak, Z., Rough Sets, *International Journal of Computer and Information Sciences*, 11, 1982, 341-356
17. Pawlak, Z., *Rough Sets*, Kluwer, Dordrecht, 1991
18. Williamson, J., A dynamic interaction between machine learning and the philosophy of science, *Minds and Machine*, 14(4) (2004) 539-549
19. Wittgenstein, L., *Tractatus Logico-Philosophicus*. Routledge and Kegan Paul, London, 1922; fifth impression 1951
20. Zadeh, L. A., Fuzzy sets, *Information and Control*, 8, 1965, 338-353

Fuzzy Spatial Relationships for Model-Based Pattern Recognition in Images and Spatial Reasoning Under Imprecision

Isabelle Bloch

Ecole Nationale Supérieure des Télécommunications,
Dept. TSI - CNRS UMR 5141 LTCI,
46 rue Barrault, 75013 Paris, France
Isabelle.Bloch@enst.fr

Abstract. We show in this paper that mathematical morphology provides a unified and consistent framework to express different types of spatial relationships and to answer different questions about them, with good properties. We show then how to use these fuzzy relationships in model-based pattern recognition and spatial reasoning under imprecision. Two examples are presented, one where recognition of face features is expressed as non bijective correspondence between graphs representing regions and spatial relations, and one where anatomical expert knowledge involving spatial relationships is used to guide the recognition of brain structures.

1 Introduction

Fuzzy set theory provides a good theoretical basis to represent imprecision of information, at different levels of representation, in particular in image processing and interpretation. It constitutes a unified framework for representing and processing both numerical and symbolic information, as well as structural information (constituted mainly by spatial relationships in image processing). The interest of spatial relationships between objects has been highlighted in very different types of works. Indeed, the spatial arrangement of objects in images provides important information for recognition and interpretation tasks, in particular when the objects are embedded in a complex environment like in medical or remote sensing images. We distinguish between relationships that are mathematically well defined and relationships that are intrinsically vague. Topological relationships (such as set relationships and adjacency) and distances belong to the first class. If the objects are precisely defined, their relationships can be defined and computed in a numerical (purely quantitative) setting. But if the objects are imprecise, as is often the case if they are extracted from images, then the semi-quantitative framework of fuzzy sets proved to be useful for their representation, as spatial fuzzy sets. Definitions of relationships have then to be extended to be applicable on fuzzy objects. Results can also be semi-quantitative, and provided in the form of intervals or fuzzy numbers. Some metric relationships, like relative directional position, belong to the second class. Even for crisp objects, fuzzy definitions are then appropriate.

V. Di Gesú, F. Masulli, and A. Petrosino (Eds.): WILF 2003, LNAI 2955, pp. 164–173, 2006.
© Springer-Verlag Berlin Heidelberg 2006

We show in this paper that mathematical morphology provides a unified and consistent framework to express different types of spatial relationships and to answer different questions about them, with good properties (Section 2). We show then through two examples how to use these fuzzy relationships in model-based pattern recognition and spatial reasoning under imprecision (Section 3).

2 Mathematical Morphology as a Unified Framework for Defining Spatial Relationships

In this Section we address the problem of modeling spatial relationships in the fuzzy set framework. This framework is interesting here for several reasons:

- the objects of interest can be imprecisely defined, for instance due to the segmentation step;
- some relations are imprecise, such as *to be left of*, and find a more suitable definition in the fuzzy set framework;
- the type of knowledge available about the structures or the type of question we would like to answer can be imprecise too.

We consider here adjacency (as one example of topological relation), distances, and directional relative position. Some of them have led to a rich literature in the fuzzy set community, like distances which have been defined using a lot of different approaches, while others have not raised so much attention. We summarize here our work based on fuzzy mathematical morphology [1], which allows us to represent in a unified way various spatial relationships [2].

Two types of questions are important for applications in structural pattern recognition:

1. given two objects (possibly fuzzy), assess the degree to which a relation is satisfied;
2. given one reference object, define the area of the space in which a relation to this reference is satisfied (to some degree).

Our approach provides answers to these two types of questions. The second one will be illustrated only for distances and directional position here (see [2] for the other relations).

We consider the general case of a 3D space $\mathcal{S}$ (typically $\mathbb{R}^3$ or $\mathbb{Z}^3$ in the digital case), where objects can have any shape and any topology, and can be crisp or fuzzy.

Adjacency. Adjacency has a large interest in image processing and pattern recognition, since it denotes an important relationship between image objects or regions [3], widely used as a feature in model-based pattern recognition. In the crisp case, it is defined based on the digital connectivity $n_c(x, y)$ defined on the image: two subsets X and Y in $\mathcal{S}$ are adjacent according to the c-connectivity if: $X \cap Y = \emptyset$ *and* $\exists x \in X, \exists y \in Y : n_c(x, y)$. This definition can also be expressed equivalently in terms of morphological dilation, as: $X \cap Y = \emptyset$ *and* $D_B(X) \cap Y \neq$

$\emptyset$, $D_B(Y) \cap X \neq \emptyset$, where B denotes the elementary structuring element associated to the c-connectivity and $D_B(X)$ denotes the dilation of X by B.

This morphological expression can be extended to the fuzzy case, leading to the following degree of adjacency between two fuzzy sets [4]:

$$\mu_{adj}(\mu, \nu) = t[\mu_{\neg int}(\mu, \nu), \mu_{int}[D_B(\mu), \nu], \mu_{int}[D_B(\nu), \mu]], \qquad (1)$$

where $D_B(\mu)$ denotes the fuzzy dilation of μ by B. This definition represents a conjunctive combination (through a t-norm t) of a degree of non-intersection $\mu_{\neg int}$ between μ and ν and a degree of intersection μ_{int} between one fuzzy set and the dilation of the other. B can be taken as the elementary structuring element related to the considered connectivity, or as a fuzzy structuring element, representing for instance spatial imprecision (i.e. the possibility distribution of the location of each point). We proved that this definition is symmetrical, consistent with the binary definition if μ, ν and B are binary, decreases if the distance between μ and ν increases, and is invariant with respect to geometrical transformations [4].

Distances. The importance of distances in image processing is well established. Their extensions to fuzzy sets can be useful in several parts of image processing under imprecision (classification and clustering, skeletonization, registration, structural pattern recognition, since distances constitute a major component of the spatial arrangement of objects).

Several definitions can be found in the literature for distances between fuzzy sets (which is the main addressed problem). They can be roughly divided in two classes: distances that take only membership functions into account and that compare them point-wise, and distances that additionally include spatial distances [5]. The definitions which combine spatial distance and fuzzy membership comparison allow for a more general analysis of structures in images, for applications where topological and spatial arrangement of the structures of interest is important (segmentation, classification, scene interpretation). These distances combine membership values at different points in the space, and take into account their proximity or distance in $\mathcal{S}$. The price to pay is an increased complexity, generally quadratic in the cardinality of $\mathcal{S}$.

We proposed in [5] original approaches for defining fuzzy distances taking into account spatial information, which are based on fuzzy mathematical morphology. The idea is that in the binary case, there exist strong links between mathematical morphology (in particular dilation) and distances (from a point to a set, and between two sets), and this can also be exploited in the fuzzy case. The advantage is that distances are expressed in set theoretical terms, and are therefore easier to translate to the fuzzy case with nice properties than usual analytical expressions. Definitions of nearest point distance between two fuzzy sets and of Hausdorff distance can be obtained this way, and provide evaluations as fuzzy numbers. These definitions are not detailed here, but the reader can refer to [5] for these, as well as for properties and examples.

Let us now consider the second question, i.e. defining the area of space that satisfies some distance property with respect to a reference object. We assume that a set A is known as one already recognized object, or a known area of $\mathcal{S}$, and we want to determine B, subject to satisfy some distance relationship with A. According to the algebraic expressions of distances, dilation of A is an adequate tool for this. For instance if the knowledge expresses that $d(A, B) \geq n$, then B should be looked for in $D^{n-1}(A)^C$ ($D^n(A)$ denotes the dilation of size n of A). As another example, expressing that B should lay between a distance n_1 and a distance n_2 of A can be obtained by considering both minimum and maximum (Hausdorff) distances: the minimum distance should be greater than n_1 and the maximum distance should be less than n_2. In this case, the volume of interest for B is reduced to $D^{n_2}(A) \setminus D^{n_1-1}(A)$.

In cases where imprecision has to be taken into account, fuzzy dilations are used, with the corresponding equivalences with fuzzy distances [1,5]. The extension to approximate distances calls for fuzzy structuring elements. We define these structuring elements through their membership function ν on $\mathcal{S}$. Structuring elements with a spherical symmetry can typically be used, where the membership degree only depends on the distance to the center of the structuring element.

Let us consider the generalization to the fuzzy case of the last case (minimum distance of at least n_1 and maximum distance of at most n_2 to a fuzzy set μ). Instead of defining an interval $[n_1, n_2]$, we consider a fuzzy interval, defined as a fuzzy set on $\mathbb{R}^+$ having a core equal to the interval $[n_1, n_2]$. The membership function μ_n is increasing between 0 and n_1 and decreasing after n_2 (this is but one example). Then we define two structuring elements, as:

$$\nu_1(v) = \begin{cases} 1 - \mu_n(d_E(v,0)) & \text{if } d_E(v,0) \leq n_1 \\ 0 & \text{else} \end{cases} \tag{2}$$

$$\nu_2(v) = \begin{cases} 1 & \text{if } d_E(v,0) \leq n_2 \\ \mu_n(d_E(v,0)) & \text{else} \end{cases} \tag{3}$$

where d_E is the Euclidean distance in $\mathcal{S}$ and O the origin. The spatial fuzzy set expressing the approximate relationship about distance to μ is then defined as:

$$\mu_{distance} = t[D_{\nu_2}(\mu), 1 - D_{\nu_1}(\mu)] \tag{4}$$

if $n_1 \neq 0$, and $\mu_{distance} = D_{\nu_2}(\mu)$ if $n_1 = 0$. The increasingness of fuzzy dilation with respect to both the set to be dilated and the structuring element [1] guarantees that these expressions do not lead to inconsistencies: we have $\nu_1 \subseteq \nu_2$, $\nu_1(0) = \nu_2(0) = 1$, and therefore $\mu \subseteq D_{\nu_1}(\mu) \subseteq D_{\nu_2}(\mu)$. In the case where $n_1 = 0$, we do not have $\nu_1(0) = 1$ any longer, but in this case, only the dilation by ν_2 is considered. This case corresponds actually to a distance to μ less than "about n_2". These properties are indeed expected for representations of distance knowledge.

Directional Relative Position. This type of relation is ambiguous and imprecise even if objects are crisp. Therefore, relative position concepts may find a better understanding in the framework of fuzzy sets, as fuzzy relationships, even for crisp objects. This framework makes it possible to propose flexible definitions which fit the intuition and may include subjective aspects, depending on the application and on the requirements of the user. The few existing fuzzy approaches in the literature mostly rely on angle histogram [6, 7] or extensions of it [8]. Our approach is completely different since it works directly in the spatial domain.

Let us consider a reference object R and an object A for which the relative position with respect to R has to be evaluated. In order to evaluate the degree to which A is in some direction with respect to R, we propose the following approach [9]:

1. We first define a fuzzy "landscape" around the reference object R as a fuzzy set such that the membership value of each point corresponds to the degree of satisfaction of the spatial relation under examination. This is formally defined by a fuzzy dilation of R by a fuzzy structuring element representing the desired relation with respect to the origin.
2. We then compare the object A to the fuzzy landscape attached to R, in order to evaluate how well the object matches with the areas having high membership values (i.e. areas that are in the desired direction). This is done using a fuzzy pattern matching approach [10], providing an evaluation consisting of two numbers, a necessity degree N (a pessimistic evaluation) and a possibility degree Π (an optimistic evaluation), as often used in the fuzzy set community. An average measure can also be useful from a practical point of view.

The first step answers the second type of question, while the second one answers the first type. Details about the formalization and the properties, as well as some algorithmical and computational aspects, can be found in [9].

3   Examples in Model-Based Pattern Recognition and Spatial Reasoning

Spatial reasoning is a research field dedicated to reasoning about spatial entities and spatial relations. It is particularly developed in artificial intelligence and several formal theories have been developed (see e.g. [11] for a survey) but much less in image interpretation. An example of application concerns structural recognition in images under imprecision.

Let us now briefly illustrate how fuzzy spatial relations can be used for recognizing structures in a scene based on a model of this scene. Two types of approaches can be developed, corresponding to the two types of questions mentioned in Section 2.

Graph-Based Approach. In the first approach, spatial relations evaluated between spatial entities (typically objects or regions) are considered as attributes in a graph.

Graph representations are widely used for dealing with structural information, in different domains including image interpretation and model-based pattern recognition. Here, we assume that the model is represented as a graph where nodes are objects and edges represent links between these objects. Both nodes and edges are attributed. Node attributes are characteristics of the objects, while edge attributes quantify spatial relationships between the objects. A data graph is then constructed from each image where the recognition has to be performed. Since it is usually difficult to segment directly the objects, usually the graph is based on an over-segmentation of the image, for instance based on watersheds. Each region constitutes a node of this data graph, and edges represent links between regions. Attributes are computed as for the model. The use of fuzzy relations is particularly useful in order to be less sensitive to the segmentation.

One important problem to be solved then is graph matching. In order to achieve a good correspondence between both graphs, the most used concept is the one of graph isomorphism and a lot of work is dedicated to the search for the best isomorphism between two graphs or subgraphs. However, in a number of cases, the bijective condition is too strong: because of the schematic aspect of the model and of the difficulty to segment the image into meaningful entities, no isomorphism can be expected between both graphs. In particular, several regions of the image can be assigned to the same node of the model graph. Such problems call for inexact graph matching. It constitutes generally in finding a morphism, which furthermore optimizes an objective function based on similarities between attributes. The morphism aims at preserving the structure of the graphs, while the objective function privileges the association between nodes, respectively between edges, with similar attribute values. This approach can benefit from the huge literature on fuzzy comparison tools (see e.g. [12]) and from recent developments on fuzzy morphisms [13]. The optimization is not an easy task since the problem is NP-hard. Genetic algorithms, estimation of distribution algorithms (EDA) and tree search methods have been developed towards this aim [14, 15, 16].

This approach has been applied in brain imaging, in order to recognize brain structures in a 3D magnetic resonance image (MRI) based on an anatomical atlas [14], and in face feature recognition, based on a rough model of a face constructed from a different person image [16] (an example is shown in Figure 1).

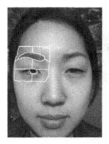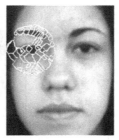

Fig. 1. Left: model; middle: over-segmented image (subset); right: results on a few face features obtained with EDA (from [16])

Focusing Attention Based on Spatial Representation of Spatial Knowledge. In the second type of approach, we use the spatial representation of spatial knowledge. Each relation is then represented as a spatial fuzzy set, constraining the search for the object that should satisfy this relation. This region of interest allows to focus attention towards the only region satisfying the relation (to some degree). Since usually several relations are represented in the model for describing one structure, fusion of these representations should be performed. The fuzzy set framework offers a large set of fusion operators, varying from conjunctive to disjunctive ones, including adaptive operators [17]. The fusion of all regions of interest leads to a fuzzy region representing the combination of all relationships concerning one structure. Then segmentation of the structure can be based on image information (typically grey levels) focused in the obtained fuzzy region.

A recognition procedure based on this type of representation has been developed for the recognition of internal brain structures in MRI [18, 19]. The model has an iconic part (digital atlas) and a symbolic part (linguistic descriptions of relationships between anatomical structures). The procedure consists in recognizing first simple structures (typically brain and lateral ventricles), and then progressively more and more difficult structures, based on relationships between these structures and previously recognized structures. Each relationship describing the structure to be recognized is translated into a spatial fuzzy set representing the area satisfying this relation, to some degrees. The fuzzy sets representing all relationships involved in the recognition process are fused using a numerical fusion operator. In the obtained fuzzy region of interest, a segmentation procedure is performed, and the quality of the results is guaranteed by the very restricted (focused) area in which the structure of interest is searched. This approach typically belongs to the field of spatial reasoning under imprecision in images.

For instance, the recognition of a caudate nucleus in a 3D MRI image uses the results of recognition of brain and lateral ventricles and the following pieces of knowledge, illustrated in Figure 2:

– rough shape and localization are provided by the representation of the caudate nucleus in the atlas, and its fuzzy dilation to account for variability and for inexact matching between the model and the image,

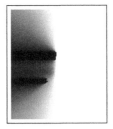

Fig. 2. Knowledge representation in the image space (only one slice of the 3D volume is shown), illustrating knowledge about one caudate nucleus: shape information (left), set relationships (middle), and relative directional relationship (right). Membership values vary from 0 (white) to 1 (black).

  - the caudate nucleus belongs to the brain (black) but is outside from both
    lateral ventricles (white components inside the brain),
  - the caudate nucleus is lateral to the lateral ventricle.

These pieces of knowledge are then combined (also with information extracted
from the image itself), which leads to a successful recognition of the caudate
nucleus.

Figure 3 illustrates the spatial representation of some knowledge about distances, used for several structures.

Figure 4 shows 3D views of some cerebral objects as defined in the atlas and
as recognized in an MR image with our method. They are correctly recognized
although the size, the location and the morphology of these objects in the image

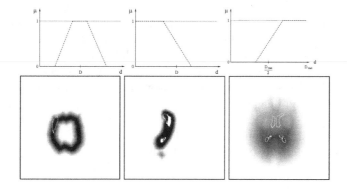

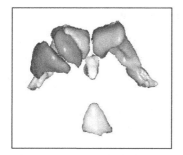

Fig. 3. Representation of knowledge about distances. Top: membership functions μ_n.
Bottom: spatial fuzzy sets. The following examples are illustrated: the putamen has
an approximately constant distance to the brain surface (left), the caudate nucleus is
at a distance about less than D from the lateral ventricles (in white) (middle), lateral
ventricles are inside the brain and at a distance larger than about D from the brain
surface (right). The contours of the objects we are looking at are shown in white.

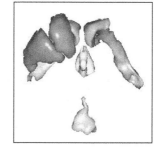

Fig. 4. Recognition results. The left view represents six objects from the model atlas: lateral ventricles (medium grey), third and fourth ventricles (light grey), caudate
nucleus and putamen (dark grey). The right view represents the equivalent objects
recognized from a MRI acquisition. (From [18].)

significantly differ from their definitions in the atlas. Note in particular the good recognition of third and fourth ventricles, that are very difficult to segment directly from the image. Here the help of relationships to other structures is very important.

The segmentation can be further improved once recognition is achieved by integrating the fuzzy regions representing the spatial relations as new energy terms in deformable models [20].

This approach has been used in other domains, for instance in mobile robotics to reason about the spatial position of the robot and the structure of its environment [21].

4   Conclusion

As illustrated in this paper, the semi-qualitative fuzzy set framework shows interesting features both for knowledge representation (of spatial relations, of imprecision existing both in the objects and in the relations), and for reasoning and recognition. We have also shown the usefulness of fuzzy mathematical morphology in this context. This work opens new perspectives for spatial reasoning under imprecision in image interpretation.

Acknowledgments. The author would like to thank Alfredo Petrosino for his invitation to present this paper at the WILF conference.

References

1. Bloch, I., Maître, H.: Fuzzy Mathematical Morphologies: A Comparative Study. Pattern Recognition **28** (1995) 1341–1387
2. Bloch, I.: Mathematical Morphology and Spatial Relationships: Quantitative, Semi-Quantitative and Symbolic Settings. In Sztandera, L., Matsakis, P., eds.: Applying Soft Computing in Defining Spatial Relationships. Physica Verlag, Springer (2002) 63–98
3. Rosenfeld, A., Kak, A.C.: Digital Picture Processing. Academic Press, New-York (1976)
4. Bloch, I., Maître, H., Anvari, M.: Fuzzy Adjacency between Image Objects. International Journal of Uncertainty, Fuzziness and Knowledge-Based Systems **5** (1997) 615–653
5. Bloch, I.: On Fuzzy Distances and their Use in Image Processing under Imprecision. Pattern Recognition **32** (1999) 1873–1895
6. Miyajima, K., Ralescu, A.: Spatial Organization in 2D Segmented Images: Representation and Recognition of Primitive Spatial Relations. Fuzzy Sets and Systems **65** (1994) 225–236
7. Keller, J.M., Wang, X.: Comparison of Spatial Relation Definitions in Computer Vision. In: ISUMA-NAFIPS'95, College Park, MD (1995) 679–684
8. Matsakis, P., Wendling, L.: A New Way to Represent the Relative Position between Areal Objects. IEEE Trans. on Pattern Analysis and Machine Intelligence **21** (1999) 634–642

9. Bloch, I.: Fuzzy Relative Position between Objects in Image Processing: a Morphological Approach. IEEE Transactions on Pattern Analysis and Machine Intelligence **21** (1999) 657–664
10. Dubois, D., Prade, H., Testemale, C.: Weighted Fuzzy Pattern Matching. Fuzzy Sets and Systems **28** (1988) 313–331
11. Vieu, L.: Spatial Representation and Reasoning in Artificial Intelligence. In Stock, O., ed.: Spatial and Temporal Reasoning. Kluwer (1997) 5–41
12. Bouchon-Meunier, B., Rifqi, M., Bothorel, S.: Towards General Measures of Comparison of Objects. Fuzzy Sets and Systems **84** (1996) 143–153
13. Perchant, A., Bloch, I.: Fuzzy Morphisms between Graphs. Fuzzy Sets and Systems **128** (2002) 149–168
14. Perchant, A., Boeres, C., Bloch, I., Roux, M., Ribeiro, C.: Model-based Scene Recognition Using Graph Fuzzy Homomorphism Solved by Genetic Algorithm. In: GbR'99 2nd International Workshop on Graph-Based Representations in Pattern Recognition, Castle of Haindorf, Austria (1999) 61–70
15. Bengoetxea, E., Larranaga, P., Bloch, I., Perchant, A., Boeres, C.: Inexact Graph Matching by Means of Estimation of Distribution Algorithms. Pattern Recognition **35** (2002) 2867–2880
16. Cesar, R., Bengoetxea, E., Bloch, I.: Inexact Graph Matching using Stochastic Optimization Techniques for Facial Feature Recognition. In: International Conference on Pattern Recognition ICPR 2002. Volume 2., Québec (2002) 465–468
17. Bloch, I.: Information Combination Operators for Data Fusion: A Comparative Review with Classification. IEEE Transactions on Systems, Man, and Cybernetics **26** (1996) 52–67
18. Géraud, T., Bloch, I., Maître, H.: Atlas-guided Recognition of Cerebral Structures in MRI using Fusion of Fuzzy Structural Information. In: CIMAF'99 Symposium on Artificial Intelligence, La Havana, Cuba (1999) 99–106
19. Bloch, I., Géraud, T., Maître, H.: Representation and Fusion of Heterogeneous Fuzzy Information in the 3D Space for Model-Based Structural Recognition - Application to 3D Brain Imaging. Artificial Intelligence Journal **148** (2003) 141–175
20. Colliot, O.: Représentation, évaluation et utilisation de relations spatiales pour l'interprétation d'images, application à la reconnaissance de structures anatomiques en imagerie médicale. PhD thesis, Ecole Nationale Supérieure des Télécommunications (2003)
21. Bloch, I., Saffiotti, A.: On the Representation of Fuzzy Spatial Relations in Robot Maps. In: IPMU 2002. Volume III., Annecy, France (2002) 1587–1594

Classification of Digital Terrain Models Through Fuzzy Clustering: An Application

G. Antoniol[1], M. Ceccarelli[1], A. Maratea[1], and F. Russo[2]

[1] Research Center On Software Technology,
University of Sannio, Via Traiano 11, Benevento, Italy
{antoniol, ceccarelli, maratea}@unisannio.it
[2] Dep.of Geological and Environmental Studies,
University of Sannio, via Port'Arsa 11, Benevento, Italy
filrusso@unisannio.it

Abstract. Experts classifications of spatial data are strongly affected by subjectivity and rigidity of rules. They do not take into account, in a quantitative way, the overlap of classes and as a major consequence, their classifications are often not reproducibles. To overcome this subjectivity, exploratory techniques can suggest a coherent set of rules that will produce suitable polythetic and overlapping classes. The aim of this paper is to validate the unsupervised method of fuzzy clustering applied to classification of raster spatial data.

Keywords: Fuzzy Clustering, Digital Terrain Model, Validity Index.

1 Introduction

The identification of geomorphological or functional units (Correlative Complex [8]), where the whole environment is strongly characterized, is extremely difficult to be done by hand and needs a well trained expert geographer. It is well known that different experts tend to describe the same area in different ways, depending on their background and their personal insigths and consequently classifications performed are often very subjective and not reproducible. On the other hand, the utility of this work is enormous in planning surveys, analysis or simply in reducing the causal factors to be analyzed for a generic environmental phenomenon. A limited number of easily discernible functional units is much more manageable than a complex of correlated and overlapping variables for discovering characteristic of, e.g., surface hydrology, soil properties or site stability. To define classes limits unambiguosly can be feasible when there is just one variable, but it's an ambitious task when there are multiple variables that overlaps each other in various ways. There is the need of modelling the fact that most of points do not belong to just one unit. In this situation, choosing hard or crisp boundaries for the classes will lead to an increment of casual errors, especially in points near the boundaries [7].

In this work we have validated a method that uses fuzzy logic in classification of landscapes morphological units: the fuzzy c-means [1]. We applied the clustering algorithm to the Digital Terrain Model (DTM) representing the territory

V. Di Gesú, F. Masulli, and A. Petrosino (Eds.): WILF 2003, LNAI 2955, pp. 174–182, 2006.
© Springer-Verlag Berlin Heidelberg 2006

of the Caudina Valley (Benevento Italy), starting from a set of morphometrical parameters derived from the DTM, and then we have tested the results for various parameter values trough differents validity indexes. As it has been shown in others works as well (e.g. [2] [4]), this has proven to be an efficient and fast method to represent in a less subjective way the morphological units in the area of study and to allow for overlap among classes.

The paper is organized as follows: in section 2, after illustrating the data and briefly introducing the fuzzy c-means algorithm, we explain the validation procedure and the adopted validation indexes; in section 3 we present the results and the geographical characterization of the membership functions of the optimal solution; in section 4, we draw our conclusion and highlight method's limits.

2   Data, Method and Validation

2.1   The Data

The starting DTM is a high resolution altimetric matrix of Caudina Valley (Benevento Italy), with square grid of 1000 cells per side; the resolution is 20 meters and it has 1000000 points. As proposed in [2] we have derived the morphometrical parameters that mostly characterize the relief and for each of them we have generated the relative thematic map. The list of the variables used is the following: Heigth, Slope, Plan Curvature, Profile Curvature, and Ridge Proximity. Whereas all such variables are continuous the DTM data are based on a raster format, so they are sampled in a finite number of points. Hence differentials values such as the slope and the curvature are obtained using finite difference computed on a windows centered at each point of sampling grid [13]. For each sample of the DTM we have a 5-dimentional vector. All components have been normalized to avoid differences of weight.

2.2   The Method

In general, given a certain number of statistical units on which it's possible to observe a certain number of variables, the unsupervised technique that groups them in a given number of clusters based on the similarity of the variable and observation values is known as Cluster Analysis. It divides the given data set in groups such that they are the most possible homogeneous within them and the most possible heterogeneous between them; it searches for the most similar units in the data and groups them toghether [9].

The adopted algorithm is the fuzzy c-means [1]. It is an iterative stochastic hill-climbing procedure: it generates the cluster centers randomly, then it allocates the points to the cluster, computes again cluster centers and reallocate points, until convergence. Let $X = \{x_1, \ldots, x_N\}$ be a set of N k-dimensional samples and $m_1, \ldots, m_c$ a set of vectors representing the cluster centers. The fuzzy c-means algorithm aims to generate a convergent sequence of vectors $m_1(t), \ldots, m_c(t)$, such that the limit point of this sequence is a local minimum of the objective function

$$J_b = \sum_i^c \sum_j^N d(x_j, m_i)\mu_{ij}^b \tag{1}$$

where $d(\cdot, \cdot)$ is a scalar product induced by the adopted norm; μ_{ij} are free parameters such that $\mu_{ij} \geq 0$ and $\sum_i^c \mu_{ij} = 1$; $b \geq 1$ is a costant (*fuzzifier* or index
of overlap). The value μ_{ij} is the degree of membership of observation i to cluster j and is called *membership function*. It varies between 0 (minimum) and 1
(maximum). This algorithm has been used extensively in a number of vectorial
quantization and pattern recognition problems (e.g.[3]).

To reduce the computational cost of this method we have calculated cluster
centroids on a subset of the whole data set, extracting a sample of 25% from the
original DTM an thus working separately for centroids on a matrix 500 × 500.
At the end of process, points have been also deffuzzified to allow drawing of line
boundaries among morphological units, assigning every point to the cluster with
the higher membership value (figure 1).

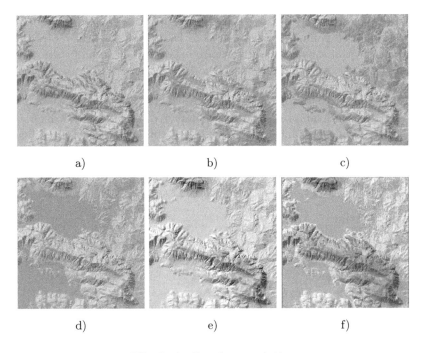

a)   b)   c)

d)   e)   f)

Fig. 1. the five cluster solution

The only critical free parameter is the amount of fuzziness b, wich measures
the overlap. Actually there is no formal method to choose the optimal value of
overlapping (although its asymptotic properties have been studied [11]) and it's
very application dependent. After extensive experiments, we have found that for
this case the best value is 1.5.

2.3   The Validation

The choice of the rigth number of clusters, is one of the main open questions in Clustering. We have a lot of solutions proposed for this non trivial problem, but none of them can be considered the best in sense of being optimal in every situation. We have choosen a set of indexes that seem to be the most reliable for our case, but much depends on the degree of detail required. All indexes have been calculated for a range of clusters number from 3 to 10 and plotted versus the number of clusters.

The Partition Coefficient (PC) and the Partition Entropy (PE) [1] are validity indexes involving only the membership values, not the data. The first is simply the mean of all squared membership and the second is the entropy of all membership values. The closer to unity the PC index (and the closer to 0 the PE index), the crisper the clustering is.

$$PC = \frac{1}{N} \sum_i^c \sum_j^N \mu_{ij}^2 \tag{2}$$

$$PE = \frac{1}{N} \sum_i^c \sum_j^N \mu_{ij} \log_a \mu_{ij} \tag{3}$$

where N is the number of points in the data set, μ_{ij} are the membership values and c is the number of clusters. The known drawbacks of this indexes are their monotonous dependency on the number of clusters and the lack of a direct connection to the geometry of the data. In our case both the PC and the PE show a very regular trend (decreasing and increasing respectively), with no significant knee for none of the cluster numbers (figure 2).

The Xie-Beni index [12] (XB), also called the compactness and separation validity function, is a function of both the data set and the centroids of the clusters, so it accounts for data geometry. It is the ratio of the total variation of the partition divided for the size of the data set (the compactness) and the minimum distance between cluster centroids (the separation). Minimum values support best partitions. It is known that XB decreases monotonically when c is close to N. We have plotted the values of this index versus the number of clusters and it has clear minimum for the five clusters solution (figure 2).

$$XB = \frac{\sum_i^c \sum_j^N \mu_{ij}^2 \|m_i - x_j\|^2}{N \min_{ij} \|m_i - m_j\|} \tag{4}$$

Another frequently used index is the Fukuyama-Sugeno index [5] (FS), which is characterized by the difference of two terms, the first term measuring the compactness of the clusters and the second one measuring the distances of the clusters centroids from the grand mean of the data. The minimum values of this index also propose a good partition.

$$FS = \sum_i^c \sum_j^N \mu_{ij}^b (\|x_j - m_i\|_A^2 - \|m_i - m\|_A^2) \tag{5}$$

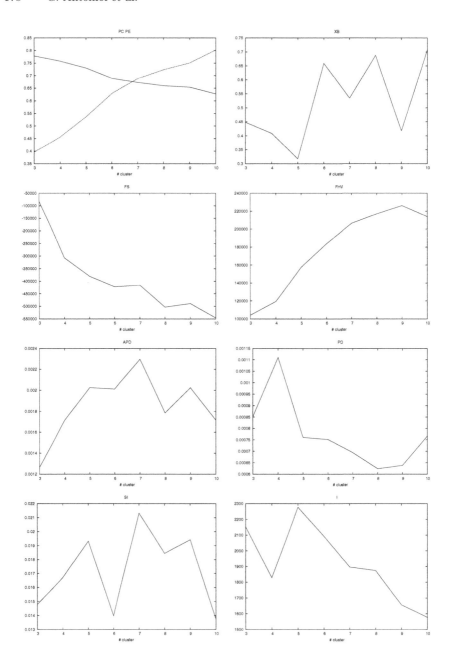

Fig. 2. validity indexes plot: on the top left corner PC&PE; on the top rigth corner XB; under the top left corner FS; under the top rigth corner FHV; over the bottom left corner APD; over the bottom rigth corner PD; on the bottom left corner SI; on the bottom rigth corner I

where A is a $k \times k$ positive definite, symmetric matrix and m is the grand mean of the data. When $A = I$, the distance become the squared Euclidean distance. In our case it has an almost regular decreasing trend with the increment of clusters number, with a pair of steps for 7 and 9 clusters (figure 2).

Other validity indices are proposed in [6], based on the heuristics that a better clustering assumes clear separation between the clusters, minimal volume of the clusters and maximal number of data points concentrated in proximity of cluster centroids. The volume of clusters and the physical density of membership values are used to quantify this considerations. We calculated all three index proposed, the Fuzzy Hyper Volume (FHV), the Partition Density (PD) and the Average Partition Density (APD).

$$FHV = \sum_i^c \det F_i^{\frac{1}{2}} \qquad (6)$$

$$APD = \frac{1}{c} \sum_i^c \frac{S_i}{\det F_i^{\frac{1}{2}}} \qquad (7)$$

$$PD = \frac{S}{FHV} \qquad (8)$$

where F_i is the fuzzy covariance matrix of the i-th cluster; $S_i = \sum_j^N \mu_{ij} \ \forall x_j \in \{X : (x - m_i)F_i^{-1}(x - m_i) < 1\}$ is "the sum of central members", taking into account only those member within the hyperellipsoids whose radii are standard deviations of the cluster features; $S = \sum_i^c S_i$. The hypervolume criterion is related to the within-cluster scatter, but due to its fuzzy characteristics the FHV is in general not a monotone function of c. In our case, however, it shows a regular increasing trend with the increase of clusters number (figure 2). The PD and APD are the general density and the mean density of points in cluster, the first being more stable but less connected to geometry and the second being more sensible to single anomalous cluster but more connected to the geometry. In our case they have an absolute maximum for 4 and 7 clusters respectively (figure 2).

We calculated also the Separation Index (SI also called CS Index), defined as the ratio between the mean diameter of each cluster and the minimum distance between that cluster centroid and all others. This index assumes that data are in some ways defuzzified to be calculated, that a hard partition is derived from the fuzzy one. It answers the question if the clusters are compact and separated, and has a mainly geometrical nature. Unfortunately it is often computationally infeasible for big data sets since a distance matrix between all the data membership values has to be calculated. Clearly minor values support best partitions.

$$SI = \frac{\sum_i^c \frac{1}{|C_i|} \sum_{x_j \in C_i} \max_{x_k \in C_i} \|x_j - x_k\|}{\sum_i^c \min_{j \in \{1,...,c\}, j \neq i} \|m_i - m_j\|} \qquad (9)$$

where C_i is the set whose elements are the data points assigned to the i-th cluster and $|C_i|$ is the number of elements of C_i. In our case it shows its minimum for the 6 classes solution (figure 2).

Finally, we calculated a fuzzy version of a recently developed index I [10], that seems to show very interesting performances for validation of various heterogeneous data sets. It is the product of three factors: the first being a correction factor needed to remove increasing trend with number of cluster of other two; the second being the ratio the total mass of the data set and the sum of all distances from centroids weighted with the membership; the third which measures the maximum separation between two clusters over all possible pairs of clusters. The three factors are found to compete with and balance each other critically.

$$I = (\frac{1}{c} \times \frac{E_1}{E_c} \times D_c)^p \tag{10}$$

where $E_c = \sum_i^c \sum_j^N \mu_{ij} \|x_j - m_i\|$; $D_c = \max_{i,j}^c \|m_i - m_j\|$ and $E_1 = \sum_j^N \|x_j - m\|$. The power p is used to control the contrast between the different cluster configurations. As in the original work [10], in this article we have taken $p = 2$. In our case I shows a unique maximum in correspondence of the 5 classes solution (figure 2).

To analyze all these results we have to do some considerations first. Most of this validity indexes presume that a "crisper" partition is better than a "fuzzier", and if it isn't necessarily true in general, especially in our case, where we know a priori that our classification will contain a significant amount of fuzziness, this paradigm is inappropriate. All of them depends also implicitly on fuzzifier value b and show a variable behaviour (some more than others) changing its value, and as we have already said, there's no formal method to choose b optimal value. Moreover, most of these validity indices usually assume tacitly that data points have constant density into the clusters, and of course this is never true in real problems. In spite of this considerations, with the appropriate care, these indexes can actually help in recognizing the clustering structure of our data.

The PC and the PE can be considered as a general measure of fuzziness. Both show a regular trend, even after scaling. This makes virtually impossible to choose the breakpoint and confirms to us that the data have a significant overlap. Due to this overlap, the FHV also has a regular increasing trend and shows us that our clusters are quite regularly spaced, not helping us otherwise. The Gath and Geva indexes PD and APD, taking into account only central members and being average quantities, are not enough reliable since density measure in this condition are too rough. The FS index also, being characterized by a sum, it's more sensible to single anomalous values with respect to XB, that's a ratio and has a better balance. Moreover recent studies [11] emphasize how the FS is very sensitive to the value of the fuzzifier b and thus in general much more unreliable of XB (that in sensible only to very large values of b). Index I instead balances well its three factors and is less sensitive to anomalous clusters. The SI index works geometrically on defuzzified data and is not too much affected by the overlap: it gives us values nearby XB and I. Concluding, we can say that there is a substantial agreement between the two theoretically more reliable indexes (XB and I), and a slight variation for SI, while the others are affected by the remarkable amount of fuzziness.

3   Results

Once obtained the classification through the cited method, results have been submitted to qualitative judgement of experts geographers, which have found as optimal the five classes solution. They recognized the solution with five classes as the most readable and as that in which are better highlighted the most meaningful morphological structures, agreeing with the validation results. In detail, the membership functions have been characterized as explained below:

In the first cluster (figure 1 (a)) the membership function has higher values in ripid areas, mainly convex, and lower values in the valley bottom and near the ridges. In the second cluster (figure 1 (b)) the membership function has higher values in the lower ridges and where the slope isn't too high. It has lower values in the valley bottom and near the higher ridges. In the third cluster (figure 1 (c)) the membership function has higher values in areas almost plain, with low heigth, and lower values in the valley bottom and on the mountains. In the fourth cluster (figure 1 (d)) the membership function has higher values in the concave valley bottom and has lower values in all convex areas and ridges. In the fifth cluster (figure 1 (e)) the membership function has higher values in the higher ridges, mainly convex, and has lower values in areas where the slope or the heigth are medium or low.

4   Conclusions

Analyzing the complex of results, it turns out that the fuzzy c-means has been confirmed a viable solution in reducing and controlling both the variability and the subjectivity of the classifications of environmental data. It has been shown that the general procedure of sampling, training and tuning the parameters of the classification is an effective way to proceed that concurs to save time and resources. The validation procedure trough various indexes can help in finding the right values of the parameters, and should be easily generalized. Experts geographers have recognized also the output as coherent and meaningful. Finally, a warning: the amount of overlap b needs to be tuned with care, it should be chosen and dosed in relation to the morphological structure of the landscape and with respect to the selected variables. Variables, or zones, with a different geomorfological structure (e.g. a valley and a ripid mountain) involve differents values of the parameters, such as the maximum number of iterations allowed, the overlap coefficient b, and the number of clusters.

References

1. Bezdek J. C. (1981), *Pattern Recognition with Fuzzy Objective Function Algorithms*, Plenum Press, NY
2. Burrogh P. A., Van Gaans P.F.M., MacMillan R.A. (2000), High Resolution Landform Classification using Fuzzy k-means, *Fuzzy sets and systems*, 113: 37-52

3. Ceccarelli M., Farina A., Petrosino A. (1995), fuzzy unsupervised terrain classification based on a multiresolution approach, *New Trends in Fuzzy Logic*, World Scientific, 151-159
4. De Bruin S., Stein A. (1998), Soil-Landscape Modelling using Fuzzy c-means Clustering of Attribute Data derived from DTM, *Geoderma*, 83: 17-33
5. Y. Fukuyama and M. Sugeno (1989), A new method of choosing the number of clusters for the fuzzy c-means method, *Proc. 5th Fuzzy Syst. Symp.*, 247-250 (in japanese)
6. I. Gath and A. B. Geva (1989), Unsupervised Optimal Fuzzy Clustering, *IEEE Transactions on Pattern Analysis and Machine Intelligence*, 7:773-781
7. Heuveling E., Burrogh P.A. (1993), Error Propagation in Cartographic Modelling using Boolean Logic and Continuos Classification ,*Internal Journal of GIS* ,7: 231-246
8. Hopkins L. D. (1977), Methods for Generating Land Suitability Maps: a Comparative Evaluation, *American Institute of Planners Journal* (Oct), 386-400
9. Kaufman L., Rouseeuw P. J. (1990), *Finding Groups in Data: an introduction to Cluster Analysis*, Wiley, NY.
10. Maulik U., Bandyopadhyay S. (2002), Performance Evaluation of Some Clustering Algorithms and Validity Indices, *IEEE Transactions On Pattern Analysis And Machine Intelligence*, 24:1650-1654
11. Nikhil R. P., Bezdek J.C. (1995), On cluster validity for the fuzzy c-means model, *IEEE Transactions on Fuzzy Systems*, 3:370-379
12. L. X. Xie and G. Beni (1991), Validity measure for fuzzy clustering,*IEEE Transactions on Pattern Analysis and Machine Intelligence*, 8: 841-847
13. Zevenbergen L.W., Thorne C. R. (1987), Quantitative Analysis of Land Surface Topography, *Earth surface Processes and Landforms*, 12: 47-56

Evolutionary Approach to Inverse Planning in Coplanar Radiotherapy

V. Bevilacqua, G. Mastronardi, and G. Piscopo

Dipartimento di Elettrotecnica ed Elettronica, Politecnico di Bari,
Via Re David 200, 70125 Bari, Italy
{bevilacqua, mastrona}@poliba.it, giuseppe.piscopo@katamail.com

Abstract. In this paper we present an evolutionary optimisation technique to search for full beam configurations, that is beam intensity, beam
shape and especially beam orientation in three different kinds of radiation
therapy. This method automatically determines exact beam angles not
relaying solely on a geometrical basis but involving beam intensity profiles, thus considering the effective delivered dose. Experimental results
have been carried out comparing the obtained dose distribution model
with that obtained with a commercial system. As stated by physician
and by simulation with the same commercial system, our tools found
good solutions for some real clinical cases.

1 Introduction

Radiation therapy treatment of cancers is typically achieved using an array of
external X-ray beams directed at the tumour from different angles. The treatment's goal is to deliver a high dose of radiation to the diseased tissue (target)
while partially or totally avoiding normal tissue and organs at risk (OARs). In
our work we have considered three among the most used kinds of radiation therapy techniques: conformal radiation therapy (3D-CRT), so-called aperture-based
radiation therapy (ABRT) and intensity-modulated radiation therapy (IMRT).
Their main difference lies in beam intensity profile: constant for 3D-CRT, piecewise constant over discrete levels for ABRT, almost continuous for IMRT. *Forward planning* is the manual process of finding the best beams configuration
with respect to the specialist prescribed dose. The operator decides some configuration parameters based on his experience, then executes a simulation to see
the resulting dose distribution and repeats the process until some satisfactory
treatment plan is found. *Inverse planning* is the automated computation of the
therapy treatment plan that satisfies the prescribed dose over the target and
over all critical structures (OARs with/out normal tissue). Usually to achieve
this result an optimisation algorithm is used to find the best solution, which
is classified in terms of an objective function (or cost function). This describes
how good (or bad) is a proposed solution with respect to the inverse planning
problem. Many methods can be found in literature to solve different kinds of
optimisation problems for different kinds of radiation therapies [1], but only few
examples exist about utilization of evolutionary techniques in inverse treatment

V. Di Gesú, F. Masulli, and A. Petrosino (Eds.): WILF 2003, LNAI 2955, pp. 183–190, 2006.
© Springer-Verlag Berlin Heidelberg 2006

planning [2, 3, 4, 5]. Thanks to genetic algorithms, a particular implementation of evolutionary algorithms, we have been able to find the optimal beam configuration, including beam orientation angles. It must be noticed that, to our best knowledge, only few recent articles give a proposal solution for the angles optimisation [5, 6, 7, 8]. In [5, 6, 7] such a solution is found relaying solely on a geometrical basis; in a second phase beam weights and shapes are calculated. In [8] hints on preferred beam directions are given through a so-called "beam selection" metric. According to the physician judgment and to the executed simulations on a forward planning commercial system [9], the results obtained for real clinical cases are suitable for effective radiation treatments. They show that 3D-CRT can be used for simple clinical situations but then it fails for more complex cases, when ABRT and IMRT are needed. All three inverse planning problems have been solved using the same evolutionary-based framework, while in literature different algorithms are proposed for different kinds of therapies.

2   Algorithm Proposed

The designed algorithm is made of two main parts: the dose distribution model and the optimisation algorithm itself. The former takes into account the way radiation propagates through the volume. Because this doesn't depend on intensity profile, the model is the same for every kind of therapy. The latter is the actual implementation of genetic algorithm and varies with therapy, although it shares the same structure and the same cost-function evaluation.

2.1   Dose Distribution Model

Implemented model is based on single ray tracing from one fixed direction. Before the projection/retro-projection a rotation from generic angle to the fixed direction must occur. After retro-projection only, an inverse rotation is needed to obtain correct dose distribution over each section. Because of coplanar directions, an axis of symmetry exists (z) and all rotations are intended around this axis (in xy-plane). Absorption of radiation through body volume is taken into account multiplying intensity by a function of depth along the path. This function approximates an experimental absorption curve given by the physician. It takes care of lateral beam diffraction in a simple way, having a maximum just after skin surface and then exponentially decaying. In this first approach to inverse planning problem horizontal beam divergence is not modelled, nor is vertical beam divergence. In such context the *isocenter* position is a trivial matter, so it has been fixed at the centre of given volume. Easy modifications are needed to change this feature and let isocenter position free to be set.

2.2   Optimisation

Genetic algorithms have been chosen mainly because of the inverse planning problem complexity. Their stochastic nature permits to investigate fast enough for enough possible solutions in a huge search space, as the one determined by the many variables involved. Besides, these techniques are suitable for problems with a global optimum and multiple local optimal solutions. This especially holds when beam angles are optimised, as it has been stressed that in such a scenario many local maxima (minima) appear in objective (cost) function [10, 11]. Genetic algorithms emulate natural evolution of species, evolving a population according to the principles of *natural selection* and *survival of the fittest*. Every individual in a population represents a possible solution to the given problem. For our purposes, every individual must represent a possible treatment plan. The *genes* that define an individual are the parameters that define a plan (beam configuration parameters). This part of implementation changes accordingly to the radiation therapy considered, as change the parameters that define some treatment plan. These comprise beam direction, beam aperture for each vertical section and beam intensity profile for each vertical section. Especially the last one changes from therapy to therapy: a single scalar value in 3D-CRT or a function for each section in ABRT and IMRT. These parameters characterise every beam in the treatment plan. The number of beams used in the treatment is fixed for all individuals. Starting from genes, the dose distribution model enables to calculate the dose distribution associated with some plan. Then a specially designed cost function gives the penalty for the individual: this represents the *distance* of the realized distribution dose from the ideal one prescribed by the physician. Prescriptions limits change for every noticeable structure and also change the rules in evaluating the distance for each one of these. Guided by the physician knowledge, we have classified six different kinds of tissue with their respective dose limits (d_x) and penalty rules (p) once given the delivered dose (d) over a region voxel. Rules are shown in formulas below and, for some tissues, in Fig.1.

$$- \text{``Target'' (T)} \qquad p = \begin{cases} c_{T1} \cdot (d_{T1} - d) + s_{T1} & \text{if } d < d_{T1} \\ 0 & \text{if } d_{T1} \leq d \leq d_{T2} \\ c_{T2} \cdot (d_{T2} - d) + s_{T2} & \text{if } d_{T2} < d \leq d_{Tmax} \\ \infty & \text{if } d > d_{Tmax} \end{cases} \tag{1}$$

$$- \text{``Partially Critical'' (PC)} \qquad p = \begin{cases} c_P \cdot d & \text{if } d \leq d_P \\ \infty & \text{if } d > d_P \end{cases} \tag{2}$$

$$- \text{``Absolutely Critical'' (AC)} \qquad p = \begin{cases} 0 & \text{if } d = 0 \\ \infty & \text{if } d > 0 \end{cases} \tag{3}$$

$$- \text{``Minimally Critical'' (MC)} \qquad p = c_M \cdot d \tag{4}$$

$$- \text{``Normal'' (N)} \qquad p = c_N \cdot d \tag{5}$$

$$- \text{``Outside'' (O) (don't care)} \qquad p = 0. \tag{6}$$

The cost of a single plan is obtained by summing the average penalty over each kind of region: it is a typical implementation of *dose-based* cost. This part must be carefully designed, as cost function guides genetic algorithm in evolving the population and little mistakes can lead to totally wrong results. Cost functions must be minimised by optimisation algorithms, so higher (lower) fitness is assigned to individuals with less (more) cost in the population. After this,

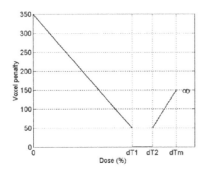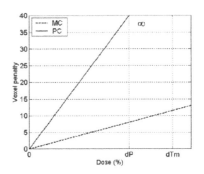

Fig. 1. Target penalty rule (left) and two OARs penalty rules (right)

the selection of parents comes, then the reproduction phase (*crossover*): genes from two parents are mutually exchanged with some probability so that two new individuals are created. To keep congruent treatment plans, to exchange a gene between two plans actually means to exchange a whole beam. After crossover comes *mutation*, i.e. a single gene in every descendant can be randomly changed with low probability. Depending on radiation therapy, the gene could be a beam angle or a beam weight. Newly created offsprings make up a new population for the next generation. Evolution is obtained repeating this process, until some convergence criterion is reached. In this case we have fixed a maximum number of generations, which seemed to be valid for all three kinds of therapies and for all tests considered. Designed genetic algorithm implements *elitism* [12], i.e. one copy of the best individual from a generation must pass unchanged to the next. The algorithm is also *adaptive*, i.e. mutation probability is increased when population becomes more homogeneous, and vice versa. This tries to find alternative solutions in search space even when population is converging to some optimum, thus giving the chance to still explore good areas of the solutions space. We have found that this evolutionary approach is robust enough to be quite insensitive with respect to parameters set-up. Only mutation probability has been adaptively set to high values (1%÷10%), but mutation happens on a single gene.

3   Results

We have tested our algorithm with real clinical cases. These involved both simple (i.e. convex target, far OARs) and complex (i.e. concave target, close OARs) cases, as it can be seen in Fig.2 (left and right respectively). It must be noticed that tests comprise full volumes and not only these single 2D images. Fixed dose limits are: d_P=80%, d_{T1}=94%, d_T=100%, d_{T2}=106%, d_{Tmax}=115%. Dose is not expressed in Gy units but in terms of percentage of the dose prescribed at the target (100%). Fixed beam number is 5 for all kinds of therapy. Fixed genetic algorithm parameters are: population size 100, number of generations 35, crossover probability 80%, initial mutation probability 1%.

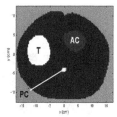

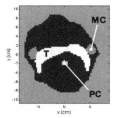

Fig. 2. Sample slice of simple clinical case (left) and of complex clinical case (right)

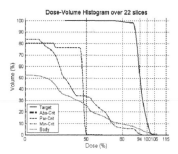

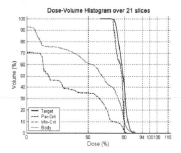

Fig. 3. DVH for 3D-CRT, simple case (left) and complex case (right)

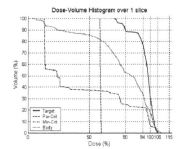

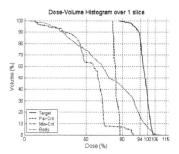

Fig. 4. DVH for ABRT (left) and IMRT (right), both complex case

Among other graphs, the software produces a diagram widely used in clinical practice: Dose-Volume Histogram (DVH). Given a tissue and its corresponding curve in this graph, if point (d, V) lies on the curve then $V\%$ of tissue volume receives a dose equal to or greater than $d\%$. DVH of a perfect dose distribution would have for the target a step function with corner (100%, 100%) and for other tissues some curves close to y-axis. Because of its use in the real world, this diagram seems to us the best way to evaluate the quality of proposed treatment plans. Figure 3 shows (left and right respectively) DVH for simple and complex case, both treated and resolved with 3D-CRT. These confirm that such a therapy is suitable for simple situations, and accordingly the software is able to find a

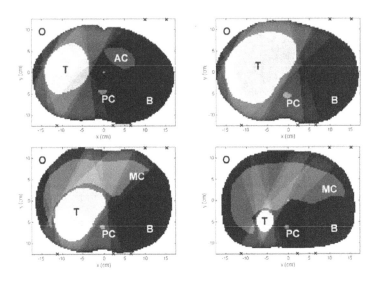

Fig. 5. Delivered dose overlapped to prescribed dose for subsequent 2D slices

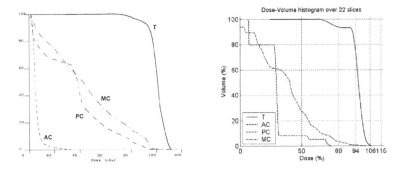

Fig. 6. DVHs calculated by commercial system (left) and by designed software (right)

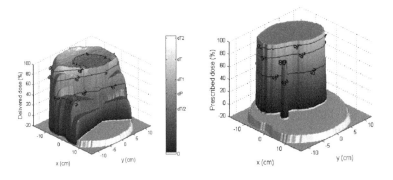

Fig. 7. 3D view of delivered dose (left) and prescribed dose (right) of over single slice

good solution. About 50% of target volume receives a dose in acceptable interval [94%, 106%]. 3D-CRT fails instead for complex situations, and the software is not able to find a good solution too. This can be noticed from the "Target" and "Par-Crit" curves almost overlapped. They receive the same radiation, because dose on the former is limited by constraints on the latter. The curve of absolutely critical OAR lies on y-axis, thus confirming the absence of radiation over it.

Figure 4 shows (left and right respectively) DVH for complex case only, treated and resolved with ABRT and IMRT. It must be noticed that these graphs refer to runs on a single 2D slice (Fig.2 right) in order to show how the method is able to work with this target geometry. Anyway the algorithm has been tested with full volumes, when entire tissue shapes are taken into account and averaging over several slices makes this capability less noticeable. These DVHs confirm that such therapies are suitable for complex cases: accordingly, the software is able to find a dose distribution that "follows" complex target shape. With ABRT almost 75% of target volume receives acceptable dose and then this steeply decreases. With IMRT the fraction raises to 85% and dose decreases more slowly. Delivered dose over subsequent slices is shown in Fig.5 by means of several 2D splash-diagrams. Beam shapes determined by the software have been successfully compared with those computed by the forward planning commercial system. Fixed the same beam angle set they give the same beam shapes, thus confirming the correctness of the system geometry and ray projection technique. With the same beam configuration, dose distribution has been generated for both commercial system and our software: Fig.6 shows the respective DVHs (again, in our diagram AC curve lies on y-axis). In Fig.7 (left) an example dose distribution over a single slice is presented in a 3D fashion, with height corresponding to delivered dose. This can be compared with prescribed dose over the same slice shown in Fig.7 (right), where height represents ideal values to obtain over the target, or limits to respect over critical structures.

4 Conclusions

A unified evolutionary approach to inverse planning for three different kinds of coplanar radiotherapies has been proposed. Thanks to genetic algorithm optimisation we have been able to search for full beam configurations: beam intensity, beam shape and especially beam orientation. To our best knowledge, only few recent articles give a proposal solution for the angles optimisation and even fewer make use of evolutionary techniques. Our implemented framework has the advantage of being simple and modular, with several small "parts" that can be modified to take care of different scenarios. Modelling of 3D-CRT, ABRT and IMRT inverse planning with one common approach is a result of this. Cost function can be easily altered to give different importance to different features required for dose distribution, such as homogeneity or *hot/cold spots*. Results are given through the same tools which physicians are used to: dose distribution over 2D sections, BEV, DVH, resuming tables. Approximations have been introduced only in dose distribution model, about various kinds of divergences and other effects of radiation propagation. Simple modifications are required in order to improve it and make it closer to standard simulation systems (divergence, electron transport). Our dose distribution model has been validated through comparison with commercial system, and the whole optimisation algorithm has been tested with real clinical cases, both simple and complex. As stated by physician and by simulation with the same commercial system, our algorithm found good solutions in simple and complex cases using corresponding correct therapy, with direct chance to use them in real clinical treatment.

References

1. S. Webb: Intensity-Modulated Radiation Therapy. Institute of Physics Publishing, Bristol, UK (2000)
2. N. Milickovic, M. Lahanas, D. Baltas, N. Zamboglou. Intensity Modulated Beam Radiation Therapy Dose Optimisation with Multiobjective Evolutionary Algorithms. EMO (2003)
3. G.A. Ezzell. Genetic and Geometric Optimisation of Three-dimensiona Radiation Therapy Treatment Planning. Medical Physics **23** (1996) 293–305
4. J. Knowles, D. Corne, M. Bishop. Evolutionary training of artificial neural networks for radiotherapy treatment of cancers. Proc. IEEE Int. Conf. on Evolutionary Computation, Alaska (1998) 398–403
5. O.C.L. Haas, K.J. Burnham, J.A. Mills. Optimisation of Beam Orientation in Radiotherapy using Planar Geometry. J. of Phys. in Med. and Biol. **43** (1998) 2179–2193
6. E. Schreibmann, R. Uricchio, M. Lahanas, K. Theodorou, N. Zamboglou, C. Kappas, D. Baltas. A Geometry Based Optimisation Algorithm for Conformal External Beam Orientation. Germany (2001)
7. A. Pugachev, J.G. Li, A.L. Boyer, S.L. Hancock, Q.T. Le, S.S. Donaldson, L. Xing. Role of Beam Orientation Optimisation in Intensity-Modulated Radiation Therapy. Int. J. of Radiation, Oncology, Biol., Phys. **50(2)** (2001) 551–560
8. M. Braunstein, R.Y. Levine. Optimum Beam Configurations in Tomographic Intensity Modulated Radiation Therapy. Spectral Sciences, Inc., Burlington, MA, USA (2000)
9. PLATO complete System. http://www.nucletron.com
10. S. Webb. Optimizing the Planning of Intensity-Modulated Radiotherapy. Phys. in Med. and Biol. **39** (1994) 2229–2246
11. S. Marzi, M. Mattia, P. Del Giudice, B. Caccia, M. Benassi. Optimisation of Intensity Modulated Radiation Therapy, Assessing the Complexity of the Problem. Ann. Istituto Superiore di Sanit **37(2)** (2001) 225–230
12. D. Beasley, R. Bull, R.R. Martin. An Overview of Genetic Algorithms, Part 1: Fundamentals. University Computing **15** (1993) 58–69

Soft Pyramid Symmetry Transforms

Bertrand Zavidovique[1] and Vito Di Gesú[1,2]

[1] IEF University of PARIS XI - ORSAY, France
zavido@ief.u-psud.fr
[2] DMA University of Palermo, Palermo, Italy
digesu@math.unipa.it

Abstract. Pyramid computation is a natural paradigm of computation in planning strategies and multi-resolution image analysis. This paper introduces a new paradigm that is based on the concept of soft-hierarchical operators implemented in a pyramid architecture to retrieve global versus local symmetries. The concept of symmetry is mathematically well defined in geometry whenever patterns are crisp images (two levels). Necessity for a soft approach occurs whenever images are multi-levels and the separation between object and background is subjective or not well defined. The paper describes a new pyramid operator to detect symmetries and shows some experiments supporting the approach. This work has been partially supported by the French Ministry of Research and the University Paris XI and the Agenzia Spaziale Italiana.

1   Introduction

Pyramid computation has been introduced to design efficient vision algorithms [1], [2] based on both *top-down* and *bottom-up* strategies. It was suggested too by biological arguments that show a correspondence between pyramid architectures and the mammalian visual pathway, starting from the retina and ending in the deepest layers of the visual cortex.

This paradigm of computation can also be related to the work made by Pomerantz and Sager [3] in their study on visual perception; the authors describe the visual perception as a transition in which the attention goes from global to local features, (*olystic* phase), and from local to global features, (*analytic* phase). In [4] Navon synthesizes this perception mechanism in one sentence: *Are we seeing the forest before trees or trees before the forest?* the author supports the precedence of global features in visual perception.

Pyramid computation has suggested both new data structures (quad-trees, multi-resolution), and new machine vision architectures (PAPIA) [5], (SPHINX) [6]. The concept of irregular pyramid has been introduced in [7] to handle connectivity problems that can arise when spatial data are mapped through the pyramid layers. The computation in a pyramid structure allows us to detect image features at different level of *resolution*. For example, at the higher resolution Figure 1 represents three objects with global vertical symmetry, the same symmetry is preserved at lower resolution where the computation is easier and faster.

V. Di Gesú, F. Masulli, and A. Petrosino (Eds.): WILF 2003, LNAI 2955, pp. 191–199, 2006.

Fig. 1. Capturing features at different resolution levels

On the other hand, symmetry operators have been included in vision systems to perform different visual tasks. For example, a set of annular operators can be used to identify enclosed symmetry points, and then a grouping algorithm is applied to represent and to describe object-parts [9]; axial symmetry properties have been applied to perform image segmentation [10].

A major problem with symmetry is capturing the right size of symmetric objects, that is the correct resolution which to analyze the object with. Moreover, considering texture for instance, several symmetries could be of interest for a single pattern. Then another perceptual difficulty, leading to paradox or ambiguity, is to balance between symmetry from edges (global, pattern) and symmetry from texture (local, core). Aiming to solve the latter difficulty we proposed to combine a morphological erosion with a symmetry detector in a repeated way. Still a bound of the object size needs to be known for it to be checked symmetric. We thus aim at exhibiting a computationally efficient iterative process of the kind to capture object symmetries, the most as possible independent from *their size, their balance between texture and edge symmetry, their position in the picture.*

A system is said to exhibit symmetry if the application of certain isometries, called symmetry operators, leaves it unchanged while permuting parts. More formally, a variable p of a system, S, is said symmetric with respect to a given transformation T if: $S(p) = S(T(p))$. In words p is a symmetric variable if it is an invariant with respect to T. In mathematics we may define several classes of symmetries.

However, the concept of symmetry is mathematically well defined whenever images are crisp (fixed number of levels), noiseless, and the separation between object and background is unambiguous. Often, images contain random noise and the separation between objects and background is subjective or not well defined (see Figure 2).

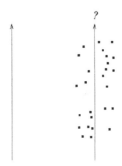

Fig. 2. Mathematical (left) and fuzzy (right) vertical symmetry

Moreover, subjectiveness may influence the perception of symmetry. For example, the mirror symmetry of dots in the left image of Figure 3 pops out, while it is less evident to recognize that the right image is obtained by translating few points. Colors too may privilege some symmetries (diagonal axis) to the detriment of others based on texture for instance (vertical axis). In these situations soft approaches [11] are likely to provide better solutions, because of both their ability to model subjectiveness and their flexible behavior.

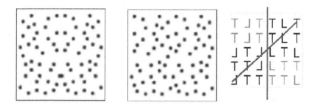

Fig. 3. Symmetry helps to perceive internal order (left); color may influence the perception of symmetry (right)

In this paper, the computation paradigm is soft because of the fuzziness of the image operators introduced in computing object symmetry and because of the kind of transition functions that are defined between layers of the pyramid structure. The goal is to study soft symmetry operators that detect regions of interest in a pyramidal environment. In Section 2 some examples of fuzzy measures of symmetry are suggested. Section 3 describes the pyramid implementation. Experimental results and applications are presented in Section 4. Concluding remarks are made in Section 5.

2   Fuzzy Symmetry Measures

In computer vision tasks symmetry can be *global* and *local* . Global symmetry regards either a single object (principal axes of a $2D$ object, principal axes and planes of a $3D$ object) or the spatial position of objects in a scene (regularity and periodicity). Several computation paradigms were proposed:

The use of gray level information was firstly investigated in [13]; where the measure of symmetry of a given object is based on a cross correlation operator evaluated on the gray levels.

In [14] authors introduce several measures for the analysis of object symmetries. The methods are based on the concept that any real function is the sum of a symmetric and an asymmetric function. In particular a measure, based on the Radom and the Fourier transforms, is developed. Scale dependency is considered to detect global symmetries in an image without using a segmentation procedure. The proposed algorithm is based on a *global optimization* approach that is implemented by a probabilistic genetic algorithm in order to speedup the computation.

In [15] a point of interest detector is presented for real-time implementation. It does not require the gradient to be quantized into angular bins and the contribution of every orientation is computed in a single pass over the whole image. This new approach determines the contribution that each pixel makes to the symmetry of pixels around it, rather than considering the contribution of a local neighborhood to a given central pixel. The transform is defined as the sum of the symmetry obtained for a range of different kernel sizes. A Gaussian low-pass filter is applied to spread the influence of the noise and to reduce the quantization error. The algorithm can be tuned for different vision tasks, by varying the size of the kernel and by looking only for dark or bright regions. In the following we will describe some fuzzy operators to detect local and global symmetry. A vector notation will be used to lighten the notation.

The Discrete Symmetry Transform (DST) computes symmetries based on the measure of *axial moments* of a body around its center of gravity. In the image case, gray levels g are considered the point masses. This measure has been applied for local level operation to detect local symmetries. The DST computed for pixel (i, j) with radius r on n axes is:

$$DST_{i,j} = \left(1 - \text{stddev}_k\left(T_{i,j}^k\right)\right) \cdot E_{i,j}$$

where *stddev* returns the standard deviation, for $k = 0, \ldots, n - 1$, of the first order moment relative to the angle $\alpha_k = k\pi/n$:

$$T_{i,j}^k = \sum_{(x,y) \in C_r} \left|(x - i)\sin\alpha_k - (y - j)\cos\alpha_k\right| \cdot g_{x,y}.$$

The second operator weighs the previous one according to the local smoothness of the image:

$$E_{i,j} = \sum_{\substack{(x,y) \in \partial C_r \\ (s,t) \in \partial C_{r+1}}} \left|g_{x,y} - g_{s,t}\right| \text{ for } |x - r| + |y - s| = 1.$$

Obviously $E_{i,j} = 0$ iff the image is locally flat.

The Object Symmetry Transform (OST) is an example of global measure of an object symmetry [16]. It is given by:

$$OST(k, i)(O) = MS_k(O)$$

where:

$$MS_\theta(O) = 1 - A_\theta(O) \text{ and } A_\theta(O) = \frac{\int_C |O(\underline{p}) - O(\underline{p}_s)| h(\underline{p}) d\underline{p}}{(G-1)\int_C h(\underline{p}) d\underline{p}}$$

here, C is the support of the object O. The point p_s is the mirror point of p with respect to a given axis $\underline{r}$ with direction θ, and passing trough the center of gravity of the frame, O, selected, for example, by an active contour algorithm [18] or from peculiar level-sets.

The term $(G-1)\int_C h(\underline{p})d\underline{p}$ normalizes $MS_\theta(O)$ in the interval $[0,1]$, while $h > 0$ is a function of the distance, d, of the point, $\underline{p}$ from the axis $\underline{r}$.

Note that, the choice of h depends on the influence that is given to the distance d. Examples of h-functions are: $h(\underline{p}) = d$, $h(\underline{p}) = 1/d$, $h(\underline{p}) = e^{-d^2}$, and $h(\underline{p}) = d^2 e^{-d^2}$, usually chosen according to *a priori* knowledge about the object.

The Iterative Object Transform (IOT) is performed by applying, in an alternated way, the OST operator, S, and the erosion, E, to the input image, X.

$$IOT_{\theta,0}(X) = X$$

$$IOT_{\theta,n}(X) = S \circ (E)_\theta^{n-1}(X) \quad for \ \ n \geq 1$$

where, $\bullet^n$ denotes the application of an operator $\bullet$, n times.

The erosion on gray level images can be implemented using the *min* operation [19]. The S operator has been implemented computing the normalized axial moments of an object around its center of mass with increments of angle by $\Delta\theta = \frac{\pi}{16}$. This is explained and justified in [12].

In words, the IOT computes the S transform on steadily intensity reduced versions of the input image, until a minimum of intensity is reached. The number of iterations depends on both the size of the input image and the distribution of the gray levels.

Indeed, a valid question about symmetry is: considering that a pattern is a geometric projection of an object onto the focal plane, which importance should be attributed respectively to contours $C(X)$ and grey-level distribution X, in the symmetry detection? It can be measured from the ratio $\frac{S_\theta(X)}{S_\theta(CX)}$. If the silhouette is predominating, then any prior adequate binarization or edge detection would do, sending back to the binary case, and the ratio can be trimmed to 1. Same, when texture and contours agree on the symmetry.

In the case edges and texture disagree, two more situations occur: a) if texture is not symmetric then the above ratio decreases in favor of edges; b) if texture is symmetric but in a different direction than edges or if edges are not symmetric at all, (possibly due to numerical truncation, ill-detection etc.), then one could think of resorting to a simple cooperative method *edge-symmetry/region-symmetry* in the fashion of [17], with a loop on the axis direction to check the discrepancy.

After the IOT definition, the iterated elongation, $\eta_X(n)$, and iterated circularity, $circle_n(X)$, can be introduced as follows:

$$\eta_n(X) = \frac{\min_{\theta \in [0,\phi[} \{IOT_{\theta,n}(X)\}}{\max_{\theta \in [0,\phi[} \{IOT_{\theta,n}(X)\}}$$

$$circle_n(X) = 1 - var(IOT_{\theta,n}(X) \ \ for \ \ \theta \in [0,\pi[.$$

In case of digital images the $IOT_{\theta,n}(X)$ can be considered a novel image representation of the inner structure of X. The shape operators $\eta_n(X)$ and $circle_n(X)$ indicate dynamic changes of X shapes versus n.

3   The Pyramid Computation

In the following we propose three pyramidal schemes for the implementation of symmetry operators introduced above, all of them will be denoted by, S. An image, I, is a set of triplets $\{(i, j, g_{ij})\}$ on which are defined two projections: $fI = \{(i, j)\}$ and $vI = \{g_{ij}\}$.

A pyramid is a sequence of images $PI = (I_0, I_1, \ldots, I_{L-1})$ with decreasing resolution, $|I_0| > |I_1| > \ldots > |I_{L-1}|$. The dimension and the intensity of each pyramid layer are determined by the following mapping function:

$$F : fI_r^{(k)} \rightarrow I_{r+1} \; pixel \; mapping$$
$$V : vI_r^{(k)} \rightarrow I_{r+1} \; intensity \; mapping$$

where, the lower index, r, indicates the pyramid layer and the upper index, k, indicates the number of pixels that are mapped from layer r to one given pixel of the layer $r + 1$. For sake of simplicity, the dimension of the input image will be a power of a window dimension p, $|I_0| = p^m \times p^m$ $(k = p^2)$. In the following we will consider regular pyramids showed in Figure 4; the V-mapping depends on the problem and it characterizes the evolution of the pyramid computation. Examples of V-mapping are: *max, min, and, or, average, median*. Note that symmetry values range in the interval $[0, 1]$ and they can be interpreted as a belonging degree for a fuzzy set *to be symmetric*. Then more complex V-mapping can be defined using min/max.

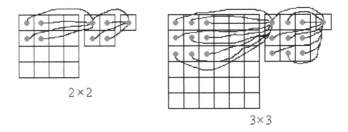

$$2 \times 2$$

$$3 \times 3$$

Fig. 4. The 2×2 and 3×3 pyramids

In the following the whole operator that generates the pyramid representation of the input, X, is denoted by $\wp(X)$. The three pyramid computation are:

Direct computation. In this case, the symmetry operator, $PS = \wp(S)$, is applied on each layer of the $PI = \wp(I)$ and the result is the pyramid $PT = PS(PI)$.

Indirect computation. In this case, the symmetry operator, S, is applied on the first level of PI and then the pyramid of the $S(I_0)$ is built, $PT = \wp(S(I_0))$.

Hierarchical Symmetries. In this case, the symmetry operator is applied recursively on each level of the pyramid:

$$PT_0 = PS_0(I_0) \qquad first\ level$$
$$PT_r = PS_r(PT_{r-1})\ r > 0$$

Note that in general the three computations produce different results.

4   Some Experiments

The pyramid algorithms have been tested on simulated and real data under uncontrolled illumination conditions. For example the pyramid version of the *IOT* has been applied to detect global *vertical* symmetries under different spatial conditions.

In Figure 5a the global vertical symmetry of the input image on the left is detected in the second layer; In Figure 5b the global vertical symmetry disappears in the second layer, because the spatial frequency of the vertical segments

(a)   (b)

Fig. 5. Sampling effects: a) spatial frequency $\leq 2k + 1$; b) spatial frequency $> 2k + 1$

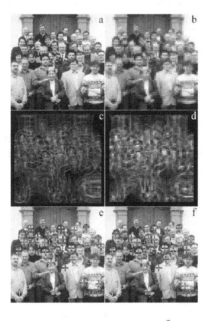

Fig. 6. a) Input image D_0; b) $DST(D_0)$; c) D_2; d) $\wp^{-2}DST(D_0)$; e) zones of interest obtained via direct computation; f) zones of interest obtained via indirect computation

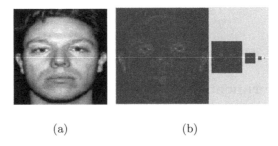

(a)   (b)

Fig. 7. An example of pyramid computation: a) the input image; b) the full convolution; c) the sampled convolution

is greater than 2 pixels. However, the vertical symmetry is detected in the third level. These examples illustrate relations between symmetry, spatial sampling and pyramid computation.

Figures 6a,c,e show the areas of interest as detected by the direct computation of the DST; Figures 6b,d,f show the indirect computations of the DST. They have been obtained using the mean value for the V-mapping and it can be shown that, using a proper sampling that is related to the maximum frequency, ν_{max}, of the input signal, the two transformations are very close.

Figure 7 shows application results of the hierarchical computation of the DST when applied to a face of size 243×243, using a kernel of size 3×3. This example demonstrates the ability of this fuzzy operator to detect correct areas of interest (eyes, nose, mouth) at higher level in the pyramid. Note that in the fourth level the highest value of the DST is in the center of the frame, and this is a global image feature.

5   Final Remarks

This paper describes some examples of symmetry measure based on fuzzy operators. These measures are embedded in a pyramid computation scheme showing the power of hierarchical systems in detecting global features from local ones. Results are preliminary and future work will be done to study the relations between local versus global computation.

References

1. Uhr L.: Layered Recognition Cone Networks that Preprocess, Classify and Describe. *IEEE Trans.Comput.*, C-21, 1972.
2. Pavlidis T.A., Tanimoto S.L.: A Hierarchical Data Structure for Picture Processing. *Comp.Graphycs & Image Processing*, Vol.4, 1975.
3. Pomeranzt J.R. and Sager L.C.: Asymmetric integrality with dimensions of visual pattern. *Perception & Psycophysics*, Vol.18, 460-466, 1975.
4. Navon D.: Forest befor trees: the precedence of global features in visual perception. *Cognitive Psychology* , Vol.9, 353-385, 1977.

5. Cantoni V., Di Gesú V.: Ferretti M., Levialdi S., Negrini R., Stefanelli R.: The Papia System. *Journal of VLSI Signal Processing*, Vol.2, 195-217, 1991.
6. Mrigot A., Zavidovique B.: Image Analysis on Massively Parallel Computers: An Architectural Point of View. *IJPRAI*, Vol.6, N.2 & 3, pp 387–393, 1992.
7. Kropatsch W.G.: Building Irregular Pyramids by Dual Graph Contraction. *Technical Report PRIP-TR-35*, Institute f. Automation 183/2, Dept.for Pattern Recognition and Image Processing, TU Wien, Austria, 1995.
8. Khöler W. and Wallach H.: Figural after-effects:an investigation of visual processes. *Proc. Amer. Phil. Soc.*, Vol.88, 269-357, 1944.
9. Kelly M.F. and Levine M.D.: From symmetry to representation. *Technical Report*, TR-CIM-94-12, Center for Intelligent Machines. McGill University, Montreal, Canada, 1994.
10. Gauch J.M. and Pizer S.M.: The intensity axis of symmetry application to image segmentation. *IEEE Trans. PAMI*, Vol.15, N.8, 753-770, 1993.
11. L.A.Zadeh, "Fuzzy Logic, Neural Networks, and Soft Computing", in *Communication of the ACM*, Vol.37, N.3, pp.77-84, 1994.
12. Di Gesú V., Valenti C.: Symmetry operators in computer vision. in *Vistas in Astronomy*, Pergamon, Vol.40, No.4, pp.461-468,1996.
13. Marola G.: On the detection of the axes of symmetric and almost symmetric planar images. *IEEE Trans. on PAMI*, Vol.11, pp.104–108, 1989.
14. Kiryati N., Gofman Y.: Detecting symmetry in grey level images (the global optimization approach. Preprint, 1997.
15. G.Loy and A.Zelinsky, A Fast Radial Symmetry Transform for Detecting Points of Interest, Proceedings of European Conference on Computer Vision (ECCV2002), Copenhagen, 2002.
16. Di Gesú V., Intravaia D.: A new approach to face analysis. DMA-IR-05/98, University of Palermo, 1998.
17. Milgram D.L.: Region extraction using convergent evidence. *CGIP*, Vol.1, pp.1–12, 1979.
18. Blake A., Isard M.: Active Contours. Springer, 1998.
19. Vincent L., Soille P.: Watersheds in digital spaces: an efficient algorithm based on immersion simulations. IEEE Transactions on Pattern Analysis and Machine intelligence, Vol.13, N.6, pp.583–598, 1991.

Image File Compression Using Approximation and Fuzzy Logic[*]

Antonio Di Nola[1] and Barnabás Bede[2]

[1] Dipartamento di Matematicae Informatica, Universitá di Salerno,
Via S. Allende, 84081 Baronissi (Salerno), Italy
dinola@unisa.it
[2] Department of Mathematics, University of Oradea,
str. Armatei Române no. 5, 3700 Oradea, Romania
bbede@uoradea.ro

Abstract. We combine tools provided by approximation theory and by fuzzy logic, in order to improve image file compression methods. For this aim we use logical operators, $t-$norms and fuzzy sets to obtain a compressed file and approximate the function obtained this way, by some polynomial, rational function, trigonometric polynomial or spline for decompression. Error estimates and experimental results for the proposed method are presented.

1   Introduction

The applications of Approximation Theory to Image Processing are well-known. For example, Fourier transforms and Bi-cubic splines are widely used for image file compression and zooming.

Another approach to image processing uses fuzzy logic. In this setting, using logical operators and fuzzy relations, image file compression is also possible (see [6], [7]).

The aim of this paper is to combine these techniques. So, it could be possible to obtain better compression rates and better quality of the compressed image.

The idea of this approach is very simple. We will use logical operators and fuzzy relations to obtain a compressed file (as in [6]) and we approximate the image by some polynomials, rational functions, trigonometric polynomials or splines, for decompression. The algebraic and topological structure in which such a combination becomes possible is the Riesz MV-algebra (here we have MV-algebra structure and some basic facts from analysis, see [4]).

Let us recall some definitions and properties needed in what follows. We denote $\mathbb{R}_+ = \{x \in \mathbb{R} : x \geq 0\}$ and $\mathbb{R}_+^*$ stands for $\mathbb{R}_+$ without 0.

First of all it is necessary to remind the definition and some properties of MV-algebras (see e.g. [1], [2]).

---

[*] The idea of the paper was raised while the second author was visiting Soft Computing Laboratory at Salerno University.

V. Di Gesú, F. Masulli, and A. Petrosino (Eds.): WILF 2003, LNAI 2955, pp. 200–207, 2006.
© Springer-Verlag Berlin Heidelberg 2006

Definition 1. *An MV-algebra is an algebra* $\langle A, \oplus, \neg, 0_A \rangle$ *with a binary opera-tion* $\oplus$, *a unary operation* $\neg$ *and a constant* 0_A *satisfying the following equations:*

MV1) $x \oplus (y \oplus z) = (x \oplus y) \oplus z$;

MV2) $x \oplus y = y \oplus x$;

MV3) $x \oplus 0_A = x$;

MV4) $\neg\neg x = x$;

MV5) $x \oplus \neg 0_A = \neg 0_A$;

MV6) $\neg(\neg x \oplus y) \oplus y = \neg(\neg y \oplus x) \oplus x$.

On each MV-algebra A is defined the constant 1_A and the operations $\odot$ and $\ominus$ as follows:

i) $1_A =_{def} \neg 0_A$;

ii) $x \odot y =_{def} \neg(\neg x \oplus \neg y)$;

iii) $x \ominus y =_{def} x \odot \neg y$.

Let A be an MV-algebra and $x, y \in A$. We say that $x \leq y$ if and only if x and y satisfy one of the bellow equivalent conditions:

i) $\neg x \oplus y = 1_A$;

ii) $x \odot \neg y = 0_A$;

iii) $y = x \oplus (y \ominus x)$;

iv) there is an element $z \in A$ such that $x \oplus z = y$.

It follows that $\leq$ is a partial order, called the natural order of A. On each MV-algebra A the natural order determines a lattice structure.

The distance function $d : A \times A \to A$ is defined by

$$d(x, y) =_{def} (x \ominus y) \oplus (y \ominus x).$$

In every MV-algebra A we have:

i) $d(x, y) = 0_A$ if and only if $x = y$;

ii) $d(x, y) = d(y, x)$;

iii) $d(x, z) \leq d(x, y) \oplus d(y, z)$;

iv) $d(x, y) = d(\neg x, \neg y)$;

v) $d(x \oplus s, y \oplus t) \leq d(x, y) \oplus d(s, t)$.

Definition 2. *(see [8])We say that an MV-algebra A, is a vectorial MV-algebra, if there is defined a multiplicative, external operation* $\bullet : \mathbb{R}_+ \times A \to A$ *having the following properties:*

i) $1 \bullet x = x$ for any $x \in A$;

ii) $(a + b) \bullet x = a \bullet x \oplus b \bullet x$ for any $x \in A$ and $a, b \in \mathbb{R}_+$;

iii) $a \bullet (b \bullet x) \leq (a \cdot b) \bullet x$ for any $x \in A$ and $a, b \in \mathbb{R}_+$;

iv) $d(a \bullet x, a \bullet y) \leq a \bullet d(x, y)$, for any $x, y \in A$ and $a \in \mathbb{R}_+$;

Recall the definition of truncated modules (see [5])

Definition 3. *An MV-algebra A is a truncated module over a unital lattice or-dered ring (R, v) if there is defined an external operation* $\bullet : R_+ \times A \to A$ *such that the following properties hold for any $\alpha, \beta \in R_+$ and $x, y \in A$.*

(1) $(\alpha + \beta) \bullet x = \alpha \bullet x \oplus \beta \bullet x$;

(2) $\alpha \bullet (x \oplus y) = \alpha \bullet x \oplus \alpha \bullet y$ if $x \leq \neg y$

(3) $\alpha \bullet (\beta \bullet x) = (\alpha \cdot \beta) \bullet x$ *if* $\alpha, \beta \in [0, v]$;
If moreover holds
(4) $v \bullet x = x$
then A *is called a unital MV-module over* (R, v).

Definition 4. *An MV-algebra* A *will be called a Riesz MV-algebra if it is a unital truncated module over* $(\mathbb{R}, 1)$.

In [4] it is proved that Riesz MV-algebras are the appropiate algebraic and topological structures for development of some image file compression methods.

2   The Compression and Decompression Algorithm

It is well-known that a triangular norm t (or $t-$norm) is a binary operation $t : [0, 1]^2 \rightarrow [0, 1]$, which is commutative, associative, non-decreasing in both arguments and $t(0, x) = 0$, $t(1, x) = x$ for any $x \in [0, 1]$. We denote $t(x, y)$ by xty. Some examples of $t-$norms are the following:

Lukasiewicz $t-$norm
$xty = \max\{0, x + y - 1\}$,
Gödel $t-$norm
$xty = \min\{x, y\}$,
Goguen (or product) $t-$norm
$xty = x \cdot y$.

These $t-$norms will play an important role in compression.

Let us recall the definitions of some well-known bivariate operators from approximation theory. These bivariate operators are obtained as tensor products of univariate operators. This method is usual in Approximation Theory. For the definitions in the univariate case see e.g. [3].

Let $f : [0, 1] \times [0, 1] \rightarrow \mathbb{R}^3$ be continuous. The bivariate Bernstein polynomial is defined as follows:

$$B_{n,m}(f)(x, y) = \sum_{k=0}^{n} \sum_{l=0}^{m} p_{n,k}(x) p_{m,l}(y) f\left(\frac{k}{n}, \frac{l}{m}\right),$$

where $x, y \in [0, 1]$ and $p_{n,k}(x) = \binom{n}{k} x^k (1 - x)^{n-k}$, $k = 0, ..., n$.

Let $f : \left[-\frac{1}{4}, \frac{1}{4}\right] \times \left[-\frac{1}{4}, \frac{1}{4}\right] \rightarrow \mathbb{R}^3$, be continuous. Then

$$R_{n,m}(f, x, y) = \sum_{k=-n}^{n} \sum_{l=-m}^{m} r_{n,k}(x) r_{m,l}(y) f(x_k, y_l),$$

with $r_{n,k}(x) = \frac{(x-x_k)^{-2p}}{\sum_{j=-n}^{n}(x-x_j)^{-2p}}$ and $x_k = \frac{k}{4n}$, $y_l = \frac{l}{4m}$, $k = -n, ..., n$, $l = -m, ..., m$ is the Shepard operator of order p, with $p \geq 1$.

The bivariate Shepard operator can also be defined as follows:

$$R_{n,m}(f, x, y) = \sum_{k=-n}^{n} \sum_{l=-m}^{m} r_{n,m,k,l}(x, y) f(x_k, y_l),$$

where $r_{n,m,k,l}(x, y) = \frac{[(x-x_k)^2 + (y-y_l)^2]^{-p}}{\sum_{i=-n}^{n} \sum_{j=-n}^{n} [(x-x_i)^2 + (y-y_j)^2]^{-p}}$, $p \geq 1$.

The Jackson operator associated to $f : [-\pi, \pi] \times [-\pi, \pi] \to \mathbb{R}^3$ is given by

$$J_{n,m}(f)(x,y) = \int_{-\pi}^{\pi} \int_{-\pi}^{\pi} K_n(t)K_m(s)f(x+t, y+s)dsdt,$$

where $K_n(t) = L_{n'}(t)$, $n' = [n/2] + 1$,

$$L_{n'}(t) = \frac{3}{2\pi n'[2(n')^2 + 1]} \left[\frac{\sin(n't/2)}{\sin(t/2)} \right]^4, \quad \int_{-\pi}^{\pi} L_{n'}(t)dt = 1.$$

Other approximation operators as e.g. bivariate splines can be also considered. The description of the compression method is given below (see [6]).

Let A, B be fuzzy sets ($A : \{1, ..., k\} \to [0, 1]$ and $B : \{1, ..., l\} \to [0, 1]$, $k, l \in \mathbb{N}$). We model the image as a function $f : [0, 1] \times [0, 1] \to [0, 1]^3$ (we have normalized each component of RGB-model to be in $[0, 1]$). In order to compress the file we divide it in blocks of $k \times l$ pixels (blocks may overlap). From the block of coordinates u, v we store only one value

$$g(u,v) = \bigvee_{j=1}^{l} \bigvee_{i=1}^{k} [(A(i)tB(j))tf(x_i, y_j)], \tag{1}$$

where t is a $t-$norm (we define $\alpha t(a, b, c) = (\alpha ta, \alpha tb, \alpha tc)$, $\forall \alpha \in [0, 1]$ and $(a, b, c) \in [0, 1]^3$). The value of g is stored in the position indexed by the coordinates of the block in which it is obtained. The compression is done.

For decompression we shall approximate the above obtained function g by some (trigonometric) approximation polynomial, rational function or spline in the Riesz MV-algebra $[0, 1]^3$ on each block of dimension $(n+1) \times (m+1)$ pixels. Let $f : [0, 1] \times [0, 1] \to [0, 1]^3$.

The bivariate Bernstein polynomial in the Riesz MV-algebra $[0, 1]^3$ is

$$B_{n,m}(f)(x,y) = \bigoplus_{k=0}^{n} \bigoplus_{l=0}^{m} p_{n,k}(x)p_{m,l}(y) \bullet g\left(\frac{k}{n}, \frac{l}{m} \right),$$

where $x, y \in [0, 1]$ and $p_{n,k}(x) = \binom{n}{k} x^k (1 - x)^{n-k}$, $k = 0, ..., n$.
The bivariate Shepard operator in the Riesz MV-algebra $[0, 1]^3$ is

$$R_{n,m}(f, x, y) = \bigoplus_{k=-n}^{n} \bigoplus_{l=-m}^{m} r_{n,k}(x)r_{m,l}(y) \bullet g(x_k, y_l),$$

with $r_{n,k}(x) = \frac{(x-x_k)^{-2p}}{\sum_{j=-n}^{n}(x-x_j)^{-2p}}$ and $x_k = \frac{k}{4n}$, $y_l = \frac{l}{4m}$, $k = \overline{-n, n}$, $l = \overline{-m, m}$, $p \geq 1$, or

$$R'_{n,m}(f, x, y) = \bigoplus_{k=-n}^{n} \bigoplus_{l=-m}^{m} r_{n,m,k,l}(x, y) \bullet g(x_k, y_l),$$

where $r_{n,m,k,l}(x, y) = \frac{[(x-x_k)^2+(y-y_l)^2]^{-p}}{\sum_{i=-n}^{n} \sum_{j=-n}^{n}[(x-x_i)^2+(y-y_j)^2]^{-p}}$, $p \geq 1$.

The Jackson operator associated to g is

$$J_{n,m}(f)(x,y) = \int_{-\pi}^{\pi} \int_{-\pi}^{\pi} K_n(t)K_m(s) \bullet g(x+t, y+s)dsdt,$$

where the integral sign is considered in the Riesz MV-algebra $[0,1]^3$ and this type of integral is defined in [4].

Lagrange interpolation polynomials can also be used, but with other truncation procedure since a truncated addition destroys all the properties of Lagrange polynomials.

Now, from each block of dimension $m \times n$ pixels we have to obtain $k \cdot m \times l \cdot n$ pixels. Let $h(i,j) = P\left(\frac{i}{k \cdot m}, \frac{j}{l \cdot n}\right)$, $i = 0, ..., k \cdot m$, $j = 0, ..., l \cdot n$ be the approximate value to g, where P is one of the above defined approximation polynomials. These values give us the decompressed file.

The steps of the compression-decompression algorithm are given below.

Let $f : [0,1] \times [0,1] \to [0,1]^3$ denote an image with $M \times N$ pixels, $M, N \in \mathbb{N}$, file which will be compressed.

Compression
Step 1: Divide the file in blocks of dimension $k \times l$ pixels.
Step 2: For the block of coordinates (u,v), $u = 1, ..., M/k$, $v = 1, ..., N/l$, store the value

$$g(u,v) = \bigvee_{j=1}^{l} \bigvee_{i=1}^{k} [(A(i)tB(j))tf(x_i, y_j)].$$

The file in which we stored the values $g(u,v)$ is the compressed file.

Decompression
Step 1: Divide the compressed file in blocks of dimension $(n+1) \times (m+1)$ if we use Lagrange or Bernstein polynomials or splines. For Shepard-type operators we divide the file in blocks of dimension $(2n+1) \times (2m+1)$. For Jackson and Bojanic-DeVore-type operators, the dimension of the block is not correlated with the number of interpolation points.
Step 2: Compute the value $P(x,y)$ given above.
Step 3: Store the values $h(i,j) = P\left(\frac{i}{k \cdot m}, \frac{j}{l \cdot n}\right)$, $i = 0, ..., k \cdot n$, $j = 0, ..., l \cdot n$.
The file in which we stored all the values $h(i,j)$ for all blocks is the decompressed file.

If different $t-$norms and different approximation polynomials are used, different image file compression-decompression methods are obtained. Also, let us observe that this is a generalization of existing methods based only on approximation theory, since if the fuzzy set A is a crisp set consisting only of one element i_0, i.e. $A(i) = \delta_{i,i_0}$ (Kronecker δ) and so is also B, $B(j) = \delta_{j,j_0}$, then $g(u,v) = f(x_{i_0}, y_{j_0})$, i.e. a single value of the function f. The use of fuzzy logic allows a better choice of the values that should be approximated. So, depending on the choice of the membership functions of the fuzzy sets A and B we can have a better control on the interpolation points. For example in [7] these membership functions are of gaussian-type. In our interpretation this means the choice of a "maximum value" of f, around the middle point of a given block, value influenced by the rest of values of the function f.

A primary general estimate on the order of approximation is given below.

Theorem 1. *Let* $f : [0, 1]^2 \to [0, 1]^3$, *an image and* $P(x, y)$ *be an approximation polynomial (except the Lagrange Polynomial) constructed as above. Then we have*

$$d(f(x, y), P(x, y)) \leq \left| f(x, y) - \bigvee_{i=1}^{l} \bigvee_{j=1}^{k} [(A(i)tB(j))tf(x_i, y_j)] \right|.$$

Proof. We make the proof for Bernstein and Jackson type operators the other operators defined above have similar properties. For Bernstein polynomials it is well known that $\sum_{i=0}^{n} \sum_{j=0}^{m} p_{i,j}(x, y) = 1$, (see e.g. [3]). Then we obtain:

$$\bigoplus_{i=0}^{n} \bigoplus_{j=0}^{m} p_{i,j}(x, y) = 1 \qquad (2)$$

(since in $[0, 1]$, $\oplus$ denotes truncated addition). Let

$$P(x, y) = \bigoplus_{u=0}^{n} \bigoplus_{v=0}^{m} p_{n,u}(x) p_{m,v}(y) \bullet g\left(\frac{u}{n}, \frac{v}{m} \right),$$

the Bernstein polynomial associated to g. We denote $x_u = \frac{u}{n}$ and $y_v = \frac{v}{m}$. By the properties of a Riesz MV-algebra and the properties of the distance function on an MV-algebra, we have successively

$$d(f(x, y), P(x, y)) = d\left(f(x, y), \bigoplus_{u=0}^{m} \bigoplus_{v=0}^{n} p_{u,v}(x, y) \bullet g(x_u, y_v) \right) =$$

$$= d\left(\bigoplus_{u=0}^{m} \bigoplus_{v=0}^{n} p_{u,v}(x, y) \bullet f(x, y), \bigoplus_{u=0}^{m} \bigoplus_{v=0}^{n} p_{u,v}(x, y) \bullet g(x_u, y_v) \right) \leq$$

$$\bigoplus_{u=0}^{m} \bigoplus_{v=0}^{n} p_{u,v}(x, y) \bullet d(f(x, y), g(x_u, y_v)).$$

By (1) and (2) we have

$$d(f(x, y), P(x, y)) \leq d\left(f(x, y), \bigvee_{i=1}^{l} \bigvee_{j=1}^{k} [(A(i)tB(j))tf(x_i, y_j)] \right).$$

By definition, the distance function is the truncated absolute value of the difference, fact which leads to the required conclusion. For the Jackson operator associated to g

$$P(x, y) = \int_{-\pi}^{\pi} \int_{-\pi}^{\pi} K_n(t) K_m(s) \bullet g(x + t, y + s) ds dt,$$

since $\int_{-\pi}^{\pi}\int_{-\pi}^{\pi}K_n(t)K_m(s)dsdt = 1$, we have

$$d(f(x,y), P(x,y)) = d\left(f(x,y), \int_{-\pi}^{\pi}\int_{-\pi}^{\pi}K_n(t)K_m(s) \bullet g(x+t,y+s)dsdt\right)$$

$$\leq \int_{-\pi}^{\pi}\int_{-\pi}^{\pi}K_n(t)K_m(s) \bullet d(f(x,y), g(x_u, y_v))dsdt = d(f(x,y), g(x_u, y_v)).$$

The expression in the preceding theorem is complicated, but it shows that the error of the compression-decompression method described in this paper contains not only the properties of the function which is approximated, but also some fuzzy sets. As a consequence, if we choose them conveniently, we can obtain better compression rates. Observe that particular error bounds can be obtained separately for each pair consisting of a $t-$norm and an approximation operator.

We conclude this section with some experiments on the proposed method. The size of a block in the compression Step 1. is 3×3. In these experiments we have used product t-norm and the fuzzy sets A and B have exponential membership functions, i.e.

$$A(i) = e^{-\alpha|i-u|}, \ B(j) = e^{-\alpha|j-v|},$$

where (u,v) denote the coordinates of the middle point of the curent block and α is a parameter (in these eperiments we consiered $\alpha = 0.4$). For decompression we have used Shepard-type local approximation operators. The compression rate for "Lenna" image is $1/4$, and the block size for decompression is 11×11 pixels. For image "Cameraman" the compression rate is $1/16$ and the block size for decompression was set to 17×17 pixels.

Fig. 1. Original image 'Lenna' (left), compressed-decompressed files using crisp approximation (middle) and proposed method (right)(compression rate $1/4$)

3   Conclusions and Further Research

We developed a new algorithm for image file compression which is a combination of two existing approaches (the use of fuzzy logic and approximation theory). These could provide better compression rates, or improve the quality of

Fig. 2. Original image 'Cameraman' (left), compressed-decompressed files using crisp approximation (middle) and proposed method (right) (compression rate 1/16)

a zoomed image. The big number of possibilities for the choice of the $t-$norm and the approximation polynomial for which tests and error analysis can be made (in this paper are presented 18) makes possible to choose different compression algorithms for different types of images. Tests on these various algorithms is a challenging research topic.

References

1. C.C. Chang, Algebraic analysis of many-valued logic, Trans. Amer. Math. Soc. 88(1958), 467-490.
2. R. Cignoli, I.M.L. D'Ottaviano, D. Mundici, Algebraic Foundations of many-valued Reasoning, Kluwer Academic Publishers, trends in Logic, vol 7, 2000.
3. R.A. Devore, G.G. Lorentz Constructive approximation, polynomials and splines approximation, Springer Verlag, Berlin-Heidelberg, 1993.
4. B. Bede, A. Di Nola, Elementary calculus in Riesz MV-algebras, International Journal of Approximate Reasoning, to appear.
5. A. Di Nola, P. Flondor, I. Leustean, MV-modules, Journal of Algebra, 261,1(2003), 21-40.
6. V. Loia, S. Sessa, Compression and Decompression of Fuzzy Relations in the Basic Logic over [0,1], to appear.
7. H. Nobuhara, W. Pedrycz and K. Hirota, Fast solving method of fuzzy relational equations and its applications to lossy image compression/reconstruction, IEEE Trans. on Fuzzy Systems, 8(2000), 325-334.
8. D. Noje, B. Bede Vectorial MV-algebras, Soft Computing, 7(2003) 258-262.

Fuzzy Information Fusion Scheme
Used to Segment Brain Tumor from MR Images

Weibei Dou[1,2], Su Ruan[1], Qingmin Liao[2],
Daniel Bloyet[1], Jean-Marc Constans[3], and Yanping Chen[4]

[1] GREYC-CNRS UMR 6072, 6 Boulevard Maréchal Juin, 14050 Caen, France
[2] Department of Electronic Engineering, Tsinghua University, 100084 Beijing, China
[3] Unité d'IRM, CHRU, Caen, France
[4] Imaging Diagnostic Center, Nanfang Hospital, Guangzhou, China
douwb@tsinghua.edu.cn, wdou@greyc.ismra.fr

Abstract. A fuzzy information fusion scheme is proposed in this paper
to automatically segment tumor areas of human brain from multispectral magnetic resonance images such as T1-weighted, T2-weighted and
Proton Density (PD) feature images. The proposed scheme consists of
four stages: data-level fusion, space creation of fuzzy features, fusion of
fuzzy features and fuzzy decision. Several fuzzy operators are proposed to
create the feature-level fusion. The fuzzy information models describing
the characteristics of tumor areas in human brain are also established.
A fuzzy region growing based on fuzzy connecting is presented to obtain
the final segmentation result. The comparison between the result of our
method and the hand-labeled segmentation of a radiology expert shows
that this scheme is efficient. The experimental results (based on 4 patients studied) show an average probability of correct detection equal to
96% and an average probability of false detection equal to 5%.

1 Introduction

Magnetic Resonance Imaging (MRI) can provide much information about brain
tissues from a variety of excitation sequences. The segmentation of brain tissues
from MR images is a hot issue in many applications, especially for representation
of tissue abnormalities. A lot of studies have been done and are described in the
literature. Some methods, by deforming standard images, templates, or atlases
using elastic matching techniques, or deformable models [1][2] have proven to be
reliable and efficient for small and local shape changes [3], especially for normal
tissue segmentation. Some approaches start from a parametric statistical model,
such as Gaussian intensity models [4][5], Explicit models [6],Markov random
field models [7]. They are effective on large and general tissue segmentation,
but not for various abnormal tissues. Others have introduced knowledge-based
techniques [8] to make more intelligent classification and segmentation decisions.
By using fuzzy clustering and information fusion technique, this kind of approach
is very powerful for addressing the problem of abnormal tissue segmentation
and classification. But some of them rely on manual tracing [9], and some fuzzy

V. Di Gesú, F. Masulli, and A. Petrosino (Eds.): WILF 2003, LNAI 2955, pp. 208–215, 2006.
© Springer-Verlag Berlin Heidelberg 2006

models are built, based on limited pathologic information, because few MRI sequences, such as T1-weighted or T1 Gadolinium enhancement sequences, have been used [8][10].

To diagnose tissue abnormalities, e.g. tumor, it's necessary to utilize multispectral MR images for finding some of its properties such as size, position, type, and relationship with other tissues, etc... Imagine a process of tumor diagnosis in the clinic, radiology experts always checking different MRI sequences of a patient, according to their *a priori* knowledge to combine the information provided by each sequence resulting in the determination of location, extension, prognosis and diagnosis. The fact that fuzzy information fusion could reproduce the process of human image reading induces ideas of segmentation-method designing. A fuzzy information fusion scheme from multiple sources is preferable to capture redundancy and complementary information.

Considering the ambiguous, complementary and redundant character of different MR images, the fuzzy logic and information fusion techniques are a first choice [3][9]. Our fuzzy information fusion scheme is introduced, consisting of four steps: (1) data-level fusion (2) creation of fuzzy feature space (3) fusion of fuzzy feature, and (4) fuzzy decision. The linear registration method presented in [11] is employed for data-level fusion to establish a common coordinate system among different data sources. Some membership functions are proposed for fuzzy information modeling to create fuzzy feature spaces for different sources. We utilize a fuzzy relation to combine these fuzzy feature spaces into a joined feature space. To obtain the segmentation result, a decision by fuzzy region growing is presented. One study using three MR image sequences, T1-weighted (T1), T2-weighted (T2) and Proton Density (PD) features images of a single patient taken as an example to illustrate the method's efficiency. The results are appreciated by radiology experts.

2   Scheme of Fuzzy Information Fusion

Based on a functional model for the fusion process presented in [12], A scheme for fusing fuzzy information is proposed in figure 1.

- The multiple information to be fused is captured from multispectral MR images $(S_1, S_2 \ldots S_N)$.
- Due to the various voxel sizes and the quantization levels in different spectral MRI and movement of the patient during the process of image capture, a data alignment is necessary to transform the multiple data source into a common coordinate system called " Source Matched"(SM).
- The information of interest from each source is then projected onto a fuzzy feature space by a fuzzy feature model. Various approaches of feature modelling are applied to the SM, because the different sources represent the same object with different gray level information.
- For combination of these fuzzy features from different sources, a fuzzy feature-level fusion creates the joined feature space through fuzzy relation or fuzzy set operation.

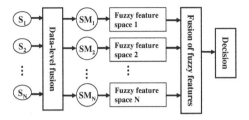

Tissues	Signal Intensity		
	$T1$	$T2$	PD
Tumor	$-$	$++$	$++$
Edema	$-+$	$+$	$+$
CSF	$--$	$++$	$+-$

Fig. 2. Intensity characteristics of brain tissues on MR images

Fig. 1. Architecture of the fuzzy information fusion

- A decision step is necessary to obtain the segmentation result from the joined feature space. Different techniques of decision-level fusion can be used in this step. We propose here a fuzzy-region growing method to obtain the segmentation.

3   Creation of Fuzzy Feature Space

The brain tumor area observed in an MR image can be defined as fuzzy sets. For this specific observation universal, we propose several definitions that we use about these sets:

Set 1: Let B be a space with the generic element of B denoted by v. Thus, $B = \{v\}$. In fact, B is the set of human brain volume and v is the coordinate of voxel, $v = (x, y, z)$.

Set 2: Let a fuzzy set T be a fuzzy subset on B, that is $T = \{v, \mu_T(v) \mid v \in B\}$ where $\mu_T : B \to [0, 1]$ is a membership function of T on B. In this application, T is a fuzzy set of the fuzzy object called human brain tumor of B.

Set 3: Let S^i be a universal set about the scene of MR image, where $I = \{i\}$, I is the index set of multispectral. S^i presents the scene of T1-weighted image when $i = 1$, T2-weighted image when $i = 2$, and Proton Density image when $i = 3$. The element of S^i is denoted by s_i, thus, $S^i = \{s_i\}$. In fact, the S^i is the set of signal intensity of MRI image.

Set 4: The Cartesian product of B and S^i forms a universal set of human brain MRI image; that is $B \times S^i = \{(v, s_i), v \in B, s_i \in (S)^i\}$ $i \in I$.

Set 5: Let the fuzzy set TS^i be a fuzzy feature space set as a fuzzy subset on $B \times S^i$. It is the feature set of the human brain tumor observed in the scene S^i and defined by $TS^i = \{(v, s_i), \mu_{TS^i} \mid v \in B, s_i \in S^i\}$ $i \in I$ where $\mu_{TS^i} : B \times S_i \to [0, 1]$ is the membership function of TS^i on $B \times S^i$.

According to the description of radiology experts, a knowledge–based fuzzy model of the brain tumor characteristics on the three types of MR images can be presented in Table 2. The symbol "+" presents a hyper-signal, it means the image intensity is very bright; "-" presents a hypo-signal, the intensity is very dark; "-+" means that the signal intensity is brighter than hypo-signal, and "+-" means that it is darker than hyper-signal; "–" means that the signal intensity is darker than the hypo-signal, and "++" means that it is brighter than the hyper-signal.

We can conclude that the signal intensity of tumor is neither very bright nor very dark in T1, except for necrotic parts, but it is the brightest in T2 and PD. We propose several mathematical functions to model the fuzzy information presented in table 2. The membership functions of tumor area corresponding to TS^1, TS^2 and TS^3 that is μ_{TS^1}, μ_{TS^2} and μ_{TS^3} respectively, are defined as follows:

$$\mu_{TS^1}(v, s_1) = \begin{cases} 0, & s_1 \leq a_1 \\ \frac{1}{2} + \frac{1}{2}\sin[(\frac{\pi}{b_1-a_1})(s_1 + \frac{b_1+a_1}{2})], & a_1 < s_1 \leq b_1 \\ 1, & b_1 < s_1 \leq c_1 \\ \frac{1}{2} - \frac{1}{2}\sin[(\frac{\pi}{d_1-c_1})(s_1 - \frac{d_1+c_1}{2})], & c_1 < s_1 \leq d_1 \\ 0, & d_1 < s_1 \end{cases} \tag{1}$$

$$\mu_{TS^2}(v, s_2) = \frac{1}{2} + \frac{1}{2}\sin[(s_2 - \frac{a_2+b_2}{2})(\frac{\pi}{b_2-a_2})], \quad a_2 < s_2 \leq b_2 \tag{2}$$

$$\mu_{TS^3}(v, s_3) = \begin{cases} 0, & s_3 \leq a_3 \\ \frac{1}{2}(\frac{s_3-a_3}{a_3-b_3})^2, & a_3 < s_3 \leq b_3 \\ 1 - \frac{1}{2}(\frac{s_3-c_3}{c_3-b_3})^2, & b_3 < s_3 \leq c_3 \\ 1, & c_3 < s_3 \end{cases} \tag{3}$$

where $(a_1, b_1, c_1, d_1), (a_2, b_2)$ and (a_3, b_3, c_3) are parameters of μ_{TS^1}, μ_{TS^2} and μ_{TS^3} respectively. The variables s_1, s_2 and s_3 are signal intensities and correspond to T1, T2 and PD images respectively. The parameters will be estimated through statistical values taken from these image volumes.

The fuzzy Markovian segmentation method proposed in [7] can successfully segment three main brain tissues, WM (white matter), GM (gray matter), and CSF (cerebrospinal fluid), from T1 images. It's used in our system to pre-segment T1 image of tumorous brain into 11 classes. Some characteristics of the tumor area are evident from the result of tissue segmentation: (1) tumor area isn't present in classes 1 (CSF), 10 (WM) and 11 (WM); (2) essential regions are present in classes 3 and 4; (3) edema region is present in classes 4, 5 and 6; its center is found in classes 5.

The pre-segmentation result of T1 image can be projected onto the registered T2 and PD images. The statistical means of signal intensity in each class are called class mean. The relationship between the class mean and possibility of that a voxel belongs to a tumor area is determined as follows: (1) the voxels having intensity close to maximal class mean are considered as probable tumor region on T2 and also on PD (2) also the linear distribution of class means of T1 image shows that the minimal and maximal class means do not correspond to the region of interest, and (3) the values close to minimum have a strong correlation with this region. These statistical characteristics have been used to create a selection rule of parameters for fuzzy models (Eq. 1, 2 and 3). The minimal redundancy and the maximal inclusion are basic rules.

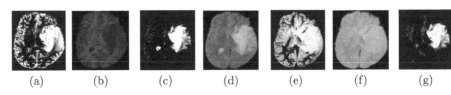

(a)	(b)	(c)	(d)	(e)	(f)	(g)

Fig. 3. Fuzzy feature spaces corresponding their SM, $\boldsymbol{TS}^1/SM_{T1}$: (a)/(b), $\boldsymbol{TS}^2/SM_{T2}$: (c)/(d), $\boldsymbol{TS}^3/SM_{PD}$: (e)/(f), and joined fuzzy feature space $\boldsymbol{T}$ (g)

The fuzzy models project the fuzzy features of brain tumor image onto the corresponding fuzzy feature spaces $\boldsymbol{TS}^1, \boldsymbol{TS}^2$, and $\boldsymbol{TS}^3$. They are illustrated in figure 3(a), (c) and (e).

4   Fuzzy Feature Fusion

A combination of these three feature spaces induce a joined fuzzy feature space and give us a better feature description of tumor area. This operation is called feature-level fusion.

From *Set 2* and *Set 4*, we can infer that $\boldsymbol{T}$ should be formed from the fuzzy relation of the Cartesian product of fuzzy set $\boldsymbol{TS}^i$ defined by $\boldsymbol{T} : \boldsymbol{TS}^1 \times \boldsymbol{TS}^2 \times \boldsymbol{TS}^3 \to [0,1]$. There is a practical fuzzy relation in our application, such that: $\exists v$ of $\boldsymbol{B}$, $v \in \boldsymbol{T}$ with higher membership degree $\mu_{\boldsymbol{T}}(v)$ if and only if $v \in \boldsymbol{TS}^i$ with higher membership degree, where $i = 1, 2, 3$. Here, we propose a geometric mean of fuzzy values presented in equation 4 to build a joined feature space $\boldsymbol{T}$ (see figure 3(g)). The typical tumorous area has been kept in $\boldsymbol{T}$.

$$\mu_{\boldsymbol{T}}(v) = (\mu_{\boldsymbol{TS}^1}(v, s_1) \cdot \mu_{\boldsymbol{TS}^2}(v, s_2) \cdot \mu_{\boldsymbol{TS}^3}(v, s_3))^{1/3} \qquad (4)$$

Any fuzzy intersection operator can be used for fusing these features, for example, Zadeh intersection, Yager intersection, or Hamacher intersection, etc. We have tested these fuzzy intersection operators. They are found to produce similar spaces, also similar to the result of the geometric mean operation.

5   Fuzzy Region Growing

We propose a fuzzy decision called fuzzy region growing. Firstly, the joined feature space is divided into several fuzzy subsets by using fuzzy set α-cut representation. The seed of fuzzy growing is the α-cut subset with α as maximal as possible. Then, a 6-near voxel fuzzy relation is applied to the interior region connection in subsets and exterior region growing between subsets.

Let $^{\alpha}\boldsymbol{T}$ denote the α-cut of $\boldsymbol{T}$. $\boldsymbol{\alpha}$ is a vector with elements $k, k = 1, 2, \ldots, N$, and $\boldsymbol{\alpha} = [1, (N-1)/N, \ldots, 1/N]$, where N is the total number of fuzzy subsets. The subset of $\boldsymbol{T}$, denoted by $_{\alpha}\boldsymbol{T}$, can be used to present different regions and be defined as $_{\alpha_k}\boldsymbol{T} = \overline{^{\alpha_k}\boldsymbol{T}} \cap {^{\alpha_{k+1}}\boldsymbol{T}}$, where $^{\alpha_k}\boldsymbol{T}$ presents the kth fuzzy subset and $\overline{^{\alpha_k}\boldsymbol{T}}$ is the complement of $^{\alpha_k}\boldsymbol{T}$.

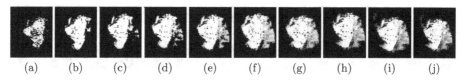

Fig. 4. Fuzzy region growing result with, from (a) to (j), $\alpha > 0.95, \alpha > 0.9, \alpha > 0.8, \alpha > 0.7, \alpha > 0.6, \alpha > 0.5, \alpha > 0.4, \alpha > 0.3, \alpha > 0.2, \alpha > 0.1$, respectively

A fuzzy adjacency relation δ is defined in equation 5 to present the 6-near neighbor relation of a voxel.

$$\delta(v_i, v_j) = \begin{cases} 1, & \text{if } \|v_i - v_j\| = 1, i \neq j \\ 0, & \text{otherwise} \end{cases} \tag{5}$$

Let C_k be the kth grown region which corresponds to fuzzy subset $_{\alpha_k}T$, and produced by the following operation:

- The growing seed C_1 is given by $C_1 = \delta(v_i, v_j) \times {}^{\alpha_2}T, \quad v_i, v_j \in {}^{\alpha_2}T$ where α_2 is decided by $(N-1)/N$ and N should be selected according to that α_2 will be as great as possible.
- Let R be a set of positive whole numbers, and $R = \{r\}$. The probable connected regions $C_k{}^r$ which is one of interior region on $_{\alpha_k}T$ is taken by $C_k{}^r = \delta(v_i, v_j) \times {}_{\alpha_k}T, \quad v_i, v_j \in {}_{\alpha_k}T, \quad k > 2$; where $C_k{}^r$ is a probable subregion of C_k and represents the rth probable connected region which belongs to C_k and $r = 1, 2, \ldots$ Let A denote a subset of R, if $C_k{}^r$ should be used for growing exterior region of C_k, then we have $r \in A$. that is $A = \{r \mid \delta(v_i, v_j) \times C_k{}^r \neq 0, v_i \in C_{k-1}, v_j \in C_k{}^r\}, \quad k > 2$.
- The grown region C_k is the union of $C_k{}^r$ with $r \in A$, that is $C_k = \bigcup_{r \in A} C_k{}^r \quad k > 2$; This means that $C_k{}^r$ belongs to C_k, if and only if at least one of their voxels is adjacent to C_{k-1} in terms of 6-near neighbors.
- The decision result is given by $T = \bigcup_k C_k \quad k = 1, 2, \ldots N$.

Figure 4 is an example of the fuzzy region growing from joined feature space shown in figure 3(g). The seed of growing is the fuzzy subset α-cut with $\alpha > 0.95$. The different k values produce varied decisions. A small k corresponds to a high probability of decision region that the belongs to tumorous area.

6   Result Validation

The MR images of 4 patients with glial cerebral tumor are given in this paper to present the effect of our method. Each of the 4 patients was imaged with a 1.5T GE using an axial 3D IR T1-weighted (TI/TR/TE: 600/10/2), an axial FSE T2-weighted(TR/TE: 3500/102) and an axial FSE PDweighted(TR/TE: 3500/11). The image specifications for T1 image are that the total number of slices is 124, the thickness of each slice is $1.5mm$, and the pixel size is $0.94 \times 0.94mm^2$; for

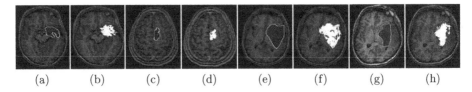

(a)   (b)   (c)   (d)   (e)   (f)   (g)   (h)

Fig. 5. Segmentation results: (a), (c), (e) and (g) are hand-labeled by an expert for 4 patients, respectively. The corresponding results using the proposed method is shown in (b), (d), (f) and (h).

T2 and PD images are that the total number of slices is 20, the thickness of each slice is $5mm$, and the pixel size is $0.47 \times 0.47mm^2$. They were registered by a software tool called FLIRT provided by the Oxford Center for Functional Magnetic Resonance Imaging of the Brain.

Two probability measures, correct detection and false detection, defined by

$$P_c = \frac{N_B}{N_R} \quad \text{and} \quad P_f = \frac{N_D - N_R}{N_{norm}}$$

were used to evaluate the efficiency of the proposed method, where N_R is the number of reference voxels marked by the expert, N_B is the number of voxels detected which are correct relative to the reference, P_c is the probability of correct detection relative to the reference by using the proposed automatic segmentation. N_D is the total number of voxels detected, N_{norm} is the number of voxel of normal tissue which is marked by an expert on the concerned abnormal MR slices. P_f is the probability of false detection, it presents the rate of incorrect detection: that is, our method gives a true result while the reference marks it false. The reference used here is the hand-labeled segmentation by a radiology expert shown in figure 5(a) (c) (e) and (g) for 4 patients while the result of our method is given in figure 5(b) (d) (f) and (h). The average probability of correct detection is equal to 96% and the average probability of false alarm is equal to 5% from a study on 4 patients.

7   Conclusion

We have proposed in this paper a fuzzy information fusion scheme to automatically segment tumor areas of human brain from multispectral MR images. Some mathematic models are introduced to extract fuzzy features from different MR image sequences for creating fuzzy feature spaces corresponding to these sequences. The fuzzy relationship established among these feature spaces is a fusion operator of fuzzy feature. Using the proposed fuzzy region growing, the final segmentation by our method presents a good efficiency than to a synergy of the information acquired from different image sources. The result is appreciated by radiology experts. In comparison with some existing methods [8][9][13], Our method offers some advantages such as full automation, taking into consideration more general and complete pathologic information, and segmentation starting directly from full volume and ending in a more complete result. In a further work, we will continue to develop fuzzy modelling of tumorous tissue and to study fuzzy information fusion operators in more patients with glial tumors and other types of brain tumors in order to improve the robustness of our method and confirm the preceding results.

References

1. Pitiot, A., Toga, A.W., Thompson, P.M.: Adaptive Elastic Segmentation of Brain MRI via Shape-Model-Guided Evolutionary Programming. IEEE Trans. on med. imag. **21** (2002) 910–923
2. Fan,Y., Jiang, T., Evans, D.J.: Volumetric Segmentation of Brain Images Using Parallel Genetic Algorithms. IEEE Trans. on med. imag. **21** (2002) 904–909.
3. Barra, V., Boire, J.: Automatic Segmentation of Subcortical Brain Structures in MR Images Using Information Fusion. IEEE Trans. on Med. Imag. **20** (2001) 549–558
4. Styner, M., Brechbühler, C., Székely,G., Gerig, G.: Parametric estimate of intensity inhomogeneities applied to MRI. IEEE Trans. on Med. Imag. **19** (2000) 153–165.
5. Schroeter, P., Vesin, J-M., Langenberger, T., Meuli, R.: Robust Parameter Estimation of Intensity Distributions for Brain Magnetic Resonance Images. IEEE Trans. on Med. Imag. **17** (1998) 172–186.
6. Leemput, K.V., Maes, F., Vandermeulen, D., Suetens, P.: A Unifying Framework for Partial Volume Segmentation of Brain MR Images. IEEE Trans. on Med. Imag. **22** (2003) 105–119
7. Ruan, S., Moretti, B., Fadili, J., and Bloyet, D.: Fuzzy Markovian Segmentation in Application of Magnetic Resonance Images. Computer Vision and Image Understanding, **85** (2002) 54–69
8. Clark, M.C., Hall, L.O., Goldgof, D.B., Velthuizen, R. Murtagh, F.R., Silbiger, M.S.: Automatic Tumor Segmentation Using Knowledge-Based Techniques. IEEE Trans. on Med. Imag. **17** (1998) 187–201
9. Udupa, J.K., Wei, L., Samarasekera, S., Miki, Y., van Buchem, M.A., Grossman, R.I.: Multiple Sclerosis Lesion Quantification using Fuzzy-Connectedness Principles. IEEE Trans. on Med. Imag. **16** (1997) 598–609
10. Clark, M.C., Hall, L.O., Goldgof, D.B., Clarke, L.P., Velthuizen, R.P., Silbiger, M.S.: MRI Segmentation using Fuzzy Clustering Techniques. IEEE Engineering in Medicine and biology, November/December (1994) 730–742
11. Jenkinson, M., and Smith, S.: Optimization in Robust Linear Registration of Brain Images. FMRIB Technical Report TR00MJ2.
12. Hall, D.L.: Mathematical Techniques in Multisensor Data Fusion. ARTECH HOUSE, INC. (1992)
13. Warfield, S.K., Kaus, M., Jolesz, F.A., Kikinis, R.: Adaptive, Template Moderated, Spatially Varying Statistical Classification. Medical Image Analysis **4** (2000) 43–55

Out-of-Core Segmentation by Deformable Models

Gilson Giraldi, Leandro Schaefer, Ricardo Farias, and Rodrigo Silva

LNCC - National Laboratory for Scientific Computing,
Av. Getulio Vargas, 333 25651-070, Petrópolis, RJ, Brazil
Tel (55) 24 - 2233-6088 Fax (55) 24 - 2231-5595
{gilson, schaefer, rfarias, rodrigo}@lncc.br

Abstract. Memory limitations can lower the performance of segmentation applications for large images or even make it undoable. In this paper we address this problem through out-of-core techniques. Specifically, we integrate the T-Surfaces model, and out-of-core isosurface generation methods in a general framework for segmentation of large image volumes. T-Surfaces is a parametric deformable model based on a triangulation of the image domain, a discrete surface model and an image threshold. Isosurface generation techniques have been implemented through an out-of-core method that uses a k-d-tree-like structures, called *meta-cell* technique. By using the meta-cell framework, we present an out-of-core version of a segmentation method based on T-Surfaces and isosurface extraction. We demonstrate our out-of-core methodology (Meta-Cell, Isosurfaces, T-Surfaces) for segmentation of grey level images.

1 Introduction

Image segmentation is useful in fields like robot vision [1], and medical diagnosis [8], among a large variety of application areas [5]. From the segmentation results, it is possible to identify regions of interest and objects in the scene.

In this paper, we focus on parametric deformable surface models for segmentation of large image volumes. These models consist basically of an elastic surface (or curve) which can dynamically conform to object shapes in response to internal (elastic) forces and external forces (image and constraint ones).

In general, deformable surface models make use of only the data information along the surface when evolving the model towards the object boundary [7, 8]. However, state-of-the-art implementations of these models do not account for this fact and fetch the whole volume from disk at the initialization. Such procedure brings limitations for large size image volumes, mainly if we consider that, in general, deformable models need not only the image intensity but also the image gradient [6, 8]. That is the starting point of this work.

The analysis of large datasets is a known problem in the context of scientific visualization [11, 2, 4]. Out-of-core techniques have been developed for scalar and vector fields visualization and new proposals are still in progress.

V. Di Gesú, F. Masulli, and A. Petrosino (Eds.): WILF 2003, LNAI 2955, pp. 216–223, 2006.

These methods partition the dataset into clusters that are stored in disk blocks, and build a data structure to index the blocks (*Preprocessing step*). At run-time, the data structure is read to main memory for information retrieval. The most commonly used data structures, for scientific visualization applications, are the octrees [11, 10] and a *k-d*-tree based technique called *meta-cell* [2].

In this paper we present a segmentation approach, based on an out-of-core T-Surfaces implementation, using the meta-cell structure (section 5). Up to our knowledge, it is the first out-of-core algorithm for deformable surface model reported in the literature. It is important to highlight that the proposed structure is useful not only to efficiently swap data between memory and disk, but also to accelerate the segmentation process, as we shall demonstrate on the experimental results (section 6).

2   Meta-cell Technique

Meta-cell Constrution: Sort all data points by the x-values, and partition them into H consecutive chunks. Then, for each such chunk, sort its data points by the y-values, and partition them into H consecutive chunks. For $3D$ images, we must repeat the procedure for the z-values. Each generated chunk (*meta-cell*) stores the minimum and the maximum of its image scalar values.

Given a point (q_1, q_2, q_3), inside the domain, the corresponding meta-cell is given by:

$$MCell = \lfloor q_i/C_i \rfloor, i = 0, 1, 2, \tag{1}$$

where C_i is the number of data points of each chunk in the direction i. To each meta-cell, it is associated a set of meta-intervals (connected components among the intensity intervals of the meta-cell). These meta-intervals are used to construct an interval tree, which will be used to optimize I/O operations.

When used for isosurface generation, the meta-cell technique proposed by Chiang at al. [3] works as follows: Given an *isovalue*, the query pipeline follows the next steps: (a) Query the interval tree to find all meta-cells which meta-intervals contain the *isovalue* (*active meta-cells*); (b) Sort the reported meta-cell ID's properly to allow sequential disk reads; (c) For active meta-cell, read it from disk to main memory, and compute the corresponding isosurface patches.

This minimizes the impact of the I/O bottleneck by reading from disk only those portions of the search structure and data set necessary to construct the current isosurface.

3   T-Surfaces Model

The T-Surfaces approach is composed basically by three components [8]: (1) a tetrahedral decomposition (CF-Triangulation) of the image domain $D \subset \Re^3$; (2) a particle model of the deformable surface; (3) a *Characteristic Function* χ defined on the grid nodes which distinguishes the interior ($Int(S)$) from the exterior ($Ext(S)$) of a surface S: $\chi : D \subset \Re^3 \rightarrow \{0, 1\}$, where $\chi(p) = 1$ if $p \in Int(S)$ and $\chi(p) = 0$, otherwise, where p is a node of the grid.

Following the classical nomenclature, a tetrahedron (also called a simplex) σ is a *transverse* one if the characteristic function χ changes its value in σ. Analogously, for an edge.

In this framework, the reparameterization of a surface is done by [8]: (1)Taking the intersections points of the surface with the grid; (2)Find the set of transverse tetrahedra; (3)For each transverse edge choose an intersection point belonging to it; (4) Connect these points properly.

In this reparameterization process, the transverse simplices play a central role. Given such a simplex, we choose in each transverse edge an intersection point to generate the new surface patch. In general, we will have three or four transverse edges in each transverse tetrahedron. The former gives a triangular patch and the later defines two triangles. So, at the end of the step (4) we have a triangular mesh. Each triangle is called a *triangular element* [8].

Dynamically, a T-Surfaces can be seen as a closed elastic mesh. Each node is called a *node element* and each pair of connected nodes v_i, v_j is called a *model element*.

The node elements are linked by springs, whose natural length we set to zero. Hence, a tensile force can be defined by:

$$\vec{\alpha_i} = \sum_j \vec{S}_{ij} \text{ where } \vec{S}_{ij} = c\left(r_{ij}\right), \tag{2}$$

c is a scale factor and $r_{ij} = \|v_i - v_j\|$ is the length of the corresponding model element. The model also has a normal force which can be weight as follows [8]:

$$F_i = k\left(sign_i\right) n_i, \tag{3}$$

where n_i is the normal vector at node i, k is a scale factor, and $sign_i = +1$ if $I\left(v_i\right) > T$ and $sign_i = -1$ otherwise (T is a threshold for image I). This force is used to push the model towards image edges until it is opposed by external image forces.

The forces given in (2)-(3) are internal forces. The external force is defined as a function of the image data, according to the features we seek. One possibility is:

$$Image\ Force\ f_i^t = -\gamma_i \nabla P; \quad P = \|\nabla I\|^2. \tag{4}$$

The evolution of the surface is governed by the following explicit numerical method:

$$v_i^{(t+\Delta t)} = v_i^t + h_i\left(\vec{\alpha_i}^t + \vec{F}_i^t + \vec{f}_i^t\right), \tag{5}$$

where h_i is an evolution step. During the T-Surfaces evolution some grid nodes become interior to a surface. Such nodes are called *burnt nodes* and its identification is fundamental to update the characteristic function [8]. To deal with self-intersections of the surface the T-Surfaces model incorporates an entropy condition: *once a node is burnt it stays burnt*. A termination condition is obtained based on the number of deformations steps that a simplex has remained a transverse one.

4   Segmentation Framework

We propose in [9] a segmentation approach which is based on two steps: First, a rough approximation of the target surfaces is obtained by isosurfaces generation methods; Then, a T-Surfaces is applied to improve the result.

The main idea is pictured on Figure 1. In the Figure 1.a we have a CF triangulation with grid resolution is 10×10. In a first stage, we use the T-Surfaces grid to define a coarser image resolution by sampling the image field over the grid nodes. Now, the obtained field is thresholded to define a simple function, called an *Object Characteristic Function*:

$$\chi(p) = 1, \quad if \quad I(p) < T, \tag{6}$$

$$\chi(p) = 0, \quad otherwise,$$

where p is a node of the triangulation (grid nodes marked on Figure 1.a). We can perform a further step, shown in Figure 1.b, where we present a curve which belongs to the triangles in which the characteristic function (marked nodes) changes its value. Observe that this curve approximates the boundary we seek. These curves (or surfaces for $3D$) can be obtained by isosurface extraction methods and can be used to initialize the T-Surfaces model [9].

We can summarize the segmentation method above described as follows: (1) Extract region based statistics; (2) Coarser image resolution; (3) Define the *Object Characteristic Function*; (4) Extract isosurfaces; (5) Apply T-Surfaces model.

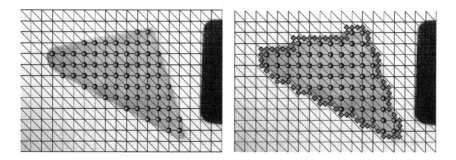

Fig. 1. (a) Original image and Characteristic Function. (b) Boundary approximation.

5   Out-of-Core Segmentation Approach

In this section we present the out-of-core version of the segmentation framework described above.

The algorithm is interesting for this work because of two aspects. First, it uses the T-Surfaces model which uses auxiliary and very memory consuming data structures. Second, it needs both the two queries found in segmentation algorithms: (a) Given a reference value q, find all image points p such that $I(p) = q$; (b) Given a point p find the image intensity $I(p)$.

The algorithm use the meta-cell technique described in section 2 and has the following elements.

Meta-Cell Partition: The meta-cell size is application dependent. Basically, it depends on the dataset size, disk block size, and the amount of memory available.

Interval Tree: Let us consider the worst case, for which the meta intervals are of the form: $I_0 = [0,0]; I_1 = [2,2]; ...; I_{127} = [254, 254]$. For a $2^9 \times 2^9 \times 2^9$ data set, if we take meta-cells with $2^4 \times 2^4 \times 2^4$ data points, we find $2^{15} = 32KB$ meta-cells. Thus, we will need an amount of $2 \cdot 128 \cdot 32KB = 8.0MB$, which is not restrictive for usual workstations. Besides, in general, interval tree sizes are much smaller than this bound (see section 6).

Data Cache: To avoid memory swap, we must control the memory allocation at run time. This can be done through a data cache, which can store a pre-defined number M of meta-cells. When the cache fills, the least recently used (LRU) meta-cell will be replaced [10].

Query Algorithm:(a)Given an isovalue q, find all meta-intervals (and the corresponding meta-cell ID's) containing q, by querying the I/O interval tree defined on section 2; (b) Given a point $q = (q_1, q_2, q_3)$, find the corresponding meta-cell ID through the expression (1).

insert_neighbors(p): For each neighbor q of a node element p, verifies if q has not been evolved by equation (5) and if $q \notin processing\_list$. In this case, insert q in *processing_list*. The key idea behind the *processing_list* construction is to update node elements according to a *breadth-first-search algorithm* (**BFS**); that is, we consider neighbors of a node as predecessors in the search: starting at a seed (a node element for which neighbors belong to the same meta-cell), the algorithm visits all the neighbors; then it visits all the neighbors of neighbors, etc..., until it runs out of neighbors to visit (see Figure 2).

Next, we outline the algorithm. We suppose that the object of interest has intensity pattern inside the range $[I_1, I_2]$.

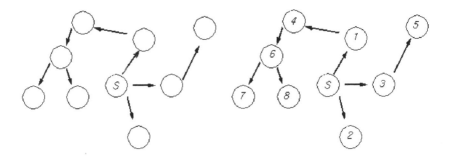

Fig. 2. (a) Example of BFS algorithm in graphs. (b) Possible order of visiting nodes after BFS with seed S.

Out-of-Core Segmentation Algorithm:

1: Compute Object_Characteristic_Function
2: Traverse interval tree to find the list L of active meta-cells
3: **while** L is not NULL **do**
4:    Read M active meta-cells to main memory
5:    Take a *metacell*. Given a grid node $p \in metacell$
6:    If $I(p) \in [I_1, I_2]$ then $\chi(p) = 1$
7: **end while**
8: Extract isosurfaces. If needed, increase grid resolution. Go to step (1)
9: Find a seed and insert it into *processing_list*
10: Begin T-Surfaces model
11: **while** *processing_list* is not empty **do**
12:    Pop a point p from *processing_list*
13:    Find the corresponding meta-cell(p)
14:    **if** meta-cell(p) is not in memory **then**
15:       read meta-cell(p)
16:    **end if**
17:    Find $I(p)$ and $\nabla I(p)$
18:    Update p according to the equation (5)
19:    Call *insert_neighbors(p)*
20: **end while**
21: Update function χ
22: Reparameterization of T-Surfaces (section 3)
23: If termination condition is not reached go to (9)

6   Experimental Results

In this section, we attempt to experimentally demonstrate our out-of-core segmentation technique. We consider three grey level datasets (Table 1.a). The machine used was a Pentium III, 863MHz with 512M of RAM, and 768M of swap space.

There are three main steps to be considered: Preprocessing, Isosurfaces Generation and T-Surfaces Evolution. Preprocessing encompasses the gradient computation and meta-cell generation. Meta-Cell generation is basically divided in two steps: (a) Mapping data points into meta-cells and writing data information to the corresponding meta-cells; (b) Find meta-intervals and computing the interval tree. Preprocessing step can be expensive due to the gradient computation.

Isosurfaces Generation encompasses steps (1) and (2) of the algorithm of section 5. It is important to observe that, in general, the smaller meta-cell size, the faster the isosurface search. This fact is verified on Table 1.b. For instance, when using 7.600 meta-cells the algorithm can fetch all the set of active meta-cells from disk. Thus, there is not extra I/O operations during steps (1) of the segmentation algorithm. Also, the meta-cell technique minimizes the effect of the I/O bottleneck by reading from disk only those portions of the data necessary for step (1). Besides, the time for an interval tree query was approximately $1s$. The final step, the T-Surfaces evolution is globally reported on Table 1.c for the Kidney dataset, maintaining the same partitions of Table 1.b.

Table 1. (a) Statistics for preprocessing: number of meta-cells (No. MC), times for meta-cell generation (MC Generation), gradient computation (Gradient), and interval tree construction (IT), size of each meta-cell (MC size) and size of the interval tree (IT size). (b) Statistics for isosurface generation on the Kidney dataset. This table reports the no. of meta-cells (No. MC), no. of active meta-cells (ActiveMC), interval tree (IT) information, and total time for isosurface generation (IsoTime). The Data Cache size used is 15MB. (c) T-Surfaces on the Kidney dataset. This table reports the no. of meta-cells (No. MC), no. of meta-cells that have been cut (CutMC), no. of I/O operations (No. I/O), and the total clock time for evolution (Time).

(a)

DataSet	Artery	Artery2	Kidney
Size (MB)	3.37	20.97	4.57
No. MC	125	1000	7600
MC Gene.	3s	25s	5s
Gradient	16s	88s	24s
IT	0.5s	0.5s	0.5s
Total	20s	114s	30s
MC size(KB)	343.04	285.69	8.2944
IT size(KB)	38.62	379.13	938.95

(b)

No. MC	7600	1000	288	125
ActiveMC	1140	474	256	125
IT size(KB)	938.95	203.56	61.23	21.25
IT time	1s	1s	1s	1s
IsoTime	13s	15s	15s	20s

(c)

No. MC	7600	1000	288	125
No. I/O	1244	4780	1818	1458
CutMC	1074	325	125	70
Time	503s	570s	584s	600s

 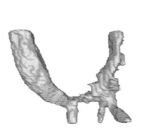 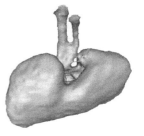

Fig. 3. Extracted surfaces for: (a) Artery dataset; (b) Artery2; (c)Kidney dataset

Again, the smaller the meta-cell size, the faster the whole process. Despite of the high number of I/O operations reported on line 2 of Table 1.c we must highlight that the total time for T-Surfaces evolution without using the meta-cell was 623s, against 600s of the worst case reported on Table 1.c . For the best case, we observe a performance improvement of 120s, which is an important result. The final surface (Figure 3.c) has 34, 624 triangular elements.

The parameters used in the T-Surfaces for the above experiments are: grid $4 \times 4 \times 4$, freezing point $= 10$, $\gamma = 0.01$, $k = 1.222$; $c = 0.750$. The intensity pattern of the targets are given by the following ranges: $[10, 22]$ for dataset, $[195, 255]$ for Kidney, $[15, 30]$ for Artery2. Figure 3 shows the extracted surfaces.

7 Conclusions

In this paper we demonstrate the efficiency of an out-of-core implementation of the segmentation framework proposed in [9]. The methodology presented is based on the meta-cell technique and an out-of-core version of T-Surfaces model. Future directions for this work will be to implement out-of-core Level Sets and region growing methods as well as to minimize I/O operations during T-Surfaces evolution.

References

1. J. Bruce, T. Balch, and M. Veloso. Fast and inexpensive color image segmentation for interactive robots, 2000.
2. Y.-J. Chiang, R. Farias, C. Silva, and B. Wei. A unified infrastructure for parallel out-of-core isosurface and volume rendering of unstructured grids. In *IEEE Parallel and Large-Data Vis. and Graph.*, 2001.
3. Y.-J. Chiang, C. Silva, and W. J. Schroeder. Interactive out-of-core isosurface extraction. In *IEEE Visualization*, pages 67–174, 1998.
4. R. Farias and C. Silva. Out-of-core rendering of large unstructured grids. *IEEE Computer Graphics & Applications*, 21(4):42–50, July 2001.
5. Anil K. Jain. *Fundamentals of Digital Image Processing*. Prentice-Hall, Inc., 1989.
6. M. Kass, A. Witkin, and D. Terzopoulos. Snakes: Active contour models. *International Journal of Computer Vision*, 1(4):321–331, 1988.
7. T. McInerney and D. Terzopoulos. Deformable models in medical image analysis: A survey. *Medical Image Analysis*, 1(2), 1996.
8. T. McInerney and D. Terzopoulos. Topology adaptive deformable surfaces for medical image volume segmentation. *IEEE Trans. on Medical Imaging*, 18(10):840–850, October 1999.
9. E. Strauss, W. Jimenez, G. A. Giraldi, R. Silva, and A. F. Oliveira. A semi-automatic surface reconstruction framework based on t-surfaces and isosurface extraction methods. In *International Symposium on Computer Graphics, Image Processing and Vision (SIBGRAPI)*, 2002.
10. P. Sutton and C. Hansen. Accelerated isosurface extraction in time-varying fields. *IEEE Trans. on Visualization*, 6(2):98–107, 2001.
11. Shyh-Kuang Ueng, C. Sikorski, and Kwan-Liu Ma. Out-of-core streamline visualization on large unstructured meshes. *IEEE Trans. on Vis. and Computer Graphics*, 3(4):370–380, 1997.

Rough Set Approach for Classification of Breast Cancer Mammogram Images

Aboul Ella Hassanien and Jafar M. Ali

Kuwait University, Collegue of Business Administration,
Quantitative Methods and Information Systems Department,
P.O. Box 5969 Safat, code no. 13060, Kuwait
Abo@cba.edu.kw
http://www.cba.edu.kw/abo

Abstract. This paper presents a study on classification of breast cancers in digital mammography images, using rough set theory in conjunction with statistical feature extraction techniques. First, we improve the contrast of the digitized mammograms by applying computer image processing techniques to enhance x-ray images and then subsequently extract features from suspicious regions characterizing the underlying texture of the breast regions. Feature extractions are derived from the gray-level co-occurrence matrix, then the features were normalized and the rough set dependency rules are generated directly from the real value attribute vector. These rules can then be passed to a classifier for discrimination for different regions of interest to test whether they are normal or abnormal. The experimental results show that the proposed algorithm performs well reaching over 98 % in accuracy. . . .

1   Introduction

Currently, digital mammography (Kok, 2003 and Nico 1998) is one of the most promising cancer control strategies since the cause of breast cancer is still unknown. Mammography is a specific type of imaging that uses a low-dose X-ray system and high-contrast, high-resolution film for examination of the breasts. Most medical experts agree that successful treatment of breast cancer often is linked to early diagnosis. Mammography plays a central part in early detection of breast cancers because it can show changes in the breast up to two years before a patient or physician can feel them. Classification is a form of medical data analysis, which can be used to extract models describing important data classes or to predict future data trends. In other words, classification is to identify essential features of different classes based on a training set and then classify new instances into the appropriate classes. Recently various published algorithms have been applied to handle the classification problem in medical field. The most commonly algorithms used in medical fields are neural networks, Bayesian classifier, genetic algorithms, decision trees, and fuzzy theory (Lavrac, 1999). Recently, rough sets (Aboul Ella, 2003, Grzymala, 1999 and Pawlak, 1982) have been also applied in this field. In this paper, we introduce an efficient classification approach based on the context of rough set theory which applied on five

V. Di Gesú, F. Masulli, and A. Petrosino (Eds.): WILF 2003, LNAI 2955, pp. 224–231, 2006.
© Springer-Verlag Berlin Heidelberg 2006

statistical extracted features from the digital mammograms. Rough set concept was introduced by Polish logician, Pawlak in early eighties (Pawlak, 1982). This theory become very popular among scientists around the world and the rough set is now one of the most developing intelligent data analysis. Rough sets data analysis was used for the discovery of data dependencies, data reduction, approximate set classification, and rule induction from databases. The generated rules represent the underlying semantic content of the images in the database. A classification mechanism is developed by which the images are classified according to the generated rules. This paper is organized as follows. Feature extraction based on Gray-level Co-occurrence Matrix is presented in Section 2. In section 3, the fundamental of rough set theory and the rule generation algorithm are introduced. The rule classification algorithm is discussed in Section 4. Experimental results are given and discussed in section 5. The paper is concluded in section 6.

2   Texture Feature Extraction

Texture is one of the most important defining characteristics of an image. It is characterized by the spatial distribution of gray levels in a neighborhood. In order to capture the spatial dependence of gray-level values which contribute to the perception of texture, a two-dimensional dependence texture analysis matrix is discussed for texture consideration. Since texture shows its characteristics by both each pixel and pixel values. There are many approaches using for texture classification. The gray-level co-occurrence matrix seems to be a well-know statistical technique for feature extraction (Ahuja, 1978 and Haralick, 1979).

2.1   Gray-Level Co-occurrence Matrix

Co-occurrence matrix, the second-order histogram, is the two dimensional matrix of joint probabilities $P_{d,r}(i,j)$ between pairs of pixels, separated by a distance d in a given direction r. Haralick et al., 1979 define 14 texture features derived from the co-occurrence matrix. In this paper, five features were selected for further study; maximum probability, contrast, inverse different moment, angular second moment, and entropy. Table (1) gives the description of these selected features. Where $P(i,j)$ refers to the normalized entry of the co-occurrence matrices. That is $P(i,j) = P_d(i,j)/R$ where R is the total number of pixel pairs (i,j). For a displacement $d = (dx, dy)$ vector and image of size NxM is given by $(N - dx)(M - dy)$.

3   Rough Set Theory: Theoretical Background

Let us present here some preliminaries of rough set theory, which are relevant to this work. For details one may refer to (AboulElla, 2003, Grzymala, 1999 and Pawlak, 1982).

3.1   Information Systems

Knowledge representation in rough sets is done via information systems, which are a tabular form of an OBJECT ATTRIBUTE VALUE relationship. More precisely, an information system, $\Gamma = < U, \Omega, V_q, f_q >_{q \in \Omega}$, where

Table 1. Texture features extracted from Co-occurrence matrix

Feature	Equation	Description
Maximum probability)	$\max \sum_{i,j} P(i,j)$	This is simply the largest entry in the matrix, and corresponds to the strongest response.
Contrast	$\sum_{i,j} (i,j)^2 P(i,j)$	A measure of the image contrast or the amount of local variations present in an image.
Inverse different moment	$\sum_{i,j} \frac{1}{1+(i-j)^2} P(i,j)$	This descriptor has large values in cases where the largest elements in P are along the principal diagonal.
Angular second moment	$\sum_{i,j} P(i,j)^2$	A measure of the homogeneity of an image. Hence it is a suitable measure for detection of disorders in textures. For homogeneous textures value of angular second moment turns out to be small compared to non-homogeneous ones.
Entropy	$\sum_{i,j} P(i,j) \log(P(i,j))$	Measures the randomness of intensity distribution.

- U is a finite set of objects, $U = \{x_1, x_2, \ldots, x_n\}$
- Ω is a finite set of attributes (features), the attributes in Ω are further classified into disjoint condition attributes A and decision attributes D, $\Omega = A \cup D$
- For each $q \in \Omega$,
- V_q is a set of objects
- Each $f_q : U \longrightarrow V_q$ is an information function which assigns particular values from domains of attributes to objects such that $f_q(x_i) \in V_q$ for all $x_i \in U$ and $q \in \Omega$:

$$R_q = \{x : x \in U \wedge f(x,q) = f(x_0, q) \forall x_0 \in U\} . \tag{1}$$

With respect to a given q, the functions partitions the universe into a set of pairwise disjoints subsets of U:

$$U/IND(P) = \cap \{q \in P : U/IND(P)(\{q\})\} . \tag{2}$$

Assume a subset of the set of attributes,$P \subseteq A$. Two samples x and $y$in U are indiscernible with respect to P if and only if $f(x,q) = f(y,q) \forall q \in P$. The indiscernibility relation for all $P \subseteq A$ is written as $IND(P)$. Where $U/IND(P)$ is used to denote the partition of U given $IND(P)$ and is calculated as follows:

$$A \cap B = \{X \cap Y : \forall q \in A, \forall Y \in B, X \cap Y \neq \{\}\} . \tag{3}$$

3.2 Approximation Spaces

A rough set approximates traditional sets using a pair of sets named the lower and upper approximation of the set. The lower and upper approximations of a set $P \subseteq U$, are defined by equations (4) and (5), respectively.

$$\underline{P}Y = \cup\{X :\in U/IND(P), X \subseteq Y\} . \tag{4}$$

$$\overline{P}Y = \cup\{X :\in U/IND(P), X \cup Y \neq \{\}\} . \tag{5}$$

Assuming P and Q are equivalence relations in U, the important concept positive region $POS_P(Q)$ is defined as:

$$POS_p(Q) = \bigcup_{X \in Q} PX . \tag{6}$$

A positive region contains all patterns in U that can be classified in attribute set Q using the information in attribute set P.

3.3 Degree of Dependency

The degree of dependency $\gamma(P, Q)$ of a set P of attributes with respect to a set Q of class labeling is defined as:

$$\gamma(P, Q) = \frac{|POS_p(Q)|}{|U|} . \tag{7}$$

Where $|S|$ denotes the cardinality of set.

The degree of dependency provides a measure of how important P is in mapping the dataset examples into Q. If $\gamma(P, Q) = 0$, then classification Q is independent of the attributes in P, hence the decision attributes are of no use to this classification. If $\gamma(P, Q) = 1$, then Q is completely dependent on P hence the attributes are indispensable. Values $0 < \gamma(P, Q) < 1$ denote partial dependency, which shows that only some of the attributes in P may be useful, or that the dataset was flawed to begin with. In addition, the complement of $\gamma(P, Q)$ gives a measure of the contradictions in the selected subset of the dataset.

3.4 Attribute Reduction

In an information system there often exist some condition attributes that do not provide any additional information about the objects in U. So, we should remove those attributes since the complexity and cost of decision process can be reduced if those condition attributes are eliminated (Kryszkiewicz, 1993).

Reduct: Given a classification task mapping a set of variables C to a set of labeling D, a reduct is defined as any $R \subseteq C$, such that $\gamma(C, D) = \gamma(R, D)$.

Reduct Set: Given a classification task mapping a set of variables C to a set of labeling D, a reduct set is defined with respect to the power set $P(C)$ as the set $R \subseteq P(C)$ such that $R = \{A \in P(C) : \gamma(A, D) = \gamma(C, D)\}$. That is, the reduct set is the set of all possible reducts of the equivalence relation denoted by C and D.

It is now possible to define the significance of an attribute. This is done by calculating the change of dependency when removing the attribute from the set of considered conditional attributes. Given P, Q and an $x \in P$, the significant $\sigma_x(P, Q)$ of x in the equivalence relation denoted by P and Q is $\sigma_x(P, Q) = \gamma(P, Q) - \gamma(P - \{x\}, Q)$.

Now, attribute reduction involves removing attributes that have no significance to the classification at hand. It is obvious that a dataset may have more than one attribute reduct set.

4   Rule Generation and Building the Classifier

The main task of the rule generation method is to compute reducts relative to a particular kind of information system. The goal of classification is to assign a new object to a class from a given set of classes based on the attribute values of this object. To classify objects, which has never been seen before, rules generated from a training set will be used. These rules represent the actual classifier. This classifier is used to predict to which classes new objects are attached. Given a new image, the classification process searches in this set of rules for finding the class that is the closest to be attached with the object presented for classification [1]. This section describes how the classification system is built and how a new pattern can be classified using this system. Given an object to classify, the features discussed in section (2) are extracted. The features in the object would yield a list of applicable rules. Then the applicable rules are grouped by class in their consequent part and the groups are ordered by the sum of rules confidences, the ordered groups would indicate the most significant class that should be attached to the object to be classified. We use the already generated rules to classify new objects. Given a new image, its feature vector is first extracted and then the attribute vector is computed. The nearest matching rule is determined as the one whose condition part differs from the attribute vector of re-image by the minimum number of attributes. When there is more than one matching rule, we use a voting mechanism to choose the decision value. Every matched rule contributes votes to its decision value, which are equal to the t times number of objects matched by the rule. The votes are added and the decision with the largest number of votes is chosen as the correct class. Here t represents the validity of the rule. The classification algorithm is given as follows:

Input: A new image to be classified, the attribute vector, and the set of rules
Output: The final classification
Processing:
(1)   For each rule in Rule set Do
(2)   If match (rule, new object) Then
(3) $Measure = |Objects|$
(4) $K \rightarrow |Classes|$
(5)   For i=1 to K Do
(6)   Collect the set of objects defining the concept X^i
(7)   Extract $Mrule(X^i, u^t) = r \in Rule$
(8)   For any rule $r \in Mrule(X^i, u^t)$ Do
(9) $T = Match_A(r) \cap X^i and LL = LL \cup T$
(10) $Strength = Card(LL)/Card(X^i)$
(11) $Vote = Measure * Strength$
(12)   Give $Vote(Class(Rule), Vote)$
(13)   Return Class with highest Vote

5   Results and Discussion

The data sets that we used in this work were taken from the Mammography Image Analysis Society (MIAS) (Mini Mammography database, 2003). It contains 320 images, which belong to three normal categories: normal, benign and malign. There are 206 normal images, 63 benign and 51 malign, which are considered abnormal. In addition, the abnormal case are further divided in six categories: microcalcification, circumscribed masses, speculated masses, ill-defined masses, architectural distortion and asymmetry. All the images also include the locations of any abnormities that may be present. We divide the 320 samples of mammogram images into 10 equal size folders, such that a single folder is used for testing the model that has been developed from the remaining nine sets. The evaluation statistics for each method is then assessed as an average of 10 experiments.

Table 2. Classification accuracy over the 10-folder

Folder	Number of rules	Accuracy
1	22	97.2
2	18	98.8
3	22	98.3
4	22	98.8
5	40	99.7
6	34	99.0
7	32	100
8	25	99.3
9	16	98.9
10	17	98.4
Ave(%)	24.8%	98.46%

The query was performed by providing a query image from a data set and the selected five texture features: maximum probability, contrast, inverse difference moment, angular second moment and entropy calculated from each occurrence matrix and their values are saved in the feature vector of the corresponding image. Then the rules will be generated and ordered. The similarity between images is estimated by summing up the distance between corresponding features in their feature vectors. Images having feature vectors closest to feature vector of the query image are returned as best matches. The results were then numerically sorted and the best images were displayed along with the query image.

The results show that the algorithm was able to classify breast cancer in digital mammogram images with high accuracy rate and with small number of rules. Table (2) shows the number of generated rule with the overall classification accuracy based on 10-fold cross validation. The overall accuracy rate and the average number of generated rules were 98.46% and 24.8%, respectively.

A comparison between the obtained results of applying rough set and neural networks (Jelonek et. al., 1993) has been made. Table (3) shows the comparison of rough sets and neural networks results. Rough set results were much better in terms of the number of rules and the classification accuracy.

Table 3. Number of generated rules and accuracy results

Algorithm	Number of rules	classification Accuracy
Neural netwroks		85.25%
Rough sets		98%

From Table (3) we observe that the rough set algorithm seem the best in finding out a small set of interesting rules for effective classification using possibly large and simplified patterns. Also, it could be used for extracting knowledge from incomplete data. Furthermore, rough set approximations enable to describe the decision classes, regarded as the sets of objects satisfying some predefined conditions, by means of indiscernibility relations grouping into classes the objects with the same (similar) values of the considered attributes. On the other hand, rule-based classification process associated with neural networks is not easy to explain as rules that are meaningful to the user. Moreover, in the neural networks, more robust features are required to improve the performance of the neural networks.

6   Conclusion

Mammography is one of the best methods in breast cancer analysis, but in some cases, radiologists can not analysis tumors despite their experiences. Such computer-aided methods like the work presented in this paper could assist medical staff and improve the accuracy of detection. This paper presents an efficient classification based on texture features to classify from medical databases in the context of rough set theory. Five features generated form the co-occurrence matrix are extracted and represented in attribute vector, and then the decision rules within the data are extracted. Therefore, the classifier model was built and the quadratic distance similarly is used for matching process. The experimental results show that the algorithm performs well reaching over 98% in accuracy with less number of rules.

Acknowledgement. This work was supported by Kuwait University, Reserach Grant No. IQ03/02.

References

1. Aboul Ella H., Jafar M. H. Ali.:An Efficient Classification and Image Retrieval Algorithm based on Rough Set Theory. In: 5th International Conference On Enterprise Information Systems Ecole Supérieure d' Electronique de l' Ouest - Angers - France - 23-26 April, (2003) 141–147
2. Ahuja N., Rosefeld A. :A Note on the Use of Second-order Gray-level Statistics for Threshold Selection. In: IEEE Trans. Systems, Man, and Cybernatics, SMC-8912, (1978) 895-898
3. Grzymala-Busse J., Pawlak Z., Slowinski R., Ziarko W.:Rough Sets. In: Communications of the ACM, vol.38, no. 11, 1999.
4. Haralick R.M. :Statistical and Structural Approaches to Texture. In: Proceeding of the IEEE, vol.67, no.5, May 1979.
5. http://www.wiau.man.ac.uk/services/MIAS/MIASmini.htm.:The Mammographic Image Analysis Society: Mini Mammography Database. 2003
6. Kok S.L. : Computer Interpretation of X-ray Mammography. Department of Engineering Science, University of Oxford, web site http://www.eng.ox.ac.uk, 2003
7. Lavrac N. : Machine Learning for Data Mining in Medicine. In AIMDM'99, (1999) 47–64
8. Nico K., Martin T., Jan H., Leon V. E.:Digital Mammography: Computational Imaging and Vision. In: Kluwer academic publication, (1998)
9. Pawlak Z.:Rough sets. In: Int. J. Computer and Information Science, vol. 11, (1982) 341-356
10. Kryszkiewicz M., Rybinski H.: Finding reducts in composed information systems. In: W. Ziarko (ed.), Rough Sets, Fuzzy Sets and Knowledge Discovery. Proceedings of the International Workshop on Rough Sets and Knowledge Discovery (RSKD'93), Banff, Alberta, Canada, October 12-15, Springer-Verlag, Berlin, (1993) 261–273
11. Jelonek J., et. al.:Neural networks and rough sets - comparison and combination for classification of histological pictures. In: Proceedings of the International Workshop on Rough Sets and Knowledge Discovery (RSKD'93), Banff, Alberta, Canada, October 12-15, Springer-Verlag, Berlin,(1993) 426–433

Genetic Fourier Descriptor
for the Detection of Rotational Symmetry

Raymond K.K. Yip

Department of Information and Applied Technology,
Hong Kong Institute of Education
10 Lo Ping Road, Tai Po, New Territories, Hong Kong
hkryyip@ied.edu.hk

Abstract. In this paper, a Genetic Fourier Descriptors is proposed to detect rotational symmetry. Rotational symmetry is one of the important features for image decoding and object recognition in computer vision systems. In the Genetic Fourier algorithm, the Fourier descriptors are chromosomes and fitting function of the GA. The Genetic Fourier method has the following advantages. (1) It can handle partially occurred contour and opened contour, (2) It can handle complex point pattern, (3) It can obtain multiple perceptions and (4) It is highly parallel and its efficient can be greatly improved if parallel processors are used. Experimental results show that it can handle complex symmetry figures, these symmetry figures may be formed by separated curves, points or partially occurred or partially missed (open contour).

1 Introduction

In this paper, a Genetic Fourier Descriptors is proposed to detect rotational symmetry. Rotational symmetry is one of the important features for image decoding and object recognition in computer vision systems

Rotational symmetry is one of the important features for image decoding and object recognition in computer vision systems. It plays an important role in pattern recognition, especially when extracting a planar symmetric figure from a single image without the need of models. In the recent years, many methods have been proposed for the detection of rotational symmetry. However most of the methods are difficult to handle complex symmetry figure, e.g. figure 5-7. Some methods, like Hough transform [8] can handle these situation but they only extract the symmetric points and the problem of finding the connected contour (connectivity problem) and equation (parameterization problem) of the figure still left open.

Fourier descriptors, FDs [1-4] are one of the powerful tools for object recognition and symmetry detection. However, it cannot handle partially occurred symmetry figure, symmetric point pattern and open contour situation.

On the other hand, Genetic Algorithms (GAs) [5-7] are powerful tools in the areas of computer vision. It employs the evolution process of natural selection to find (search) the optimal solution of a desired problem. GA works with a

V. Di Gesú, F. Masulli, and A. Petrosino (Eds.): WILF 2003, LNAI 2955, pp. 232–239, 2006.

population of chromosomes, each represents a potential solution and fitness value to a desired problem. Chromosomes with the higher fitness have a better chance to progress their information to the next generation through the chromosomes crossover and gene mutation process. If a GA is designed well, the population will finally converge to an optimal solution. In this paper, Fourier descriptors are selected as the fitting function and its coefficients become the chromosomes of the GA. Experimental results show that it can handle complex symmetry figures, these symmetry figures may be formed by separated curves, points or partially occurred or partially missed (open contour).

2 Elliptic Fourier Descriptors

Fourier descriptors (FD's) are useful in describing and recognizing the shapes of 2-D closed contours. The basic idea is, a closed curve may be represented by a periodic function of a continuous parameter t, or alternatively, by a set of Fourier coefficients of this function.   In general, there exists infinitude ways to parameterize a 2-D closed curve to form the FD's. The reason for the infinitude is that t is an implicit (hidden) parameter. Therefore, there exists an infinite number of ways to distribute its values along the curve. The most common (familiar) way is based on the arc length l ($t = 2\pi l/L$ where L is the perimeter of the contour) parameterization. As the calculation of the parameter t using arc length (constant speed assumption) is simple, this parameterization method is widely used by many researchers.

The basic idea of elliptic Fourier descriptors is as follows. A closed curve may be represented by a periodic function of a continuous parameter t, eqt. (1)

$$\begin{bmatrix} X(t) \\ Y(t) \end{bmatrix} = \begin{bmatrix} a_0 \\ c_0 \end{bmatrix} + \sum_{k=1}^{\infty} \begin{bmatrix} a_k & b_k \\ c_k & d_k \end{bmatrix} \begin{bmatrix} \cos kt \\ \sin kt \end{bmatrix} \tag{1}$$

where $t = 0$ to 2π and $k = 0, 1, 2, \ldots$, $(X(t), Y(t))$ is the coordinates of the contour in the image planes and $[a_k \ b_k \ c_k \ d_k]$ are the kth coefficients of the FD.

In using Fourier descriptors for pattern recognition, a curve representation must be normalized with respect to a desired transformation domain so that the FD's are invariant with respect to the specified domain. Invariant of FDs for object recognition and symmetry detection under 2D and 3D (affine) transform have been widely investigated. However, using arc length parameterization FD for object recognition and symmetry detection has the following limitation.

(1) Image points must be connected (e.g. chain coded) to form a closed contour before FDs can be applied, this leads to great difficulties when the point patterns are complex (e.g. figure 5a)
(2) It cannot handle partially occurred object (e.g. figure 6a)
(3) It cannot handle opened contour (e.g. figure 7a)

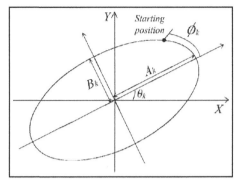

$$\begin{bmatrix} X_k(t) \\ Y_k(t) \end{bmatrix} = \begin{bmatrix} \cos\theta_k & -\sin\theta_k \\ \sin\theta_k & \cos\theta_k \end{bmatrix} \begin{bmatrix} A_k & 0 \\ 0 & B_k \end{bmatrix} \begin{bmatrix} \cos\phi_k & -\sin\phi_k \\ \sin\phi_k & \cos\phi_k \end{bmatrix} \begin{bmatrix} \cos kt \\ \sin kt \end{bmatrix} \quad (2)$$

Fig. 1. The rotation an starting phase of an ellipse of the kth harmonic

This paper proposes a new strategy using a Genetic-Fourier (GFD) algorithm for the extraction of rotational symmetry. The proposed method has the following advantages.

(1) It eliminates the arc length parameterization method so it can handle partially occurred contour and opened contour
(2) It eliminates the image points' connection process so it can handle complex point pattern.
(3) It is highly parallel and its efficient can be greatly improved if parallel processors are used.

2.1 FD Invariants of Rotational Symmetry

Elliptic Fourier descriptors invariants of symmetry have been explored in [4]. Recall properties 1 and 2, for a N order rotational symmetry, the following properties hold.

Property 1: For the coefficients of the kth harmonic,
    if $k \neq nN_s + 1$ and $k \neq nN_s - 1$, then $a_k = b_k = c_k = d_k = 0$.
    where $n = 1, 2, 3, \ldots$

Property 2: For the coefficients of the kth harmonic,
    if $k = nN_s - 1$, then $A_k = -B_k$
    if $k = nN_s + 1$, then $A_k = B_k$
    i.e. $|a_k| = |d_k|$, $|b_k| = |c_k|$. and $\theta_k = 0$ where $n = 1, 2, 3, \ldots$

From equation (1), (2), and property 1, it can be obtained that

$$\begin{bmatrix} X(t) \\ Y(t) \end{bmatrix} = \begin{bmatrix} x_0 \\ y_0 \end{bmatrix} + \sum_{k=1}^{\infty} \begin{bmatrix} A_k & 0 \\ 0 & B_k \end{bmatrix} \begin{bmatrix} \cos(kt+\phi_k) \\ \sin(kt+\phi_k) \end{bmatrix} \qquad \text{where } x_0 = a_0, \ y_0 = c_0,$$

From properties 2, it can be obtained that

$$\begin{bmatrix} X(t) \\ Y(t) \end{bmatrix} = \begin{bmatrix} x_0 \\ y_0 \end{bmatrix} + \sum_{n=1}^{\infty} \left\{ A_{nN-1} \begin{bmatrix} 1 & 0 \\ 0 & -1 \end{bmatrix} \begin{bmatrix} \cos((nN-1)t+\phi_{nN-1}) \\ \sin((nN-1)t+\phi_{nN-1}) \end{bmatrix} + A_{nN+1} \begin{bmatrix} 1 & 0 \\ 0 & 1 \end{bmatrix} \begin{bmatrix} \cos((nN+1)t+\phi_{nN+1}) \\ \sin((nN+1)t+\phi_{nN+1}) \end{bmatrix} \right\}$$

Furthermore, ϕ_1 is arbitrary and can be selected as 0. Hence, the detection of a N order rotational symmetry can be considered as finding the best fit for the FD parameters $(x_0, y_0, A_1, A_{N-1}, \phi_{N-1}, A_{N+1}, \phi_{N+1}, \ldots\ldots, A_{nN-1}, \phi_{nN-1}, , A_{nN+1}, \phi_{nN+1}, \ldots\ldots).$

3 Genetic Algorithm (GA)

GA is a searching (optimization) method using procedures that are inspired by natural evolution, it involves population (chromosomes), mating, crossover, mutation, natural selection (fitness measure) and generation (iteration).

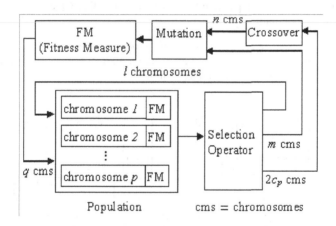

Fig. 2. The general flow of genetic algorithm

The population consists of fixed- or variable-length chromosomes (potential solutions). The chromosomes are formed by real value or binary format to represent the parameters of the problem domain. Figure 2 shows that there are p chromosomes in the population. In each update,

1) b chromosomes are selected and remain in the population, usually they are the first b best fit (FM) chromosomes.
2) m chromosomes are selected for mutation and produces m new chromosomes (self reproduction),
3) c_p pairs chromosomes are selected for crossover to produces n new chromosomes, these n new chromosomes with further go to the mutation process. In general, n is either equal to c_p (2 to 1) or 2 c_p (2 to 2).
4) All the new chromosomes produced in the mutation process will then perform the fitness measure and q new chromosomes will be used to update the population. In general $q = m + n$.

In general, the number of population, p can be fixed or varies. If p is fixed, then $q = p - b$, $n = p - b - m$.

The selection mechanism takes many forms, yet it always ensures that the best fit chromosomes have a higher probability to be selected for reproduction.

3.1 Defining Genetic Chromosomes, Parameters and Operators

Coding chromosomes: The chromosome of the GFD is formed by the parameters of the FDs, i.e. $(x_0$, y_0, A_1, A_2, ϕ_2, ... , A_k, ϕ_k , ..., A_{2N+1} , ϕ_{2N+1}) with the maximum harmonic being $2N+1$. Here, real value is used.

Selection: selection operator is used to select good chromosomes for the progress of their inherited knowledge to the next generation. In the proposed algorithm, the selection probability is proportional to the square root of its fitness value.

Direct selection: It is used to maintain those chromosomes that have the highest chance to success. In this paper, the top l chromosomes that have the best fit will be maintained in the population.

Crossover: Crossover operator is used to produce new chromosomes through combining partial structure of two father individuals. Figure below shows the crossover mechanism of the proposed algorithm.

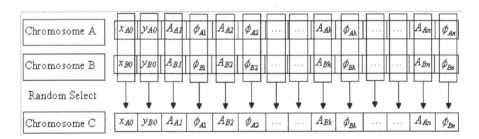

Fig. 3. The crossover process

Mutation: In order to prevent the loss of diversity in the evolutionary process, a mutation process is designed and operates to represent a sudden change in a small area of a chromosome. The mutation process will directly obtain a small among (m) of chromosomes from the population. In this paper, the top m chromosomes that have the best fit will be selected. The probability P_m of the individual FD coefficients undergo the mutation process is set to 0.5 with the following process is used for the selected FD coefficients

$$A_k = A_k + 32 \, (\text{Rnd} - 0.5)$$
$$\phi_k = \phi_k + 32 \, (\text{Rnd} - 0.5)$$

where Rnd is a random generator between 0 to 0.999.

Fitness function: In this paper, the following fitness function is used.

$$FD_{fitness} = FD_{energy} \frac{FD_{energy}}{5FD_{pts}}$$

FD_{energy} is an energy function represents a distances measure between the FD and the image points.

FD_{pts} is the number of image pixels passed by the FD and $FD_{energy}/5FD_{pts}$ is a completeness measure.

Consider figure 4, figure 4a shows a 7x7 image with (1) 7 image points and (2) a FD curve passing through it. Figure 4b shows the energy measure of the figure 4a, the position of an image point will have the highest value 5 and the value will gradually decrease as the distance is away from the image points. For figure 4,

$FD_{energy} = 1.5+2.8+5+2.8+1.5 = 13.6$, $FD_{pts} = 7$.
Therefore, $FD_{fitness} = 13.6 \times 13.6/(5 \times 7) = 5.28$.

1			2			
	1		2			
		1	2			
		1	2			
			2	1		
			2		1	
			2			1

5	2.8	1.5	0	0	0	0
2.8	5	2.8	1.5	0	0	0
1.5	2.8	5	2.8	1.5	0	0
0	1.5	2.8	5	2.8	1.5	0
0	0	1.5	2.8	5	2.8	1.5
0	0	0	1.5	2.8	5	2.8
0	0	0	0	1.5	2.8	5

Fig. 4a. (1) Image points and (2) the FD curve passing through the image

Fig. 4b. Energy measures of figure 4a

Parameter and Initial setting: In this paper, the following parameters are used. $P = 100$, $b = 10$, $m = 10$, $c_p = 80$ and $n = 80$. N is fixed at the beginning of the iteration and the initial values of x_0, y_0 and A_k are set using the following processes.

A_1 is randomly selected between 0 to 128 (for a 256 x 256 image)

ψ is randomly selected between 0 to 360°
$x_0 = I_i(x) + A_1 \cos \psi$, $y_0 = I_i(y) + A_1 \sin \psi$
$A_k = 0 \; \forall k > 0$, $\phi_k = 0 \; \forall k > 0$

where I_i is an image point randomly selected from the input image and $I_i(x)$ and $I_i(y)$ are the corresponding x and y co-ordinators of the i image.

4   Experimental Results

In order to verify the proposed algorithm, lots of experiments have been performed. This section presents some of these experiments.

Experiment 1 shows the algorithm performed well for complex symmetry figure. Experiment 2 shows the algorithm can handle complex symmetry figure even it is partially occurred. The experiment also shows the Genetic Fourier algorithm can obtain different perceptions (different solutions). Experiment 3 shows that the algorithm can handle symmetry formed by separate curves and different solutions (interpretation) may be obtained.

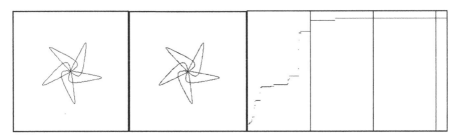

Fig. 5a. Input image **Fig. 5b.** Results of 250   500   generation
of experiment 1   experiment 1   **Fig. 5c.** The fitness value of the best
chromosome

Table 1. FD coefficients obtained in experiment 1

N	x_0	y_0	A_1	ϕ_1	A_4	ϕ_4	A_6	ϕ_6
5	128	128	30	$0°$	30	$16°$	-12	$-36°$

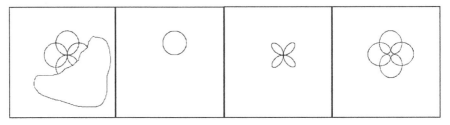

Fig. 6a. Input image   **Fig. 6b.** Solution 1   **Fig. 6c.** Solution 2   **Fig. 6d.** Solution 3
of experiment 2.   (local maximum) .   (local maximum).   (global maximum).

Table 2. FD coefficients obtained in experiment 2

Solution	N	x_0	y_0	A_1	ϕ_1	A_4	ϕ_4	A_6	ϕ_6	A_4	ϕ_4	A_6	ϕ_6
1	5	140	83	28	$0°$	$0°$	$0°$	0	$0°$	0	$0°$	0	$0°$
2	5	140	111	20	$0°$	8	$180°$	9	$0°$	0	$0°$	0	$0°$
3	5	140	111	31	$0°$	5	$0°$	20	$180°$	1	$180°$	1	$0°$

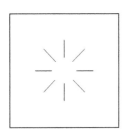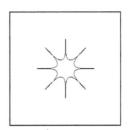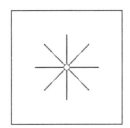

Fig. 7a. Experiment 3   **Fig. 7b.** Solution 1   **Fig. 7c.** Solution 2

Table 3. FD coefficients of figure 7

Solution	N	θ	x_0	y_0	A_1	ϕ_1	A_7	ϕ_7	A_9	ϕ_9
1	8	$0°$	128	128	44	$0°$	16	$0°$	-7	$0°$
2	8	$0°$	128	128	40	$0°$	21	$0°$	-13	$0°$

5 Conclusion

In this paper, a Genetic-Fourier algorithm is proposed for the detection of rotational symmetry. Experimental results show that it can handle different complex situations. The proposed method has the following advantages.

(1) It can handle partially occurred contour and opened contour.
(2) It can handle complex point pattern.
(3) It can obtain multiple perceptions.
(4) It is highly parallel and its efficient can be greatly improved if parallel processors are used.

References

1. Granlund, G.H., "Fourier preprocessing for hand print character recognition", *IEEE Trans. Comput.*, vol. C-21, pp.195-201, Feb. 1972.
2. Han, K.P., Song, K.W., Chung, E.Y., Cho, S.J., Ha, Y.H., "Stereo matching using genetic algorithm with adaptive chromosomes", *Pattern Recognition* 34, pp. 1729 -1740, 2001
3. Lin, C.S. and Hwang, C.L., "New forms of shape invariants from elliptic Fourier descriptors", *Pattern Recognition*, Vol. 20, no. 5, pp. 535-545, 1987.
4. Yip, K.K. and Tam, K. S., "Application of Elliptic Fourier Descriptors to Symmetry Detection Under Parallel Projection", *IEEE Trans. on PAMI*, vol. 16, No. 3, March 1994.
5. Yip, K.K., "A Hough Transform Technique for the Detection of Parallel Projected Rotational Symmetry", *Pattern Recognition Letters*, Vol. 20, pp.991 – 1004, 1999.
6. Yuen, S.Y. and Ma, C.H., "Genetic algorithm with competitive image labelling and least square", *Pattern Recognition* 33, pp. 1949 -1966, 1999.
7. Zhan, C.T. and Roskies, R.Z., "Fourier descriptors for plane closed curves", *IEEE Trans. Comput.*, vol. C-21, no. 3, pp.269-281, Mar. 1972.
8. Zhang, L., Xu, W. and Chang, C., "Genetic algorithm for affine point pattern matching", *Pattern Recognition Letters* 24, pp. 9 -19, 2003.

Fourier Transform Based Column-Block and Row-Block Matching Procedure for Document Image Mosaicing

P. Shivakumara[*], G. Hemantha Kumar, D.S. Guru, and P. Nagabhushan

Department of Studies in Computer Science, Manasagangotri,
University of Mysore, Mysore, 570006, Karnataka, India
Phone: 0821-2510789
hudempsk@yahoo.com

Abstract. There are situations where it is not possible to capture or scan a large document with given imaging media such as Xerox machine or scanner as a single image in a single exposure because of their inherent limitations. This results in capturing or scanning of large document into number of split components of a document. Hence, there is a lot of scope for mosaicing the several split images into a single large document image.

In this work, we present a novel technique Fourier Transform (FT) based Column-Block (CB) and Row-Block (RB) matching procedure to mosaic the two split images of a large document in order to build an original and single large document image. The FT is rarely used in the analysis of documents since it provides only the global information of the document. The global information doesn't help in analyzing the documents of split images since the mosaicing of split document images requires local information rather than global information. Hence, in this work, we explore a novel idea to obtain local values of the split documents by applying FT for smaller sized split documents of split document images. The proposed method assumes that the overlapping region is present at the right end of split image 1 and the left end of split image 2. The overlapping region is a common region, which helps in mosaicing.

Keywords: Fourier transform, Column-Block matching, Row-Block matching, Overlapping region, Document image mosaicing.

1 Introduction

The concept of mosaicing is essential because it may not be possible to capture a large document with a given camera or Xerox machine or a scanner in a single exposure. It has got to be captured as two or more split images due to inherent limitations of the capturing medium. In such man made multiple camera exposures to cover a large image, the split images should necessarily contain OLR between the split images, so that the stitching of two or more such split images into a single image becomes easier. Therefore, the proposed technique demands that a small amount of OLR is present at the right end of the first image and the left end of second split image respectively.

---

[*] Corresponding author.

V. Di Gesú, F. Masulli, and A. Petrosino (Eds.): WILF 2003, LNAI 2955, pp. 240–254, 2006.

Thus, mosaicing is defined as the process of assembling the multiple components that are obtained either by scanning or capturing a large image part by part, in order to restore an original image without any duplication of portions. For example, a Xerox machine handles the documents of size A_4 (210mm X 297mm) and A3 (297mm X 420mm). But, the documents of sizes A_2 (420mm X 594mm) such as a full newspaper cannot be scanned in a single stroke because of its inherent limitation. Hence, bigger sized documents such as newspapers have got to be split into number of smaller documents of A_4 and A_3 dimension with little overlap between the split images.

Several researchers addressed the methods for obtaining the large image from its split images. (Schutte and Vossepoe, 1995) described the usage of flat bed scanner to capture large utility map. The method selects the control points in different utility maps to find the displacement required for shifting from one map to the next. These control points are found from pair of edges common to both the maps. However, the process requires human intervention to mask out the region not common to both the split images in image mosaicing.

The researchers (Zappala et al., 1997; Peleg, 1997) have worked on DIM. A feature-based approach through estimation of the motion from point correspondence is proposed. They have exploited domain knowledge, instead of using generic corner features, to extract a more organized set of features. The exhaustive search adopted was computationally expensive because of the rotation of an image employed during matching. However, the approaches are limited to only text documents and are prone to failure in case of general documents containing pictures. But in practice, a typical document contains both text and pictures.

An automatic mosaicing process for split document images containing both texts and pictures, based on correlation technique is proposed by (Whichello and Yan, 1997). Here correlation technique is used to find the position of the best match in the split images. However, accuracy is lost at the edges of the images. Moreover, the correlation of two images of practical size is computationally very expensive. In order to find a solution, additional constraints like *a priori* knowledge were introduced. Here, the sequence in which the images were captured and their placement (generally, referred as image sequencing) is known. Template matching procedure was used to search OLRs, present in the split document images. Usually, template-matching procedure is a time consuming method. In addition, this approach assumes that the printed text lies on straight and horizontal baselines, which is not always possible in many of the pragmatic applications.

The authors of this paper propose a novel technique for mosaicing of two split images containing text as well as picture based on Pattern Matching Approach (PMA). The proposed approach generates Strings of Column Sums (SCS) of split images. The SCS is defined as the sum of values of pixels present in each column of the split images. The PMA is employed to identify the overlapping region in the split images by generating identical longest suffix and prefix sub strings of column sums of split image1 and split image 2 respectively. The proposed method demands one pixel wide OLR in the split images. The method requires $O(n^2)$ search time for finding OLR in the split images which in turn helps in generating mosaiced image from its split images. However, the method is said to be a time consuming method.

A few FT based methods have been addressed the problem of mosaicing of images but not document images in literature. (Jharna Majumdar and Vanathy, 2001) have proposed the FT based method for mosaicing of satellite split images. In this method, they extract invariant features to register the sequence of frames obtained by satellite to produce single large frame using FT. However this method is very sensitive to noise and control points of overlapping region in the split images. In addition, it works only for general images and not document images. (Postal et al, 1986) have proposed a method detection of liner oblique structures and skew in digitized documents. In this method, they used FT for finding skew angle for skewed document.

From the above literature, it is evident that there is a need for mosaicing of split documents into single large document image using Fourier Transform.

In this paper, we propose a novel technique Fourier Transform based Column-Block and Row-Block matching procedure for mosaicing of split document images to produce one single large document image. The proposed method obtains local values of the split documents by implementing FT in new form. These values are used to identify the overlapping region in the split images. The overlapping region is determined by the methods of Column-Block and Row-Block. The column-block method finds the overlapping region in the split images by comparing the Fourier values present in the column of the split images. Similarly, the row-block method is used to find overlapping region in the split images by comparing the Fourier values present in rows of the split images. Of course, the column-block and row-block matching procedures require that the small amount of overlapping region at the right end of split image 1 and the left end of split image 2.

The rest of the paper is organized as follows. The section 2 describes the proposed methodology for obtaining mosaiced image and algorithms. The comparative study of two methods is given in section 3. The experimental results are reported in section 4. Finally the conclusion is given in section 5.

2   Proposed Methodology

In this section, we propose FT based approach for obtaining mosaiced image from split images using Column-Block (CB) and Row-Block (RB) matching procedures. The proposed approach assumes that overlapping region is present at the right end of split image 1 and the left end of the split image 2 respectively. The FT is applied here to obtain local values of split document images. The following sub sections explains the methodology for obtaining for local values using FT and the column-block procedure for obtaining mosaiced image from its split images by finding overlapping region in the split images. And one more sub section explains row-block procedure for obtaining mosaiced image from its split images by finding overlapping region in the split images.

2.1 Fourier Transform for Obtaining Local Values of Split Document Images

The FT of $f(x,y)m$, denoted by $£\{f(x,y)\}$, is defined by the equation

$$£\{f(x,y)\} = F(u, v) = \int_{-\infty}^{\infty}\int_{-\infty}^{\infty} f(x, y)\exp[-j2\Pi(ux+vy)]dxdy \quad \text{where } j = \sqrt{-1}.$$

Given F(u, v) , f(x,y) can be obtained using inverse Fourier transform

$$\pounds^{-1}\{F(u,v)\} = f(x,y) = \int_{-\infty}^{\infty}\int_{-\infty}^{\infty}f(u,v)\exp[-j2\Pi(ux+vy)]dudv \quad \text{where } u, v \text{ are}$$

frequency variables. These two equations, called the Fourier transform pair, exist if f(x, y) is continuous and integrable and F(u, v) is integrable. These conditions are almost always satisfied in practice.   The variables u, v appearing in the FT often is called the frequency variables. This name arises from expression of the exponential term. Interpreting the integral in equation as a limit summation of discrete terms makes evident that F(u , v) is composed of an infinite sum of sine and cosine terms and that each value of u and v determines the frequency of its corresponding sine cosine pair.

Suppose that a continuous function f(x, y) is discretized into a sequence $f(x_0 + x\Delta x, y_0 + y\Delta y)$ and so on by taking N samples Δx units apart. So the discrete Fourier transform pair is

$$F(u, v) = \frac{1}{MN}\sum_{x=0}^{M-1}\sum_{y=0}^{N-1}f(x,y)\exp\left[-j2\Pi\left(\frac{ux}{M}+\frac{vy}{N}\right)\right] \quad \text{for } u = 0, 1, 2, ...M\text{-}1, v = 0, 1,$$

2, ...N-1. and $f(x, y) = \frac{1}{MN}\sum_{x=0}^{M-1}\sum_{y=0}^{N-1}f(u,v)\exp\left[j2\Pi\left(\frac{ux}{M}+\frac{vy}{N}\right)\right]$ for x = 0, 1, 2, 3, ... M-1

and y = 0, 1, 2, 3, ...N-1. sampling of a continuous function is now in 2-D grid, with divisions of width Δx and Δy in the x and y axis, respectively. When images are sampled in square array, M = N and

$$F(u, v) = \frac{1}{N}\sum_{x=0}^{N-1}\sum_{y=0}^{N-1}f(x,y)\exp\left[-j2\Pi\left(\frac{ux+vy}{N}\right)\right] \quad \text{for } u, v = 0, 1, 2, ..., N\text{-}1, \text{ and}$$

$$F(x, y) = \frac{1}{N}\sum_{x=0}^{N-1}\sum_{y=0}^{N-1}f(u,v)\exp\left[j2\Pi\left(\frac{ux+vy}{N}\right)\right] \quad \text{for } x, y = 0, 1, 2, ..., N\text{-}1. \text{ Note the}$$

inclusion of a 1/N term in both the above equations. Because F(u, v) and f(x, y) are a Fourier transform pair, the grouping of these constant multiplicative terms is arbitrary. In practice, images typically are digitized in square arrays, so we will be concerned mostly with the Fourier transform pair in the above equations (Gonzalez et al, 2000).

The above Fourier transform requires more time to obtain Fourier coefficients. Hence an alternate method to reduce the time and computations is as follows

$$F_{even}(u) = \frac{1}{M}\sum_{x=0}^{M-1}f(2x)W_m^{ux} \tag{1}$$

for u = 0, 1, 2...m - 1

$$F_{odd}(u) = \frac{1}{M}\sum_{x=0}^{M-1}f(2x+1)W_m^{ux} \tag{2}$$

for u = 0, 1, 2.....m-1

The number of complex multiplications and additions required to implement is proportional to N^2. That is for each of the N values of u, expansion of the summation requires N complex multiplications of f(x) by exp[-jΠux/N] and N-1 additions of the results. The terms of exp[-jΠux/N] can be computed once and stored in table for all subsequent applications. For this reason, the multiplication of u by x in these terms is usually not considered a direct part of the implementation. Proper decomposition can make the number of multiplication and addition operations proportional to $N\log_2 N$. The decomposition procedure is called the fast Fourier transform (FFT) algorithm. The reduction in proportionality from N^2 to $N\log_2 N$ operations represents a significant saving in computational effort. Obviously, the FFT approach offers considerable computational advantage over direct implementation of the Fourier transform, particularly when N is relatively large. A 2-D Fourier transform can be obtained by successive passes of the 1-D transform. For example consider the set of samples { f(0), f(1) ......f(7) } Equation (1) uses samples with even arguments { f(0), f(2), f(4), f(6)} and equation (2) uses samples with odd arguments {f(1), f(3), f(5), f(7)}. Thus to compute FFT of the first set above, we must divide it into its even part {f(0), f(4)} and odd part {f(2), f(6)}. Similarly, the second set is divided into {f(1), f(5)} for equation (1) and {f(30, f(7)) for equation (2). No further rearrangement is required because each two element set is considered as having one even and one odd element. Combining these results requires that the input array be expressed in the form {f(0), f(4), f(2), f(6), f(1), f(5), f(3), f(5)}. The successive doubling algorithm operates on the array in the manner shown in the following Fig.1.

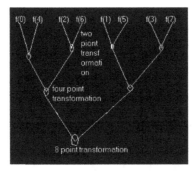

Fig. 1. Ordered input array and its use in successive doubling method

This FT is used in this work to get local values of the split documents of a document. Simple method is that the FT is applied for smaller sized windows of 3X3 dimension. The sum of the Fourier values of the 3X3 window is considered as one local value of the split document. This procedure is repeated for all windows of split documents of a document. In this passion we pass the 3X3 windows for each split document. The sums of all the Fourier values of all windows are used for identifying the overlapping region.

Algorithm for local FT values

Input: Split image 1(S_1) and Split image 2 (S_2)
Output: Local FT values for S_1 and S_2
Method:
        Step 1: For each 3X3 window of S_1 and S_2
                        Call FFT

$$Sum_1 = \sum_{i=1}^{3}\sum_{j=1}^{3} W_{i,j} \quad \text{for } S_1$$

$$Sum_2 = \sum_{i=1}^{3}\sum_{j=1}^{3} W_{i,j} \quad \text{for } S_2$$

$Mat_1 = Sum_1$ (this contains local FT values of S_1)

$Mat_2 = Sum_2$ (this contains local FT values of S_2)

For end

Method ends

Algorithm ends

2.2 Algorithm for Column-Block Matching Procedure for Mosaicing

In this section, we present an algorithm to mosaic two split images using CB matching procedure to produce a single large document image. Let S_1 and S_2 be the given two split images containing local FT coefficients obtained by the above algorithm (section 2.1) The algorithm begins by matching the pixel values of F_c (First column) of S_1 with F_c of S_2. IF match is found then it goes to next pixel values of corresponding columns of S_1 and S_2. After finding whole column match (CM) the algorithm considers rest of the portion in the split images as a block from next to CM to end of S_1. Similarly in S_2 also. Next the method computes total sum of the values of pixels in both the blocks of S_1 and S_2. If sums are match then that portion is considered as actual overlapping region in the split images. If the pixel values in the column or sums do not match then the pointer C_p pointing to S_1 moves to next column mean while the pointer C_p pointing to S_2 comes back to F_c. This is because of assumption that the overlapping region is present at the ends of the split images. That means the overlapping region in S_1 begins at middle column and in S_2 the overlapping region begins from first column of S_2. The algorithm terminates when C_p of S_1 reaches n where n is the end of column of S_1 without overlapping region. The algorithm also terminates if the overlapping region is found in the split images.

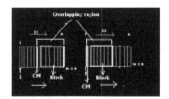

Fig. 2. The method to finds overlapping region in the split images

In Fig. 2, the Column Match (CM) denotes the matching column in the split images and Blocks denotes rest of the overlapping region in the split images. i and j are the pointers pointing to split image 1(S_1) and split image 2 (S_2). The actual overlapping region is represented by both CM and Blocks of split images.

Algorithm for CB

Input: S_1 and S_2 containing local FT coefficients
Output: Mosaiced image
Method:

Step1: For each Column (C) of S_1 and S_2
For each pixel value of C of S_1 and S_2
If $(P_i = P_j)$ in C_i of S_1 and S_2 (Where P_i is the pixel values of column of S_1 and P_j is the pixel values of column of S_2)
$i = i + 1$ and $j = j + 1$ (i is pointing to Column values of S_1 and j is pointing to column values of S_2)
if $(P_i = P_j)$ and $(i = E_c$ of $S_1)$ (here E_c is represents the end of column in)
CM = 1(if the whole column matches in S_1 and S_2)
Else exit from the for loop
else exit from for loop
for end
Step2: If (CM = 1) then $B_1 = N - CM + 1^{th} = W$ in S_1
$B_2 = CM + 1^{th}$ to W in S_2 (B_1 represents the Block of S_1, N is number of column in the S_1, W is the width of Block of S_1 and B_2 represents the Block of S_2)
Else $C_p = C_p + 1$ in S_1 and C_p in S_2 comes back to F_c (C_p is the pointer pointing to Column of S_1 and S_2)
For end
Step3: For B_1 of S_1

$$Sum_1 = \sum_{p=1}^{N}\sum_{q=1}^{M} B_{pq}$$ (Where p and q are the pointers of

Block and N is the number of rows in Block and M is the number of column in the Block)
For B_2 of S_2

$$Sum_2 = \sum_{p=1}^{N}\sum_{q=1}^{M} B_{pq}$$

Step4: If $(Sum_1 = Sum_2$) then OLR = 1 (overlapping region is found)
Else OLR = 0
If (OLR = 1) Mosaic the split images
Else if (i = n) algorithm terminates with overlapping region is not found
Method ends
Algorithm ends

2.3 Algorithm for Row-Block Matching Procedure for Mosaicing

In this section, we present a similar algorithm given in the above section (section 2.2) by changing a column. That means in the above section the algorithm considers column block for obtaining mosaiced image but here the algorithm considers the row instead of column to generate mosaiced image.

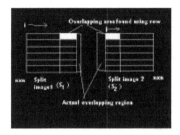

Fig. 3. Row-Block method for finding overlapping region

In Fig. 3. the overlapping region is found out by using the row as shown in Fig. 3.

Algorithm is as follows

Input: Split image 1 and split image 2
Output: Mosaiced image
Method:
      Step1: Obtain local FT coefficients for both split image 1 and split image2
      Step2: Invoke the above algorithm (section 2.2) by translating the given split
           images.
Method ends
Algorithm ends

3 Comparative Study

In this section, we present comparative study of two methods for particular data set. From the table it is noticed that for text graph images which is given in next section (example 1 in section 4) the method CB takes less time and less number of comparisons compared to RB. This is because in the given data set of text graph images (example 1 in section 4) the split images contain more white space at the top. So Row match occurs in the split images but Block which is rest of portions will not match in the split images. This procedure is repeated till it gets actual overlapping region or end of the split images. Hence, the Row-Block procedure takes more time compared to CB procedure since the given split image contains no white space at the left ends. Generally, we get this type of split images in practice. If more white space is present at the ends of the split images then CB becomes worst method but RB becomes good method. This is very rare case. Therefore, we conclude that the CB procedure is better for solving real world applications. For experimentation we use the system with configuration of 128 MB RAM, 6 GB and 650 MHZ

Table 1. Comparative study of CB and RB for text graph images (example 1in section 4)

Method	Time for FFT conversion	No. of comparisons	Time for comparisons
CB	18.13 sec	172	0.05 sec
RB	18.07 sec	14983	14.55 sec

4   Experimental Results

This section presents experimental results based on proposed methodology. We have presented different kinds of split images for obtaining mosaiced image. In the following examples Fig. (a) and (b) are the input images, Fig. (c) is the overlapped image and Fig. (d) is the mosaiced image.

Example1: Here, the split images contain text with graph

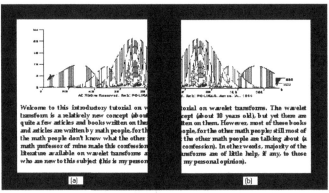

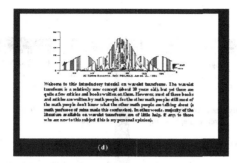

Fig. 4. (a) and (b) are the input image (c) is the overlapping region and (d) is the output image

Example 2: Here, the split images contain Kannada with picture

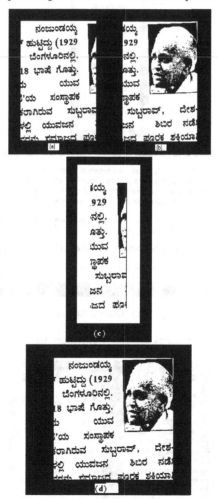

Fig. 5. (a) and (b) are the input image (c) is the overlapping region and (d) is the output image

Example 3: Here, the split images contain only English text

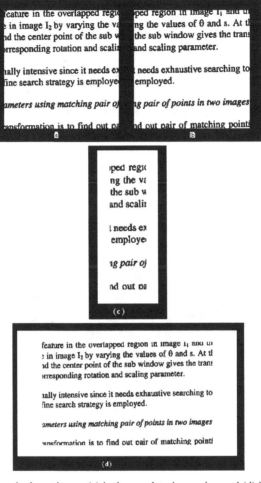

Fig. 6. (a) and (b) are the input image (c) is the overlapping region and (d) is the output image

Example 4: Here, the split images contain Malayalam language

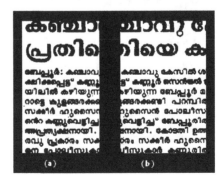

Fig. 7. (a) and (b) are the input image (c) is the overlapping region and (d) is the output image

Example 5: Here, the split images contain English text with pictures

Fig. 8. (a) and (b) are the input image (c) is the overlapping region and (d) is the output image

Example 6: Here, the split images contain the Urdu language

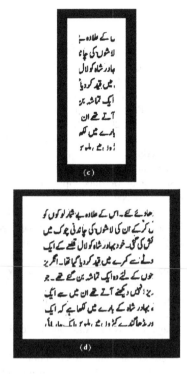

Fig. 9. (a) and (b) are the input image (c) is the overlapping region and (d) is the output image

5 Conclusion

In this work, we have proposed a novel method to produce mosaiced image from its split components using Fourier transform. We have showed in this work that the FT could be used to obtain local values for document image mosaicing. Of course the method becomes computationally expensive since it involves many FTs to obtain local Fourier coefficients. In order to identify and mosaic the split images we have introduced CB method and RB method. The comparative study is also given for particular data set. And also it is conclude that based on comparative study the CB method is better for solving real world applications. The proposed method demands the overlapping region in the split images of size at least 3X3 dimension since to obtain local FT coefficients the method uses 3X3 sized window. However, the method fails when the split images are skewed, rotated differently. In addition, if overlapping region is present at the centre in any one of the split images then the method fails.

Acknowledgment

One of the authors (Mr. Shivakumara .P) wishes to place on record his gratitude to the fellowship sponsoring agency AICTE, vide sanction number F.No/8020/RID/ R&D – 50.2001-01, New Delhi, for pursuing his work.

References

[1] Shivakumara et al., Document Image Mosaicing: A Novel Technique Based on Pattern Matching Approach. Proceedings of the National Conference on Recent Trends in Advanced Computing (NCRTAC-2001), Tamil Nadu, Feb 9-10, 2001, pp 01-08.

[2] Shivakumara et al., Pattern Matching Approach based Image Sequencing useful for Document Image Mosaicing. Proceedings of the National Conference on Document Analysis and Recognition (NCDAR-2001), Mandya, Karnataka, July 13-14, 2001.

[3] Shivakumara et al., Mosaicing of Color Documents: A Technique based on Pattern Matching Approach. Proceedings of National Conference on NCCIT, Kilakarai, Tamilnadu, 24th and 25th September, 2001, pp 69-74.

[4] Shivakumara et al., Mosaicing of Scrolled Split Images Based on Pattern Matching Approach. Proceedings of Third National Conference on Recent Trends in Advanced Computing (NCRTAC – 2002), Tamil Nadu, Feb 13-15, 200

[5] Adrian Philip Whichello and Hong Yan Document Image Mosaicing, Imaging Science and Engineering laboratory, Department of Electrical Engineering, University of Sydney, NSW 2006,1997.

[6] Shmuel Peleg, Andrew Gee, Haifa Research Laboratory, Virtual Cameras using Image mosaicing, Hebrews University, October 1997

[7] Zappala, et. al. Document Mosaicing. In proceedings of the British Machine Vision Conference, volume2, pages 600-609, Colchester, 1997

[8] Gonzalez et al., Digital Image processing, Addison-Wesley Publishing company, 2000.

[9] Postl. W Detection of liner oblique structure and skew scan in digitized documents. In Proc. of International Conference on Pattern Recognition, 1986, pp 687-689

[10] Jharna Majumadar and Vanathy, Image Mosaicing from Video Sequences. Proceedings of NCDAR -2001, pp 149-156.

Object Recognition by Recursive Learning of Multiscale Trees

Luca Lombardi[1] and Alfredo Petrosino[2]

[1] Dipartimento di Informatica e Sistemistica,
Universitá di Pavia, Via Ferrata 1, 27100 Pavia, Italy
`luca.lombardi@unipv.it`
[2] Dipartimento di Scienze Applicate,
Universitá di Napoli "Parthenope", Via A. De Gasperi 5, 80131, Napoli, Italy
`alfredo.petrosino@unipartehnope.it`

Abstract. In this paper we present an efficient and fully parallel 2D object recognition method based on the use of a multiscale tree representation of the object boundary and recursive learning of trees. Specifically, the object is represented by means of a tree where each node, corresponding to a boundary segment at some level of resolution, is characterized by a real vector containing curvature, lenght, simmetry of the boundary segment, while the nodes are connected by arcs when segments at successive levels are spatially related. The recognition procedure is formulated as a training procedure made by Recursive Neural Networks followed by a testing procedure over unknown tree structured patterns.

1 Introduction

Syntactic pattern recognition [1, 2] represents a possible meaningful step in the designing of an artificial vision system. Pattern classes contain objects, such as geometric figures, with an identifiable hierarchical structure that can be described by a formal grammar. The idea behind is the specification of a set of pattern primitives, a set of rules in the form of a grammar that governs their interconnection and a recognizer (an automaton) whose structure is determined by the set of rules in the grammar. The patterns could be not only structured (usually tree structured), but each pattern primitive could possess a sub-symbolic nature and possibly a fuzziness degree, measuring the inherent vagueness and the imprecise nature of patterns, is attached to it.

On the basis of the fact that coarse-to-fine strategies have been successfully used in a variety of image processing and vision applications (see for instance [3]), including stereo matching, optical flow computation, etc., a pattern may be also represented at various resolution levels by a graph of primitives and their relations. In such a case, production rules describe the evolution of the object primitives at increasing resolution levels. Approaches to organise data and associate information with the elements of the structures include pattern tree [4], model-feature graph [5]. Both structures suffer from the disadvantage that mis-matches at a coarse scale cause errors from which it is impossible to recover since the algorithms usually proceed by sub-dividing the corresponding coarse elements into

V. Di Gesú, F. Masulli, and A. Petrosino (Eds.): WILF 2003, LNAI 2955, pp. 255–262, 2006.

sub-elements. We follow the approach introduced by Ueda and Suzuki [6] and adopted in [7], where it is also proposed an efficient dynamic programming matching algorithm for 2D object recognition. The shape contours, extracted by a heat-diffusion process [8], are represented at all scales by a sequence of concave/convex segments identified by the inflection points along the curves. In this paper, we propose an hybrid model for syntactic object recognition based on the use of recursive learning, as introduced in [9], capable to process streams of structured data by neural networks, where the temporal processing which takes place in recurrent neural networks is extended to the case of graphs by connectionist models. The model uses symbolic grammars to build and represent syntactic structures and neural networks to rank these structures on the basis of the experience. Recursive neural networks are initialised with prior knowledge about training structured data; this ability makes recursive neural networks useful tools for modeling (eventually fuzzy) tree automata [10, 11], where prior knowledge is available. We demonstrate, by testing the model on car silhouettes data set, some of which are depicted in Fig. 1, the effectiveness of the model, the completely parallel nature of it, and the particularly encouraging performance.

2   Multiscale Tree Representation

We are interested in describing the patterns with a representation which takes into account both thier structure and the sub-symbolic information. To derive tree representations of planar shapes from images, a full Gaussian pyramid of images, taken at various levels of resolution, is first constructed. After the application of an edge detector and a contour following procedure to all resolution levels, each object boundary present in the scene is decomposed into a sequence of feature primitives, i.e. curve segments. The boundary decomposition procedure, detailed in [8], is based on the analogy with a heat-diffusion process acting on a physical object with the same shape as the given digital object. By assigning a non-zero value to all contour pixels of the digital object, an isotropic diffusion process propagating from each element to its neighbours towards the interior of the object is performed. In formula:

$$I_{t+1}(p) = I_t(p) + D(\sum_{q \in N(p)} (I_t(q) - I_t(p)))$$
(1)

where $I_t(p)$ represents the value of the pixel p at time t and D is the diffusion coefficient that describes the sharing factor of the local value of each pixel content among all its neighbours $N(p)$, in the number of 9. After a number of steps the contour elements that preserve high values correspond to local convexities and those in which a sharp decrement is produced correspond to local concavities.

These boundary descriptions at different scales induce a tree structure. Each node in the tree corresponds to a segment (concave, convex, etc.), connecting segments at consecutive levels that are spatially related. The children of a node correspond to consecutive segments at the next level of resolution that can be seen as one global segment at that level, giving a more detailed description of the same portion of the boundary as the parent node. The simblings of a node correspond to a given orientation of the curve boundary, while the leaves of the tree correspond to the segments at the finest level of resolution. Curvature values corresponding to the labels like <very_concave>, <concave>, <straight>, <convex> and <very_convex> are associated to the segments along with corresponding attributes, like the segment lenght and a measure of the simmetry, providing a quantitative description in terms of geometric features as well as a qualitative description of the spatial arrangement of the segments. In Fig. 2 the constructed tree representation of Fig. 1 is given.

Specifically, each node is charcterized by a 3-dimensional real feature vector, coming from the curvature segment it represents. Firstly, the temperature values obtained on the border of the shape after a given number of iterations are measured at each pixel; assuming the object is thermally insulated from the background, a set of thresholds is chosen so as to associate values exceeding these thresholds with a shape-related code words. The second and third attributes are computed as follows, letting $f(l)$ be the curvature function along a segment c:

$$L_c = \int dl \tag{2}$$

$$S_c = \int_0^{L_c} \left(\int_0^s f(l)dl - 1/2 \int_0^{L_c} f(l)dl \right) ds \tag{3}$$

From the above formulae, L_c gives the total lenght of the segment, while S_c represents the degree of simmetry. If $S_c = 0$ the segment is intended to be symmetric, while if S_c gets positive or negative value, the segment is intended to be inclined to the left or to the right respectively. These attributes, normalized, are used in the learning procedure to measure the similarity or dissimilarity of a pairing between segments of two different given shapes.

3   Recursive Neural Networks

To process data represented by multiscale trees, a computational model based on neural units is adopted [9]. In particular, the model realizes mappings from Directed Ordered Acyclic Graphs (DOAGs) (in our case ordered trees) to n-dimensional vectors using recursive neural networks. Recursive neural networks are characterized not to possess explicit feedback connections; the recurrent processing is then driven by the inherent recursive structure of the patterns in the training domain. Consider that instances in the training domain are structured patterns of information described by *ordered r*-ary trees. Here by an *ordered r*-ary tree we mean an r-ary tree where for each vertex a *total order* on the edges leaving from it is defined. A total order can be induced on the tree nodes by topologically sorting the nodes with a linear order $<$, such that $v < w$ if there exists an edge (v, w). Informally speaking, the encoding of a given tree into a distributed network is achieved by recursively setting the previously computed representation for the direct subtrees together with the representation of the label attached to the root. By starting this process from the leaves to the tree root, a representation of the whole tree is achieved and can be mapped to a particular user-specified output (structured or not).

To define the dynamics of the network, the *generalized shift operator* is adopted [9]. For $k = 1, \ldots, r$, the generalized shift operator is denoted by q_k^{-1} and is associated to the k-th child of a given vertex, such that when applied to a node x_v returns the variable attached to the k-th child of that node, with x_v denoting the value of a tree vertex labelled v.

Denoting uniformly labeled r-ary trees by the boldface uppercase letters corresponding to the label space of the tree, i.e. $\mathbf{Y}$ denotes a tree with labels in $\mathcal{Y}$, labels are accessed by vertex subscripts, i.e. $\mathbf{Y}_v$ denotes the label attached to vertex v. Given a tree structure $\mathbf{Y}$, the tree obtained by ignoring all node labels will be referred to as the *skeleton* of $\mathbf{Y}$, denoted by skel($\mathbf{Y}$). Two structures $\mathbf{Y}$ and $\mathbf{Z}$ can be distinguished because they have different skeletons, i.e. skel($\mathbf{Y}$) $\neq$ skel($\mathbf{Z}$), or they have the same skeleton but different vertex labels. The class of trees defined over the local universe domain $\mathcal{Y}$ and skeleton in $\#^{(1,o)}$, i.e. the set of graphs whose vertices have in-degree 1 and maximum out-degree o, will be denoted as $\mathcal{Y}^{\#^{(1,o)}}$. In the following, the training set comprises couples $(\mathbf{U}, \mathbf{Y})$, where $\mathbf{U} \in \mathcal{U}^{\#(1,o)}$ are input trees with symbols s_k in Σ, each converted into a vector $\mathbf{U}_k$ in $\mathcal{R}^n$, attached to nodes; the same is true for $\mathbf{Y} = \tau(\mathbf{U}) \in \mathcal{Y}^{\#^{(1,o)}}$ which represent output trees. Since $\tau(\cdot)$ is a binary transduction between input and output trees, $\tau \subseteq \mathcal{U}^{\#^{(1,o)}} \times \mathcal{Y}^{\#^{(1,o)}}$ the aim of any supervised learning algorithm is to estimate the transduction $\tau(\cdot)$. In particular, we consider transductions from $\mathbf{U} \in \mathcal{U}^{\#(1,o)}$ to $\mathbf{Y} \in \mathcal{Y}^{\#^{(1,o)}}$, which are: a) *IO-isomorph*, i.e. skel($\tau(\mathbf{U})$) = skel($\mathbf{U}$); b) *causal*, i.e. $\tau(\mathbf{U})_v$ only depends on the sub-tree of $\mathbf{U}$ induced by v and its descendants, $\forall v$.

Such an IO-isomorph transduction $\tau(\cdot)$ admits a *recursive state representation* if there exists a structure space $\mathcal{X}^{\#^{(i,o)}}$ such that for each $\mathbf{U}, \mathbf{Y}$ there exists $\mathbf{X} \in \mathcal{X}^{\#^{(i,o)}}$ with skel($\mathbf{X}$) = skel($\mathbf{U}$) = skel($\mathbf{Y}$) and for each vertex $v \in$ skel($\mathbf{U}$):

$$\mathbf{X}_v = f(\mathbf{X}_{\text{ch}[v]}, \mathbf{U}_v) \tag{4}$$
$$\mathbf{Y}_v = g(\mathbf{X}_v, \mathbf{U}_v) \tag{5}$$

where $\mathbf{X}_{\text{ch}[v]}$ is a fixed size array of labels attached to the (ordered) children of v and

$$f : \mathcal{X}^r \times \mathcal{U} \to \mathcal{X} \tag{6}$$
$$g : \mathcal{X} \times \mathcal{U} \to \mathcal{Y} \tag{7}$$

According to the total order induced on the tree nodes, the states are updated following a recursive message passing scheme such that a state label $\mathbf{X}_v$ is updated after the state labels corresponding to the children of v in the order defined, as instance, by any reversed topological sort of the tree nodes.

We consider that f and g are implemented by single-layer MLPs; each neuron possesses r recursive connections (the valence of the domain is r), even if not all of them will be used for computing the output of a node x with out-degree less than r. The output of the recursive neuron is defined as:

$$X_{i,v} = \sigma(\alpha_{i,v}) = \frac{1}{1 + e^{-\alpha_{i,v}}}$$

$$\alpha_{i,v} = \theta_i + \sum_{j_1} \cdots \sum_{j_r} \sum_{k} W_{i,j_1,\ldots,j_r,k} \prod_{p=1}^{r} (q_p^{-1}\mathbf{X}_v)_{j_p} U_{k,v} \qquad (8)$$

where $W_{i,j_1,\ldots,j_r,k}$ are the weights of the recursive neurons. Due to the recursive nature of the network dynamics, the stability is guaranteed only if the function $\sigma(\cdot)$ asimptotically converges towards its fixed points in the saturation regions; some conditions in different cases can be shown to be valid [11].

The supervised learning problem in recursive neural networks is solved in the usual framework of error minimization, by searching the parameters θ_i and $W_{i,j_1,\ldots,j_r,k}$ by gradient descent techniques. The gradients can be efficiently computed using the Backpropagation through structure (BPTS) algorithm, an extension of Backpropagation through time that unrolls the recursive network in a larger feedforward network, following the ordered tree structure [12]

4   Experimental Results

A set of experiments has been designed to settle a preliminary evaluation of the multicale tree based object recognition algorithm. The class of the objects considered here as example are car silhouttes. In all the experiments, the application of the boundary description procedure sets the diffusion coefficient D to 0.625 and the number of steps N to 80 after extensive experiments as reported in reference [8].

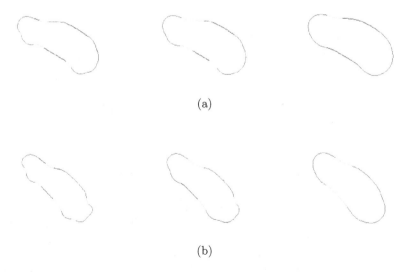

(a)

(b)

Fig. 1. Two different colour labelled silhouttes at rotation of 30 degree (a) and 45 degree (b) at three levels of representation of the contours extracted after the application of a Gaussian Pyramid

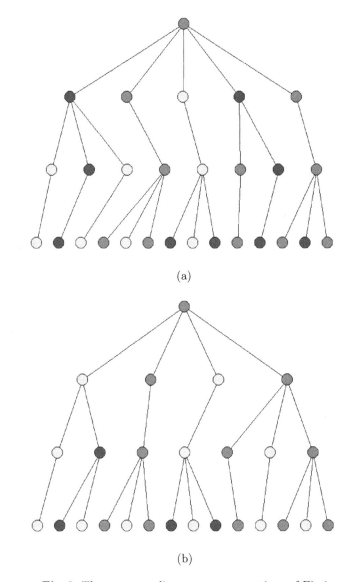

(a)

(b)

Fig. 2. The corresponding tree representations of Fig.1

Three different rotated versions were produced with planar rotation angles $\alpha = 15$, $\beta = 30$, $\eta = 45$. For each image, once the boundary decomposition is obtained, the tree structure representing the multi-resolution profiles shown in Fig. 1 is constructed as may be seen in Fig. 2.

Table 1 summarizes the results obtained using recursive neural networks on 8-ary multiscale ordered trees. Recursive nets trained with BPTS (kindly provided to us by Marco Maggini, Siena University) had 8, 6 and 4 state units as shown in the table, while in all the experiments the learning rate was initially fixed to

Table 1. Experimental results in terms of recognition accuracy and rejection

Network	Estimated Accuracy (%)	Rejection Rate (%)
8 State neurons	96.75	0.15
6 State neurons	96.40	0.25
2 State neurons	96.15	0.40

0.02 and the rejection threshold to 0.5. The table shows the accuracies % for the testing set computed as the percentage of the correct classification number over the total number of patterns and the rejection rate % as the percentage of the number of rejected patterns over the total number of patterns for learning set. Although different numbers of state neurons were adopted, the recursive neural networks appear to have similar performances, which have been better than those achieved by using other methods on the same data set, like tree matching by dynamic programming (see [7]).

5   Conclusions

This paper presented an algorithm for the recognition of two dimensional objects using a multiscale tree representation. The boundary of each object has been described in terms of segments which correspond to nodes on a tree and, for each resolution level, a set of nodes fully describes the image at that level. The tree representation is thus further processed with Recursive Neural Networks in order to obtain a fixed size vector which can be used to define topological relations between the curvature segments describing the shape boundaries of the objects. The preliminary results, achieved on the data set of car silhouettes, are shown to produce good retrieval of exact classes, validating the promising properties of the proposed scheme. We are currently investigating the applcation of the proposed technique (multiscale tree learning) to more complex tasks, also in cases of the presence of occluded objects. We confide that occlusion should be better dealt with recursive neural networks than tree matching algorithms, due to the neural network tolerance to noise and invariance, together with a multiscale tree representation; both characteristics should assure that the general tree structure could be learned also in the case the occlusion partially hides salient features.

References

1. K.S. Fu, Syntactic Methods in Pattern Recognition, New York: Academic (1974).
2. F.S. Fu, B.K. Bargava, Tree systems for syntactic pattern recognition, IEEE Transactions on Computer, vol. C-22 no. 12 (1973) pp. 1087-1099.
3. A. Rosenfeld, ed. Multiresolution Image Processing and Analysis, Springer, Berlin (1984).
4. P. S. Burt, Attention mechanism for vision in a dynamic world, Proc. 11th Int. Conf. on Pattern Recognition (1988) pp. 977-987.

5. C. R. Dyer, Multiscale image understanding, in Parallel Computer Vision, L. Uhr, ed. 171-213, Academic Press, New York (1987).

6. N. Ueda, S. Suzuki, Learning visual models from shape contours using multi-scale convex/concave structure matching, IEEE Trans. Pattern Anal. Mach. Intell., vol. 15 no. 4 (1993) pp. 337-352.

7. V. Cantoni, L. Cinque, C. Guerra, S. Levialdi, L. Lombardi, 2-D object recognition by multiscale tree matching, Pattern Recognition, vol. 31 no. 10 (1998) pp. 1443-1454.

8. L. Cinque, L. Lombardi, A. Rosenfeld, Evaluating digital angles by a parallel diffusion process, Pattern Recognition Letters, vol. 16 (1995) pp. 1097-1104.

9. P. Frasconi, M. Gori, A. Sperduti, A general framework for adaptive processing of data structures', IEEE Transactions on Neural Networks, vol. 9 no. 5 (1998) pp. 768-786.

10. C. W. Omlin, C. L. Giles, "Constructing deterministic finite-state automata in recurrent neural networks", Journal of ACM, vol. 43 no. 2 (1996) pp. 937-972.

11. M. Gori, A. Petrosino, Encoding Nondeterministic Fuzzy Tree Automata into Recursive Neural Networks, submitted to IEEE Trans. on Neural Networks (2001).

12. A. Sperduti, A. Starita, "Supervised neural networks for the classification of structures", IEEE Transactions on Neural Networks, vol. 8 no. 3 (1997) pp. 714-735.

An Integrated Fuzzy Cells-Classifier

Giosuè Lo Bosco

Dipartmento di Matematica e Applicazioni,
University of Palermo, Palermo, Italy
lobosco@dipmat.math.unipa.it

Abstract. The term *soft-computing* has been introduced by Zadeh in 1994. Soft-computing provides an appropriate paradigm to program malleable and smooth concepts. In this paper a genetic algorithm is proposed to fuse the classification results due to different distance functions. The combination is based on the optimization of a vote strategy and it is applied to cells classification.

1 Introduction

Clustering and classification problems are often hard or vague, in spite of the simplicity of their formulation. For example, a good knowledge of the probability distribution of the feature space is not always available, the Gaussian assumption, often considered as valid, is wrong, and linear separation between classes is usually a rough approximation.

Moreover, features and parameters representing each element of the universe U, may be non-numerical; so that, their interpretation becomes subjective and does not follow any statistical model.

In such a situation, both the "heuristic" and the "user expertise" allow us to find suitable approximate solutions; therefore an automatic data-analysis system should include a suitable "fuzzy" representation of both data-model, and expert-knowledge.

Fuzzy-clustering approaches have been considered to overcome some of the problems, mentioned above. Fuzzy-clustering algorithms are, usually, objective functional; i.e. the clustering criteria is based on the maximization (minimization) of a gain (lost) function, which is computed, for example, on the basis of a possibility model [1] of the data provided, for example, by experts.

Fuzzy-clustering has been studied by several authors, [2], [3], [4]. For example, the fuzzy c-mean (FCM) algorithm has produced fairly good results when applied to the analysis of multi-spectra thematic maps [5], FCM has been also applied to the analysis of Magnetic Resonance Images [6].

In the following a genetic method is proposed to integrate the classification results coming from three different distance functions. The combination strategy is based on the optimization of the integration coefficients deriving from a vote strategy. The methodology has been applied to classify cells representing bacteria, white blood cell casts, non squamous renal epithelial, and non squamous transitional epithelial (see Figure 1). The classification problem is quite hard

V. Di Gesú, F. Masulli, and A. Petrosino (Eds.): WILF 2003, LNAI 2955, pp. 263–270, 2006.
© Springer-Verlag Berlin Heidelberg 2006

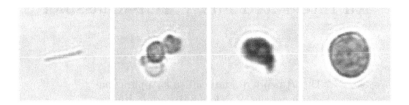

Fig. 1. Examples of input cell images; from left to right, bacteria, white blood cell casts, non squamous renal epithelial, non squamous transitional epithelial

because non squamous renal epithelial and non squamous transitional epithelial classes have similar shape features and texture.

In Section 2 the integration problem is outlined. Section 3 describes the classifier and the distances used to discriminate different classes. Section 4 describes the genetic algorithm used to optimize the voting strategy. Experimental results are shown in Section 5. Section 6 is dedicated to final remarks and future developments.

2   Integrated Fuzzy Algorithm

In the last decade, several methods for combining multiple classifier has been developed [10, 11]. These methods uses different combination techniques such as ensemble averaging [13], where the outputs of different classifiers are linearly combined; boosting and bagging [14], where each classifier is applied to different subset of training set; mixture of experts where the outputs of the classifier are not linearly combined [16].

Integrated Fuzzy Classification (IFC) consists in the weighted combination of more then one classification methods $Cl_1, Cl_2, ..., Cl_S$, in order to increase the performance and the accuracy of data grouping. For example, weighted-vote functions may be used to model the accuracy related to each classification algorithm.

For example in [7] three hierarchical algorithm have been integrated to perform the analysis of medical MRI images. One motivation for considering this combined technique is the fact that also humans use more than one evaluation paradigm and usually a complex decision is taken by more than one expert. To each Cl_s ($1 \le s \le S$) of an IFC a weighting coefficient, $0 \le \pi_s \le 1$, is assigned. These coefficients can be derived from both the accuracy of each classification method or by the user on the basis of his experience.

Let us denote with $M \equiv \{M^{(1)}, M(2), ..., M^{(s)}, ..., M^{(S)}\}$ the confusion matrices computed by the classification algorithms $Cl_1, Cl_2, ..., Cl_s, ..., Cl_S$, and by

$$\Pi_M = (M^{(1)}/\pi_1, M^{(2)}/\pi_2, \ldots, M^{(s)}/\pi_s, \ldots, M^{(S)}/\pi_S)$$

an initial possibility distribution of M, with $\pi_s \in [0, 1]$. The meaning of Π_M depends on the experimental situation and it could be determined as described before.

More formally, IFC consists in the evaluation of the final M and π by means of two functions $G(M; \Pi_M)$, and $m(\Pi_M)$ respectively. Their explicit forms depends on the kind of integration paradigm used in combining methods.

In the literature, two main strategies have been considered: the *global combination* (IFC-global) and the *chain combination* (IFC-chain).

In the first case classification algorithms are executed independently. IFC-global approach should be preferred whenever the classification algorithms do not need to exchange information during the computation. The evaluation of Π_M is the crucial point, and it is related to the relevance of each classification algorithm. The evaluation of M and π can be expressed by the equations:

$$M = G(M^{(1)}, M^{(2)}, ..., M^{(S)}; \pi_1, \pi_2, ..., \pi_S)$$
$$\pi = m(\pi_1, \pi_2, ..., \pi_S)$$

In the case of chain combination, the confusion matrices, $M^{(s)}$, and the possibility value π_s, at the stage s_{th} depend on both the algorithm Cl_s, and the matrices obtained at the previous stage $(s-1)_{th}$:

$$M^{(s)} = G(M^{(s)}, M^{(s-1)}, \pi_s, \pi_{s-1})$$
$$\pi_s = m(\pi_s, \pi_{s-1}) \text{ for } 1 < s \le S$$
$$M = M^{(S)} \text{ and } \pi = \pi_S$$

Note that in the IFC-chain procedure, the updating of π_s is performed after the computation of $M^{(s)}$. It must be point out that the result, obtained from the application of an IFC-chain algorithm, may depend on the order of execution of each classifier. Chain combination musts be preferred whenever classifiers interact in finding the best solution.

3   The Cell-Classifier

Here, the data set U is composed of gray level images representing four different kind of cells. For each images, $X \in U$, a set of different features, F, is extracted:

$$F(X) = (f_1(X), f_2(X), ..., f_n(X))$$

The classification algorithm is supervised and it is based on a KNN that assign each cell to the closest class. In order to define the representative of each class a training set $T \subset U$ is considered:

$$T = \{t_1^{(1)}, t_1^{(2)}, ..., t_1^{(n_1)}, ..., t_4^{(n_4)}\}$$

where $t_j^{(h)}$ is the h_th element of the j_th class. In our case, we use the same classification schema for all classifiers, but the discrimination is based on different distance functions between images. In particular, three different distances function have been used.

The first distance evaluates the closeness of an unclassified cell to the center of mass, $\mu_k \equiv (\mu_k^{(1)}, \mu_k^{(2)}, ..., \mu_k^{(n)})$ of the k_th class:

$$d_1(X, k) = \sum_{i=1}^{n} \frac{|F_i(X) - \mu_k^{(i)}|}{max(F_i(X), \mu_k^{(i)})} \times \frac{1}{1 + P_{\mu_k^{(i)}, \sigma_i}(F_i(X))}$$

where $P_{\mu, \sigma}$ is the normal probability density function with parameters μ and σ. This term has been added to consider the dispersion of the data.

The other two distances are rank defined:

$$d_i(X, k) = 1 - \frac{c_i(X, k)}{r} \quad \text{for} \quad i = 2, 3$$

The term $c_i(X, k)$ counts how many training images of class k are in the set of the r nearest neighbors to X evaluated considering distance δ_i for $i = 2, 3$, where δ_i is so defined :

$$\delta_2(a, b) = \frac{1}{n} \sum_{i=1}^{n} \frac{|a_i - b_i|}{max(a_i, b_i)}$$

$$\delta_3(a, b) = \frac{1}{n} \sqrt{\sum_{i=1}^{n} \frac{(a_i - b_i)^2}{max(a_i^2, b_i^2)}}$$

More formally if $T_{nn}(X)$ is a set of training which are the r nearest neighbors of X evaluated considering distance δ_i, and $T_{nn}^{(k)}(X) \subseteq T_{nn}(X)$ is the subset of those in class k,

$$c_i(X, k) = |T_{nn}^{(k)}(X)|$$

4   The Integration Strategy

The described distances provide different classification results and our goal is their integration using the IFC-global combination paradigm:

$$D(X, k) = \sum_{j=1}^{3} \pi_k^{(j)} \times d_j(X, k)$$

where $\Pi = \{\pi_k^{(j)}\}$ is the vector of weighting coefficients. The problem of fusion can be stated informally as it follows: *found the vector Π that maximize the diagonal of the confusion matrices.*

The decision rule to assign each image $Y \in U - T$ to the class j is:

Assign Y to class $j = 1, 2, 3, 4 \Leftrightarrow j = arg(min_{k=1,4}D(Y, k))$

Therefore, the integration strategy consists on obtaining the best weights Π_b such that:

$$\Pi_b = arg(max_{\Pi}(\sum_{i=1}^{4} M_{\Pi}(i, i)))$$

The search of the best combination coefficients can be formulated as a global optimization problem.

Genetic Algorithm (GA) [8, 12, 15] have been already used in clustering problems [9]. They are search methods that take their inspiration from natural selection and survival of the fittest in the biological world. *GA*s differ from more traditional optimization techniques in that they involve a search from a *population* of solutions, not from a single point. Each iteration of an *GA* involves a competitive selection that weeds out poor solutions. The solutions with high *fitness* are *recombined* with other solutions by *swapping* parts of a solution with another. Solutions are also "mutated" by making a small change to a single element of the solution. Cross-over and mutation are used to generate new solutions that are biased towards regions of the space for which good solutions have already been seen.

The genetic optimization algorithm, below described, has been chosen because it allow us to find more robust approximated solutions. Here, chromosomes are vectors of floating point values of length 4×3 (number of classes $\times$ number of distances) that are exactly the values of the Π's.

A key point of a *GA* is the choice of the so named *fitting function* that depends on the Global optimization problem to be solved; in our case it correspond to the sum of the diagonal elements of M_Π:

$$f(\Pi) = \sum_{i=1}^{4} M_\Pi(i, i)$$

and the matrix M_Π is build using the decision rule above described.

To evolve the population the classical *single point crossover* has been used. The used *mutation* operator differs from classical ones because it is non uniform with the iterations; it has been used to reduce the disadvantage of random mutation in the floating point representation of chromosomes [17].

If Π is a chromosome at a generation g, $\Pi(g) = \pi_1^{(1)}(g), \pi_1^{(2)}(g), ..., \pi_4^{(3)}(g)$ and $\pi_r^{(h)}(g)$ has been decided for mutation, the new chromosome $\Pi'(g)$ is evaluated as follows:

$$\pi_r^{(h)'}(g) = \begin{cases} \pi_r^{(h)}(g) + \Delta(g, 1 - \pi_r^{(h)}(g)) & \text{if a random digit is 0} \\ \pi_r^{(h)}(g) - \Delta(g, \pi_r^{(h)}(g)) & \text{if a random digit is 1} \end{cases}$$

where $\Delta(t, y) = y * (1 - rand^{(1 - \frac{g}{G})})$, G is the maximum number of iteration, and *rand* is a random number in the interval $[0, 1]$.

In the case of the floating point representation the cross-over operator does not change the global content of each chromosome, while the mutation is the main responsible for changing the population space. The mutation rule used in this paper allows us an adaptive mutation that generate a wider kind of chromosomes initially and very selected ones in the later stages. After the application of crossover and mutation, we select the chromosomes using the *binary tournament method*. The genetic operator and the selection process are applied until maximum fixed number G of iteration is reached.

5   Experimental Results

The used data set U [1] is composed of 560 pre-classified images representing four different kind of cells: bacteria (class A), white blood cell casts (class B), non squamous renal epithelial (class C) , non squamous transitional epithelial (class D). Examples of those images are in Figure 1.

The features vector $F(X) = (f_1(X), f_2(X), ..., f_8(X))$ is composed by eight shape indicators which are respectively the mean and standard deviation values of the elongation, the mean and standard deviation values of the circularity, the horizontal and vertical histogram, the convex hull area, and the perimeter of a cell image.

Tables 1 show the confusion matrices obtained using separately the three distances d_1, d_2, d_3 on 560 pre-classified cells.

Table 1. Cells classification results using d_1, d_2, d_3

d_1	A	B	C	D	d_2	A	B	C	D	d_3	A	B	C	D
A	0,95	0,01	0,02	0,02	A	0,93	0,02	0,05	0	A	0,93	0,01	0,05	0,01
B	0,01	0,62	0,29	0,08	B	0,01	0,58	0,35	0,04	B	0,02	0,34	0,22	0,42
C	0,08	0,3	0,55	0,07	C	0,06	0,26	0,64	0,04	C	0,03	0,17	0,6	0,2
D	0,01	0,36	0,18	0,45	D	0,01	0,37	0,17	0,45	D	0,01	0,18	0,16	0,65

Table 2 show the confusion matrices obtained using the genetic algorithm integration rule, the best Π founded by the algorithm is

$$\Pi_b = \begin{vmatrix} 0.78 & 0.51 & 0 \\ 0.76 & 0.46 & 1 \\ 0.96 & 0.3 & 0 \\ 0.77 & 0.48 & 0.51 \end{vmatrix}$$

Table 2. Cells classification results using the integration rule

	A	B	C	D
A	0,97	0,01	0,02	0
B	0,02	0,65	0,24	0,09
C	0,03	0,21	0,69	0,07
D	0,02	0,37	0,16	0,45

Table 3 shows the mean values of correct and uncorrect classification for d_1, d_2, d_3 and for the integrated method.

The values Π_b has been found by the genetic algorithm after 2000 iteration using a crossover probability of 0.8 and a mutation probability of 0.02. Figure 2 show the convergence of the algorithm finding solution.

The results show that the integration method provides a better results in the average. Only for class D the results were the same as distances d_1 and d_2 and worst than distance d_3.

---

[1] Data sets have been kindly provided by IRIS Diagnostic, CA, USA

Table 3. The mean values of correct and uncorrect classification

	correct	uncorrect
$d1$	0, 64	0, 36
$d2$	0, 65	0, 35
$d3$	0, 63	0, 37
integrated	0, 69	0, 31

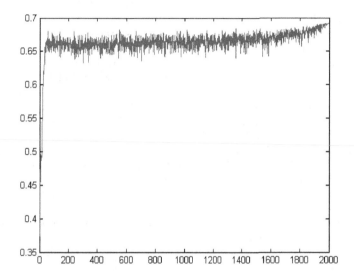

Fig. 2. The plot of the mean fitness versus the iteration number

6   Conclusions

The integration procedure described in this paper is based on a GA approach. The genetic paradigm has been chosen because it allow us to search in a large solution space that can be defined subjectively. In our case the performances of three separated distance functions are combined to reach a better classification. We aim to compare the method with other standard integration procedures and its validation will be tested on different kind of data.

References

1. R.R.Yager, "A Foundation for a Theory of Possibility", *Journal of Cybernetics*, Vol.10, pp.177-204, 1980.
2. E.Ruspini, "A New Approach to Clustering", in *Information & Control*, Vol.15, pp.22-23, 1969.
3. E.Backer and A.K.Jain, "A Clustering Performance Measure Based on Fuzzy Set Decomposition", in *IEEE Trans.PAMI* , Vol.3, N.1, pp.66-74, 1981.

4. J.C.Bezdek, "Pattern Recognition with Fuzzy Objective Function Algorithms", Plenum Press, NY, 1987.
5. R.L.Cannon, J.V.Dave, J.C.Bezdek, M.M.Trivedi, "Segmentation of a Thematic Mapper Image Using the Fuzzy c-Means Clustering Algorithm", *IEEE Trans. on Geoscience and Remote Sensing*, Vol.24, No.3, pp.400-408, 1986.
6. V.Di Gesù, R.De La Paz, W.A.Hanson, R.Bernstein, "Clustering Algorithms for MRI", in *Lecture Notes in Medical Informatics*, K.P.Adlassing, G.Grabner, S.Bengtsson, R.Hansen (Eds.), Springer-Verlag, pp.534-539, 1991.
7. V.Di Gesù, "Integrated Fuzzy Clustering", in *Fuzzy Sets and Systems*, Vol.68, pp.293-308, 1994.
8. J.H. Holland, "Adaption in natural and artificial systems", the University of Michigan Press, Ann Arbor, MI, 1975.
9. L.O. Hall, I.B. Ozyurt, J.C.Bezdek, Clustering with a genetically optimized approach, *IEEE Transactions on Evolutionary Computation*, Vol.3, N.2, pp.103–112, 1999.
10. T.G.Dietterich, "Ensemble methods in machine learning",in *Multiple calssifier systems, MCS 2000* J.Kittler, F. Roli (Eds.), Series Lecture Notes in Computer Science, Vol.1857, pp.1–15, Springer Verlag, Cagliari, Italy, 2000.
11. G. Valentini, F. Masulli, "Ensembles of learning machines, in R. Tagliaferri and M. Marinaro (Eds.) Neural Nets WIRN Vietri-2002, Series Lecture Notes in Computer Sciences, Vol.2486, pp.3–19, Springer Verlag, 2002
12. D.E.Goldberg, Genetic algorithms in search, optimization and machine leraring. Addison Wesley, Reading, MA, 1989.
13. S.Hashem , "Optimal linear combination of neural networks", *Neural computation*, Vol 10, pp.519–614 , 1997.
14. R.E.Shapire, Y. Freund, P.Barlett, W. Lee, "Boosting the margin. A new explanation for the effectiveness of voting methods" ,*The annals of statistics*, Vol 26, N.5, pp.1651–1686, 1998.
15. Michalewicz, Z.: Genetic Algorithms + Data Structures = Evolution Programs. 3rd edn. Springer-Verlag, Berlin Heidelberg New York, 1996.
16. M.I.Jordan, R.A. Jacobs, "Hierarchical mixture of experts and the EM algorithm", Neural Computation, Vol 6, pp.181–214, 1994.
17. C.Z. Janikowa, Z. Michalewicz, "An experimental comparison of binary and floating point representations in genetic algorithms", Proceedings of the Fourth International Conference Genetic Algorithms, R.K. Belew and J.B. Booker (Eds.), pp.31–36, 1991.

A Neural Network for Classification of Chambers Arrangement in Foraminifera

Roberto Marmo[1] and Sabrina Amodio[2,3]

[1] Dipartimento di Informatica e Sistemistica, University of Pavia,
Via Ferrata 1, 27100 Pavia, Italy
marmo@vision.unipv.it
[2] Dipartimento di Scienze della Terra, University Federico II,
Largo San Marcellino 10, 80138 Napoli, Italy
ciclisti@gms01.geomare.na.cnr.it
[3] Istituto per l'Ambiente Marino Costiero (IAMC),
Geomare, National Research Council,
Calata Porta Di Massa, Porto di Napoli, 80133 Napoli, Italy

Abstract. Foraminifera are very important microfossils to determine geological age of marine rocks. Image analysis techniques are used to compute two set of shape features describing the shape of the most common foraminifera shells. A k-nearest neighbor and a multiplayer perceptron classifiers are compared for automated classification of the chambers arrangement. Experimental results show 87.1 and 97.1% of accuracy using, respectively, k-nearest neighbor and multiplayer perceptron.

1 Introduction

Foraminifera are single-celled organisms (protists) with minelarized shells [3, 6] and they are abundant and widespread as microfossils (size 100μm - 20cm) in marine environments from the last 540 million years. They have showed fairly continuous evolutionary development, so that different species are found at different times. Some species was short-lived and widespread in the sea; for this reason foraminifera are very important to determine the geological age of the marine rocks. Since the 1920's the oil industry has been an important employer of paleontologists who specialize in these microfossils.

Foraminifera shells are built of chambers which are added during growth and are separated by partitions with small openings called "foramina" connecting the chambers. They get their name from these foramina [3, 6]. The most common forms of chambers arrangements are (Fig. 1):

1. biserial: chambers added in a double linear series
2. irregular: without any definite arrangement of the chambers, these forms usually live attached to a solid surface
3. milioline: chambers arranged in a series where each chamber extends the length of the test, and each successive chamber is placed at an angle of up to 180 degrees from the previous one

V. Di Gesú, F. Masulli, and A. Petrosino (Eds.): WILF 2003, LNAI 2955, pp. 271–278, 2006.

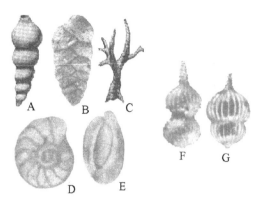

Fig. 1. The most common forms of chambers arrangement in foraminifera: (A) unise-rial, (B) biserial, (C) irregular, (D) spiral, (E) milioline, (A,F,G) uniserial forms that have very different shapes

4. spiral: chambers added in a coil within a single plane, the center of the coil is called the umbilicus
5. uniserial: chambers added in a single linear series (Fig. 1.A,F,G).

Several attempts have been made in developing computer systems to auto-matically classify the foraminifera. Belyea [1] developed a shape Fourier analysis used to assess the evolutionary relationship between two foraminiferal genera. Liu et al. [7] developed a knowledge-based system for the identification by com-puter vision of some species of the group Globotruncanids, a representative group of the Late Cretaceous foraminifera. Schiebel et al. [8] developed a software for classification of only six species of foraminifera on digital images, using neural network structures designed by operator.

We have been able to overcome some of the difficulties on the description of the chambers arrangement.

2 Image Acquisition

The microfossils were examined with an optical microscope and acquired by a digital camera. The image is acquired with magnification about 20-25X, and digitized with 150 dots per inch 256 8-bits linear grey levels. These digitized images are taken from a set of photo collections. The white pixels corresponding to the background and the grey pixels corresponding to the image of foraminifera.

The image is converted in a black-white image, in which the grey pixels of original image become black and the white pixels is due to the original back-ground. In the image matrix, the white pixel is represented by 1 and the black pixel is represented by 0.

3 Measurements of Features

Foraminifera have a lot of shapes (Fig. 1) and the use of shape description and analysis algorithms [1, 5] are not useful. As the surface of the fossil is irregular, segmentation algorithms cannot individuate the singular chambers; as a consequence their counting is not possible. Due to wide variety of shapes, features such as eccentricity, moments, roundness, ecc. are not useful.

The chambers arrangement determines the shape of the shells characterizing each class. In this way a specific pattern of horizontal lines has been individuated that allow the five classes (chambers arrangement) to be recognize. These horizontal lines measure the width variations of the shell providing a useful set of features. Considering these horizontal lines as rows of an image matrix, the width measurements of a shell are given by the number of black pixels.

In order to compare the width variations of the objects, the black object is rotated in a counter-clockwise direction, through degrees resulting from the difference between the x-axis and the major axis in the cartesian plane. In this way, the major axis is perpendicular.

Using the nearest neighbor interpolation method, the black object is resized to obtain a major axis measuring 300 pixels. This parameter was established after many experiments.

We chose two set of shape features corresponding to 11 horizontal lines. The set FC (Fig. 2) is composed by equidistant choice of rows: 25, 50, 75, 100, 125, 150, 175, 200, 225, 250, 275. The set FA (Fig. 2) is composed by non-equidistant choice of rows: 10, 30, 50, 80, 110, 150, 190, 220, 250, 270, 290. In this set we chose more width measurements at top and bottom of the shape, in order to distinguish the shapes better.

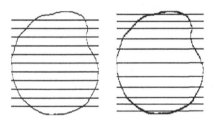

Fig. 2. Horizontal lines showing the shape feature set FC (left) and FA (right) of width variations of the spiral arrangement in Fig. 1.D

The index of rows were established using a sequential backward feature elimination. Starting with a 20 features, at each stage the feature chosen for elimination is the one corresponding to the largest reduction in classification error.

A linear transformation provide for all the inputs to have values in the range [0.0, 1.0], to prevent singular features from dominating the others.

The Principal Component Analysis (PCA) technique arranges the orthogonal components (principal components that are uncorrelated with each other) in decreasing order, respect to the variance in the feature set. In this way, 7 from the 11 features are selected as inputs after a lot of experiments.

The confusion matrix C allows to summarize the classification results: the columns represent the true classes and the rows the predicted classes.

Table 1. Loss matrix. The columns represent the true classes and the rows the predicted classes: the element (j,k) specify the penalty associated with assigning a pattern to class j when in fact it belongs to class k.

	B	I	M	S	U
B	0	9	9	9	2
I	9	0	9	9	9
M	9	9	0	2	9
S	9	9	2	0	9
U	2	9	9	9	0

The loss matrix L (Tab. 1) allows to summarize the performance of the classifier. The elements in (j,k) specifying the penalty associated to the assignment of a pattern to class j when in fact it belongs to class k. Each penalty is chosen by hand in the set $\{0,2,5,9\}$ corresponding to penalty {null, low, sufficient , high}. The total penalty is the sum of $L(i,j) \times C(i,j)$ i,j=1..5.

4   K-Nearest Neighbor

The k-nearest neighbor (k-NN) classifier is a nonparametric classifier [4]. Each class is represented by a set of prototype vectors. A test sample is assigned the class most frequently represented among the k nearest training samples. The best value of k produces the lowest misclassification rate on the validation set is chosen.

The training set was composed by 207 images in this class order: 48 biserial, 13 irregular, 49 milioline arrangement, 49 spiral, 50 uniserial. The validation set was composed by 68 images, according to the previous class order: 16, 4, 16, 16, 16. The test set was composed by 70 images, according to the previous class order: 17, 4, 17, 16, 16. Table 2 shows some values of k and the validation error for the two features choice. The best choice is k=4 (4-NN) and FA.

Table 2. Some percentages of correct performance on validation set on k-NN corresponding to two sets of shape features

k	FC	FA
1	58.8	55.9
2	58.8	61.8
3	80.9	86.8
4	79.4	88.2
5	79.4	85.3
6	83.8	85.2
7	80.9	82.3
8	80.9	82.3
9	82.3	83.8

Table 3 shows the confusion matrix on test set corresponding to two sets of shape features and k=4.

Table 3. Confusion matrix on test set classified by 4-NN corresponding to two sets of shape features. The columns represent the true classes and the rows the predicted classes the element (j,k) specify the number of shapes associated to class j when in fact they belong to class k. B = biserial; I= irregular; M = milioline; S = spiral; U = uniserial.

FC	B	I	M	S	U
B	16	0	1	0	2
I	0	0	0	0	0
M	1	1	16	1	3
S	0	0	0	15	0
U	0	3	0	0	11

FA	B	I	M	S	U
B	17	2	0	0	0
I	0	0	0	0	0
M	0	0	16	0	4
S	0	0	1	16	0
U	0	2	0	0	12

5   Neural Networks

Neural networks have been widely used in artificial intelligence because they are models for expressing knowledge using a connectionist paradigm inspired by the mechanism of the human brain. Bishop [2] describes all the mathematical details related to supervised neural networks.

The neural networks classify a chambers arrangement after a training on a specific data set by taking into account all extracted features. Each output of the neural network is the probability to classify an input section belonging to a specific arrangement. We assign the input section to the class associated with the highest value to the output.

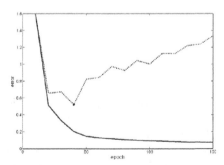

Fig. 3. Evaluation of the training set and validation set errors as training progresses. The training and validation error are shown by the solid and dotted line, respectively. The minimum error for the validation set is shown by the black circle on dotted line.

The input layer of the Multi Layer Perceptron (MLP) has 7 neurons, the output layer has 5 neurons corresponding to each class, the hidden layer has 6 neurons. The hidden units use the tanh activation function, and the output units use the sigmoid activation function in order to interpret the output values as probabilities. We choose the cross-entropy error function and the quasi-Newton minimization error function. These parameters were established following experiments by varying the number of neurons in the hidden layer: the chosen architecture reaches a small training error.

The data set used for the experiments was the same used for the k-NN.

We used the early stopping method to control the effectiveness of the training step. The training error monotonically decreases as training progresses, while the validation set error only decreases up to a certain point, after which it increases (Fig. 3).

Table 4 shows the confusion matrix on test set corresponding to two sets of shape features. The results have been obtained using a strategy based on the choice of the class suggested by the highest output

Table 4. Confusion matrix of test set classified by MLP corresponding to two sets of shape features. The columns represent the true classes and the rows the predicted classes the element (j,k) specify the number of shapes associated to class j when in fact they belong to class k. B = biserial; I= irregular; M = milioline; S = spiral; U = uniserial.

FC	B	I	M	S	U
B	15	1	0	0	0
I	1	3	0	0	0
M	0	0	16	0	2
S	0	0	0	16	0
U	1	0	1	0	14

FA	B	I	M	S	U
B	17	0	0	0	1
I	0	4	0	0	0
M	0	0	16	0	0
S	0	0	0	16	0
U	0	0	1	0	15

When the output values of the MLP are very similar among them, so that the highest value is very far from 1.0, the MLP classifies the image with high probability of uncertainty. Only with a support of the micropaleontologist it is possible to exactly classify the above images, that are selected on the basis of the following threshold decision rule: if the highest output value is less than (or equal to) the rejection threshold, then the corresponding image has to be classified by the micropaleontologist; in other case the MLP classification may be accepted. It is important to choose an optimal rejection threshold: more images are rejected and fewer errors are made if the value of the rejection threshold is increasing. Each highest output value is compared with a rejection value in

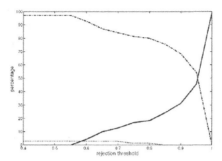

Fig. 4. The percentage of classification for each value of the rejection threshold in the range [0.0,1.0]. The percentage of correct classifications is shown by the dash-dot line, the percentage of wrong classifications is shown by the dotted line, the percentage of uncertain classifications is shown by the solid line.

the range [0.0, 1.0]. Fig. 4 shows these curves for each rejection value and the value 0.65 made an acceptable percentage of the images classified as uncertain. This value discriminates 7 uncertain images (10.0%), 2 images wrongly classified (2.9%) and 61 images well classified (87.1%).

6   Discussion

Tables 3,4 show that shape feature FA is better than FC, in particular in detecting irregular shapes. Table 5 shows that MLP is better than 4-NN, whichever choice of shape features is done.

Table 5. Comparison of penalty and percentages of correct performances on test set. MLP with set FA is the best choice.

	4-NN		MLP	
	FC	FA	FC	FA
test set	82.9	87.1	91.4	97.1
penalty	71	58	35	7

7   Conclusions

We have proposed a new numerical approach based on image analysis, k-NN and MLP, that allowed us to classify the chambers arrangement of foraminifera by grey level digitalized images. A series of experiments were also carried out to compare the performance of the two classifiers. These test results have led to the selection of a set of shape features and a MLP as the preferred methods for doing the classification in a machine vision systeme. This technique predicts the type of arrangement with 97.1% accuracy on a test set of 70 images. Accuracy may be improved using larger training and test sets. This set of features can be useful as key indexes for image retrieval in database of fossil images, because it is possible to store only these features in order to describe a particular shape.

To conclude, the present results indicate a wide potential range of neural networks applications to the micropaleontology.

We also note that this methodology is implemented in MatLab (The Math-Works Inc.) code. This software allows to visualize and to export the data processing with simple graphical interfaces. The codes have been written as part of a package, which can be used and extended for future applications.

Acknowledgments

The authors would like to thanks Prof. Tagliaferri for his kind suggestions about Neural networks and Prof. D'Argenio and Prof. Ferreri for their kind helps on the geological arguments.

References

1. Belyea, P. R.: Fourier shape analysis and planktonic foraminiferal evolution: the Neogloboquadrina-Pulleniatina lineages. Journal of Paleontology, **58** (1984) 1026-1040
2. Bishop, C.M.: Neural networks for pattern recognition. Clarendon Press, Oxford (1998)
3. Culver, S.J.: Foraminifera, 169-212. In: T.W. Broadhead, Fossil Prokaryotes and Protists, notes for a short course. University of Tennessee, Department of Geological Sciences, Studies in Geology (1987).
4. Dasarathy, B. V.: Nearest neighbor pattern classification techniques. IEEE Computer Society Press, (1991)
5. Gonzalez, R.C.: Digital image analysis. Addison Wesley Publishing Company (1992)
6. Haynes, J.: Foraminifera. John Wiley and Sons, New York (1981)
7. Liu-Yu, S., Saint-Marc, P., Thonnat, M., Berthod, M.: Feasibility study of automatic identification of planktic foraminifera by computer vision. Journal of Foraminiferal Research, **26** (1996) 113-123
8. Schiebel, R.; Bollmann, J; Quinn, P S; Vela, M; Schmidt, D.H R Thierstein.: Automated analysis of planktic foraminifers part III: neural network classification. Geophysical Research Abstracts **5** (2003) 12531

Fuzzy Concepts in Vector Quantization Training

Francesco Masulli[1,3] and Stefano Rovetta[2,3]

[1] Department of Computer Science, University of Pisa, Italy
[2] Department of Computer and Information Sciences, University of Genoa, Italy
[3] INFM - National Institute for the Physics of Matter

Abstract. Vector quantization and clustering are two different problems for which similar techniques are used. We analyze some approaches to the synthesis of a vector quantization codebook, and their similarities with corresponding clustering algorithms. We outline the role of fuzzy concepts in the performance of these algorithms, and propose an alternative way to use fuzzy concepts as a modeling tool for physical vector quantization systems, Neural Gas with a fuzzy rank function.

Keywords: Vector quantization; Neural Gas; Fuzzy clustering.

1 Introduction

The problem of clustering [1] is often addressed with the partitive, centroid-based approach of the c-Means procedure and many other derived algorithms. In this approach clustering is viewed as *finding the reference vectors (centroids) which best explain the input data distribution according to some cost criterion.*

Vector quantization [2][3] is a different technical problem, which can be stated as follows: *find the reference vectors (codevectors) which approximate with the minimum error the input data according to some distortion criterion.* (Usually the problem is also constrained by some resource limits: Rate/Distortion or Distortion/Rate approaches.)

In this work, we analyze some approaches to the synthesis of a vector quantization codebook, and their similarities with corresponding clustering algorithms. We outline the role of fuzzy concepts (such as membership in more than one Voronoi polyhedron) in the performance of these algorithms. Then, we propose an alternative use of the fuzzy paradigm in the vector quantization training algorithm by Martinetz *et al.*, the "Neural Gas" [4].

2 Clustering, Vector Quantization, and Fuzzy Concepts

We have outlined some differences between clustering and vector quantization, and yet the synthesis of a codebook for vector quantization is often approached with algorithms derived from c-Means (a standard clustering technique). One usual difference is that, since vector quantization is typically adopted for large-dimensional, large-sized training sets, minimization is performed by stochastic gradient descent (*online* training) rather than by deterministic (or *batch*) algorithms. This is because the curse of local minima is worsened by the large dimensionality and codebook size.

V. Di Gesú, F. Masulli, and A. Petrosino (Eds.): WILF 2003, LNAI 2955, pp. 279–288, 2006.

Several clustering algorithms have been modified in the direction of incorporating fuzzy concepts (starting with the Fuzzy c-Means algorithm [5]). A review of fuzzy concepts in clustering is provided in [6, 7].

The relationship between the clustering and quantization problems is of a geometrical nature. In both cases, the input space is partitioned by a *Voronoi tessellation* [8], representing regions of data sharing similar properties by means of a single reference point or site or (in vector quantization jargon) codevector. However, in clustering, data points belonging in a single region should be the largest group of data that can be reasonably gathered in a single cluster (clusters should be as few as possible to enable understanding the structure of data), whereas in vector quantization points in a region must be so similar that the approximation error obtained by substituting data with codevectors is negligible (thus codevectors should be as many as possible, within the resource limits imposed by the overall system design).

The introduction of a fuzzy membership has a twofold meaning in clustering. On one side, data can be partially belonging to more than one cluster, and this has a conceptual interpretation. On the other side, fuzziness is a way to fight local minima during optimization. In vector quantization, the first aspect is irrelevant, since at the end of training a crisp decision must always be made. The other aspect is more important, since in the typical vector quantization application local minima are a serious issue.

3   Codebook Design (Training)

In the following we review how typical algorithms for the synthesis of vector quantization codebooks introduce fuzzy concepts in the minimization procedure, and what is their effect. We will assume that N training points (individually denoted with $\mathbf{x}$) of dimensionality d are used to design a codebook $\{\mathbf{y}_1, \ldots \mathbf{y}_c\}$ of c reference points. The distorsion assumed is the Euclidean distance $d_i = ||\mathbf{x} - \mathbf{y}_i||$.

The classical approach is Lloyd/MacQueen's method [9][10][11], the standard c-Means clustering procedure; MacQueen's method is the online version. The k-th input vector is attributed to the Voronoi polyhedron defined by reference vector $\mathbf{y}_i$ if $u_{ik} = 1$, where u_{ik} is a crisp membership value which is 1 if $d_{ik} = \min\{d_{1k}, \ldots, d_{Nk}\}$ and 0 for all other reference vectors. The closest reference vector for a data point wil be called the "winner" for that point. The updating rule is:

$$\mathbf{y}_i^{(t+1)} = \frac{\sum_{k=1}^N \mathbf{x}_k u_{ik}}{\sum_{k=1}^N \mathbf{x}_k} \tag{1}$$

This algorithm finds the minimum of a cost function based on the mean square error as a distortion criterion. Its well-known drawback lies in the huge number of local minima (for practical d and N). The on-line version transforms the Picard iteration of the standard version, in which at each step a necessary minimum condition is satisfied, in a stochastic optimization process. Input vectors are randomly selected, adding noise to the cost function, now optimized on the average. The updating rule is therefore:

$$\mathbf{y}_i^{(t+1)} = \mathbf{y}_i^{(t)} + \eta^{(t)} u_{ik} (\mathbf{x}_k - \mathbf{y}_i) \tag{2}$$

where t indexes the training steps, $\eta^{(t)}$ is an updating coefficient, and k is a random function of t.

Convergence is usually much slower, but local minima are escaped thanks to the "statistical" behaviour of the updating procedure, which does not necessarily reduce the cost at each step and therefore does not necessarily get trapped into sub-optimal basins.

The law for varying $\eta^{(t)}$ to ensure convergence (annealing schedule) has been studied in [12]. MacQueen [10] adopts an individual coefficient for every reference vector, equal to $1/t_i$ where t_i is the number of updates for reference vector $\mathbf{y}_i$ so far, thus retaining the exact equivalence between the online and batch versions of c-means. Ritter *et al.* [13] propose instead an exponential decay rate $\eta^{(t)} = \eta_i \left(\eta_f/\eta_i\right)^{t/t_{max}}$ from η_i to η_f in t_{max} steps. This law has been used also in the Neural Gas algorithm.

The maximum entropy approach of the Deterministic Annealing technique by Rose [14] builds on a different concept. Here a fuzzy membership in clusters is introduced by substituting the "min" selection criterion, by which a single reference vector is selected for updating on a minimum-distance basis, with a "softmin" criterion:

$$u_i = \frac{e^{-d_i/\beta}}{\sum_{j=1}^{c} e^{-d_j/\beta}} \tag{3}$$

The parameter β governs the fuzziness of this criterion; for $\beta \to 0$ it turns back into the crisp "min" criterion. The Deterministic Annealing approach is a sequence of deterministic minimizations (made by Picard iterations), with β decreasing at each minimization. Therefore the first minimizations are done with a high degree of fuzziness, that is, high β (with few local minima), whereas the last minimizations, with $\beta \to 0$, are potentially subject to local minima, but they take advantage of the good initialization provided by previous steps.

The Neural Gas algorithm by Martinetz *et al.* [4] combines fuzzy membership in partitions with stochastic minimization. This algorithm has the interesting feature that membership in a Voronoi polyhedron is not defined as a direct function of the distance from the data point to the reference vector, but rather as a function of its rank with respect to the list of distances from all reference vectors. Distance d_i has the rank ρ_i in the set $\{d_1, \ldots, d_N\}$ when ordered decreasingly with respect to values, and this value can be written in an algebraic fashion as:

$$\rho_i = \sum_{j=1}^{c} \theta\left(d_i - d_j\right) \tag{4}$$

$\theta(x)$ is the Heaviside step function, taking on the values 0 for $x < 0$, 1 for $x > 0$, and 0.5 for $x = 0$. This extension is needed in the case of ties, very uncommon if the distances are real numbers; however this is the standard way to deal with ties in rank-order statistics. Notice that $\rho_{winner} = 0$ rather than 1, so $\rho_i \in \{0, \ldots, c-1\} \; \forall i \in \{1, \ldots, c\}$.

The membership of the data point to the i-th encoding polyhedron is:

$$u(\mathbf{x}) = e^{-\rho_i/\lambda} \tag{5}$$

where λ is a parameter which is annealed (made smaller) during training, thereby progressively reducing the extent to which reference vectors, other than the nearest (the "winner"), are included in the updating process.

When vectors other than the winner get updated a correlation is introduced between reference vectors, thus effectively reducing the learning capacity of the vector quantizer. As the annealing proceeds, the range of the correlation shrinks gradually, and the capacity is correspondingly increased; however, at the same time the learning coefficient is reduced, so that it is progressively more difficult to fall into local minima.

4   A Fuzzy Model of the Ranking Function

The performance of the Neural Gas algorithm is remarkably good, as found in previous research by the present and other authors. This is probably due to the combination of fuzzy membership, stochastic optimization and robust evaluation through ranking. Therefore it is not surprising that this algorithm has been used as the basis for improvements [15] as well as hardware implementations [16]. In the case of analog hardware implementations, other algorithms either perform worse, as we have reviewed, or imply very complex circuit structures. The Neural Gas seems the best choice in view of this trade-off.

In analog hardware, when the functions implemented are non-ideal there can be a variable effect on training performances. In particular, the rank function (4) uses the Heaviside step as a crisp distance comparison.

The step function in analog hardware is simply built by means of a saturating amplifier with large gain, which means typically an open-loop operational amplifier. However, Equation (4) has a c^2 space complexity, so circuit topologies should be made very inexpensive in terms of silicon area. Consequently, the operational amplifier will feature a finite gain which implies a deviation from the ideal behavior.

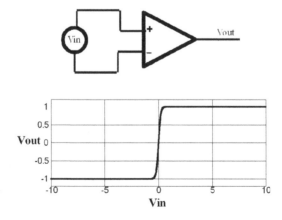

Fig. 1. A low-performance operational amplifier implements an approximate step function

The input-output relationship of an operational amplifier at middle frequencies is a hyperbolic tangent saturating (about) at the $+$ and $-$ power voltages. This suggests a very natural fuzzy model for the non-ideal rank function.

In a fuzzy perspective, it is more natural to define the relation "larger" among two (conventional) numbers as a degree to which one number is larger than another. We should mention that the problem of ranking fuzzy quantities has been reviewed for instance by Bortolan and Degani [17]. However, we are not dealing with fuzzy quantities, but with a *fuzzy evaluation* of crisp quantities.

For instance, suppose that we are to compare (a) $d_1 = 3$ with $d_2 = 4$, and (b) $d_1 = 3$ with $d_2 = 3.01$. Clearly in both case (a) and case (b) we can rightfully say that $d_2 > d_1$, but it is also clear that in (a) this is "more true" than in (b).

Therefore, we can make the following substitution:

$$\theta(d_j - d_i) \approx \frac{1}{1 + e^{(d_j - d_i)/\beta}} \qquad \text{and} \qquad \frac{1}{1 + e^{(d_j - d_i)/\beta}} \xrightarrow[\beta \to 0]{} \theta(d_j - d_i) \qquad (6)$$

so the computation of fuzzy rank can be expressed as

$$\rho_j = \sum_{i=1, j \neq i}^{n} \frac{1}{1 + e^{(d_j - d_i)/\beta}} \qquad (7)$$

The parameter β here acts as a fuzzification parameter, such that for large β the ranking function is definitely fuzzy, while for $\beta = 0$ we obtain the original, crisp ranking function.

The two expressions (4) and (7) for the rank function $\rho(\cdot)$ are compared in a simple example, illustrated in Figure 2, where the following set of values is used: $\{d, 2, 3, 5\}$. The diagram is a plot of $\rho(d)$ (in the two expressions, crisp and fuzzy) for d in the range $[0, 7]$. Two plots are shown for the fuzzy expression, one for $\beta = 0.05$ and another for $\beta = 0.25$ (smoother).

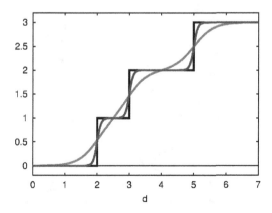

Fig. 2. Comparing crisp and fuzzy rank functions

The fuzzy ranking function is directly implemented by the op-amp-based circuitry outlined above. The fuzzification parameter is the inverse of the amplifier gain (the crisp and fuzzy version coincide for gain $\rightarrow \infty$ or for $\beta \rightarrow 0$). Therefore the fuzzy Neural Gas is a realistic model for the hardware implementation of the algorithm.

5   Experimental Performance

The fuzzy model for the Neural Gas has been tested by comparison with the standard version on some problems, both artificial and real:

1. Centers-only (toy problem, very trivial): place three codevectors on three points. For initial "consistency checks".
2. Centers-plus-noise (toy problem): place three codevectors on a set of points generated by a superposition of three Gaussians plus 60% random points.
3. Lena (real problem). Vector quantization of the standard benchmark image "Lena", shown in Figure 3, with codebooks of size 16 and 256.
4. Four images (real problem). Vector quantization of more benchmark images, shown in Figure 4.

The training of both algorithms was performed with identical initialization parameters (for the scheduling of updating coefficient and of range of influence of non-winners,

The first problem was used to ensure that the training steps were not too different, to validate the software (written in C). For $\beta = 0$ the two algorithms are indeed identical.

The second problem highlighted that, for low values of β, there are no significant differences in performance between the two algorithms. In some experiments the fuzzy version outperformed the standard version, but this is not a typical behavior.

Fig. 3. The "Lena" image

Fig. 4. Four benchmark images (from `http://links.uwaterloo.ca/bragzone.base.html`)

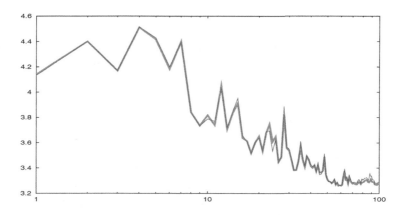

Fig. 5. Trace of mean square error during training on the "Lena" image

The training on the Lena image was a test of these outcomes on a real problem. In Figure 5 is shown a typical training trace (mean square error versus training steps), put on a logarithmic scale to show that the two traces are different, but converge to the same solution. The thin trace is standard Neural Gas and the thick trace (only slightly different in some locations) is the fuzzy modification.

Finally, the four additional images (greyscale 256x256) were used to confirm the previous results. Codevector sizes used are 16, 64 and 256. Results on the concordance of the two methods are outlined in the following table. For each test, the maximum deviation of the fuzzy version over the standard version (in percentage of RMS error) is indicated. The final codebooks have always been found to be equal according to the following definition. Two codebooks A and B are considered equal if, for any codevector in codebook A, the closest codevector in codebook B is within a preselected distance threshold. This threshold has to be selected case by case, taking into account codebook cardinality and making it less than the minimum distance between two codevectors of any codebook.

Test	Max. discordance in RMS
goldhill 16	0.8%
goldhill 64	0.9%
goldhill 256	1.3%
bridge 16	0.0%
bridge 64	0.5%
bridge 256	0.5%
bird 16	0.2%
bird 64	1.0%
bird 256	2.1%
camera 16	1.7%
camera 64	1.7%
camera 256	1.1%

The acceptable value of β depends linearly on the difference between distances that has to be resolved. The nomogram in Figure 6 is a plot of β versus $d_i - d_j$ for different values of the accepted error (annotated on the right margin).

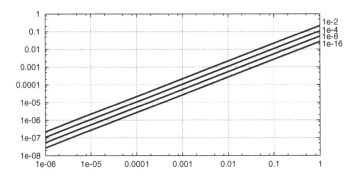

Fig. 6. Nomogram for the calculation of β

6   Conclusion

In this paper we have reviewed some uses of fuzzy concepts in vector quantization training. The main application is to enhance convergence, but we have also proposed using fuzzy ranking for the modeling of hardware implementations.

Acknowledgments

This work was funded by the Italian National Institute for the Physics of Matter (INFM) and by the Italian Ministry of Education, University and Research under a "PRIN - Cofin2002" grant.

References

1. Anil K. Jain and Richard C. Dubes, *Algorithms for Clustering Data*, Prentice Hall, Englewood Cliffs, New Jersey, USA, 1988.
2. Allen Gersho, "On the structure of vector quantizers", *IEEE Transactions on Information Theory*, vol. 28, no. 2, pp. 157–166, March 1982.
3. R.M. Gray, "Vector quantization", *IEEE Acoustic, Speech and Signal Processing Magazine*, vol. 1, pp. 4–29, 1984.
4. T.M. Martinetz, S.G. Berkovich, and K.J. Schulten, "'Neural gas' network for vector quantization and its application to time-series prediction", *IEEE Transactions on Neural Networks*, vol. 4, no. 4, pp. 558–569, 1993.
5. James C. Bezdek, *Pattern recognition with fuzzy objective function algorithms*, Plenum, New York, 1981.
6. A. Baraldi and P. Blonda, "A survey of fuzzy clustering algorithms for pattern recognition. I", *IEEE Transactions on Systems, Man and Cybernetics, Part B (Cybernetics)*, vol. 29, pp. 778–785, 1999.
7. A. Baraldi and P. Blonda, "A survey of fuzzy clustering algorithms for pattern recognition. II", *IEEE Transactions on Systems, Man and Cybernetics, Part B (Cybernetics)*, vol. 29, pp. 786–801, 1999.
8. Franz Aurenhammer, "Voronoi diagrams-a survey of a fundamental geometric data structure", *ACM Computing Surveys*, vol. 23, no. 3, pp. 345–405, 1991.
9. S. LLoyd, "Least squares quantization in pcm", *IEEE Transactions on Information Theory*, vol. 28, pp. 129–137, 1982.
10. J. MacQueen, "Some methods for classification and analysis of multivariate observations", in *Proceedings of the Fifth Berkeley Symposium on Mathematical Statistics and Probability*, L. Le Cam and J. Neyman, Eds. University of California, January 1967, vol. I, pp. 281–297.
11. Y. Linde, A. Buzo, and R.M. Gray, "An algorithm for vector quantizers design", *IEEE Transactions on Communications*, vol. COM-28, pp. 84–95, January 1980.
12. G. Geman and D. Geman, "Stochastic relaxation, gibbs distribution and bayesian restoration of images", *IEEE Transactions on Pattern Analysis and Machine Intelligence*, vol. PAMI-6, no. 6, pp. 721–741, 1984.
13. H.J. Ritter, T.M. Martinetz, and K.J. Schulten, *Neuronale Netze*, Addison-Wesley, München, Germany, 1991.

14. Kenneth Rose, "Deterministic annealing for clustering, compression, classification, regression, and related optimization problems", *Proceedings of IEEE*, vol. 86, no. 11, pp. 2210–2239, November 1998.

15. T. Hoffmann and J.M. Buhmann, "An annealed neural gas network for robust vector quantization", in *Proceedings of the International Conference on Artificial Neural Networks – ICANN96, Bochum, Germany*, 1996, pp. 151–156.

16. Stefano Rovetta and Rodolfo Zunino, "Efficient training of vector quantizers with analog circuit implementation", *IEEE Transactions on Circuits and Systems, Part II*, vol. 46, no. 6, pp. 688–698, June 1999.

17. G. Bortolan and R. Degani, "A review of some methods for ranking fuzzy sets", *Fuzzy sets and systems*, vol. 15, pp. 1–19, 1985.

Some Component Analysis Based on Fuzzy Relational Structure

Hajime Nobuhara and Kaoru Hirota

Department of Computational Intelligence and Systems Science,
Tokyo Institute of Technology, 4259 Nagatsuta, Midiri-ku,
Yokohama 226-8502, Japan
{nobuhara, hirota}@hrt.dis.titech.ac.jp
http://www.hrt.dis.titech.ac.jp/

Abstract. Two component analysis methods based on the fuzzy relational structure are proposed. First one is a component analysis based on the decomposition of fuzzy relation into fuzzy bases. Second one corresponds to a component analysis based on the eigen fuzzy sets of fuzzy relation. It is confirmed that results of application of the proposed methods to images extracted from SIDBA and 'View Sphere Database' are useful for various image application fields.

1 Introduction

As image analysis techniques, many component analysis have been developed in the framework of linear algebra [1], [4]. These methods are based on a space-frequency structure or multi-resolution space one. By using the image intensity normalization of each pixel into [0,1], an original image can be regarded as a fuzzy relation [8]. The fuzzy relational calculus, i.e., any fuzzy operation for fuzzy relation is based on ordered structure. In this paper, by using the fuzzy relational calculus, two component analysis methods based on ordered structure are proposed. First one is a component analysis based on a decomposition of fuzzy relation into fuzzy bases [5] [7]. Second one is based on the eigen fuzzy sets that correspond to the component of images [9]. By using the two proposed methods, analytical results of images (extracted from SIDBA and 'View Sphere Database') are presented, respectively.

2 Component Analysis Method (I)

2.1 Problem Formulation

A component analysis method based on a decomposition of fuzzy relation and its application to image processing, are shown. An original image of size $M \times N$ (pixels) can be treated as a fuzzy relation $R \in F(\mathbf{X} \times \mathbf{Y})$, $\mathbf{X} = \{x_1, x_2, \ldots, x_M\}$, $\mathbf{Y} = \{y_1, y_2, \ldots, y_N\}$, by normalizing the intensity range of each pixel into $[0, 1]$. The original image R is approximated by the composition of two pairs of fuzzy bases, $\{A_i \in F(\mathbf{X}) | i = 1, \ldots, c\}$ and $\{B_i \in F(\mathbf{Y}) | i = 1, \ldots, c\}$ such that

V. Di Gesú, F. Masulli, and A. Petrosino (Eds.): WILF 2003, LNAI 2955, pp. 289–296, 2006.
© Springer-Verlag Berlin Heidelberg 2006

$$R(x,y) \approx \tilde{R}(x,y) = \bigvee_{i=1}^{c} (A_i(x) \wedge B_i(y)), \tag{1}$$

for all $x \in \mathbf{X}$, $y \in \mathbf{Y}$, where c denotes the Schein rank [3] of the fuzzy relation R, that is the smallest integer satisfying Eq. (1). As it can be seen from Eq. (1), the fuzzy bases $\mathbf{A}$ and $\mathbf{B}$ express components of the original images. Obviously c measures the approximate performance $\tilde{R}$ of R, in the sense that the possible larger the value c, the better approximation $\tilde{R}$ is. The approximation problem (Eq. (1)) can be seen as an optimization that minimizes the cost function:

$$Q = \sum_{(x,y) \in \mathbf{X} \times \mathbf{Y}} \left(R(x,y) - \bigvee_{i=1}^{c} (A_i(x) \wedge B_i(y)) \right)^2. \tag{2}$$

A solution of the optimization problem based on the gradient method has been presented in [7], and its improvement, i.e., a fast solution of the optimization problem has been proposed by [5]. Here, an overview of the detailed notation shown in [7], [5] is given as follows:

$$A_i^{(iter+1)}(x) = A_i^{(iter)}(x) - \alpha \frac{\partial Q_{iter}}{\partial A_i^{(iter)}(x)}, \tag{3}$$

$$B_i^{(iter+1)}(y) = B_i^{(iter)}(y) - \alpha \frac{\partial Q_{iter}}{\partial B_i^{(iter)}(y)}, \tag{4}$$

for all $x \in \mathbf{X}$, $y \in \mathbf{Y}$, where "iter" denotes the iteration number of the gradient method. For simplicity of notation, by setting $Q = Q_{iter}$, $A_i = A_i^{(iter)}$ and $B_i = B_i^{(iter)}$, the derivation of the cost function Q with respect to $A_l(x')$ can be written for $l = 1, 2, \ldots, c$, as

$$\frac{\partial Q}{\partial A_l(x')} = \frac{\partial}{\partial A_l(x')} \sum_{(x,y) \in \mathbf{X} \times \mathbf{Y}} \left(R(x,y) - \bigvee_{i=1}^{c} (A_i(x) \wedge B_i(y)) \right)^2$$

$$= -2 \sum_{y \in \mathbf{Y}} \left(R(x',y) - \bigvee_{i=1}^{c} (A_i(x') \wedge B_i(y)) \right) \cdot \frac{\partial}{\partial A_l(x')} \left(\bigvee_{i=1}^{c} (A_i(x') \wedge B_i(y)) \right)$$

$$= -2 \sum_{y \in \mathbf{Y}} \left(R(x',y) - \bigvee_{i=1}^{c} (A_i(x') \wedge B_i(y)) \right)$$

$$\cdot \varphi \left(A_l(x') \wedge B_l(y), \bigvee_{i=1,i \neq l}^{c} (A_i(x') \wedge B_i(y)) \right) \cdot \psi(A_l(x'), B_l(y)), \tag{5}$$

being the functions φ and ψ defined by

$$\varphi(a,b) = \begin{cases} 1 \; if & a \geq b, \\ 0 & otherwise, \end{cases} \tag{6}$$

$$\psi(a,b) = \begin{cases} 1 \; if & a \leq b, \\ 0 & otherwise, \end{cases} \tag{7}$$

and α is a learning rate. The above process is performed until a final criterion, e.g., if

$$Q_{iter+1} - Q_{iter} < \epsilon, \tag{8}$$

is satisfied, where ϵ is a required threshold. For the computation of the second fuzzy basis B_i, the derivation follows the same scheme as above and we get

$$\frac{\partial Q}{\partial B_l(y')} = -2 \sum_{x \in \mathbf{X}} \left(R(x, y') - \bigvee_{i=1}^{c} \left(A_i(x) \wedge B_i(y') \right) \right)$$
$$\cdot \varphi \left(A_l(x) \wedge B_l(y'), \bigvee_{i=1, i \neq l}^{c} \left(A_i(x) \wedge B_i(y') \right) \right) \cdot \psi(B_l(y'), A_l(x)). \tag{9}$$

In [5], an efficient formula of the derivative (5) is shown as follows:

$$\frac{\partial Q}{\partial A_l(x')} = -2 \sum_{y \in \mathbf{Y}} \left(R(x', y) - \bigvee_{i=1}^{c} \left(A_i(x') \wedge B_i(y) \right) \right) \cdot \phi(A_l(x'), \tilde{R}(x', y)). \tag{10}$$

Similarly, reasoning as in the previous schema, we can transform the derivative (9) in the following formula:

$$\frac{\partial Q}{\partial B_l(y')} = -2 \sum_{x \in \mathbf{X}} \left(R(x, y') - \bigvee_{i=1}^{c} \left(A_i(x') \wedge B_i(y') \right) \right) \cdot \phi(B_l(y'), \tilde{R}(x, y')). \tag{11}$$

2.2   Experiments

A result of application of the component analysis (I) to an image extracted from Standard Image DataBAse (SIDBA), is presented. Figure 1 (left) shows an original image 'girl'. Under the condition that the learning rate α is set at 0.005, the approximated image $\tilde{R}$ is obtained. The approximated image $\tilde{R}$ with the Schein rank being 25, 50, and 100 are shown in Figs. 1 (right) - 2, respectively. The value of the cost function Q with respect to *iter* is shown in Fig. 6. The Fuzzy bases **A** and **B** with the Schein rank being 25, 50, and 100, are shown in Figs. 3 - 5, respectively. As it can be seen from Figs. 1 - 6, if the Schein rank is higher, the approximation of $\tilde{R}$ is better. In other words, the Schein rank is higher, the component of the original image included in the fuzzy bases **A** and **B** is larger.

Fig. 1. Original image (left) and approximated image $\tilde{R}$, Schein rank = 25, (right)

Fig. 2. Approximated image $\tilde{R}$, Schein rank = 50 (left), and Schein rank = 100 (right)

Fig. 3. Fuzzy bases **A** and **B**, Schein rank = 25

Fig. 4. Fuzzy bases **A** and **B**, Schein rank = 50

Fig. 5. Fuzzy bases **A** and **B**, Schein rank = 100

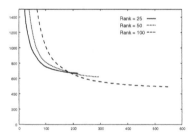

Fig. 6. The value of the cost function Q with respect to *iter*

2.3   Extension Proposals

A lossy image compression method based on fuzzy relational structure (fuzzy relational equations), has been proposed in [2], [6]. The component analysis method (I) can be a candidate of the design of appropriate coders in the compression scheme, in order to achieve an efficient compression. The fuzzy relation R can be regard as the concept of keywords in natural language. Therefore, the proposed component analysis method (I) can be also applied to the processing for the concept between keywords in natural language.

3   Component Analysis Method (II)

3.1   Problem Formulation

This section shows a component analysis method based on eigen fuzzy sets [9]. Specially, we focus on the eigen fuzzy sets of max-min and min-max composition type.

Let R be a fuzzy relation between a finite set $\mathbf{X}$ and A be a fuzzy subset of $\mathbf{X}$, i.e., $R \in F(\mathbf{X} \times \mathbf{X})$ and $A \in F(\mathbf{X})$.

[Max-min Composition Type]

An eigen fuzzy set associated with R, is a fuzzy set A such that

$$A = A \circ R, \tag{12}$$

where

$$A(x') = \max_{x \in \mathbf{X}}\{\min(A(x), R(x', x))\} \qquad \forall x' \in \mathbf{X}. \tag{13}$$

[Min-max Composition Type]

An eigen fuzzy set associated with R, is a fuzzy set A such that

$$A = A \bullet R, \tag{14}$$

where

$$A(x') = \min_{x \in \mathbf{X}}\{\max(A(x), R(x', x))\} \qquad \forall x' \in \mathbf{X}. \tag{15}$$

The eigen fuzzy set A corresponds to a component of the fuzzy relation R in terms of the ordered structure. The greatest eigen fuzzy set (GEFS) for max-min composition type, and the smallest eigen fuzzy set (SEFS) for min-max composition one, are presented using numerical example as follows:

[The greatest eigen fuzzy set]

Let R be given by

$$\begin{pmatrix} 0.3\,0.5\,0.9 \\ 0.6\,0.8\,0.1 \\ 0.1\,0.2\,0.4 \end{pmatrix}. \tag{16}$$

Step G-1: Find the smallest element in their corresponding columns (See Eq. (17)), and construct a candidate fuzzy set A_1 by using them (See Eq. (18)),

$$\begin{pmatrix} 0.3 & 0.5 & \boxed{0.9} \\ \boxed{0.6} & \boxed{0.8} & 0.0 \\ 0.1 & 0.2 & 0.4 \end{pmatrix}, \tag{17}$$

$$A_1 = [0.6, 0.8, 0.9]. \tag{18}$$

Step G-2: Calculate the composition of R and $A_n, (n = 1, \ldots)$ until the convergence of the fuzzy set A_n.

The composition of R and $A_n, (n = 1, \ldots)$ is shown as follows:

$$A_1 \circ R = [0.9, 0.8, 0.4] = A_2, \tag{19}$$

$$A_2 \star R = [0.5, 0.8, 0.4] = A_3, \tag{20}$$

$$A_3 \star R = [0.5, 0.8, 0.4] = A_4 = A_3. \tag{21}$$

Step G-3: When the fuzzy set A_n is converged, GEFS can be obtained as the fuzzy set A_n.

[The smallest eigen fuzzy set]

Let R be given as Eq. (22).
Step S-1: Find the smallest element in their corresponding columns (Eq. (22)), and construct a candidate fuzzy set A_1 by using them (Eq. (23)),

$$\begin{pmatrix} 0.3 & 0.5 & 0.9 \\ 0.6 & 0.8 & \boxed{0.1} \\ \boxed{0.1} & \boxed{0.2} & 0.4 \end{pmatrix}, \tag{22}$$

$$A_1 = [0.1, 0.2, 0.1]. \tag{23}$$

Step S-2: Calculate the composition of R and $A_n, (n = 1, \ldots)$ until the convergence of the fuzzy set A_n. The composition of R and $A_n, (n = 1, \ldots)$ is shown as follows:

$$A_1 \bullet R = [0.3, 0.10.1] = A_2, \tag{24}$$

$$A_2 \bullet R = [0.3, 0.1, 0.1] = A_3, \tag{25}$$

Step. S-3 When the fuzzy set A_n is converged, SEFS can be obtained as the fuzzy set A_n.

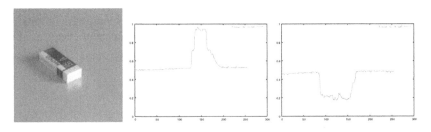

Fig. 7. Original image : File-32-36 (left) and corresponding GEFS (middle) and SEFS of (right)

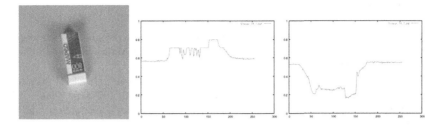

Fig. 8. Original image : File-74-0 (left) and corresponding GEFS (middle) and SEFS (right)

3.2 Experiments

A result of application of component analysis method (II) to images extracted from 'View Sphere Database' [10] is presented. The size of the original image is 256×256 pixels, therefore, $\mathbf{X} = \{x_1, x_2, \ldots, x_{256}\}$. By using image intensity normalization from $\{0, \ldots, 255\}$ into $[0, 1]$, the original images can be considered as fuzzy relations $R \in F(\mathbf{X} \times \mathbf{X})$. Two examples of the original images, GEFS, and SEFS are shown in Figs. 7 - 8.

3.3 Extension Proposals

The proposed component analysis method (II), that is, eigen fuzzy sets of the original images can be used for are useful candidate of image feature, in order to perform an image retrieval.

4 Conclusion

In terms of ordered structure, two component analysis methods have been proposed by using fuzzy relational calculus. First component analysis is based on a decomposition of fuzzy relation (original image) into fuzzy bases. The decomposition is formulated as an optimization problem and it can be solved by using a gradient method [5]. Second method corresponds to the eigen fuzzy set of the fuzzy relation under the condition that the composition type is max-min and min-max, respectively. The proposed analysis methods can be applied to various fields, e.g., an image compression based on fuzzy relational equations, an image retrieval, and a text mining. These developments should be a future study.

Acknowledgment

Support from Mizuho Foundation for the Promotion of Sciences is gratefully acknowledged.

References

1. M. S. Bartlett, J. R. Movellan, and T. J. Sejinowski, "Face recognition by independent component analysis", *IEEE Transaction on Neural Networks*, Vol. 13, No. 6, 1450–1464, 2002.

2. K. Hirota, and W. Pedrycz, "Fuzzy Relational Compression", *IEEE Transactions on Systems, Man, and Cybernetics, Part B*, Vol. 29, No. 3, 407–415, 1999.

3. K. H. Kim and F. W. Roush, "Generalized Fuzzy Matrices", *Fuzzy Sets and Systems*, Vol. 4, 293–315, 1980.

4. A. Leonardis, H. Bischof, and J. Maver, "Multiple Eigenspaces", *Pattern Recognition*, Vol. 35, No. 11, 2613–2627, 2002.

5. H. Nobuhara, K. Hirota, W. Pedrycz, and S. Sessa, "Two Iterative Methods of Decomposition of a Fuzzy Relation for Image Compression/Decomposition Processing", Soft Computing, to appear.

6. Nobuhara, H., Pedrycz, W. and Hirota, K.: Fast Solving Method of Fuzzy Relational Equation and its Application to Image Compression/Reconstruction. IEEE Transaction on Fuzzy Systems, Vol. 8, No. 3, (2000) 325–334

7. W. Pedrycz, K. Hirota, and S. Sessa, "A Decomposition of Fuzzy Relations", *IEEE Transaction on Systems, Man, and Cybernetics, Part B*, Vol. 31, No. 4, 657–663, 2001.

8. W. Pedrycz, and F. Gomide, "An Introduction to Fuzzy Sets ", *The MIT Press*, 1998.

9. Sanchez, E.: Resolution of Eigen Fuzzy Sets Equations. Fuzzy Sets and Systems, Vol. 1, No. 1, (1978) 69–74

10. http://www-prima.inrialpes.fr/

Fuzzy Technique Based Recognition
of Handwritten Characters

R.M. Suresh and S. Arumugam

Department of Computer Applications,
RMK Engineering College,
Kavaraipettai, Tamil Nadu, India
rmsuresh@hotmail.com
Department of Mathematics,
Manonmaniam Sundaranar University,
Thirunelveli, 627 012.

Abstract. The different methods for automatic pattern recognition are motivated by the way in which pattern classes are characterized and defined. In this paper, the handwritten characters (numerals) are preprocessed and segmented into primitives. These primitives are measured and labeled using *fuzzy logic*. Strings of a character are formed from these labeled primitives. To recognize the handwritten characters, conventional string matching is performed. However, the problem in this string matching has been avoided using the *membership value* of the string. This result is being compared with the *Modified Parser* generated from the *Error-free Fuzzy Context-Free Grammar*.

Keywords: Fuzzy Logic, Fuzzy Context-free Grammar, Preprocessing, Polygonal Approximation, Segmentation, Labeling, Handwritten Numerals, Modified Earley's Parsing Algorithm.

1 Introduction

A lot of research effort has been dedicated to handwritten character recognition. Number of schemes are available for this purpose. Some of the areas where the handwritten character recognition is being carried are Fuzzy Methods [2] Knowledge-based techniques [11] and Neural Networks [3-7]. The different methods for automatic pattern recognition are motivated by the way in which pattern classes are characterized and defined [1]. The idea in syntactic pattern recognition is to describe a complex pattern in terms of a hierarchical composition of simple sub-patterns [25]. In syntactic pattern recognition a basic set of primitives forms the terminal set of grammar. The pattern class is the set of strings generated by the pattern grammar. But the concept of formal grammar is too rigid to be used for the representation of real-life patterns such as handwritten documents.

This rigidity can be changed if certain fuzziness is introduced which describes the vagueness of such patterns. Accordingly a fuzzy language can handle imprecise patterns when the indeterminacy is due to inherent vagueness [16]. The conventional approaches to knowledge representation usually lack the means to represent the imprecise concepts.

V. Di Gesú, F. Masulli, and A. Petrosino (Eds.): WILF 2003, LNAI 2955, pp. 297–308, 2006.

Due to Zadeh [18], Fuzzy sets offer a theoretical basis to cope with the vagueness of patterns, which we exploited in the proposed method. First the motivation for this method is given. This is followed by the of inference of Fuzzy Context-free Grammar and its Inference method. Then the case study with results has been discussed.

2 Motivation of This Method

In recent years, some of the development tools in fuzzy software and hardware such as FuzzyClips[15], FUNN-Lab[12] have been introduced. These tools provide a convenient way to configure the membership functions, defining rules, input and output functions etc. But they are not suitable for highly structured patterns recognition. The symbolic and structural description of a pattern is more useful for analysis and recognition[14]. The allograph-based method to recognize cursive handwritten words with fuzzy logic has been proposed by Parizeau et al. [13]. The drawback of this method is that, there is no direct way of generating handwriting features all graphs automatically. Malaviya et al. [11] have proposed FOHDEL a new fuzzy language to automatic generation of a pattern description in a rule-base and the representation of patterns in a linguistic form. The problem rest in this method is that, the large number of input features make the rule-base incomprehensible and consumes more time to recognize. The theory of Fuzzy grammars and quantitative fuzzy semantics[17] give very interesting ideas like the connection between context-free grammar and natural grammar through transformational grammar and the derivation trees (structural descriptions or pattern markers). The idea here is to identify primitives using fuzzy logic and label them in the form of a compact fuzzy language (Strings). The labeled strings are parsed using a modified parser algorithm to recognize the pattern.

The purpose of this paper is to offer the system which infers a complete Error-handling Fuzzy Context-Free Grammar (FCFG) from samples and manipulates fuzzy languages as sets of trees and parse them.

3 Fuzzy Context-Free Grammar and Its Inference

It appears that much of the existing formal grammars can be extended quite readily to fuzzy grammars. The concept of fuzzy grammar and Fuzzy context-free grammar can be referred in [16,17]. The formalization of grammatical inference includes the following phases:

i)Hypothesis space is a subsets of the general rewriting systems – Context-Free grammars; ii)The *measure of adequacy* is that the grammar inferred generates all of the known strings in the language L and none of the known non-strings; iii)The *rules* by which the samples are drawn iv)The *criterion for success* in the limit of the inference process and the *source of information* about a language L is an information sequence which is an infinite sequence of strings from the obtained set; A routine has been developed [19-22] for the automatic generation of samples. From the generated samples the strings are obtained; from the strings the grammar is inferred.

3.1 Method

The method employs straight lines to build-up the prototype character patterns. For the prototype, the end points of the segments are specified as the coordinates of the end point pixels in a normalized frame. The various instances are obtained by various coordinate specifications with different length. The specification for the prototype can be made as in the following function with reference to figure 2.1. The parameters represents the starting vertex (coordinate), the number of pixels in length, the next vertex (coordinate) and the direction using which the line to be drawn. The directions are Horizontal (0), Vertical (1), Right slant (2), and Left slant (3) respectively. The function to draw the picture KA is

DRAW L ((1,10,2,0,),(2,5,3,0), (2,6,4,1),(4,8,9,0),(9,3,10,2), (10,3,11,3), (4,6,5,3), (11,16,6,0),(6,6,7,2) (7,14,4,0),(1,7,8,1)

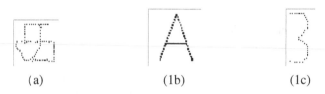

(a)   (1b)   (1c)

Fig. 1. Characters obtained from DRAW function a) Tamil Character KA b) English Alphabet A c) Numeral 3

Using such sample characters the strings are obtained and the grammar is inferred. The algorithm for the Fuzzy Context-free grammar inference is given below.

Algorithm 1. Fuzzy Context-Free Grammar Inference

Input: Finite set of sample strings

Output: The production rules.

1. Let R_s^+ denote the set of all strings in which there is no cycle or all cycles have length 1.
2. Let R_i^+ denote the set of all strings having cycle of length greater than 1.
3. Continue (repeat step 2) the process of finding subcycles in the strings in R_i^+, and determine subcycles which cannot be broken further.
4. Obtain one production rule for each such subcycle found in step 3.
5. Augment the set of production rules by using the strings of R_s^+

4 Application of Fuzzy Context-Free Grammar to Handwritten Characters Recognition

Handwritten characters are having biological origin, since as the mood of a person his handwriting varies and hence variability in all sense is possible in the input image. So it is considered to recognize such patterns. The application of the FCFG on Syntactic Pattern Recognition is described for handwritten characters in this section. The recognition of patterns is carried by the method called Syntactic String matching and parsing.

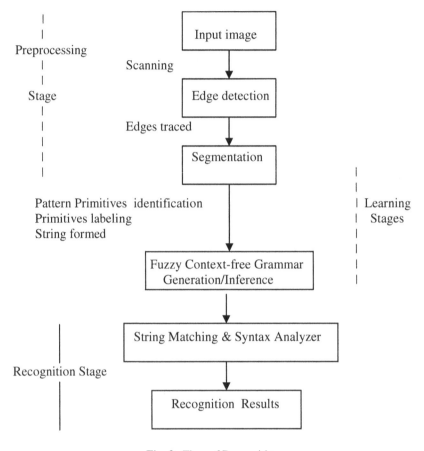

Fig. 2. Flow of Recognition

Character recognition requires a preprocessing, learning and recognition stages. The preprocessing takes different stages such as two-tone conversion, edge detection, thinning, and   segmentation. Learning Stage includes the primitive labeling and string formation and grammar inference. The recognition stage includes the string matching and parsing to classify the input pattern into a class. The general flow of the work is shown in the figure 2.

4.1 Handwritten Numerals and Tamil Characters

Handwritten numerals are considered here for case study. The numerals are very much known to every one. Where as the alphabets of Tamil need an introduction. The Tamil alphabets are very old and are organized in a systematic way. The alphabet set splits into set of vowels, consonants, composite letters, and special letter. Of course some special characters (Krantha) from Sanskrit are also being used in Tamil text for coining Tamil numbers and Tamil names. There are 12 vowels, 18 consonants, 216 composite letters, one special character (AK) and 14 special characters. A composite letters are not basic and they are derived by combining consonants and vowels as described in [24]. We have identified some 67 Tamil characters are the basic characters (Vowels, Consonants, and composite letters) and we understood that if one recognizes these 67 characters it is good-enough to recognize all 247 characters. The list of 67 characters are represented in Suresh et al [19]. An example for handwritten tamil characters are shown in figure 3 and character for digit six is shown in figure 4.

(a)   (b)

Fig. 3. (a) Gray Image (b) Two-tone Image

4.2 Preprocessing Stage (Edge Detection Smoothing and Thinning)

The scanned (digitized) input is preprocessed such as converted into a two-tone image, edge detected using Canny's algorithm and thinned using our thinning algorithm[19]. The preprocessed result for the sample image given above is shown in Figure 4.

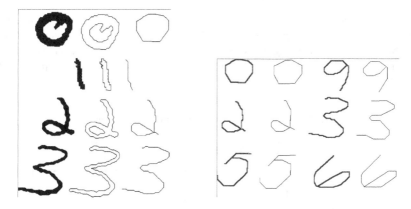

Fig. 4. Handwritten, edged, thinned   **Fig. 5.** Polygons for some of the Numerals
characters of some numerals

The result obtained in the previous section looks as such a polygonal curve. But then the real polygonal approximation [19] is necessary in cases for a number '5', '6' and '8'. Example: given in Figure 5.The advantage of this approach is that it produces a polygon with a small number of edges for any arbitrary two-dimensional digitized curves.

4.3 Feature Selection (Segmentation)/Primitive Identification(Recognition)

Feature selection and extraction are the most significant aspects of any pattern recognition problem. The features should be selected in such a way that the resulting description is independent of skew, contrast, deformation or other style of writing. In handwritten character, the normal variation due to style and other aspect of writers should not affect the feature.

Structural details like endpoints, intersections of line segments, loops, curvatures, segment lengths, etc. describing the geometry of the pattern structure are used as features. The details of feature's discriminative power is well documented in literature [8-10]. A feature is defined as a set of vertices on or near the pattern boundary (line) and the segmented line lengths are obtained from them. The structure of a character is represented by this feature. Also it is easy to reconstruct a character from them. The pattern primitives are identified, recognized (Fuzzy functions) labeled using the procedure described by Psy and Chin [26].

Feature Extraction:

The feature extraction plays the most important task in the recognition process. Particularly in the handwritten characters, based on the identification of features the strings to different character are formed and hence the recognition. Five attributes were used to describe a segment. They are

1. The type of a segment.
2. The length of the i-th segment is measured with its starting vertex.
3. Center of the i-th segment.
4. Center of the skeleton image of a the given number.
5. The predecessor and successor segments type.

The most important feature for character recognition using the syntactic approach is the type. Based on the features the membership values for a string is determined. The table1 shows the fuzzy grade membership for number of segments. The column represents the actual number of segments in a numeral and the row represents the numeral.

Table 1. Membership grade for number of segments

Number	Horizontal (h)	Vertical (v)	Right Slant (r)	Left Slant (l)
0	0.2	0.2	0.6	0.6
1	0.1	0.1	0.3	0.3
2	0.1	0.2	0.3	0.7
3	0.5	0.2	0.3	0.6
4	0.5	0.4	0.1	0.3
5	0.4	0.2	0.3	0.4
6	0.3	0.2	0.1	0.5
7	0.1	0.2	0.1	0.3
8	0.2	0.4	0.5	0.6
9	0.2	0.3	0.2	0.4

Example:

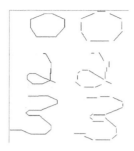

Fig. 6. Segmented Primitives of Numerals

4.4   Fuzzy Context-Free Grammar Inference

One of the first techniques suggested for grammatical inference was simple enumeration of all possible grammars in the class of interest until a suitable grammar is found. Gold [27] has pointed out that in the learning situation where a new string is presented and a new grammar is guessed at each instant of time, thus no other algorithm can uniformly reach a steady correct guess in less time for all grammars in the class and for all information sequences. Horning [28] has written an enumerative inference program which uses the class of grammars as being organized into a tree where each grammar G with n nonterminals represents a node on the tree; like wise, each grammar in the tree covers of all of the grammars below it. Pao [29] has developed a finite search algorithm for finite-state grammar inference which employs the grammar covering concept as a pruning technique. All these grammar inference procedures are expensive and consume more time also. Hence a simple algorithm has been generated to infer the grammar from the set of samples. The algorithm is given in section 4.

The inferred grammar is

S→ASB, S→SB, S→A, S→B
A →AB, A→v, A→h
B→BA, B →l, B→r

However, there is a possibility that the grammar inferred need to accommodate a string with only one change or two changes from the original string. The errors considered for the description of a pattern are

❖   An error where one symbol is changed into another (φ).
❖   An error where one symbol is deleted or missing (α).
❖   An error where one symbol is inserted or generated in addition (β).

The technique is based on first representing the productions of a grammar in equation form. This generates perfect patterns, and then applying a set of transformation to these equations yields new productions for a grammar.   Further this generates both perfect patterns and patterns containing one of (φ or α or β) three types of errors. Hence applying transformations to the productions of a new grammar, which describes not only the original patterns but also those containing specific types of errors. (or deviations from perfect formation).

φ error

Given   a grammar G , the procedure developed in this section generates a   new grammar G_φ which can handle the occurrence of a φ error in the strings of $L(G)$. A one-to-one correspondence between productions in a   FCFG G and set of defining equations of the form $A= x_1+x_2+...+x_k$.   where $A \in V_N$, $x_i \in (V_N \cup V_T)^+$, and '+' operator in the equations is the OR operator. To find the grammar G_φ the following rules are applied:

    i.   for $x_i, x_j \in (V_N \cup V_T)^+$, $\varphi(x_i+x_j) = \varphi(x_i) + \varphi(x_j)$ and $\varphi(x_i\, x_j) = \varphi(x_i)x_j + x_i\varphi(x_j)$

    ii.   for $A \in V_N$, $\varphi(A) = A_\varphi$, a new nonterminal

    iii.   for $a \in V_T$, $\varphi(a) = \{\, b \mid b \in V_T, b \neq a \}$ b is a terminal such that $b \neq a$.

α and β error

The forms of the rules for applying the φ error operator hold for the α and β operators, with the exception of rule (iii).   Rule (iii) for a deletion of symbol in α error is rewritten as

    iii.   for $a \in V_T$, $\alpha(a) = \lambda$, where λ is the empty string of length 0.

Rule (iii) for an insertion of symbol in β error is rewritten as

    iii.   for $a \in V_T$, $\beta(a) = (\{\, b \mid b \in V_T\})\, a + a\, (\{\, b \mid b \in V_T \})$.

    Considering the new production rules the new grammar inferred is

$G' = (\{\ S, A, B, S', A', B'\},$

      $\{\ h, v, l, r\}$

      $\{S \to AB,\quad S \to SB,\ S \to A,\ S \to B,$

        $S' \to A'B,\ S' \to AB',\ S' \to S'B,\ S' \to SB',\ S' \to A',\ S' \to B',$

        $A \to AB,\ A \to A,\ A \to v,\ A \to h,\ A \to \lambda,$

        $A' \to AB',\ A' \to A'B,\ A' \to A',\ A' \to h,\ A' \to v,\ A' \to \lambda,\ A' \to vh,\ A' \to hv$

        $B \to BA,\ B \to l,\ B \to r, B \to \lambda,$

        $B' \to B'A,\ B' \to BA',\ B' \to r,\ B' \to l,\ B' \to \lambda, B' \to lr, B' \to rl\ \}$

      $\{S, S'\})$

5 Parser

A general parsing algorithm for Fuzzy Context-Free Grammar is described in this section. The algorithm is a modified version of Earley's parsing algorithm for generalizing the parsing of strings for any FCFG with a complexity as $O(n^3)$.

  ❖ The first modification is the initialization, where some value in the new items is assigned to weight (membership value).

  ❖ The second modification is that the computation of weight is considered.

  ❖ The third modification introduced is to account for the case where G is ambiguous.

    We denote the unit elements for "D" and "O" as 0 and 1 respectively. A Context-Free Fuzzy Grammar is a pair (G,f), where G is a context-free grammar $G = (V_N,$

V_T, P, S) defined as V_N and V_T are finite sets of non-terminals and terminal symbols, respectively; $S \in V_N$ is the starting symbol; and $P \subset V_N \times (V_N \cup V_T)^*$ is a finite set of rules, where $(V_N \cup V_T)^*$ is the free monoid over $V_N \cup V_T$. And f is function $f: P \rightarrow W$.

Let D_l be a left derivation of $X \in V_N^*$ from S; i.e., D_i is a sequence of rules from P ($r_1^i, r_2^i, \ldots, r_n^i$) such that $S \Rightarrow X$. A weighted language is defined as

$$f: V_N^* \rightarrow W: X \in V_N^* \quad f(X) = \Pi \ (f((r_1^i) \bullet f(r_2^i) \bullet \ldots \bullet f(r_n^i)) \tag{1}$$

An extended version of Earley's parsing algorithm is used to parse a string $X \in V_N^*$ ($X = a_1 \ldots a_n$) with a given Fuzzy Grammar (G, f). The modifications are carried out in a similar way as done by Fu [25] and Casacuberta and Vidal [23] for stochastic error correcting parsers, i.e., by introducing a new definition of an item in a list I(j).

We have introduced an expanded grammar (G', f') is built from (G, f) as follows: G' = (N', E, P', S'), which accommodates all the strings including errors.

The algorithm discussed by Casacuberta et al [23] has a problem like, if (S $\rightarrow \alpha \cdot, i$, P) in I(j) then $S \Rightarrow a_{i+1}, \ldots a_j$, the inverse of this statement is not always true as it can be derived from the definition of an item.

If we could build an algorithm which verifies this statement and its inverse, the problem of substring recognition through the parsing of a given string x is solved.

Another problem, related with substring recognition, appears in step (c) of algorithm 1 if there is not any item (A→α·a_j·β, i, P) to I(j-1). In this case, no new item can be added to I(j) using steps (c) and, consequently, (A) and (B), and the parsing process is stopped.

The new modified algorithm is proposed to the earlier to overcome the problems mentioned above. The basic idea is to introduce a reintialisation, each time the construction of a list is concluded. This process can be seen as n parsings which share items. And the substring recognition consists of verifying whether a new item is of the form (S→ $\alpha \cdot, i$, P). Therefore, at the end of the parsing we know whether either X, or any of its substrings, have or have not been generated by the grammar.

Algorithm 2. Modified Parsing Algorithm for recognition of Strings

Input : An expanded Fuzzy Context-Free Grammar G', f' and a string to be recognized

Output: A parse list with starting state and ending state and membership value of the string.

```
Initialization
  I(0):=NIL;Recog:=NIL;
  add (S'→.S,0,I) to I(0);
Iteration
  for j:= 0 to n do
    repeat
      (A) for (A →α·B·β, I, P) in I(j)
            for (B→ γ) ∈ P
          add(B→·γ, j, f'(B→ γ)) to I(j);
          endfor;
        endfor;
      (B) for (A →α·, I, P) in I(j)
        for (B →β·Aγ,k, Q) in I(i)
        if (B →β·Aγ,k, r) not in I(j)
```

```
            then   add (B→β·Aγ,k,P • Q) to I(j);
            else substitute r of  (B →β·Aγ,k, r) by (r (P • Q ));
               endif;
        endfor;
        endfor;
    until no new items can be added or d=modified to I(j);
 (B') for ( S→α·, i, P)  in I(j)
         add (I+1,j,P) to Recog;
      endfor;
 (D) for (A→.α, 0, Q)  in I(0)
         add (I+1,j,P) to I(j);
      endfor;
      if j<n
      then I( j+1) := nil;
        (c ) for (A →α·a_{j+1}·β, i, P)  to  I(j)

             add (A→α·a_{j+1}·β, i, P)  to   I(j+1);

        endfor;
      endif;
    endfor;
```

In this algorithm the step D represents the reinitialization of parsing; and the step B represents the list of recognized sub-strings.

6 String Matching and Recognition

The NIST special database is used for our experiments. We have extracted 5,423 samples for testing and recognition. The experiment was conducted in a Pentium III with 64 MB RAM. The recognition time shown in the table 2.

Table 2. Recognition Performance

Techniques	Number of Samples	Performance	
		Percentage	Time in Sec.
String Comparison Parsing	2200	94.8	268
	5423	91.6	445
	2200	97.8	220
	5423	95.6	380

The experiment has been performed on handwritten Tamil characters too. Since only selected Tamil characters were considered, the result was not discussed.

7 Results and Conclusion

In this paper an unconstrained handwritten numeral is considered as an image whose position and size are considered as invariant. The concatenation among the pattern was considered as in serial and the strings obtained are by considering the trace in clockwise direction. A 20 x 20 frame is used for writing characters. Another possibility exists that this frame can be converted into 20 x 20 binary matrix and the same procedure may be followed to obtain the primitives. Prototype Numerals are used to infer the grammar. Apart from the prototype generation module a set of handwritten Numerals were collected from NIST and the experiment was conducted.

Acknowledgment

The author would like to thank **Shri. R.S. Munirathinam**, Chairman and **Shri. R. Jothi Naidu**, Director, RMK Engineering College, INDIA for their encouragement and support provided for the project.

References

1. W.Pedrycz, Fuzzy sets in Pattern Recognition: Methodology and Methods, Pattern Recognition vol 23, ½, pp 121-146, 1990.
2. I.S.I. Abhuhaiba and P.Ahmed, A Fuzzy Graph theoretic approach to recognize the totally unconstrianed handwritten Numerals, Patt. Reco. Vol 26, No. 9, pp. 1335- 1350, 1993
3. S.N. Srihari, Recognition of handwritten and machine printed text for postal address interpretation, Patt. Reco. Letters, Vol 14, pp 291-302, 1993
4. T. Wakahara, Toward robust handwritten character recognition, Patt. Reco. Letters, Vol 14, 345-354, 1993.
5. R.M.K.Sinha et al., Hybrid Contextual Text Recognition with String Matching, IEEE PAMI, Vol 15, No 9, pp 915-923, 1993.
6. Z. Chi et al., Handwritten Numeral Recognition using Self-Organizing maps and Fuzzy Rules, Patt. Reco. Vol 28, No. 1, pp 59-66, 1995.
7. J. Cao et al., Recognition of Handwritten Numerals with Multiple Feature and Multistage Classifier, Patt. Reco. Vol 28, No 2, pp 153-160, 1995.
8. A. Malaviya et al., Fuzzy Feature Description of Handwriting Patterns, Patt. Reco. Vol 30, No. 10, pp 1591-1604, 1997.
9. A.K. Jain, Representation and Recognition of Handwritten Digits using Deformable Templates, IEEE PAMI, Vol 19, No. 12, pp 1386-1391, 1997.
10. J.Cai et al., Integration of Structural and Statistical Information for Unconstrained Handwritten Numeral Recognition, IEEE PAMI, Vol 21, No. 3, pp 263-270, 1999.
11. A. Malaviya and L. Peters, Fuzzy Handwriting Description Language: FOHDEL, Patt. Reco. Vol 33, pp 119-131, 2000.
12. A.C.Downton et al., Progress in Handwriting Recognition, World Scientific, Colchester, 1996.
13. M. Parizeau et al., A Fuzzy-syntactic approach to allograph modeling for cursive script recognition, IEEE PAMI, Vol 17, No. 7, pp 707-712, 1995.
14. A.C. Shaw, A Formal picture description scheme as a basis for picture processing systems, Info. Control, Vol 14, pp 9-52, 1969.
15. M.Jamshidi, Fuzzy logic Software and Hardware, in M. Jamshidi et al (Eds), Fuzzy Logic and Control, Prentice-Hall, Englewood Cliffs, NJ 1993, pp 112-148.
16. E.T.Lee and ʟ. Zadeh, Note on fuzzy languages, Inf. Sc, Vol 1, pp 421-434, 1969.
17. M. Mizumoto et al., Some considerations on Fuzzy Automata, J. Comp. Sys. Sc. Vol 3, pp 409-422, 1969.

18. L.Zadeh, The key roles of information granulation and fuzzy logic in human reasoning, concept formulation and computing with words, Fifth FUZZ-IEEE, Lousiana, pp 1, 1996.

19. R.M.Suresh, Application of Fuzzy Technique to Pattern Recognition Problems, Ph.D. Thesis, M.S.University, 2000.

20. V.K.Govindan, Computer Recognition of Handprinted characters: An Automated approach to the design of Recognizers, Ph.D. Thesis, IISc., Bangalore, 1988.

21. S.N.S.Rajasekaran and B.L.Deekshatulu, Recognition of printed Telugu characters, Comp. Graphics Image Process.Vol 6,pp.335-360,1977.

22. R.M.K. Sinha and H.C. Karnick, PLANG based specification of patters with variations for pictorial databases, Comp. Vision Graph Image Process Vol 43, pp. 98-110, July 1988

23. F.Casacuberta et al., A parsing algorithm for weighted grammars and substring recognition, G.Ferrate et al (Eds), Syntactic and Structural Pattern Recognition, Springer-Verlag, New York, 1988.

24. P. Chinnusamy et al., "Recognition of Handprinted Tamil Characters", Pattern Recognition Vol. 12, pp141-152, 1980.

25. K.S.Fu, Syntactic Pattern Recognition and Apllications, Prentice-Hall, Englewood Cliffs, NJ, 1982.

26. P. Siy and C.S. Chen,"Fuzzy Logic for handwritten Numerical Character recognition", IEEE SMC 1,1,pp. 61- 66,1971

27. M.Gold, Language Identification in the limit, Info.Cont.,Vol 10, pp 447-474, 1967.

28. J.J.Hornings, A study of A grammatical Inference, Technical Report No CS 139, CSE Department, Stanford University, August 1969.

29. T.W.L. Pao, A solution of the syntactical Induction-inference problem for a nontrivial Subset of Context-free Languages, Report No 70-19, Department of Electrical Engineering, University of Pennsylvania, August 1969.

Optical Flow Estimation Using Genetic Algorithms

Marco Tagliasacchi

Politecnico di Milano,
Dipartimento di Elettronica e Informazione,
Piazza Leonardo da Vinci, 32,
20133 Milano, Italy
marco.tagliasacchi@polimi.it

Abstract. This paper illustrates a new optical flow estimation technique, which builds upon a genetic algorithm (GA). First, the current frame is segmented into generic shape regions, using only brightness information. For each region a two-parameter motion model is estimated using a GA. The fittest individuals identified at the end of this step are used to initialise the population of the second step of the algorithm, which estimates a six-parameter affine motion model, again using a GA. The proposed method is compared against a multiresolution version of the well-known Lukas-Kanade differential algorithm. It proved to yield the same or better results in term of energy of the residual error, yet providing a compact representation of the optical flow, making it particularly suitable to video coding applications.

1 Introduction

We refer to the optical flow as the movement of intensity patterns in the 2D space across adjacent frames of an image sequence. Usually, optical flow is the result of the projection on the 2D image plane of the true 3D motion of the objects composing the scene. Optical flow estimation tries to assign to each pixel of the current frame a two-component velocity vector indicating the position of the same pixel in the reference frame. The knowledge of the optical flow is valuable information in several applications, ranging from video coding, motion-segmentation and video surveillance just to name a few. For the rest of this paper, our main scope will be video coding. It should pointed out that a sensible optical flow might be registered also when objects do not move, due to noise, reflections or illumination changes. In this paper we do not try to track real world moving objects, but simply to provide a motion field which minimizes the energy of prediction residuals, after motion compensation. In literature there exists several methods that attempt to estimate optical flow. [1] contains a complete survey comparing most of them. Following the classification proposed in [1], we might arrange them in the following categories: differential (Lukas-Kanade [2], Horn-Schunk [3], Nagel [4]), region-based matching (Anandan [5]), energy-based (Heeger [6]) and phase correlation algorithms (Fleet-Jepson [7]). We chose the Lukas-Kanade algorithm as a benchmark because it is one of the most performing

V. Di Gesú, F. Masulli, and A. Petrosino (Eds.): WILF 2003, LNAI 2955, pp. 309–316, 2006.
© Springer-Verlag Berlin Heidelberg 2006

according to [1]. Moreover it provides a full coverage of the video frame, at least when implemented in a multiresolution fashion, as explained in greater detail in Section 3. Although our algorithm does not match exactly any of the aforementioned categories, it shares similarities with region-based matching methods. In fact both try to find those velocity vectors that maximize the correlation between a pair of consecutive frames; the substantial differences being that our approach substitutes a full search with a genetic algorithm driven search and square blocks with generic shape regions.

The remainder of this paper is organized as follows: Section 2 clarifies the metrics that can be used to assess the quality of the estimate. Section 3 summarizes the Lukas-Kanade differential algorithm. Section 4 details the genetic algorithm we employed to perform optical flow estimation. Section 5 is dedicated to experimental results. The paper concludes in Section 6.

2   Metrics to Assess Estimation

In order to assess the quality of an estimate we can use one of the following two metrics: either the average angular deviation [1] or the energy of the displaced frame difference. The former can be applied only when we are working on synthetic sequences and the real optical flow is know in advance. The deviation is not computed as the simple Euclidean distance between two velocity vectors $v_a = (v_{ax}, v_{ay})$ and $v_b = (v_{bx}, v_{by})$. Both are first converted to three component vectors having unitary norm, applying the following transformation:

$$v_e = \left(\frac{v_x}{\|v\|}, \frac{v_y}{\|v\|}, \frac{1}{\|v\|} \right) \tag{1}$$

Then, the angular displacement between the two transformed vectors turns out to be:

$$\Psi_e = \arccos \langle v_{ae}, v_{be} \rangle \tag{2}$$

The displaced frame difference (DFD) is computed as the difference between the pixel intensities of the current and the reference frame, following the motion trajectories identified by the optical flow. Stated formally:

$$DFD(x_i, y_i) = I(x_i, y_i, t) - I(x_i - v_{ix}, y - v_{iy}, t - 1) \tag{3}$$

In order to assess the estimate we can either compute the energy of the DFD (MSE - mean square error) or the MAD (mean absolute differences). The lower is the MSE or MAD, the better the estimate. It is worth pointing out that, despite average angular deviation, DFD can be applied as a metrics even if the real optical flow is not known, as it is the case for natural imagery. Furthermore, it is more suitable when we are interested in video coding, since our ultimate goal is to reduce the energy of the prediction residuals.

3   Lukas-Kanade Differential Algorithm

Lukas-Kanade estimation algorithm is one of simplest, yet powerful methods to compute optical flow. For this reason it is one of the most widely used. It builds upon the assumption that the image intensity remains unchanged along motion trajectories:

$$\frac{dI(x,y,t)}{dt} = o(t^2) \tag{4}$$

If we add to this equation the brightness smoothness constraint, i.e. that the brightness variation is linear if we look at an about of the location of interest, we obtain:

$$I_x(x,y)v_x + I_y(x,y)v_y + I_t(x,y) = 0 \tag{5}$$

Where I_x, I_y and I_t respectively the horizontal, vertical and temporal gradients. In order to enforce such a constraint, the sequence is pre-filtered along time and space with a gaussian kernel. Equation (5) represents a line in the velocity space. To find a unique solution we impose that the equation might be satisfied for all pixels falling in a window centered on the current pixel, yielding the following over-determined system (6), whose solution is computed using least squares (8):

$$\begin{bmatrix} I_{x_1} & I_{y_1} \\ I_{x_2} & I_{y_2} \\ \ldots & \ldots \\ I_{x_M} & I_{x_M} \end{bmatrix} \begin{bmatrix} v_x \\ v_y \end{bmatrix} = \begin{bmatrix} -I_{t_1} \\ -I_{t_2} \\ \ldots \\ -I_{t_M} \end{bmatrix} \tag{6}$$

$$Av = b \tag{7}$$

$$v = (A^T A)^{-1} A^T b \tag{8}$$

Lukas-Kanade algorithm suffers from the so-called aperture problem, thus it is unable to produce an accurate result when there is not enough texture within the observation window. In this situation it is able to estimate only the component that is parallel to the local gradient. The minimum eigenvalue of the matrix $A^T A$ is usually employed as a good indicator. Only when it is greater than a given threshold (approx. 1), a full velocity estimate can be accurately computed.

Another drawback of this solution is that it fails to estimate large displacements because the brightness cannot be assumed to be linear far from the observation point. In order to overcome this limitation we can apply a multiresolution approach. A low-pass laplacian pyramid is built and the Lukas-Kanade algorithm runs on the lowest resolution copy. The estimated optical flow is then interpolated and refined at the next level.

4   GA-Based Optical Flow Estimation Algorithm

The proposed algorithm starts by creating a complete segmentation of the current frame, grouping together those pixels sharing the same spatial location and having similar brightness. We accomplished this task performing a watershed algorithm on a morphological gradient, as explained in [10]. Nevertheless, the segmentation method does not affect the optical flow estimation, thus it will not be described further in this paper. It must be pointed out that there is no connection between the segmentation taking place in successive frames. Our goal is not to describe the temporal evolution of these regions, hence identifying the individual moving objects, rather to produce a dense optical field. We assume that motion field is smooth apart from abrupt changes along object boundaries. Therefore each region is a moving object (or, more likely, part of a larger moving object) and its pixels have a coherent motion that can be described with a limited number of parameters. In this paper we suppose a six-parameter affine motion model. An affine model is able to capture the motion of a rigid planar surface, which moves on the 3D space, projected on the 2D image plane. Although real objects are not planar indeed, this is a good approximation, since it allows describing complex motion such as zooming, rotation and shear. Once the six motion parameters are known, the full velocity vectors at any point (x,y) of the current region can be computed as:

$$v_{ix} = a_1 + a_3 \frac{x_i}{C_x} + a_5 \frac{y_i}{C_y} \tag{9}$$

$$v_{iy} = a_2 + a_4 \frac{x_i}{C_x} + a_6 \frac{y_i}{C_y}$$

Where $a = (a_1, a_2, a_3, a_4, a_5, a_6,)$ is the motion model vector, C_x and C_y the region centroid coordinates. Having fixed the motion model, it is matter of finding the vector a which minimize the MSE:

$$a = \arg \ \min \ \frac{1}{M} \sum_{i=1}^{M} |I(x_i, y_i, t) - I(x_i - v_{ix}, y_i - v_{iy}, t - 1)|^2 \tag{10}$$

Where M is the number of pixels in the current region.

This is an unconstrained non-linear optimization problem in a six-variable space, characterized by the following features:

- the function to be minimized should not be expressed in an explicit form
- the search space is large
- there are several local optima
- a good solution, even if it is not the global optimum, might be satisfactory

Although conventional multivariate optimization algorithm might be used, we decided to investigate the adoption of genetic algorithms in order to find the solution, since they are well suited to this class of problems.

In order to speed up the convergence, the algorithm is divided into two phases. Step I computes the estimate of a simpler two-parameter model, which is able to describe only rigid translations. The result is used to initialise Step II, which refines the solution estimating the whole six-parameter affine model. Only the fittest half of the population is selected at the end of Step I, and it is mixed with a randomly generated population.

The individuals of the genetic algorithm are encoded as 48 bits binary string chromosome, where each variable is represented with a precision of 8 bits. This allows to span the interval [-16,+16] with 1/8 pixel accuracy. The initial population is selected at random, dragging samples from a gaussian distribution. The objective function is used to provide a measure of how individuals have performed in the problem domain. In the case of a minimization problem, the fittest individuals will have the lowest numerical value of the associated objective function. In our problem scope, the objective function is the energy of the DFD, computed for a given vector $a = (a_1, a_2, a_3, a_4, a_5, a_6,)$:

$$f(x) = \frac{1}{M} \sum_{i=1}^{M} |I(x_i, y_i, t) - I(x_i - v_{ix}, y_i - v_{iy}, t - 1)|^2 = \tag{11}$$

$$= \frac{1}{M} \sum_{i=1}^{M} |I(x_i, y_i, t) +$$

$$- I(x_i - (a_1 + a_3 \frac{x_i}{C_x} + a_5 \frac{y_i}{C_y}), y_i - (a_2 + a_4 \frac{x_i}{C_x} + a_6 \frac{y_i}{C_y}), t - 1) \tag{12}$$

We make the assumption that the magnitude of v_x and v_y cannot be larger than 20 pixels. In this case the computation of the objective function is stopped prematurely, in order to speed up the evaluation. The fitness of an individual is calculated from the objective function using linear ranking, with selective pressure equal to 2.

$$F(p_i) = 2 \frac{p_i - 1}{N_{ind} - 1} \tag{13}$$

Where p_i is the position in the ordered population of individual i, using the value of the objective function as a ranking criterion. N_{ind} is the number of individuals in the current population, which has been set to 20 in our experiments. The selection phase extracts the individuals that have to be reproduced using stochastic universal sampling, which guarantees zero bias and minimum spread. A generation gap of 0.9 is chosen in order to maintain the fittest individuals. Multipoint crossover is performed on pairs of chromosomes with probability 0.7. The crossover points have fixed locations, corresponding to the boundaries between the variables, in order to preserve the building blocks. Mutation probability is set to $0.7/L_{ind}$, where L_{ind} is the length of the chromosome. This value is selected as it implies that the probability of any one element of a chromosome being mutated is approximately 0.5 [9]. Each step of the algorithm is teminated when the objective function computed for the fittest individual has not changed during the last 10 iterations. Both Step I and Step II use the same design parameters. Experiments demonstrate that with this configuration, the algorithm converges in less than 40 generations, 20 of which always spent to validate the solution. Figure 3 shows an example that illustrates the convergence.

Most of the complexity load is owed to the computation of the objective function, which grows linearly with the area of the regions. However, once the segmentation of the current frame is performed, the algorithm works independently on each region. This observation suggests that it suits a parallel implementation, where the number of simultaneous tasks matches the number of regions. Therefore, the time complexity turns out to be of the order $O(LNM/K)$, where L is the average number of iteration for the genetic algorithm to converge, N and M respectively the frame height and width, while K is the number of regions. Our algorithm does not require demanding memory requirements, since only two frame buffers are used at a time to store the current and the reference frame.

With respect to Lukas-Kanade, which requires two parameters for each pixel to be represented, our algorithm provides a more compact representation, since it uses only six parameters for each region. Despite of this, experimental results demonstrate that the accuracy of the estimate is not affected, since the affine model seems to capture adequately the motion of most natural scenes. Moreover, the algorithm does not impose the brightness smoothness constraint and it is supposed to work well even in case of poor local texturing. For this reason it always guarantees complete coverage.

5   Experimental Results

In this section we compare the results we have obtained with our algorithm (GA) with the ones of Lukas-Kanade, in its multiresolution version (LK1) as discussed in Section 3. Moreover, in order to make a fair comparison, we computed an a posteriori compact representation of the Lukas-Kanade optical flow, estimating by weighted least squares the affine motion model that best fits the data in each segmented region. In order to improve the estimate of the affine model, each pixel is assigned a weight reflecting its reliability. Pixels located close to the border and those having a non-textured neighbourhood receive a lower weight. Segmentation and optical flow estimation are performed independently and they are merged only at last. We will refer to this variant as LK2.

We performed our tests on the synthetically generated Yosemite sequence (see Figure 1). Since the real optical flow is available, we are able to compute both the MSE of the DFD and the angular deviation, which are listed in Table 1. The tabulated value of the angular deviation for LK1 differs from the one reported in literature ([1]) for two reasons: a) the latter refers to a coverage of only 40% obtained with a single resolution approach; b) a 15 pixel wide border, i.e. where most of the error is concentrated, is not considered. GA and LK1 outperform LK2 in terms of MSE. With respect to the average angular deviation, GA performs better than LK1. A closer inspection demonstrates that this is especially true along image borders. LK2 perform significantly better using this metrics. The reason is that the regularization performed by the affine model filters out outliers, improving the estimate at a cost of higher MSE. These results are confirmed by those obtained for the Foreman sequence (see Figure 2). In this case, GA reaches a MSE lower than LK1, while LK2 performs slightly worse.

We did another experiment aimed at determining the optimal stopping criterion. We stated that both Step I and Step II stop when the best individual objective function has not changed during the last G generations. Figure 4 shows the relation existing between G and the quality of the estimate for the Foreman sequence. By increasing G the average number of generations for each region and the time needed to complete the algorithm grow. For this reason, setting G equal to 10 is a good trade-off between quality and complexity.

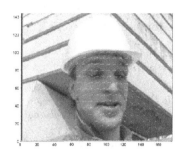

Fig. 1. Estimated optical flow of the Yosemite sequence, frame 10

Fig. 2. Estimated optical flow of the Foreman sequence, frame 193

Table 1. Yosemite

	Avg. Ang. Dev.	MSE
GA	12.1288	50.3302
LK1	14.0553	50.2521
LK2	9.7363	54.1814

Table 2. Foreman

	MSE
GA	25.9856
LK1	29.2421
LK2	34.6167

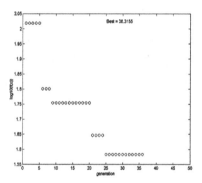

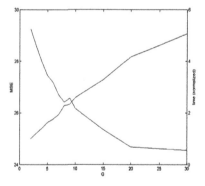

Fig. 3. Sample generations. Objective function value of the fittest individual. Red: Step I, blue: Step II.

Fig. 4. Effect of the stopping criterion G on the MSE and time complexity

6   Conclusions

In this paper we introduced a new optical flow estimation method that takes advantage of a two-step genetic algorithm. Experiments proved that it yields results comparable to the Lukas-Kanade algorithm, yet providing a compact representation of the optical flow, suitable for coding applications. We are currently working on a multiresolution version of the algorithm aiming at speeding up the computation. The presented method will be used as the core component of a motion segmentation algorithm whose goal is to isolate distinct moving objects composing the scene.

References

[1] J.L. Barron, D.J. Fleet, and S.S. Beauchemin, "Performance of Optical Flow Techniques". *In International Journal of Computer Vision*, February 1994, vol. 12(1), pp. 43–77.

[2] B. Lucas and T. Kanade. "An iterative image registration technique with an application to stereo vision". *In Proceedings of the International Joint Conference on Artificial Intelligence*, 1981.

[3] B.K.P. Horn, B.G. Schunk. "Determining optical flow". *In AI 17*, pp. 185-204, 1981

[4] H.H. Nagel. "On the estimation of optical flow: Relations between different approaches and somenew results". *In AI 33*, pp.299-324, 1987

[5] P. Anandan. "A computational framework and an algorithm for the measurement of visual motion". *In Int. J. Comp. Vision 2*, pp.283-310, 1989

[6] D.J. Heeger, "Optical flow using spatiotemporal filters". *In Int. J. Comp. Vision 1*, pp.279-302, 1988

[7] D.J. Fleet, A.D. Jepson. "Computation of component image velocity from local phase information". *In Int. J. Comp. Vision 5*, pp.77-104, 1990

[8] J.R. Bergen, P. Anandan, K.J. Hanna, and R. Hingorani. "Hierarchical model-based motion estimation". *In Proceedings of the European Conference on Computer Vision*, 1992.

[9] L. Booker, "Improving search in genetic algorithms". *In Genetic Algorithms and Simulated Annealing*, L. Davis (Ed.), pp. 61-73, Morgan Kaufmann Publishers, 1987.

[10] D. Wang, "A multiscale gradient algorithm for image segmentation using watersheds". *In Pattern Recognition*, vol. 678, no. 12, pp. 2043-2052, 1997

Neural Network Ensemble and Support Vector Machine Classifiers: An Application to Remote Sensed Data

C. Tarantino, A. D'Addabbo, L. Castellana, P. Blonda,
G. Pasquariello, N. Ancona, and G. Satalino

ISSIA-CNR, Via Amendola 166/5, 70126 Bari, Italy
Tel. +39 080 5481612
blonda@ba.issia.cnr.it

Abstract. This paper presents a comparative evaluation between two classification strategies for the analysis of remote sensed data. The first is based on the combination of the outputs of a neural network (NN) ensemble, the second concerns the application of Support Vector Machine (SVM) classifiers. Emphasis is given to the understanding of the limits and the advantages of the two strategies to design a classifier system able to provide high generalization capability. Two sets of experiments have been carried out to classify benchmark remote sensed data. In the first set a Fuzzy Integral has been used to combine the outputs of neural classifiers in an ensemble. In the second set of experiments SVM classifiers have been trained and tested on the same data set. The comparative analysis evidences that SVM classifiers outperform an ensemble of classifiers, whose partial results are combined by a Fuzzy Integral. The training complexity of SVMs seems, however, to be a limitation to the extensive use of SVMs in complex multisource-multitemporal data classification.

Keywords: SVM, Neural Network Ensemble, Fuzzy Integral, remote sensed data.

1 Introduction

To improve the generalization performance of a classification system two methodologies are investigated in recent literature. On one hand some authors suggest to combine the decisions of several classifiers in an ensemble rather than using the output of the best classifier [1], [2], [3]. In [4] - [7] non linear Fuzzy Integrals (F.I.), such as Choquet and Sugeno F.I. have been used as aggregation tools with quite encouraging results. On the other hand, a new scheme known as Support Vector Machine (SVM) [8] is proposed as a superior machine learning algorithm. The latter technique has been already used in different application domains, such as object detection and text categorization, and has outperformed the traditional NN technique in terms of generalization capability. In previous papers, the generalization performances of SVM classifiers have been generally compared with those of a single Multy-Layer Perceprton (MLP) neural classifier

V. Di Gesú, F. Masulli, and A. Petrosino (Eds.): WILF 2003, LNAI 2955, pp. 317–323, 2006.
© Springer-Verlag Berlin Heidelberg 2006

[9, 10]. The objective of this work is to compare the results of SVM classifiers with those obtained after a non linear combination of the outputs of several MLP modules in an ensemble. A benchmark remote sensed data set [11] has been used for the comparative evaluation in two sets of experiments: the first set considered the Sugeno and Choquet F.I. as non-linear combiners of the outputs of a MLP based NN ensemble; the second set has used SVM classifiers to analyze the same data. The rest of the paper is organized as follows. The second paragraph provides a brief description of the Choquet Fuzzy Integral combiner and SVM classifiers. The third section reports details on the data sets. The fourth paragraph illustrates the results. The last paragraph contains the conclusions.

2   Methodology

2.1   Non Linear Combination

The Fuzzy Integral (FI) has been already used for the combination of neural classifiers's output in the analysis of remote sensed data in [6] and [7]. In the cited papers the results have been compared with those of a single neural classifier.

In the following, only a brief description of both the Sugeno and the Choquet FIs is provided, whereas a more detailed description can be found in [5]. A FI is a non linear functional that is defined with respect to a fuzzy measure. Let $X = x_1, x_2, ..., x_n$ an ensemble of n classifiers in an ensemble and P(X) denote the power set of X or the set of all subset of X. Let $\mathbf{y}_k$ be an input pattern vector, $\mathbf{t}_k$ the associated target vector of a L-class problem, with k=1,..,L. A set function $g : P(x) \rightarrow [0, 1]$ is called a fuzzy measure over a set X if

$$g(\emptyset) = 0 \tag{1}$$

$$g(X) = 1 \tag{2}$$

$$if A, B \subset P(X) \wedge A \subset B \Rightarrow g(A) \leq g(B) \tag{3}$$

Because of monotonicity, the measure of union cannot be computed from the component meaures. Then, Sugeno introduced the so called λ fuzzy measure satisfying the additional properties: for all A, B with $A \cap B = \emptyset$ then

$$g(A \cup B) = g(A) + g(B) + \lambda g(A)g(B) \qquad for some \; \lambda > -1 \tag{4}$$

The value of λ can be found from g(X) = 1, which is equivalent to solving

$$\lambda + 1 = \prod_{i=1}^{n}(1 + \lambda g_i) \tag{5}$$

Let $A_i = x_i, x_{i+1}, ..., x_n$. When g is a λ fuzzy measure, the value of $g(A_i)$ can be computed recursively as:

$$g(A_n) = g(\{x_n\}) = g_n \tag{6}$$

$$g(A_i) = g_i + g(A_{i+1}) + \lambda g_i g(A_{i+1}) \qquad for \ 1 \leq i < n \qquad (7)$$

When a fuzzy measure is available on a finite set X, it is possible to express the Fuzzy Integral as a computational scheme to integrate all values from the individual subset nonlinearly. This means that the fuzzy integral relies on the concept of a fuzzy measure, which provides the degree to which some subset of elements satisfy some characteristic. When X is a finite set, as in the case of the classifiers in the ensemble considered in this work, the Sugeno FI [5] can be expressed as

$$e = \max_{i=1}^{n}[\min(h(x_i), g(A_i))] \qquad (8)$$

where $h : X \rightarrow [0, 1]$ is a function that denotes the decision for a class, given an input pattern vector $\mathbf{y}_k$, when the source x_i is considered. Whereas, the expression of the Choquet FI used in this work is reported in the following

$$E_g(h) = \sum_{i=1}^{n}(h(x_i)[g(A_i) - g(A_{i-1})] \qquad (9)$$

Let g_i denote the degree of importance of each specific source. In this work g_i is set equal to the value of the Overall Classification Accuracy obtained on the test data set by the *ith* classifier in the ensemble, once trained.

2.2 Support Vector Machine (SVM) Classifiers

The considerations in the following hold for the case of a two-classes classification problem, but can be generalized to a multi-class problem. A more detailed description of SVM classifiers can be found in [8]. Given a set of N examples $\mathbf{x}_i$ with their target $y_i = \{-1, +1\}$, the SVM approach consists in mapping the data in a higher dimensional feature space, where it is looked for a separation between the two classes by means of an hyper plane defined by

$$f(x) = w^* \cdot \Phi(x) + b^* \qquad (10)$$

and the membership decision rule is according to sign[f(**x**)]. Searching for a decision function $f(x_i) = y_i$, if this function exists, canonically implies

$$y_i(w \cdot \Phi(x_i) + b) \geq 1 \qquad i = 1, ...N \qquad (11)$$

In many practical applications, this separating hyper-plane does not exist because the data are not linearly separable. To deal with non separable data the so-called slack variables

$$\xi_i \geq 0 \qquad i = 1, ...N - 1 \qquad (12)$$

have been introduced, to get

$$y_i(w \cdot \Phi(x_i) + b) \geq 1 - \xi_i \qquad i = 1, ...N \qquad (13)$$

This approach is based on the Structural Risk Minimization (SRM) principle [8], i.e. the minimization of the error probability on unknown patterns, instead the usual approach is to minimize the empirical risk, that turns out not to guarantee a small actual risk (i.e. a small error on the training set does not imply a small error on a test set). According to the SRM principle, the optimal hyper-plane is the one that minimizes a cost function that expresses a combination of two criteria: margin maximization and training error minimization. It is defined as:

$$\Psi(w, \xi) = \frac{1}{2}\|w\|^2 + C \sum_{i=1}^{N} \xi_i \qquad (14)$$

subject to the constraints previously set, with C as regularization parameter. The above optimisation problem can be reformulated introducing Lagrange multipliers α_i and solving its dual problem [8]. The final result is expressed as a function of the data in the original feature space:

$$f(x) = \sum_{i=1}^{l} \alpha_i y_i \Phi(x_i) \cdot \Phi(x) + b^* \qquad (15)$$

where the training examples x_i corresponding to non zero multipliers α_i are the so-called Support Vectors: all the remaining examples of the training set are irrelevant. In some cases, the calculation of the dot product $\Phi(x_i) \cdot \Phi(x)$ can be onerous, but can be reduced by using a suitable function K satisfying the conditions of the Mercer's theorem so that it corresponds to some inner product in the transformed higher dimensional feature space

$$K(x_i, x) = \Phi(x_i) \cdot \Phi(x) \qquad (16)$$

A possible choice of K can be a polynomial expression, where k is a scale factor, such as:

$$K(x, y) = \frac{(x \cdot y)^d}{\kappa} \qquad (17)$$

3   Data

A benchmark data set was extracted from the IEEE GRSS Data Fusion reference database [11]. The data set, GRSS_DFC_0006, refers to an agricultural area near the village of Feltwell (UK). It consists of multisensor remote sensing data, acquired respectively by a radar sensor, i.e. a PLC-band fully polarimetric NASA/JPL SAR sensor and an optical Airborne Thematic Mapper scanner (ATM). Each pixel of a scene, 250x350 pixels wide, was characterized by 15 bands at: the first 9 bands from SAR sensor, the latter from ATM. Five land cover classes were considered: sugar beets, stubble, bare soil, potatoes and carrots. Some agricultural fields of known ground truth were randomly subdivided into two disjoint sets: 5124 examples were extracted from one set for training and 5820 from the fields of the other set were used for testing the classification systems. To train the SVM, the training set was subdivided in a sub-training data set, corresponding to the 70% of the whole training pixels and a validation set, the remaining 30%. The validation set was used for parameter selection, as in [12]

4   Experimental Settings and Results

4.1   Classifiers Combination Rules

In the first set of experiments, an ensemble of five MLP neural network classifiers, was considered. For each classifier in the ensemble, the number of neurons in the input layer and in the output layer was the same, i.e. 15 (the features) and 5 (the classes) respectively. The same learning parameters, i.e. learning rate equal to 0.01 and momentum equal to 0.02 were used. Only the number of nodes in the hidden layer of each classifier, varied, as follows: 5, 10, 15, 20 and 25 respectively with. The results obtained by each MLP module of the ensemble both in training and testing are reported in Table 1. The results are expressed as the percentage of the Overall Accuracy (OA). The average OA obtained in test by the whole set of classifiers was equal to 91.4%. After training, the outputs $h(x_i)$, $i = 1, \ldots, n$, of the five modules were used to train the non-linear combiners, i.e. Sugeno and Choquet F. The density values gi in the computation of FIs were set equal to the OA value, as extracted from the classification confusion matrix, obtained by each classifier in test. The results of the application of the non linear combination of the 5 MLP modules' outputs are reported in Table 2 for the Sugeno and Choquet F.I., in second line and third line, respectively. As evidenced in Table 2, the combination results by both F.I formulations are equivalent in test to the OA percentage of the best classifier in the ensemble.

Table 1. OA (%)in training and test by 5 MLP classifiers, as a function of hidden neurons number

MLP-OA(%)				
5H	10H	15H	20H	25H
TR 95.4	96.2	96.4	96.4	96.3
TE 88.8	92.0	92.4	91.8	91.9
TEST AVERAGE OA: 91.4				

Table 2. OA(%) in test obtained by the different methodologies

COMBINATION OA(%)	TE
SUGENO F.I.	92.4
CHOQUET F.I.	92.3

4.2   SVM Classifiers

In the second set of experiments SVM classifiers were applied in the recognition of the same classes. First, the SVM classifiers were trained to solve a set of 1-class problems. For each class, different trials were made by varying the polynomial degree d and the regularization parameter C to select the best SVM architecture for the specific class. For a fixed d, a smaller C value was preferred when the same number of errors was made, in order to reduce the VC-dimension. Once trained, each of the 5 SVM classifiers assigned a score to a new input pattern. In order to solve the multi-class problem with SVM classifiers the final class selection was dependent on the maximum score provided by the set of SVMs. The validation set was used to select the SVM parameters for each class. In particular, for each class the values of the d and C parameters are reported in Table 3, second and third column, respectively. Once the selection was made, the complete set of sub-training and validation data was fed to the SVM classifiers to extract the Support Vectors (SV). The number of SV for each class is reported in the last column of Table 3.

Table 3. Parameters selected for each class

CLASS	d	C	SV
1	5	500	326
2	6	500	299
3	6	1000	306
4	6	500	327
5	5	1000	316

Once trained, the SVM classifiers were used to classify test data. The results obtained in training and testing were equal to 99.8% and to 95.2%, on training and testing data, respectively. This performance was better than those obtained by the FI combination schemes, which provided an OA in test equal to 92.3%.

5   Conclusions

In this work, two sets of classification experiments were carried out on the same benchmark remote sensed data set. With respect to the application of a non-linear combination scheme, which is not based on the conditional independence of data as in the case of linear combination rules, the percentage of the OA resulted similar to the one of the best classifier in the ensemble, but it was slight better than the average OA of the single classifiers. The performance of the FI was the same for both Sugeno and Choquet formulations considered to analyze the data set. The comparison results seem to confirm that SVM classifiers can provide not only higher generalization performance than a single neural MLP classifier, but also better results than those that can be achieved by combining the partial output results of several classifiers in a neural ensemble. Still the multi-class problem and consequently the high computational cost required in training, represents a limitation in the application of SVMs to the analysis of high dimensional remote sensing data sets.

Acknowledgments

The authors would like to acknowledge the GRSS-DFC for providing the "grss_dfc_0006" data set. The research was carried with the founding of CEE project LEWIS-EVG1-CT-2001-00055.

References

1. J. Kittler, M. Hatef, R. Duin, J. Matas: On combining classifiers. IEEE Trans. Pattern Anal. Mach. Intell. vol.20 no.3 **226-238** March 1998
2. L.K. Hansen, P. Salamon: Neural network ensembles. IEEE Trans. Pattern Anal. Mach. Intell. vol.12 no.10 **993-1001** October 1990
3. G. Giacinto, F. Roli, L. Buzzone: Combination of neural and statistical algorithms for supervised classification of remote-sensing images. Pattern Recognition Letters no. 21 **385-397** 2000
4. M. Grabish and J. M. Nicolas: Classification by Fuzzy Integral: performance and tests. Fuzzy Sets and Syst. vol. 65, **255-271**, 1994
5. Jung-Hsien Chiang: Choquet Fuzzy Integral-Based Hierarchical Networks for Decision Analysis. IEEE Trans. on Fuzzy Sets Systems vol. 7 No. 1 February 1999
6. P. Blonda, C. Tarantino, A. D'Addabbo, G. Satalino: Combination of Multiple Classifiers by Fuzzy Integrals: an application to Synthetic Aperture Radar (SAR) data. IEEE Proc. of 10th Inter. Conf. On Fuzzy Systems, Melbourne, Australia, 2001, IEEE catalog No. OICH37297C, ISBN 0-7803-7295-6
7. A.S. Kumar, S.K. Basu and K.L. Majumdar: Robust classification of multispectral data using multiple neural networks and Fuzzy Integral. IEEE Trans. On Geosci. And Remote Sensing vol. 35 no.3 may 1997
8. V. Vapnik: The Nature of Statistical Learning Theory. Springer 1995
9. B. Schoelkopf: Support Vector learning thesis. Oldenbourg Verlag Munich 1997
10. C. Huang, L.S. Davis, J.R.G. Townshend: An assessment of SVM machines for land cover classification. Int. Journal of Remote Sensing vol. 23 no.4 **725-749**
11. IEEE GRSS Data Fusion reference database (http://www.dfc-grss.org/), 2001. Data set GRSS_DFC_0006
12. Chih-Wei Hsu, Chih-Jen Lin: A comparison of methods for Multiclass Support Vector Machines. IEEE Trans. On Neural Network vol.13 no.2 **415-425** March 2002

Combining Neighbourhood-Based and Histogram Similarity Measures for the Design of Image Quality Measures

Dietrich Van der Weken, Mike Nachtegael, and Etienne Kerre

Fuzziness & Uncertainty Modelling, Ghent University,
Krijgslaan 281 (building S9), 9000 Ghent, Belgium
{dietrich.vanderweken, mike.nachtegael, etienne.kerre}@rug.ac.be
http://fuzzy.rug.ac.be

Abstract. Fuzzy techniques can be applied in several domains of image processing. In this paper we will show how fuzzy set theory is used in establishing measures for image quality evaluation. Objective quality measures or measures of comparison are of great importance in the field of image processing. These measures serve as a tool to evaluate and to compare different algorithms designed to solve problems, such as noise reduction, deblurring, compression ... Consequently these measures serve as a basis on which one algorithm is preferred to another. It is well-known that classical quality measures, such as the MSE (mean square error) or the PSNR (peak signal to noise ratio), do not always correspond to visual observations. Therefore, several researchers are - and have been - looking for new quality measures, better adapted to human perception.

In [1] we illustrated how similarity measures, originally introduced to express the degree of comparison between two fuzzy sets, can be used in the construction of neighbourhood-based similarity measures which outperform the MSE in the sense of image quality evaluation because the results of the neighbourhood-based similarity measures coincide better with human perception. In this paper we show how the neighbourhood-based similarity measures can be combined with similarity measures for histogram comparison in order to improve the perceptive behaviour of these similarity measures.

1 Introduction

Objective image quality measures play important roles in various image processing applications. Basically, we can distinguish two main approaches in image quality assessment. First of all, there are mathematically defined measures such as the widely used mean square error (MSE), peak signal to noise ratio (PSNR) and root mean square error (RMSE). Secondly, there exists a class of measurement methods which try to incorporate characteristics of the human visual system in order to construct image quality measures which better coincide with human perception. Unfortunately, none of these complicated objective measures has shown any clear advantage over simple mathematical measures such as MSE and PSNR.

V. Di Gesú, F. Masulli, and A. Petrosino (Eds.): WILF 2003, LNAI 2955, pp. 324–331, 2006.

In order to design an objective quality measure we investigated [3, 4] the applicability of similarity measures, resulting from fuzzy set theory, to images. In this way we obtained several similarity measures which can be applied successfully to images. However, the pixel-based similarity measures still have some drawbacks in the sense of image quality evaluation [1]. In order to improve the perceptive behaviour of the pixel-based similarity measures we used the pixel-based measures to design neighbourhood-based measures which also incorporate homogeneity in the image quality evaluation procedure [1]. In [2] we also illustrated how similarity measures can be applied to histograms of images. Also in this case, the similarity measures do not always yield broad satisfactory results.

In this paper we propose image quality measures which are based on a twofold usage of similarity measures resulting from fuzzy set theory. First, we make use of the neighbourhood-based similarity measures introduced in [1], and second, we employ similarity measures which will be applied to histograms of images. In this way we obtain image quality measures which outperform the MSE and neighbourhood-based similarity measures in the sense of image quality evaluation.

After some preliminaries regarding similarity measures in Section 2, we will give a brief overview of the construction of the neighbourhood-based similarity measures in Section 3. The applicability of similarity measures to histograms of images is reviewed in Section 4. After this, the construction of the new image quality measure is outlined in Section 5. Finally, we illustrate the outperforming behaviour of the new image quality measures with some examples in Section 6.

2   Preliminaries

2.1   Fuzzy Sets and Digital Images

A fuzzy set A in a universe X is characterized by a $X - [0, 1]$ mapping χ_A, which associates with every element x in X a degree of membership $\chi_A(x)$ of x in the fuzzy set A. In the following, we will denote the degree of membership by $A(x)$. Note that a digital grey-scale image can be identified with a fuzzy set that takes values on the grid points (x, y), with $x, y \in \mathbb{N}$, $0 \le x \le M$ and $0 \le y \le N$ $(M, N \in \mathbb{N})$. Therefore, for two grey-scale images A and B, we have that $A, B \in \mathcal{F}(X)$, with $X = \{(x, y) | 0 \le x \le M, 0 \le y \le N\}$ a discrete set of image points, where $\mathcal{F}(X)$ is the class of fuzzy sets over the universe X. The class of crisp sets over the universe X will be denoted by $\mathcal{C}(X)$.

2.2   Similarity Measures

In the literature a lot of measures are proposed to express the similarity or equality between fuzzy sets. There is no unique definition, but the most frequently used is the following. A similarity measure [5] is a fuzzy binary relation in $\mathcal{F}(X)$, i.e. a $\mathcal{F}(X) \times \mathcal{F}(X) \to [0, 1]$ mapping that is reflexive, symmetric and min-transitive. However, not every measure in the literature satisfies this definition. Therefore, a similarity measure will here be understood as a measure we can use to compare fuzzy sets, or objects which can be identified with fuzzy sets.

3 Neighbourhood-Based Similarity Measures Which Incorporate Homogeneity of the Images

3.1 Overview of Pixel-Based Similarity Measures Which Are Applicable to Digital Images

The following similarity measures [1] out of more than 40 similarity measures were found to be appropriate for the construction of neighbourhood-based similarity measures:

$$S_1(A, B) = 1 - \left(\frac{1}{MN} \sum_{x \in X} |A(x) - B(x)|^r \right)^{\frac{1}{r}}, \text{ with } r \in \mathbb{N} \backslash \{0\}$$

$$S_3(A, B) = 1 - \frac{\sum\limits_{x \in X} |A(x) - B(x)|}{\sum\limits_{x \in X} (A(x) + B(x))}$$

$$S_4(A, B) = 1 - \frac{1}{MN \cdot 2 \ln 2} \cdot \sum_{x \in X} \left[(A(x) - B(x)) \cdot \ln \left(\frac{1 + A(x)}{1 + B(x)} \right) \right.$$
$$\left. + (B(x) - A(x)) \cdot \ln \left(\frac{2 - A(x)}{2 - B(x)} \right) \right]$$

$$S_6(A, B) = \frac{|A \cap B|}{|A \cup B|}$$

$$S_{6c}(A, B) = \frac{|A^c \cap B^c|}{|A^c \cup B^c|}$$

$$S_7(A, B) = \frac{|A \cap B|}{\max(|A|, |B|)}$$

$$S_{7c}(A, B) = \frac{|A^c \cap B^c|}{\max(|A^c|, |B^c|)}$$

$$S_{12}(A, B) = \frac{|(A \Delta B)^c|}{\max(|(A \backslash B)^c|, |(B \backslash A)^c|)}$$

$$S_{I_3}(A, B) = \frac{|(A \cap B) \cap (A^c \cap B^c)|}{|(A \cup B) \cap (A^c \cup B^c)|}$$

$$S_{I_{3c}}(A, B) = \frac{|(A^c \cap B^c) \cup (A \cap B)|}{|(A^c \cup B^c) \cup (A \cup B)|}$$

$$S_{18c}(A, B) = 1 - \frac{1}{MN} \cdot \sum_{x \in X} (A \Delta B)(x)$$

$$S_{20}(A, B) = \frac{1}{MN} \sum_{x \in X} \left[\frac{\min(A(x), B(x))}{\max(A(x), B(x))} \right].$$

3.2 Construction of Neighbourhood-Based Similarity Measures

In this section we review shortly how to construct neighbourhood-based similarity measures based on homogeneity. We start with calculating the similarity between disjoint image parts of the two images A and B. Therefore we divide both images A and B in disjoint 4×4 image parts and we calculate the similarity between each of the 4×4 image parts. To calculate the similarity between two image parts we simply apply the above pixel-based similarity measures resulting from fuzzy set theory to both image parts. Suppose the image is divided in N image parts of size 4×4, and the similarity between the image part A_i of image A and the image part B_i of image B is denoted by $S(A_i, B_i)$, then the similarity between the two images A and B is given by the weighted average of the similarities in the disjoint image parts. So, we have that

$$S(A, B) = \frac{1}{N} \sum_{i=1}^{N} w_i \cdot S(A_i, B_i),$$

where the similarity $S(A_i, B_i)$ is calculated using the similarity measures from Section 2 restricted to the image parts A_i and B_i and the weight w_i is defined as the similarity between the homogeneity h_{A_i} of image part i in image A and the homogeneity h_{B_i} of image part i in image B. The homogeneity h_{A_i} of an image part i in image A is computed as the similarity between the pixel in the image part with maximum intensity and the pixel in the image part with minimum intensity, using the similarity function s which is defined as

$$s(x, y) = \begin{cases} 1 - \frac{|x-y|}{a} & \text{if } |x - y| < a \\ 0 & \text{elsewhere} \end{cases},$$

where $1/2$ is a typical value for a.
So we have that

$$h_{A_i} = s(\max_{(x,y) \in A_i} A(x, y), \min_{(x,y) \in A_i} A(x, y))$$

and the weight w_i is then defined as follows: $w_i = s(h_{A_i}, h_{B_i})$.

Using the similarity measures from Section 4 to calculate the similarity between the image parts we obtain 13 new similarity measures which also satisfy the relevant properties and will be denoted, respectively, S_1^n, S_2^n, S_3^n, S_4^n, S_{4c}^n, S_5^n, S_{5c}^n, S_6^n, S_{6c}^n, S_7^n, S_8^n, S_9^n, and S_{10}^n, where n is the total number of elements in the universe on which the sets fuzzy A_i and B_i are defined. So, if we use 4×4 image parts, we have that $n = 16$ (using other neighbourhoods yields similar results).

4   Histogram Comparison Using Similarity Measures

Instead of a straightforward application of similarity measures to images, similarity measures can be applied to image histograms. The histogram of an image is a chart that shows the distribution of intensities in the image. So the value of the histogram of an image A in the grey value g is equal to the total number of pixels in the image A with grey value g and will be denoted as $h_A(g)$. The histogram of an image can be transformed into a fuzzy set by dividing the values of the histogram by the maximum number of pixels with the same grey value. In this way the most typical grey value has membership degree 1 in the fuzzy set associated with the histogram. So we have the following expression for the membership degree of the grey value g in the fuzzy set Fh_A associated with the histogram of the image A:

$$Fh_A(g) = \frac{h_A(g)}{\max_g h_A(g)}.$$

Now, similarity measures, introduced to express the degree of comparison between two fuzzy sets, can be applied to the fuzzy sets associated with the histogram of the images. A great advantage is that images with different dimensions can be compared and that the calculation is much faster.

In this case the following similarity measures were found to be appropriate for histogram comparison [2]:

$$H_1(A, B) = 1 - \left(\frac{1}{L} \sum_g |Fh_A(g) - Fh_B(g)|^r \right)^{\frac{1}{r}}, \text{ with } r \in \mathbb{N}\setminus\{0\}$$

$$H_3(A, B) = 1 - \frac{\sum_g |Fh_A(g) - Fh_B(g)|}{\sum_g (Fh_A(g) + Fh_B(g))}$$

$$H_4(A, B) = 1 - \frac{1}{L \cdot 2\ln 2} \cdot \sum_g \left[(Fh_A(g) - Fh_B(g)) \cdot \ln \left(\frac{1 + Fh_A(g)}{1 + Fh_B(g)} \right) \right.$$

$$\left. + (Fh_B(g) - Fh_A(g)) \cdot \ln \left(\frac{2 - Fh_A(g)}{2 - Fh_B(g)} \right) \right].$$

$$H_6(A, B) = \frac{|Fh_A \cap Fh_B|}{|Fh_A \cup Fh_B|}$$

$$H_{6c}(A, B) = \frac{|Fh_A^c \cap Fh_B^c|}{|Fh_A^c \cup Fh_B^c|}$$

$$H_7(A, B) = \frac{|Fh_A \cap Fh_B|}{\max(|Fh_A|, |Fh_B|)}$$

$$H_{7c}(A, B) = \frac{|Fh_A^c \cap Fh_B^c|}{\max(|Fh_A^c|, |Fh_B^c|)}$$

$$H_9(A, B) = \frac{\min(|Fh_A|, |Fh_B|)}{|Fh_A \cup Fh_B|}$$

$$H_{9c}(A, B) = \frac{\min(|Fh_A^c|, |Fh_B^c|)}{|Fh_A^c \cup Fh_B^c|}$$

$$H_{12}(A, B) = \frac{|(Fh_A \triangle Fh_B)^c|}{\max(|(Fh_B \setminus Fh_A)^c|, |(Fh_A \setminus Fh_B)^c|)}$$

$$H_{I_3}(A, B) = \frac{|(Fh_A \cap Fh_B) \cap (Fh_A^c \cap Fh_B^c)|}{|(Fh_A \cup Fh_B) \cap (Fh_A^c \cup Fh_B^c)|}$$

$$H_{I_{3c}}(A, B) = \frac{|(Fh_A \cap Fh_B) \cup (Fh_A^c \cap Fh_B^c)|}{|(Fh_A \cup Fh_B) \cup (Fh_A^c \cup Fh_B^c)|}$$

$$H_{18c}(A, B) = 1 - \frac{1}{L} \cdot \sum_g \min(1, \max(0, Fh_A(g) - Fh_B(g))$$

$$+ \max(0, Fh_B(g) - Fh_A(g))),$$

with L the total number of different grey levels.

5   Combined Image Quality Measures

The new combined image quality measures are simply given by the product of two components:

$$Q_{i,j}(A,B) = S_i^n(A,B) \cdot H_j(A,B).$$

In this way we obtain a mathematically defined universal image quality index. By "universal" we mean that the quality measurement does not depend on the images being tested, the viewing conditions or the individual observers. The universal behaviour of this image quality measure will be illustrated with some examples in Section 6.

6   Some Examples

In order to test the new similarity measures we use images with different types of distortions and we compare the results with the MSE and the pixel-based similarity measures. First, we add a variety of corruptions to the "Hill" image: impulsive salt & pepper noise, additive gaussian noise, enlightening, blur and JPEG compression. The original and distorted images are displayed in Figure 1 and we tuned all the distortions to yield the same MSE relative to the original image. Second, we add the same distortions to a texture image, namely a "straw" image and again we tuned all the distortions to yield the same MSE relative

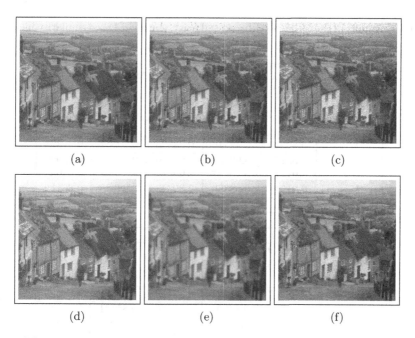

Fig. 1. (a) The original "hill" image; (b) impulsive salt & pepper noise; (c) multiplicative speckle noise; (d) enlightenend; (e) blurred; (f) JPEG-compression

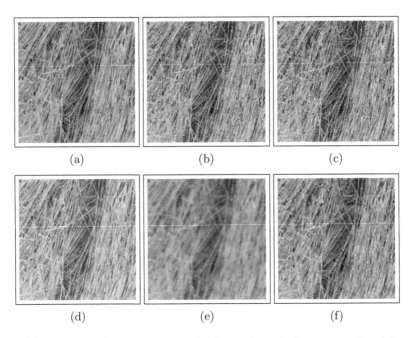

(a)　　　　　　　　　(b)　　　　　　　　　(c)

(d)　　　　　　　　　(e)　　　　　　　　　(f)

Fig. 2. (a) The original "straw" image; (b) impulsive salt & pepper noise; (c) multiplicative speckle noise; (d) enlightenend; (e) blurred; (f) JPEG-compression

Table 1. Results of the MSE, pixel-based and neighbourhood-based similarity measures

	"hill" image				
	(a) vs. (b)	(a) vs. (c)	(a) vs. (d)	(a) vs. (e)	(a) vs. (f)
$MSE(A,B)$	119.31	121.39	120.09	122.52	117.55
S_{1c}	0.83052	0.94279	0.95686	0.92818	0.93664
S_{1c}^n	0.90969	0.67821	0.95681	0.67240	0.69824
H_{1c}	0.90707	0.80235	0.87159	0.89288	0.44939
$Q_{1c,1c}$	0.82515	0.54416	0.83395	0.60037	0.31378
S_4	0.99175	0.92438	0.91070	0.93481	0.92990
S_4^n	0.91170	0.70657	0.99813	0.69608	0.72957
H_{18c}	0.91918	0.93339	0.89343	0.93725	0.66119
$Q_{4,18c}$	0.83801	0.65950	0.89175	0.65240	0.48238
	"straw" image				
$MSE(A,B)$	534.24	536.56	532.74	529.22	534.53
S_{1c}	0.79149	0.88388	0.89578	0.89148	0.89021
S_{1c}^n	0.61535	0.53995	0.77733	0.21463	0.59000
H_{1c}	0.80275	0.75047	0.73571	0.73079	0.86152
$Q_{1c,1c}$	0.49397	0.40521	0.57188	0.15684	0.50829
S_4	0.88267	0.84900	0.83576	0.85181	0.85618
S_4^n	0.67356	0.59885	0.85898	0.23056	0.64898
H_{18c}	0.95034	0.92779	0.85349	0.88699	0.94169
$Q_{4,18c}$	0.64011	0.55560	0.73313	0.20450	0.61113

to the original "straw" image. The original and distorted "straw" images are displayed in Figure 2.

As example, we illustrate the performance of the combined image quality measures $Q_{1c,1c}$, $Q_{4,18c}$ and . The results of the MSE and the similarity measures are displayed in Table 1. In this experiment, the performance of MSE is extremely poor in the sense that images with nearly identical MSE or similarity value are drastically different in perceived quality. In contrast, the proposed quality measure yields significantly better results in comparison with MSE.

7 Conclusion

In this paper we proposed image quality measures which are based on a twofold usage of similarity measures resulting from fuzzy set theory. First, we made use of the neighbourhood-based similarity measures introduced in [1], and secondly, we employed fuzzy inclusion measures which can be applied to histograms of images. In this way we obtained image quality measures which outperform the MSE and neighbourhood-based similarity measures in the sense of image quality evaluation.

References

1. D. Van der Weken, M. Nachtegael, and E.E. Kerre, *Using Similarity Measures and Homogeneity for the Comparison of Images.* Image and Vision Computing, submitted.
2. D. Van der Weken, M. Nachtegael, and E.E. Kerre, *Using Similarity Measures for Histogram Comparison.* Lecture Notes in Artificial Intelligence 2715, pp. 396-403.
3. D. Van der Weken, M. Nachtegael, and E.E. Kerre, *An overview of similarity measures for images.* Proceedings of ICASSP'2002 (IEEE International Conference on Acoustics, Speech and Signal Processing), Orlando, United States, 2002, pp. 3317-3320.
4. D. Van der Weken, M. Nachtegael, and E.E. Kerre, *The applicability of similarity measures in image processing.* To appear in Proceedings of the 8th International Conference on Intelligent Systems and Computer Sciences (December 4-9, 2000, Moscow, Russia); in Russian.
5. L.A. Zadeh, *Similarity Relations and Fuzzy Orderings.* Information Sciences, 1971, 3, 177-200.

An Automated Image Thresholding Scheme for Highly Contrast-Degraded Images Based on a-Order Fuzzy Entropy

Ioannis K. Vlachos and George D. Sergiadis

Telecommunications Laboratory,
Department of Electrical & Computer Engineering,
Faculty of Technology, Aristotle University of Thessaloniki,
University Campus, GR–54124, Thessaloniki, Greece
{ivlachos, sergiadi}@auth.gr
http://mri.ee.auth.gr

Abstract. This paper presents an automated thresholding algorithm for highly contrast-degraded images based on the minimization of the a-order fuzzy entropy of an image. The advantage of the proposed method is that it is based on a flexible parametric criterion function that can be automatically tuned according to the histogram statistics, in order for the thresholded image to preserve as much of the object properties of the initial image as possible, despite the contrast degradation. The effectiveness of the new algorithm is demonstrated by applying our method to different types of contrast-degraded images. Performance assessment is based on comparison of the results derived using the proposed method with the results obtained from various existed image thresholding algorithms using objective empirical discrepancy measures.

1 Introduction

Image thresholding is a fundamental task in image processing and machine vision. Thresholding is a simple classification procedure that assigns each pixel in the image in two classes, foreground and background, according to the intensity value of the pixel. In most real-world images there is ambiguity or fuzziness caused by the overlapping of the two class probability densities.

Fuzzy sets theory [1] provides a flexible framework to cope with the ambiguity and vagueness often present in digital images. Moreover, fuzzy sets theory offers the ability of incorporating expert knowledge into digital image processing systems.

In this paper we present an automated algorithm for thresholding highly contrast-degraded images, using the minimization of a-order fuzzy entropy criterion. Due to its parametric nature, the proposed method has the ability to tune the cost function, which is to be minimized, according to histogram statistics. Therefore, the algorithm can be used in image processing and machine vision applications when thresholding is performed in environments where illumination conditions exhibit frequent and extreme variations.

V. Di Gesú, F. Masulli, and A. Petrosino (Eds.): WILF 2003, LNAI 2955, pp. 332–339, 2006.

2   Fuzzy Sets and Fuzzy Entropies

2.1   Image Representation in the Setting of Fuzzy Sets Theory

Let us consider an image X of size $M \times N$ pixels, having L gray levels g ranging from 0 to $L - 1$. The image X can be considered as an array of fuzzy singletons. Each element of the array denotes the membership value $\mu_X(g_{ij})$ of the gray level g_{ij}, corresponding to the (i, j)-th pixel, according to a predefined image property, such as brightness, homogeneity, edgeness, etc. Using the fuzzy sets notation the image can be represented as:

$$X = \{\mu_X(g_{ij})/g_{ij} \mid i = 0, 1, \ldots, M - 1, \; j = 0, 1, \ldots, N - 1\} . \tag{1}$$

2.2   The a-Order Entropy of a Fuzzy Set

As an extension of Shannon's entropy, Renyi [2] defined the a-order entropy H_a of a probability distribution $(p_1, p_2, \ldots, p_n)$. Bhandari and Pal [3] introduced the a-order fuzzy entropy, which in the case of an image X is given by:

$$H_a(X) = \sum_{g=0}^{L-1} h_X(g) e_a(g) , \tag{2}$$

where $a(\neq 1)$ is a positive real parameter, $h_X(g)$ is the normalized frequency of occurrence of the gray level g, and $e_a(g)$ is defined as:

$$e_a(g) = \frac{1}{1-a} \log_2[\mu_X^a(g) + [1 - \mu_X(g)]^a] . \tag{3}$$

It should be mentioned that the a-order fuzzy entropy is a one-parameter generalization of the De Luca and Termini entropy H_{LT} [4] since $\lim_{a \to 1} H_a = H_{LT}$. Fig. ?? illustrates (3) for various values of the parameter a.

3   Proposed Method

3.1   Fuzzy Image Thresholding

For an image X defined as in (1) the membership function $\mu_X(g)$ can be defined to denote the relationship of gray level g belonging to one of the two classes, background and foreground. Given a certain threshold T, the membership function is defined as:

$$\mu_X(g) = \begin{cases} \dfrac{1}{1 + |g - m_0(T)|/D} & \text{if } g \leqslant T , \\[3mm] \dfrac{1}{1 + |g - m_1(T)|/D} & \text{if } g > T , \end{cases} \tag{4}$$

where $m_0(T)$ and $m_1(T)$ are the average gray levels of the background and the foreground classes respectively and D is a constant such that $0.5 \leqslant \mu_X(g) \leqslant 1$. In order to obtain the optimal image threshold, a criterion function is required. In [5] the De Luca and Termini fuzzy entropy H_{LT} was used as the optimization criterion. The minimization of fuzzy entropy implies that the pixels would have gray levels close to their class means.

3.2   Cost Function Analysis

A unified formulation of a class of image thresholding techniques was presented in [6], which shows that the difference between various methods lies in the cost functions used. This is described by the following unified equation:

$$J(T) = \sum_{g=0}^{L-1} h_X(g)c(g, T) = \sum_{g=0}^{T} h_X(g)c_0(g, T) + \sum_{g=T+1}^{L-1} h_X(g)c_1(g, T) , \quad (5)$$

where $c(g, T)$ can be considered as the cost to pixels with gray level g when the threshold is set at value T, and $J(T)$ represents the criterion function. The cost function is split into two parts, $c_0(g, T)$ and $c_1(g, T)$, which provide different weights for pixels in the two classes. Using this formulation, by changing the cost functions other thresholding methods can be derived.

In this paper we propose a parametric generalization of the algorithm presented in [5], which automatically determines the optimal threshold value even for highly contrast-degraded images. The optimization criterion used in the proposed approach is the minimization of the a-order fuzzy entropy of the image. Using the unified formulation, the cost function of the proposed method is given by:

$$c^a(g, T) = \begin{cases} \dfrac{1}{1-a} \log_2 \left[\dfrac{D^a + |g - m_0(T)|^a}{(D + |g - m_0(T)|)^a} \right] & \text{if } g \leqslant T , \\[4mm] \dfrac{1}{1-a} \log_2 \left[\dfrac{D^a + |g - m_1(T)|^a}{(D + |g - m_1(T)|)^a} \right] & \text{if } g > T . \end{cases} \quad (6)$$

Fig. ?? shows the cost function described by (6) for $D = 255$, $m_0 = 80$, $m_1 = 150$, threshold value $T = 100$ and various values of the parameter a. For the special case of $a \to 1$ the cost function coincides with the criterion function used in [5]. From Fig. ?? it is evident that for $a \in (0, 1)$ the cost function increases more rapidly as the gray level moves away from the class average gray level in each region. For values of the parameter a, such that $a > 1$, the cost function assigns smaller weights for the same departure from the class average gray level. Therefore, as a approaches 0 the criterion function becomes more discriminative against gray levels distant from their class means.

3.3   Parametric a-Order Fuzzy Image Thresholding

As mentioned above, image thresholding is a useful tool in a variety of image processing and pattern recognition applications and especially in tasks where

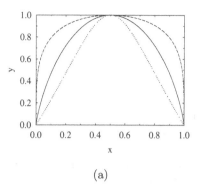 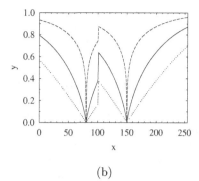

(a)   (b)

Fig. 1. (a) Plot of $e_a(x)$, and (b) cost function $c^a(g, 100)$ for various values of parameter a, that is $a \to 1$ (*solid line*), $a = 0.3$ (*dashed line*), and $a = 3.0$ (*dotted line*). For the cost function $c^a(g, 100)$ we set $D = 255$, $m_0 = 80$, $m_1 = 150$, and threshold $T = 100$.

objects must be distinguished and extracted from the background in images. Contrast-degraded images are characterized by a concentration of pixels in a narrow region of the gray-level range. Therefore, applying thresholding algorithms, which are insensitive to histogram statistics, to highly contrast-degraded images, simply fails to correctly retrieve the object. To overcome this limitation we utilize the parametric class of a-order fuzzy entropies described by (2). As the parameter a moves from 1 to 0 the sensitivity of the cost function to small derivations from the two class means increases.

Given an image X of size $M \times N$ pixels having L gray levels, we set $D = g_{max} - g_{min}$, where g_{max} and g_{min} are the maximum and the minimum gray levels of the image respectively. For a specific value of parameter a, a candidate optimal threshold T_a^* is obtained by minimizing the corresponding a-order fuzzy entropy of the image. That is:

$$T_a^* = \arg \min_{0 \leqslant T \leqslant L-1} H_a(X; T) , \qquad (7)$$

where the a-order fuzzy entropy has been considered as a function of T, since the membership function $\mu_X(g)$ is a function of the threshold.

This procedure is carried out iteratively for any $a \in (0, 1)$ and candidate optimal thresholds are obtained, which form the vector of optimal thresholds $\mathcal{T}$. It should be noted that if we have prior knowledge that the image is highly contrast-degraded, we can manually set the parameter a to a value between 0.1 and 0.5 and directly obtain the thresholded image.

After we have obtained the set of candidate optimal thresholds the selection of the overall optimal threshold value should be made. In general, the threshold is located at a deep valley of the histogram. Therefore, from the set of candidate optimal thresholds we select as the overall optimal threshold T_{opt}^* the one that is located at a valley of the histogram. The threshold T_{opt}^* can be obtained according to the following equation:

$$T^*_{opt} = \arg\min_{T \in \mathcal{T}}\{h_X(T-1) + h_X(T) + h_X(T+1)\}\,,\tag{8}$$

where $h_X(\cdot)$ is the histogram of the image.

4 Quantitative Evaluation Criteria

In [7] a detailed study on different quantitative criteria for segmentation evaluation was carried out. In order to assess the performance of the proposed algorithm, we have considered empirical discrepancy methods, which measure the disparity between the segmented image and a reference binary image. The following evaluation criteria have been selected, which are characterized by a large dynamic range and they have the discrimination capability to distinguish small segmentation degradation [7].

4.1 Misclassification Error (ME)

For bi-level thresholding, the misclassification error is expressed as:

$$ME = 1 - \frac{|B_R \cap B_S| + |F_R \cap F_S|}{|B_R| + |F_R|}\,,\tag{9}$$

where B_R and F_R denote the background and foreground pixels of the reference image, while B_S and F_S denote the background and foreground pixels of the segmented image.

4.2 Probability Error (PE)

In the case of bi-level thresholding the probability error can be calculated by:

$$PE = P(F) \times P(B|F) + P(B) \times P(F|B)\,,\tag{10}$$

where $P(B|F)$ is the probability of error in classifying foreground as background, $P(F|B)$ the probability of error in classifying background as foreground, $P(F)$ and $P(B)$ are the *a priori* probabilities of foreground and background respectively.

4.3 Normalized Discrepancy (ND)

This empirical discrepancy measure takes into account both the number of mis-segmented pixels and the spatial information of these pixels. Let n be the number of mis-segmented pixels and $d(i)$ a distance metric from the i-th mis-segmented pixel to the nearest pixel that actually belongs to the mis-segmented class. The ND measure is defined as:

$$ND = \frac{\sqrt{\sum_{i=1}^{n} d^2(i)}}{A}\,,\tag{11}$$

where A is the total number of pixels in the image. In (11) we have considered the Euclidean distance as the distance metric.

4.4   Relative Ultimate Measurement Accuracy (RUMA)

The RUMA criterion measures the discrepancy of object's features between the reference and the segmented image. If we consider the *"area"* feature, the criterion can be formulated as follows:

$$RUMA = \frac{|A_R - A_S|}{A_R},$$
(12)

where A_R and A_S are the area features of the reference and the actually segmented image respectively.

5   Experimental Results

In order to evaluate the performance of the presented technique we applied the proposed method to a number of real-world images of different types that had undergone extreme contrast degradation. The results obtained using the proposed algorithm were compared to those derived using different thresholding techniques, namely Kapur's method, Huang and Wang's method [5] and the

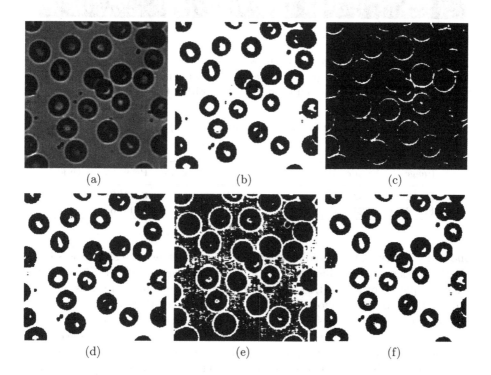

Fig. 2. (a) Contrast-degraded, and (b) reference images. Images obtained using (c) Kapur's method ($T = 105$), (d) Huang and Wang's method ($T = 9$), (e) moment-preserving method ($T = 50$), and (f) proposed algorithm ($T = 3$).

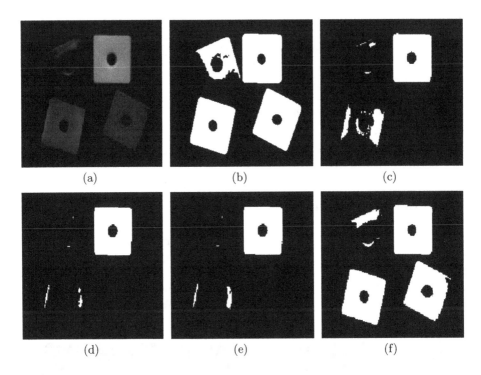

Fig. 3. (a) Contrast-degraded, and (b) reference images. Images obtained using (c) Kapur's method ($T = 21$), (d) Huang and Wang's method ($T = 40$), (e) moment-preserving method ($T = 37$), and (f) proposed algorithm ($T = 4$).

Table 1. Average errors for the images of Figs. 2(a)–3(a) using different thresholding techniques

Image	Kapur	Huang-Wang	Moment-preserving	Proposed method
Fig. 2(a)	0.5028	0.0114	0.2821	**0.0003**
Fig. 3(a)	0.2241	0.2527	0.2495	**0.0576**

moment-preserving thresholding scheme. The performance assessment was based on the average error of the above quantitative evaluation criteria. The reference image required for calculating the empirical discrepancy measures was obtained from the initial image before degradation, using Otsu's thresholding algorithm.

By observing the images of Figs. 2 and 3 we can see that the proposed method successfully retrieves the correct thresholded image. Moreover, various geometric properties of the objects, such as area, shape etc. were successfully preserved, even in cases where the image was highly contrast-degraded. This can also be verified by the average errors of Table 1 for the images used in the simulations. It should be mentioned that the proposed method was also tested using synthetic histograms, in order to simulate the histograms of contrast-degraded images.

The histograms were modelled as Gaussian mixtures with known characteristics (mean, standard deviation). The comparison of the threshold values derived using our method and the theoretical optimal thresholds obtained using the Bayes rule, showed that the presented method performs efficiently under various illumination conditions and also when images suffer from poor contrast.

6 Discussion

In this paper we have presented an algorithm for image thresholding based on the minimization of the a-order fuzzy entropy of an image. For this purpose, we have proposed a new parametric cost function, which can be adjusted according to histogram statistics. The algorithm is completely automated and delivers promising results even for highly contrast-degraded images without the need of any preprocessing, such as contrast enhancement. The algorithm can easily be extended to multilevel thresholding using the same concept. Also due to its structure, a parallel hardware implementation of the algorithm for real-time systems is also feasible. Our future work involves a locally adaptive implementation of the proposed method and also a detailed investigation on the influence of histogram statistics to the selection of the parameter a of the a-order fuzzy entropy that produces the overall optimal threshold value.

References

1. Zadeh, L.A.: Fuzzy sets. Information and Control **8** (1965) 338–353
2. Renyi, A.: On measures of entropy and information. In: Proc. Fourth Berkeley Symposium on Mathematical Statistics and Probability, Berkeley (1960) 547–561
3. Bhandari, D., Pal, N.R.: Some new information measure of fuzzy sets. Information Sciences **67** (1993) 209–228
4. Luca, A.D., Termini, S.: Definition of a nonprobabilistic entropy in the setting of fuzzy set theory. Information and Control **20** (1972) 301–312
5. Huang, L.K., Wang, M.J.: Image thresholding by minimizing the measures of fuzziness. Pattern Recognition **28** (1995) 41–51
6. Yan, H.: Unified formulation of a class of image thresholding techniques. Pattern Recognition **29** (1996) 2025–2032
7. Zhang, Y.J.: A survey on evaluation methods for image segmentation. Pattern Recognition **29** (1996) 1335–1346

Author Index

Lecture Notes in Artificial Intelligence (LNAI)